D1240243

THE TEXAS COOKBOOK

THE TEXAS COOKBOOK

From Barbecue to Banquet—an Informal View of Dining and Entertaining the Texas Way

by MARY FAULK KOOCK

with illustrations by

TOM BALLENGER

LITTLE, BROWN AND COMPANY · BOSTON · TORONTO

LIBRARY OF CONGRESS CATALOG CARD NO. 65-21362

00698 26 MI

A

The author wishes to express her thanks to the following for permission to reprint copyrighted material:

Robert Lee Brothers for his poem "Watermelon Thumpers," originally published in *Kaleidograph* magazine and included in Mr. Brothers' book *The Hidden Harp*, published by Kaleidograph Press of Dallas, Texas.

Mary Lasswell for six recipes from her book *Mrs. Rasmussen's Book of One-Arm Cookery*, published by Houghton Mifflin Company, Boston.

MV

Published simultaneously in Canada
by Little, Brown & Company (Canada) Limited

PRINTED IN THE UNITED STATES OF AMERICA

To Chester

CONTENTS

THE TEXAS COOKBOOK

PEOPLE ARE HERE!

"Mama! People are here!" The "People are here!" cry rang through the house with much excitement, relayed by various sizes of children with the same alarm as "The British are coming!" People were here! Lots of people had always been here at Green Pastures as long as I could remember. There were five of us children who had grown up in the big frame country house: nieces, nephews and cousins had come to live with us while attending school in Austin, and many others whose extended "visits" had lasted anything up to three years. If clients of my father were lonely, he'd send them out for a week or two's "pepper-upper" with his favorite diet of *Hot Water Corn Bread and the fresh buttermilk which Mama churned daily. But this time when the people were here, it was different. These people would be paying to be at Green Pastures — we were in business.

I had always been the one in the family to be in charge of getting ready for company dinner, planning the parties, decorating the house — after recruiting all sorts of "free" help, of course. I remember so well getting ready for a party Camille Long and I gave when we were in junior high school. Colored bread had just come into style, and *Good Housekeeping* magazine had a section on party sandwiches. We made pink and green ribbon sandwiches, solid pink rolled sandwiches, and pink and white checkerboard sandwiches — all day! We also made pecan fudge with heavy cream. We had an electric milk separator which separated the milk from the cream,

* Asterisks mark dishes for which recipes are given.

and this cream was much heavier than whipped cream and made terrific fudge. We also thought it would really be gay to give out fancy paper caps at the party, such as we'd seen at a New Year's Eve party in a movie; so we cut the colored crepe paper and white tissue paper for fringed tassels, but didn't have time to put them together, as making the sandwiches and fudge had taken the entire day. I desperately took all the cap-makings in to Captain Tally and Daddy, who were upstairs visiting. Captain Tally was eighty-five years old and had been a trail-driver all his life. Making party caps wasn't quite his forte — neither was it Daddy's, which he made clear as he disapprovingly wrapped the thread to secure the tassel on the end of the cap and expounded on how we were spending entirely too much time on the frivolities of life. I donned my pink organdy party dress with picoted ruffles and sallied down the stairs to greet the guests who were coming to dance to the music of our new Panatrope — which Daddy had taken as payment for a case.

I have always loved parties, and after Chester and I came to live in the big house with our seven children the trend became children's parties. Helen Posey and I would often merge talents for birthday parties, entertaining with marionette and puppet shows, and spending hours making elaborate refreshments, mostly for our own amusement, I suppose. I particularly remember a three-ring circus cake with ice cream clowns. Friends would often ask me to help them with their parties, which I loved doing. I really don't know how it did all come about, but I decided to make this a paying hobby. Heaven knows we could use a little subsidy for the increasing number of little feet pattering around. So here it was: we were having our first paying party. The people were here, dressed in their finest. Kenny, aged ten, was out in front showing the ladies where to park. Karen was helping to fill the cookie trays, and the other children scampered upstairs after sounding the alarm — "People are here!" — and peeped over the bannister to watch and later, with much enthusiasm, reported the comments of our first satisfied customers.

Twenty years ago there were few speciality restaurants in Austin, so at the insistence of friends and customers we began serving luncheon and dinner. We were truly amateurs, but the help were so loyal and interested that they turned their hands to any job to cover our inefficiency. Amy, who is still an important part of Green Pastures, mostly looked after the children. I used family recipes, and my friends were all most generous and kind in sharing ideas and recipes.

I had not been open for business very long when a lady named Mrs. Davenport (a Marie Dressler type person) came to Austin to lobby for her oil interests. She wanted to have a big party and invite all the legislators and senators, all the state officials and their wives, the governor of Texas, Beauford Jester, and the governors of the bordering states, Oklahoma, Arkansas and Louisiana; as well as, and especially, all the officials of Starr County. One definitely had to have a "title" — such as road superintendent or sheriff — to be invited to the party. Mrs. Davenport's ranch was in Starr County, and when the first oil was struck there the county officials had been very nice to her, so she surely wanted them to be invited to her first big party, which was to be a Western party. I sent out eight hundred invitations, hand-blocked on homespun-like gingham. The fifteen-piece orchestra came from Mexico City to play for dancing. A large piñata hung from one of the oak trees on the edge of the dance floor which we had built for the occasion in the front yard. The piñata was filled with all sorts of fancy-wrapped little packages from Neiman-Marcus, and with ten-dollar gold pieces which the guests scampered to catch when it was finally broken by the blindfolded governor, Beauford Jester.

We served the barbecue supper from a chuck wagon. The beef was extra fine, as it had been purchased by Provine Davenport at the 4-H Club showing. To encourage the young boy who raised it, she paid a very rewarding price. In addition to the regular barbecue supper — beef, pinto beans, potato salad, onions, pickles and so forth — Provine and her chauffeur, who was named Roosevelt, came out early the day of the party to make *Son of a Gun Stew. Many was the time she'd made it at the ranch for the cowboys, she said.

There is no such thing as a definite recipe for Son of a Gun Stew. However, Bill Kuykendall, rancher, said this is his general procedure:

★

Son of a Gun Stew (from one carcass)

Brains	**Heart**
Sweetbreads	**Liver**
Diaphragm (a little)	**Kidneys**

Cut these into bite-sized pieces, about the size of a thumb-joint. If available, use about 10 feet of marrowgut (tripe) cut in half-inch pieces. Cover with water, salt and pepper, and then add whatever is available in the way of vegetables, e.g., onions, garlic, tomatoes, English peas; but do NOT use corn. Sweet peppers, jalapeño, chili pequin, or banana peppers may be used if a hot stew is popular.

The point of this stew was that it used up, in a very palatable form, the offal from a butchered carcass which would not otherwise have kept. The meat was dried in molasses and black pepper.

This stew was served from the big black iron pot it had cooked in all day.

Provine was dressed in a shiny, purple satin cowboy suit, elaborately embroidered, and which had been specially made for her to wear when she rode her white stallion to lead the Homecoming Parade in Starr County. Games of chance were played with counterfeit money which was given to each guest as he arrived. Bars (with only the finest whiskey) were numerous. The party was a big success, and after that I felt I could tackle 'most any kind of party, and I guess I have just about done that. I was fortunate to inherit a wonderful collection of recipes from my mother, Cousin Texana and Cousin Loretta, who were truly culinary artists. I have accumulated some mighty good recipes. Still wherever I go, I always try to come home with some new dish to try on my family and customers at Green Pastures.

Madge and Ralph Janes also turned their hobby of raising turkeys into a business venture with great success. They own the Bar-Nothing Ranch, just east of Austin, and when we first started serving meals, theirs was the world's largest turkey ranch. The Janeses have contributed much knowledge to the worldwide turkey industry by their extensive research and experiments in breeding fine birds. They developed the Baby Beef turkeys about this time and they appeared on most of our menus in one form or another. The Janeses excelled not only in raising turkeys, but also in cooking and serving them to perfection. When it was their turn to host the square dance club, Madge served Fried Turkey. I have never seen any platter of food piled so high cleaned so quickly. Fried Turkey is The Best. Madge cut a five- or six-pound young turkey the same way a chicken is cut up for frying; in fact it is prepared the same way as fried chicken, only after it is browned it is removed from the skillet, covered in a heavy pan, and placed in a low oven for about thirty minutes. It is tender and juicy like good fried chicken, only more so. At Green Pastures we featured Turkey Steaks which were cut from the breast of the large birds and flattened like a cutlet. These we seasoned lightly with only a little salt, then dipped in flour and fried gently in a small amount of butter, browning on each side to a golden color. In the drippings we made a cream gravy which was served on the side. These are very delicate in flavor and were very popular with our clientele. With them we served a Waldorf salad, buttered rice with sliced stuffed olives, fresh Kentucky Wonder green beans, and hot rolls, and finished off with one of Amy's good desserts, like *Black Bottom Pie.

★

Black Bottom Pie

This is fussy to make, but once a cook gets the hang of it, it goes easily and is well worth the trouble.

CRUST

14 crisp ginger snaps **5 Tbs. melted butter**

Roll out cookies till fine. Mix with melted butter. Line a 9-inch pie tin, sides and bottom, with buttered crumbs, pressing flat and firm. Bake 10 minutes in 250-degree oven; cool.

BASIC FILLING

1 Tbs. gelatine
4 Tbs. cold water
1¾ cups milk
½ cup sugar
1 Tbs. cornstarch
Pinch salt
4 egg yolks

For chocolate layer

3 squares or 3 1-oz. bars unsweetened chocolate
1 tsp. vanilla

For rum-flavored layer

4 egg whites
½ tsp. cream of tartar
½ cup powdered sugar
1 Tbs. rum

Soak gelatine in cold water. Scald milk, add ½ cup sugar mixed with cornstarch, pinch salt, then beaten egg yolks. Cook in double boiler, stirring constantly, until custard is thick enough to coat spoon. Stir in dissolved gelatine. Divide custard in half.

(1) To one-half, add melted chocolate and vanilla. Turn while hot into the cooled crust, dipping in carefully so as not to disturb crust.

(2) Let remaining half of custard cool. Beat egg whites and cream of tartar, adding powdered sugar slowly. Blend with cooled custard. Add rum. Spread carefully over chocolate layer. Place in icebox to cool thoroughly. It may stand overnight.

TOPPING

2 Tbs. powdered sugar
1 cup whipping cream
Grated chocolate

When ready to serve, whip heavy cream stiff, add powdered sugar slowly. Pile over top of pie. Sprinkle with grated bitter or semisweet chocolate.

★

Hot Water Corn Bread

1¼ cups (approx.) of yellow cornmeal, preferably stone-ground
3 cups boiling water
4 Tbs. shortening
⅛ tsp. soda
1 tsp. salt

Add cornmeal to boiling water, stirring with wire whip constantly to prevent lumping. Stir in salt and soda. Remove from fire; this will thicken quickly.

Take by spoonfuls and pat into little oval flat cakes. Mama would always keep her hands wet when patting these. Heat shortening in iron skillet and fry cakes, browning slightly on each side. Drain on paper towel and serve with lots of butter. My! How my father loved these! Three hundred and sixty-five days of the year!

Well I remember those first frantic weeks of food operations! Every night my children had the restaurant fare of Turkey Steaks or a Filet Mignon — until they finally protested: "Are we ever gonna have any more *food*?" "What you mean, food?" asked Amy. "We want some beans" (meaning pinto beans, of course), "and no more Turkey Steaks, and no more Filet Mignon — ever!"

We have indeed been fortunate at Green Pastures in having both family and friends come to the rescue on special occasions to help with the pièce de résistance, such as when we have a dinner for Dr. John Bickley of the Business Administration Department at Texas University. Several times during the year, Dr. and Mrs. Bickley entertain the visiting insurance representatives from all over the United States, and also from foreign countries, who come to attend insurance seminars at Texas U. John really likes to go all out and serve an epicurean five- or six-course dinner, accompanied by the appropriate wines.

On such an occasion we call Esther Allidi to come and lend her expert hand to the sauces that will satisfy John's gourmet palate! Mrs. Allidi was born and grew up in Grasse, France, but now, outside of her accent and flair for French cuisine, she is a full-fledged Texan. My favorite among Esther's fine touches is Braised Duckling Country Style.

★

Braised Duckling Country Style

2 5½-lb. ducks, cleaned
Salt and pepper to taste
Bacon fat
2 medium-sized carrots, quartered
2 medium-sized onions
2 whole cloves
2 small bay leaves
8 sprigs of fresh parsley
6 sprigs of celery tops
1 cup white wine
1 cup hot consommé
½ tsp. grated orange rind
Nutmeg (optional)

Singe ducks over gas flame, then wash in hot water. Fill the cavity (which should be as small as possible) with *Rice Stuffing; sew cavity together, not too tightly. Place stuffed birds in an open roasting pan, after rubbing them with salt and pepper and a very little bacon fat. Roast in a slow (300-degree) oven, basting every 10 minutes with some of the hot drippings; this should take about an hour.

Transfer half-roasted ducks into a braising kettle; add quartered carrots, onion stuck with cloves, and the bay leaves, parsley and celery tops tied together. Cover tightly and continue cooking for 1½ hours without disturbing. Remove ducklings to a hot pan; keep hot while making the gravy as follows:

Drain all liquid from the braising kettle. To the carrots, onions, bay leaves, parsley and celery add the white wine, consommé, and grated orange rind; let this boil 5 minutes, stirring almost constantly after mashing cooked vegetables to a pulp. Strain, add salt and pepper to taste and a grating of nutmeg (optional) and serve.

RICE STUFFING

½ cup butter
2 large onions, minced
1 tsp. sage
½ cup minced celery leaves
1 qt. meat stock
¼ tsp. each: thyme, clove, mace
1 Tbs. minced parsley
1½ tsp. salt
⅛ tsp. black pepper
1½ cups washed rice (wild or white)

Melt fat and add all ingredients except rice; cook for 3 to 4 minutes over low flame. Add rice and simmer gently for 40 minutes, or until rice is tender and moisture is absorbed.

Esther's many friends kept insisting that she should open a restaurant, which finally she did; and it became famous very soon and so popular that her husband, Peter, who was an accomplished mural artist, insisted that it was too much work for her — so she sold it, much to the displeasure of her ardent clientele, and concentrated only on making salad dressings. This too soon became big business. Esther's fabulous salad dressings are now distributed to food stores throughout Texas.

The former governor of Texas, Coke Stevenson, was a great patron of the restaurant, and he asked Esther if she would cook the antelope which he had brought back from a hunting trip in New Mexico, and a good dinner to go with it, as he wanted to entertain some guests from out of the state. Esther was delighted to do so, and set about to ready her establishment for the occasion; she covered the tables with red and white checked cloths, made an arrangement of fresh fruit, autumn leaves and pine cones for a centerpiece, and placed red candles all down the table. She wrote the menus for each place on gilt-edged cards; and this is what they said:

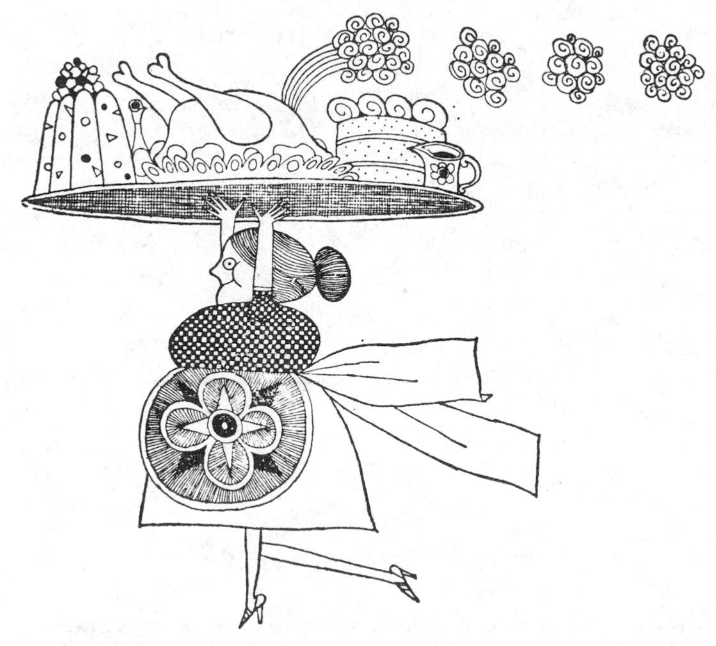

Melon with Prosciutto
* *French Onion Soup*
(I could have made that the dinner — Ester's onion soup is superb!)
Mixed green salad, with her famous French salad dressing
* *Roasted Antelope*
* *Sweet Potato Casserole*
White Asparagus on Toast with Parmesan cheese
Tray of stuffed celery and radishes
French Bread
* *Sherry Tarts*
Coffee

Esther said that after dinner Governor Stevenson put his arm round her shoulders and told her that that had been the most wonderful dinner he had ever eaten in his whole life! Another guest said that he would like to marry her, if her husband should ever die! All in good-natured fun, of course, but Peter was *very* jealous, and didn't speak to her for a week.

★

Onion Soup (*serves* 6)

4 large onions
3 Tbs. butter
3 pints of beef stock
1 tsp. Worcestershire sauce
Salt to taste
⅛ tsp. pepper
½ tsp. paprika
Thin slices of bread, toasted
Grated Parmesan cheese

Slice onions thin, and brown in butter; add more butter if necessary to keep onions moist while cooking. When onions are tender, add hot stock, Worcestershire sauce and seasoning. Bring to boil, pour soup in individual casseroles and arrange the sliced toasted bread on top. Sprinkle grated cheese generously and put under low broiler flame to brown. Serve at once.

★

Roasted Antelope

Soak overnight in marinade containing: dry red wine, thyme, sage, onion, mashed clove of garlic, salt, pepper, 1 bay leaf, 3 or 4 whole cloves, ½ cup celery tops and a little nutmeg. Remove from marinade, slit at intervals and insert cubes of salt pork. Brown in hot (400-degree) oven to form crust; then place in roasting pan with the same marinade, cover, turn oven to 300 degrees and cook slowly, allowing 20 minutes per pound.

When done, strain juice, thicken slightly with cornstarch (1 scant tsp. for each cup of liquid), add 1 cup of sauteed mushrooms and ½ cup small black pitted olives cut in half.

Guaranteed satisfaction!

★

Sweet Potato Casserole

Boil 6 medium-sized sweet potatoes in jackets till tender. Peel, put through colander, add ¼ tsp. salt, 4 Tbs. butter, ½ tsp. cinnamon. Place in buttered casserole with buttered crumbs on top, and bake in 350-degree oven for 20 minutes.

★

Sherry Tarts

SHELLS

Sift 2⅓ cups presifted pastry flour with ¾ tsp. salt. Cut into flour ⅓ cup butter, using a pastry blender or two knives, until the mixture has the consistency of cornmeal. Add ⅓ cup butter and blend till the shortening is well distributed and the particles are as big as peas. Add gradually about 5 Tbs. ice-cold water, or enough to hold the dough together, mixing it in lightly with a fork. Chill the dough for easier handling and roll it into a sheet ¼ inch thick on a lightly floured pastry board.

FILLING

Beat 6 egg yolks until light and add 1 scant cup of sugar. Soak 1 envelope gelatine in ½ cup cold water. Put the gelatine and water over a low flame till dissolved, and put into sugar-egg mixture, stirring briskly. Whip 1 pint cream until stiff, fold it into the egg mixture and flavor with ½ cup sherry.

Cool until the mixture begins to set and pour it into the shell. Let it set until firm. Sprinkle the top generously with shaved bittersweet chocolate curls, or finely chopped pistachio nuts; garnish with whipped cream and serve cold, topped with Maraschino cherries.

Another very thick chapter could be written about all the wonderful foods I have learned from this gifted lady. This *French Sauerkraut has been enjoyed often at Green Pastures, when we served it with charcoal-broiled pork chops and *Apples with Brussels Sprouts.

★

French Sauerkraut

Rinse 3 cups sauerkraut in cold water, drain and place in a heavy iron pot; add 1 medium-sized onion stuck with 6 or 8 whole cloves, 5 or 6 juniper berries, 1 sliced carrot, ¼ lb. salt pork (washed), 2 strips of lean bacon, small piece of ham hock, ¾ cup white wine.

Cover with tight-fitting lid and simmer very slowly 4 or 5 hours. Very small, raw new potatoes may be added for the last 30 minutes of cooking. When ready to serve, sprinkle with chopped parsley.

★

Apples with Brussels Sprouts

Wash, and trim if necessary, 1 lb. Brussels sprouts and drop in boiling salted water. Let cook 15 minutes or until tender, but not soft.

Core and cut in eighths 3 cooking apples. Let simmer, covered, in ¾ cup water for 10 or 15 minutes with 2 Tbs. brown sugar, till tender but not soft.

Drain Brussels sprouts; add 3 Tbs. melted butter very slightly browned, and stir in with apples.

Another delicious vegetable combination of Esther's which I often serve at Green Pastures is:

★

Zucchini Filled with Creamed Peas

Drop 4 whole zucchini into boiling water (salted) until tender; do *not* overcook. Drain well, split in halves and remove approximately 2 Tbs. of pulp in center. Cut 2 slices of bacon into small pieces and sauté until crisp with 1 Tbs. of fine-chopped onion. Add 1 tsp. of flour to thicken drippings and add 2 cups of cooked cream peas (frozen, canned or fresh). Season to taste with salt, freshly ground pepper; mix well and pile in cooked zucchini shells. Sprinkle with chopped parsley.

One of the "Cold Plates" we feature at Green Pastures is:

** Esther's Cured Ham*
** Jardinière Salad*
Cold Pickled Peaches

★

Cured Ham

Remove skin and excess fat from 12-lb. ham and brown in 375-degree oven. When brown (after 20-25 minutes) remove and make a bouquet of 6 sprigs parsley, 1 small carrot, 1 stick celery, 8 cloves, 6 or 8 whole peppercorns. Tie loosely in cheesecloth and place in pan with ham. Pour in sherry wine and enough bouillon to come up ⅓ way on ham. Cover and cook in slow (300-degree) oven approximately 3 hours. Turn at least once during baking time. Let stand in juices until cold; refrigerate. Slice cold, not too thin, and serve with this great Jardinière Salad

★

Jardinière Salad

4 medium-sized boiled potatoes
French dressing
1 8-oz. packet of frozen carrots and peas
¾ cup celery, cut
Rémoulade

Peel and dice potatoes; let marinate in French dressing for 30 minutes. Cook peas and carrots 1 minute less than time stated on packet; drain and chill. Toss all ingredients together with Rémoulade. Serve on lettuce leaf.

Everyone who eats this asks, "Where do you get this marvelous ham? What is it that makes this salad so divine?"

Two more of Esther Allidi's fabulous recipes that we use at Green Pastures:

★

Oysters Poulette

1 doz. oysters
2 Tbs. heavy cream
2 egg yolks, well beaten
1 tsp. lemon juice
1 tsp. finely chopped parsley
½ cup sliced, cooked mushrooms
Patty shells or buttered toast

Poach oysters in their own liquor for 4 minutes, or until edges curl. Remove oysters to hot serving dish. Cook oyster liquor over brisk fire until it is reduced to ½ cup, and stir in cream, to which has been added the beaten egg yolks. Bring near to boiling point, but do NOT allow to boil lest mixture curdle.

Remove from fire, add lemon juice, parsley and mushrooms. Pour sauce over poached oysters and serve either on toast, generously buttered, or in patty shells.

★

Rum Omelet

1 Tbs. butter
3 to 4 eggs
¼ tsp. salt
Apricot preserves
Sugar
¼ to ½ cup rum

Melt butter in skillet or omelet pan until it becomes hazelnut brown. Meanwhile, lightly mix eggs and salt, being careful not to overbeat.

Pour eggs into skillet and stir briskly with a fork to make sure eggs are not sticking to pan at any point. They should congeal immediately upon contact with hot, melted butter.

Spread with apricot preserves and roll the omelet by moving the skillet and folding both sides over with a fork. Invert hot serving dish over skillet, then turn over so omelet slips on to dish. Sprinkle with sugar.

Heat the rum in a small saucepan and then pour over omelet, letting it run down on the plate and over edges of omelet. Light the rum and spoon it over the omelet as it flames. Bring dish to the table while rum burns. Serves 2.

Breakfast at Memaw's was to the Koock klan as Breakfast at Brennan's in New Orleans is to visitors there. I suppose one of the most luxurious experiences our family had was Sunday morning breakfast at Memaw's. Can you imagine anyone, even your own mother-in-law, inviting the family of ten for breakfast?

Mrs. Koock and her daughter Sug and their beloved Clara would be all set for the invasion after 9 o'clock Mass. Part of the treat was that Memaw always undauntedly used her lovely china, linen and thinnest crystal on both the grown-ups' table and the children's table. She also used fascinating little jam dishes, spoon holders, and hand-painted fruit bowls.

The menu would seldom vary, for it was always popular with the multitude.

Fresh Orange Juice (or Broiled Grapefruit on cold mornings)
** German Fried Calves' Liver*
Crisp Bacon
Coffee Gravy
Jelly and Jam
Clara's Spanish Rice
Scrambled Eggs
Sliced Tomatoes
Hot Biscuits
Coffee and Milk
And Always Dessert

By the time we finished this bountiful repast, it was usually almost high noon, but this meal was intended to cover lunch too.

★

German Fried Calves' Liver

Dip thin slices of liver in cornmeal which has been seasoned with a little salt. Brown lightly and quickly on both sides in hot bacon drippings. Liver does not need to cook long to be done. Drain on absorbent paper and place on warm platter. Lay slices of crisp bacon and peeled tomatoes around it. Pour ¾ cup strong coffee in the remaining bacon and liver drippings in the skillet. Let simmer and cook down a little. Then pass it to put over liver or on biscuits.

If it was — and it usually was — near someone's birthday, there would be one of Sug's special birthday cakes for dessert. Some Sundays she served *Ambrosia, which was also a family favorite.

★

Ambrosia

6 oranges, peeled, sliced and seeded
1 whole coconut, grated
1 cup fresh or canned pineapple tidbits
Powdered sugar to taste

Arrange layers of oranges, coconut and pineapple in a large cut-glass bowl. Pour fresh orange juice sweetened with powdered sugar over the fruit. Chill overnight.

When Karen, our eldest daughter, came home from college for Christmas, she brought her roommate, Helene Redell from New York. In making plans for entertaining her house guest, Karen wrote, "And be sure to include Breakfast at Memaw's."

One day the boys, Ken and Bill, came in from dove hunting down at the farm of Oscar and Lillian Soderlund in Elroy, a small Swedish community just east of Austin. Lillian had given them some freshly baked Swedish rye bread to bring home. They enthusiastically told about the delicious dinner they had at the Soderlunds' that day. I decided to call Ellen Erickson, a friend of Lillian's in Austin and tell her the next time Lillian came to town to bring her over to Green Pastures and let's talk about having a Smorgasbord on Sunday nights. In a few days they came, and were quite excited over the project, as they both loved to cook. So we started the Sunday night Elroy Texas-style Smorgasbord, which turned out to be an overwhelming success. I can still see Lillian, who'd make a slight crack in the door leading to the dining room and stand there peeking through, mostly to hear the glowing comments of praise about her cuisine. I can give you the menu and a few of the recipes, but it was simply impossible to get the others accurately. Neither Lillian nor Ellen used any kind of written formula or standard measurements. How everything turned out so perfectly was most astounding.

GREEN PASTURES SMORGASBORD

Large baked Red Snapper, garnished with lemon boats filled with Tartare Sauce
Smoked Herring with Onions in Cream
Cottage Cheese Ring with tart jelly in the center
Tray of sliced tomatoes sprinkled with chives
Pear halves in lime gelatine mold with mayonnaise
Fruit cocktail in red gelatine ring
Pineapple rings, pecans and cream cheese in lemon gelatine mold
Large mound of Potato Salad garnished with pimento "flowers" and encircled with deviled eggs which were decorated with small pimento cut-outs, caviar and chopped parsley
A whole glazed ham garnished with flowers made of mandarin orange sections with red cherries in the center and stems of pineapple sticks tinted green
Imported sardines and crackers
* *Vegetable Mousse (very popular)*
* *Green Bean Salad*
Swedish rye bread — Hard Tack

Chafing dishes of:
Chicken à la King on rosettes
* *Tiny Swedish Meatballs*
* *Swedish Brown Beans*
* *Scalloped Oysters*
* *Vetebröd (Coffee Bread)*
Butter balls

★

Vegetable Mousse

1 envelope plain gelatine, soaked in ¼ cup cold water
1 pkg. lime-flavored gelatine, dissolved in 1 cup boiling water and ¾ cup cold water

Add plain gelatine to lime-flavored gelatine. Add:

½ cup sour cream
⅛ tsp. garlic salt
½ tsp. salt
⅛ tsp. cayenne
1 Tbs. fresh lemon juice
1 Tbs. onion juice
½ cup mayonnaise

Whip till smooth with rotary beater. Let stand until slightly thickened. Add:

¾ cup very fine cabbage
¾ cup grated carrots
¾ cup celery chopped fine

Pour in 2-qt. mold which has been rubbed with mayonnaise. Turn out on shredded red cabbage, border with shredded carrots.

★

Green Bean Salad

Drain 1 No. 2 can of tiny (No. 2 Sieve) green beans and let stand in ice water 15 minutes. Drain well again. Add 2 sliced, peeled tomatoes, removing seeds and the juice around the seeds. Add 1 onion sliced paper thin and 1 cup cut celery. Toss with an oil and vinegar dressing (approximately ¼ cup which has 1 tsp. sugar added.) Let stand at least 8 to 10 hours. Season with salt and pepper to taste.

★

Swedish Meatballs

1½ lbs. round steak, ground
1½ lbs. pork, ground
3 cups soft bread, picked small
½ cup milk
2 eggs, beaten
1 onion
½ tsp. ginger
½ tsp. ground sage
Salt and pepper
Bacon drippings
2 cans mushroom soup
1 cup sautéed mushrooms

Mix all except last three ingredients lightly and form into balls 1 inch in diameter. Put bacon drippings in skillet and brown. Remove to roaster. Make gravy in skillet by adding mushroom soup. Pour some over meat balls and bake 1½ hours at 325 degrees. When ready to serve, add mushrooms.

★

Swedish Brown Beans

Wash two cups of brown or pinto beans. Place in heavy pot, cover well with water and add 1 tsp. salt, 1 Tbs. vinegar, 1 Tbs. sugar, 1 tsp. cinnamon and 2 Tbs. sorghum syrup or molasses. Cook until beans are soft, add more water if needed, and season to taste. Add 2 Tbs. butter when done.

★

Scalloped Oysters

½ lb. crackers
1 pt. milk
1 pt. oysters

Grease casserole, roll crackers. Set a layer of crackers, wet with milk, on the bottom of the casserole. (To ensure well-soaked crackers, add milk to each layer.) Then put in several oysters and then another layer of crackers. Salt and pepper and butter each layer of oysters. Bake in 300-degree oven for about 1 hour.

★

Vetebröd

1 yeast cake
1¼ cups lukewarm milk
½ cup sugar
¼ tsp. salt
½ cup melted butter
1 tsp. ground cardamon
4 cups flour
1 egg
Sugar
Chopped almonds

Dissolve yeast in ¼ cup milk. Mix 1 cup milk, sugar, salt, butter and cardamon with a little flour, and beat smooth. Add yeast and remaining flour and beat with wooden spoon until firm. Sprinkle a little flour on dough, cover with towel and set in warm place to rise until doubled in size. Knead smooth on floured board. Cut half of the dough into three equal parts. Roll these with the hands into long ropes, then braid, forming a long loaf. Repeat with remaining dough or form twists and spirals. Let rise, covered, on buttered baking sheet. Brush with slightly beaten egg, sprinkle with sugar and chopped almonds. Bake 15 to 20 minutes at 375 degrees.

The desserts were always over on the buffet. Ellen made one of her *Baked Prune Soufflés, covered it over with whipped cream, dotted it with Maraschino cherries, and then sprinkled it with chopped toasted pecans! There were trays of wonderful little cookies and the traditional *Ostkaka, a Swedish pudding with Lingonberry Jelly.

★

Baked Prune Soufflé

Beat 12 egg whites and 1 cup sugar till it forms peaks. Then add 1½ cups cooked prunes cut in small pieces, and 2 tsp. vanilla. Continue beating. Pour in ungreased 12-inch tube cake pan, set in a shallow pan of water, and bake for approximately 1 hour in a 300-degree oven.

★

Lemon Drop Cookies

½ lb. melted butter
1 cup cornstarch
Juice and rind of 1 lemon
1½ cups white sugar
1 cup flour
2 eggs (not beaten; add one at a time)

Drop mixture with a teaspoon on cookie sheet and bake in a slow oven for about 10 to 15 minutes.

★

Fruit-Nut Cookies

½ cup butter or margarine
1 egg
1 Tbs. grated orange peel
⅛ tsp. salt
1 cup sifted cake flour
¼ cup sugar
2 tsp. vanilla
1 Tbs. lemon juice
½ cup chopped nuts
½ cup glacé fruit

Cream butter and stir in the rest of the ingredients; form into small balls and bake in 350-degree oven for 20 to 25 minutes.

★

Spritz

½ cup sugar
1 egg yolk
½ tsp. orange extract
2-2¼ cups flour
½ cup butter
¼ tsp. salt
1 tsp. grated orange rind

Press from cookie press into desired shapes. Bake at 375 degrees about 12 minutes.

★

Pepparkakor (*Swedish ginger cookies*)

⅔ cup brown sugar
1 tsp. ginger
1 tsp. cinnamon
½ tsp. cloves
⅔ cup molasses
¾ tsp. baking soda
⅔ cup butter
1 egg
5 cups flour

Heat sugar, spices and molasses to boiling point. Add soda and pour mixture over butter in a bowl and stir well. Add egg and sifted flour and blend thoroughly. Knead on floured board, chill in refrigerator. Roll out thin, form into desired shapes with cutters or knife. On greased cookie sheets, bake in 350-degree oven for 8 to 10 minutes.

Ellen used to cut the ginger cookies into fancy shapes for the children's parties; and around Christmas we'd cut patterns out of brown paper, lay them on the dough and cut around them with a sharp knife. Then Judy, Gretchen, or one of the Koock cooks would help decorate these with various colored cream icings, using a pastry tube.

I could never get an exact account of the making of the Ōstkaka from Ellen or Lillian, but Lillian's mother used to say, "Yust leave it in the oven until it yells!" But another friend of mine, Mrs. Mary Lundell, gave me her recipe, and this pudding is one of her specialities.

★

Ostkaka

½ cake rennet tablet
¼ cup lukewarm water
1 gal. whole sweet milk
2 whole eggs, beaten slightly
½ tsp. salt
½ cup flour
½ cup sugar
½ cup cream

Soak rennet in ¼ cup lukewarm water for 20 minutes. Heat milk until lukewarm and add the beaten eggs and salt. Next add the flour, which has been mixed with a little of the warm milk. Add rennet; mix well and let stand 1 hour. After the hour, pour off the whey which has formed and empty remaining solid into greased pan about 12 by 12 by 2 inches. Bake in 425-degree oven for 45 minutes. When about half done, pour over it ½ cup sugar mixed with ½ cup cream. Bake until golden brown and serve with jelly when cool, preferably Lingonberry Jelly. Serves 12.

Another dish which Ellen prepares that is a great favorite with our family is:

★

Veal Birds

¼ cup shortening
4-5 medium onions, chopped
½ cup dry breadcrumbs
Salt and pepper
Parsley
5 Tbs. cream or broth
2 lbs. veal, sliced very thin
Butter
Onions and carrots
1½ cups veal broth

Melt the shortening in a skillet and gently cook the chopped onion until tender, but not brown. Add the breadcrumbs, seasonings and parsley, and enough cream or broth to moisten. Spread this stuffing on the veal slices (you can cover with a sliver of ham if you wish). Roll up the birds and fasten with a string. Brown the rolls in butter and place in a casserole with onions and carrots enough to serve the family. Add 1½ cups broth and cover; then cook in oven about 1 hour. Thicken the broth with cornstarch or flour for gravy. Serve the Veal Birds with mashed potatoes or rice.

Mr. J. Frank Dobie, late famous writer and folklorist; Dr. Walter Prescott Webb, noted historian; Dr. Roy Bedichek, writer and naturalist; and Dr. Mody Boatright, professor of English at the University of Texas, would often come to Green Pastures with their wives, who are very talented and distinguished in their own rights. When my brother John Henry Faulk was at home from New York, he was always invited to join them for dinner. They came early and stayed late, and needless to say, never for a second did their stimulating and fascinating conversation lag. They all loved good food and good wine. We usually put their table in a small dining room where in the winter we keep a good fire cracklin' in the fireplace. One night they particularly enjoyed:

Cup of Beef Bouillon
Fresh Fruit Salad
* *Breast of White Guinea Hen, with Artichoke Sauce*
* *Baked Rice*
* *Baked Tomatoes filled with Spinach Vera Cruz*
* *Hot Crescent Rolls*
* *Sherry Almond Pudding*

Before Green Pastures was taken into the city we used to raise chickens, turkeys and guineas — guineas with black-and-white speckled feathers. They were fairly wild and when Mama wanted to cook guinea for Sunday dinner, I remember my brothers, Johnny or Hamilton, would shoot them as they flew up from the ground over the oak trees. Those guineas were all dark meat, and had to cook slowly for a long time. Not too many years ago, our friends Mr. and Mrs. Parks Johnson started raising white guineas — the first I ever heard of in Texas. Parks will be remembered for his popular nationwide radio show *Vox Pox,* before television days. When he retired from show business, he and Louise moved to their ranch near Wimberley and thought these birds had great merit. The white guineas have all white feathers and all white meat, rather like a Cornish game hen, only larger. Now that Parks has turned to other projects, we get our supply from Bill Modene and serve only the breast for dinner; and the rest goes to make delicious chicken salad.

★

Breast of White Guinea Hen
(*may also be prepared with breast of chicken*)

For 6 breasts: (approx. ¾ lb. each)
3 Tbs. butter
Salt to taste
1 tsp. white pepper
2 Tbs. flour
½ tsp. Beau Monde seasoned salt
1 garlic clove, mashed
1 Tbs. parsley, chopped very fine
1 Tbs. green onion (white and green part, chopped very fine)
3 cups rich chicken stock (all fat removed)
1 Tbs. imported Parmesan
1 tsp. Maggi Seasoning
2 Tbs. dry sherry
¾ cup sliced sautéed mushrooms
*** Baked Rice**
Hearts of artichoke
Butter

Remove skin. Rub breasts with melted butter, salt and pepper, brown lightly in heavy iron skillet and then place in roaster, meaty side down.

Make sauce by melting butter and flour and simmering 10 minutes, browning only very slightly. Add Beau Monde, garlic, pepper and salt to taste, parsley, onion and chicken stock. Then add Parmesan, Maggi and sherry and whip till smooth. This should be rather a thin sauce, so a little more chicken stock may be added if necessary. Pour over guinea breasts; cover and cook in 275-degree oven for 2 hours. Remove breasts;

strain sauce and add sautéed mushrooms. Place breasts in center of *Baked Rice; place hearts of artichoke on each side of guinea and glaze with sauce. Pass remaining sauce. Serves 6.

★

Baked Rice

- 2 Tbs. oil
- 1 cup rice
- ¼ cup chopped onion
- 1½ cups hot chicken stock (with fat removed)
- ¾ cup sautéed sliced mushrooms (optional)
- 1 cup cooked wild rice

In a heavy skillet heat oil till hot and add rice and onion. Stir till they are very light brown. Add chicken stock and mushrooms and place in 350-degree oven uncovered for approximately 30 minutes. Stir during cooking time and add more liquid if necessary. (Never let any rice overcook; grains should be tender and stand apart.) Add 1 cup of cooked wild rice; stir and season to taste.

I really think that this and the guineas are my original recipes!

★

Tomatoes Filled with Spinach Vera Cruz

- 1 small packet frozen chopped spinach
- 6 medium-sized firm tomatoes
- Salt
- 3 strips bacon
- ¼ cup chopped onion
- 1 cup sour cream
- Dash of Tabasco
- Freshly ground black pepper
- 5 slices mozzarella cheese

Thaw spinach and blanch in hot water, let drain in colander. Cut out centers of tomatoes, leaving firm outside wall. Sprinkle with salt and turn open side down to drain. Chop the part of the tomato removed from center and let it drain also in a strainer.

Fry bacon until crisp, remove from pan and drain on paper. Pour off excess bacon fat, retaining 2 Tbs. Sauté onions in bacon drippings over low fire; add spinach which has been squeezed dry. Add the chopped, well-drained tomatoes, add sour cream. Season with salt, a dash of Tabasco and freshly ground pepper. Stir well and add 2 slices of the cheese. cut fine, and stir in the bacon, which has been crumbled. When heated through, fill cavity of tomatoes. Place in slightly buttered baking pan. Top each tomato with triangle of cheese. Just before time to serve, run in oven long enough to heat through (15 minutes).

This is very pretty, and I think terrifically good; it is important not to let the tomatoes get soft by cooking too long.

★

Hot Crescent Rolls (popular at Green Pastures)

½ cup sugar
½ cup soft butter
1 tsp. salt
2 eggs
¾ cup scalded milk (scalded and then cooled to lukewarm)
2 cakes of yeast
4 cups sifted all-purpose flour

Mix sugar, butter, salt and eggs together. Beat with rotary egg beater. Stir in milk. Crumble yeast into the mixture; stir until dissolved. Beat in the flour with a spoon. Scrape dough from sides of bowl. Cover with damp cloth and let rise until double. Roll dough on floured board to ½ inch. Make pie wedges. Brush with melted butter. Roll in circles. Cut in triangular pieces. Roll and twist into crescent shapes. Let stand till double in bulk. Bake for 15 minutes in 425-degree oven. Makes 4 dozen rolls.

★

Sherry Almond Pudding

2 Tbs. unflavored gelatine
½ cup cold water
1 cup hot water
⅓ cup sherry
½ tsp. almond extract
¼ tsp. salt
6 egg whites
1½ cup sugar
1 cup heavy cream, whipped
Sherry Sauce
¼ cup toasted shredded coconut
¼ cup toasted almonds

Soak gelatine in cold water; dissolve in hot water. Cool 15 to 20 minutes. Add wine, almond extract and salt. When mixture begins to thicken, beat until frothy. Beat egg whites until foamy. Gradually add sugar and beat till stiff. Fold egg whites and whipped cream into gelatine mixture. Pour into individual molds and chill till firm. Turn out, cover with sauce and sprinkle top with 1 Tbs. each toasted coconut and almonds.

SHERRY SAUCE

6 egg yolks
¼ cup sugar
2 Tbs. flour
2 cups milk (scalded)
¼ cup sherry
1 cup heavy cream

Beat egg yolks thoroughly. Mix in sugar and flour. Gradually stir in milk. Cook over low heat until thickened, stirring constantly. Cool 15-

20 minutes. Add sherry. Chill. When ready to serve, whip cream and fold into custard.

After everyone had polished the bones of the guinea hens, Frank Dobie said, "Seeing these clean bones around the table reminds me of the time when I was a boy and living on our ranch in South Texas, and there was a lot of quail around. We never shot the quail, but would catch lots of them in a homemade trap. One day, my mother made a great big *Quail Pie for our dinner. Shortly before the time to serve, our neighbor Andrew Jackson Wright and his brother, from a nearby ranch, stopped in, and as was customary, they were asked to stay for dinner. This meant that we children had to wait for the 'second table.' As we patiently waited we peeped through the door; the guest already had a big pile of bones by his plate and was lifting another of the succulent birds from the pie. Mama was getting uneasy — and so were we! Finally he pulled the napkin from his collar, wiped his mouth and hands, and said: 'Mrs. Dobie, that was a mighty fine quail pie, but I think it would have been better if you'd fried the quail first.' "

★

Quail Pie

Split 12 quail down the back and rub with salt pork, salt and pepper. Roll in flour and brown on both sides in a little hot Crisco in a heavy iron skillet. Pour 1 qt. chicken stock over and cover. Let simmer slowly about 30 minutes, then remove to a casserole which has a sliced onion, medium-sized. Lay the birds close together and pour the hot gravy over them. Add about 1 Tbs. flour mixed smooth with a little water, ½ cup wine and a cup of small canned green peas. Cover with rich pastry dough and bake in 350-degree oven till crust is brown. Allow 3 quail per person — unless you have a greedy guest for dinner.

Mr. Dobie called me one morning and asked if I had a good recipe for beef hash. He said his mother used to make it on cold mornings and serve it with hot biscuits, and he knew of nothing he liked better. He had recently been a guest at the White House, and former President Harry Truman was also visiting there at the same time. President Johnson had very graciously asked Mr. Truman and Mr. Dobie to sit in on some of the conferences. It was about two o'clock when the three of them went up to the family dining room on the third floor of the White House for lunch. Mr. Dobie said they had a lovely lunch, but he couldn't remember anything in particular except the hash. He said it was the best he'd ever eaten; it tasted like it had a little jalapeño pepper in it. I wrote Zephyr Wright at the White House, who was probably the one who made it, and asked how she made that hash.

★

White House Hash

Zephyr said there really wasn't a definite recipe, but that it was very necessary to use only the best meat available, and make lots of gravy. She adds a few potatoes and onions, and — Mr. Dobie was right — a few jalapeño peppers. The President and his visitors from Texas always liked this little hot accent!

Living "over the store" does present some problems from time to time, I suppose, but it has also given me a great deal of pleasure to know many of the persons who come to Green Pastures to dine or for some other occasion.

Dr. and Mrs. Irl Allison, Austin folk who have known Van Cliburn most of his life and have followed his illustrious career with much interest, brought him and his parents out to Green Pastures for dinner after the magnificent concert Van played here. We were all convinced that those long legs were hollow. "That boy" ate seventeen biscuits — along with a substantial four-course dinner. The Dance Club from Burnet, a small town about fifty miles west of Austin, was having its annual Christmas dance at Green Pastures that night, and some of the members kept passing by the door of the room where Van was having dinner in order to get a glimpse of the young celebrity. When he had finished eating, two of the Burnet girls, Mary Frances Johnson and Pat Robertson, came in and asked Van if he would consent to come in to the ballroom and say hello to the dancers. Graciously, Van said that he would love to — the music sounded so *good!* When he entered the ballroom, there was a thunderous applause. Actually, the party was over; the orchestra had just played the last dance and was packing to go. Van said he'd love to dance if he could request a waltz. The orchestra obliged, and Van waltzed first with one lady and then another. Everyone joined in. He waltzes as smoothly as he runs the scales. Someone proposed making Van Cliburn an honorary member of the Burnet Dance Club, and all the members showed their agreement with another loud round of applause, whistling, and whooping. Van accepted the honor with pleasure!

A few weeks later, Van and his parents were back in Austin with our dear friend Bob Waldron, who is also a lifelong friend of Van's. Van was to play at the dinner President and Mrs. Johnson were having in honor of German Chancellor Ludwig Erhard in nearby Stonewall. After rehearsal, they came to Green Pastures for dinner. When Marie Mays heard Van was coming, she stirred up an extra supply of biscuits. The next night, after his performance in Stonewall, Van, his parents and Bob returned again to Green Pastures. It was quite late. The Koock kids were still at home for the Christmas holidays and we were just having dinner when Bob called to say they'd be out, so we made room for four more at the table and asked them to join us, which they seemed delighted to do. Everyone was in a holiday mood, and there was lots of laughing, joking, and storytelling. Van regaled us by telling stories about some of the funny and ridiculous incidents which have occurred during his tours. He has a very keen sense of humor. We all had such a good time. He had his usual hearty appetite, which is easy to understand since he naturally doesn't eat before a concert and exerts so much energy during his performance. He is starved by the time he finally gets around to having his late dinner. We were having:

Roasted Turkey and Amy's Dressing
Giblet Gravy
Hot Biscuits
Cranberry Jelly
Sweet Potatoes in Orange Cups
Fresh Green Beans

Nothing original, but the dinner was apparently enjoyed by everyone.

The hour was growing late, but Van said, "This has all been so much fun; I hate to leave. What can we do now?" Karen spoke up, "Well, usually we all gather round the piano and sing after dinner." Then glancing casually around the table, she added, "Does anyone here play the piano?"

Van held up his long arm, "I do; I can play 'Whispering Hope' all the way through with both hands." So we proceeded to the piano. Van played and we all sang variations of "The Twelve Days of Christmas" and all the other Christmas songs. This was indeed one of the gayest nights of the holidays.

Van is not only a good eater, but a pretty good cook as well. He is a great advocate of health foods — whole grain flours, raw sugar and the like. And he comes up with some mighty good results! Here are some of Van's favorite recipes. I get off on "health jags" occasionally and find that using these "off the beaten path" ingredients surely gives the jaded palate a great deal of pleasure.

Now, Van says he has a great variety of delicious health foods he eats, not just yogurt and blackstrap! For instance this:

★

Apple Pie

CRUST

2 cups whole wheat flour
1 cup soy lecithin (shortening substitute)
2 Tbs. of cold water or enough to hold crust together

FILLING

6 or 8 sliced winesap apples
1 cup brown sugar
½ tsp. each ginger, nutmeg, cinnamon
1 tsp. each wheat germ, dandelion seed
3 tsp. soy lecithin

Put filling in crust. Sprinkle with chopped pecans.

Cover with second crust and pinch the two crusts together. Cut slits in the top crust (3 or 4). Bake in hot oven at 425 degrees for 8 minutes. Lower heat to 325 degrees and continue baking 30 to 35 minutes. Van puts a thin slice of rat cheese on top of each slice while the pie is still warm.

While we were observing the fact Van ate quite a quantity of Marie's biscuits, his mother said: "Well, we just don't even try to count them when Effie George, our cook in Tucson, makes his favorite *Whole Wheat Biscuits."

★

Van Cliburn's Whole Wheat Biscuits

Sift into a mixing bowl:

1½ cups whole wheat pastry flour
½ cup wheat germ or wheat germ flour
1¼ tsp. salt
4 tsp. double-acting baking powder
¼ cup powdered milk

Add and cut in with pastry cutter:

4 Tbs. chilled soy lecithin

Add and stir with 25 strokes:

¾ cup fresh or sour milk, buttermilk, or yogurt

Turn onto floured canvas or wax paper; knead 10 times; pat 1 inch thick and cut with biscuit cutter.

Place close together on oiled baking sheet; bake in hot oven at 450 degrees for 12 to 15 minutes.

Van is also enthusiastic about another fine friend and cook Mary Brooks's *great* *Banana Pudding. She stirs up a big supply when he is home.

★

Banana Pudding

Combine and beat slightly:

¼ cup sugar stirred with
½ cup powdered milk
⅛ tsp. salt
3 whole eggs or 6 yolks
½ cup fresh milk
1 tsp. vanilla

When mixture is smooth, add and stir:

1½ cup fresh milk
½ banana, sliced
Few drops yellow food coloring

Pour into a shallow greased baking dish or custard cups; sprinkle with nutmeg. Bake in a slow oven at 300 degrees for about 40 minutes, or until center of custard is 175 degrees. Serves 4.

Texans are quite proud of the many stars in the entertainment field which have come from the Lone Star State — Mary Martin, Linda Darnell, John Boles, Zachary Scott, to mention only a few. And more recently Mrs. Bing Crosby, who was a popular Chi Omega at the University of Texas when she was Katherine Grandstaff from West Columbia. Last summer Kathy returned to her Alma Mater, where she was a "visiting professor" in the Drama Department. She brought her children, her mother, and the children's governess with her, and they lived at the Chi Omega Sorority House, which is near the campus and would have been unoccupied otherwise for the summer.

She is a tiny, winsome, pretty girl who often refers to her husband affectionately as "Harry." Kathy and Bing shoot quail and pheasant, so often she includes them in her company menus. They entertain a great deal at home and usually have only six or eight guests at a time. She invites the guests to come for dinner around six o'clock so that the children can visit, too, before going to bed. She and "Harry" like to include the children in as many of their activities as possible. A menu Kathy served the night before she came to Texas was:

** Shrimp Bisque*
Green Salad
** Roasted Pheasant*
Wild Rice
Currant Jelly
French Rolls
** Crème Brûlée*

★

Shrimp Bisque

1 onion chopped fine
Butter
1 small carrot diced fine
½ lb. shrimp, cut in thirds
1 cup dry white wine
3½ cups chicken stock
1 bay leaf
4 sprigs parsley
½ cup flour
2½ cups milk
Heavy cream

Sauté onion in 2 Tbs. butter with carrot. When slightly brown add shrimp and sauté for about 5 minutes. Then add wine and 1 cup chicken stock. Put in bay leaf and parsley; cover and let simmer 20 minutes.

In another pan melt 4 Tbs. butter. Add flour and let simmer 5 minutes without browning. Add 2½ cups chicken stock and milk and whip with wire whip till smooth. Remove shrimp from first mixture and chop fine. Strain the liquid into cream sauce and continue to whip. Pour through strainer again and then add finely chopped shrimp. Add 1 Tbs. butter and enough heavy cream to make it a cream soup consistency. It is a lovely way to start an evening. Serves 6.

★

Roasted Pheasant

Kathy said Bing likes for the pheasants to hang at least a week, as this brings out the rare rich flavor of the birds. Pheasants, like most game, are lean and must be well bardéed when cooked, so that they will not be dry. Kathy usually roasts 1 *young bird* per person.

Salt and pepper the young pheasants to taste and then rub them well with butter. Tie three strips of bacon on each bird. Place in roasting pan and roast in 350-degree oven for almost one hour, or until well done. Remove bacon before serving. Let the juice chill in the refrigerator so that all fat may be easily removed. Strain and then reheat the gravy and add seasonings. Serve over the roasted birds and garnish with lots of watercress.

★

Crème Brûlée

3 cups heavy cream
1½ inches of vanilla bean
6 egg yolks, well beaten
About ¾ cup light brown sugar

Place cream and vanilla bean in a saucepan, bring to a boil, and boil exactly 1 minute. Remove from stove, take out vanilla, and pour cream into the well-beaten egg yolks, stirring constantly. Cook in a double boiler over simmering water, stirring constantly, for five minutes or until it coats the spoon. The bottom of the pan should not touch water. Pour into a buttered baking dish and refrigerate. When thoroughly chilled and firm, cover the entire surface with the brown sugar. Place under a preheated broiler, leaving the door open, until the sugar has melted and formed a hard crust. Chill again before serving. Serves 6.

Kathy said that Harry sees to the selecting and buying of the wines which they always serve with dinner.

I don't know if Texas weddings are different from those in other parts of the country or not. In Texas, one can rarely manage to have such a thing as a small wedding. I know this is particularly true around Austin. Everyone who has ever known the bride or the groom or their parents expects an invitation. And many times if one is not received, the mother of the bride may get a phone call: "Ruth, I didn't get an invitation, but I'd love to see Sue get married," or "My cousins from San Antonio will be here. May we bring them to the wedding?"

I think, for instance, when Ed and Anne Clark's only child, Lelia, married Douglas Wynn of Greenville, Mississippi, it took some masterful planning to take care of the "over a hundred" out-of-town guests.

However, one nice thing about such an occasion is that good friends come forth and rally around to help. The usual format begins with the Announcement Party, often given by close friends or relatives of the bride. Then follows a round of parties honoring the bride and groom — brunches, luncheons, suppers, cocktail parties, dinner dances, and showers. The number of parties depends not only on the popularity of the bride, but also on her physical stamina. Then there's the Trousseau Tea — when the feminine half of the guest list is invited to come and see the gifts and peek at all the lovelies on satin sacheted hangers upstairs. There has to be a luncheon for the bridesmaids, and the Bachelors' Dinner — some grooms say this should be eliminated — and the Rehearsal Dinner given by the groom's parents. If the wedding is at night, and most of them are, due to the hot Texas sun, there is also a brunch or luncheon on the day of the wedding, given by some very dear friend for all the wedding party and out-of-town guests. Later the women don their lace dresses and everyone goes to the wedding and big reception.

For the Clark-Wynn wedding, the Greenville guests chartered a special train and had a party all the way from Mississippi to Texas.

A number of them had their chauffeurs drive their cars and meet them in Austin.

There were many beautiful parties given for the young couple, like the luncheon by the Jack Harrises. Luncheon at Rose's is always a happy and beautiful experience. She is another friend who has given me many recipes. Pink is the predominant color in the Harris dining room, and Rose used a lovely pink epergne of Venetian glass filled with sweetheart roses and lilies of the valley for a centerpiece. She served:

** Pink Crab Mold*
Hearts of Artichoke with Hollandaise
Relish tray of carrot curls, stuffed celery and olives
** Fried Dough*
Tray of fruit
** Fresh Coconut Torte*

★

Pink Crab Mold

1 can condensed tomato soup
12 oz. cream cheese
3 Tbs. gelatine and ½ cup cold water
1 cup boiling water
1 cup mayonnaise
2 Tbs. grated onion
1 cup finely chopped celery
4 Tbs. picante sauce
1 dash Tabasco sauce
3 cups white crabmeat

Barely warm the soup. Whip cheese into the soup. Soak gelatine in cold water. Add gelatine and boiling water to the cheese and soup mixture. When cool, add mayonnaise, onion, celery, picante sauce and Tabasco. Then stir in crabmeat and pour into ring mold. Turn out on fig or romaine leaves.

★

Fried Dough

Cut rich biscuit dough in strips 2 inches long, 1 inch wide, and ¼ inch thick. Place in freezer overnight. Just before serving, drop into deep fat. When light brown and puffed, remove from fat and drain on absorbent paper.

★

Coconut Torte

8-oz. package cream cheese
1 stick soft margarine
1 pkg. powdered sugar
1 Tbs. vanilla
1½ cups fresh coconut (or 1 can coconut)
2 layers sponge cake

Soften and whip the cream cheese. Add margarine. Beat in sugar and vanilla at low speed. Add coconut. Spread over cake layers.

★

Rose's Ragout

1 small baby beef sirloin, about 2 lbs.
⅔ cup beef suet, diced
1 large onion, diced
1 large green pepper, cut fine
1 can sliced mushrooms, with juice
2 Tbs. soy sauce
⅓ cup port wine
2 Tbs. flour dissolved in a little water
Salt and pepper to taste

Dice the sirloin and brown in melted suet. Add onion, green pepper, mushrooms, soy sauce and wine. Simmer slowly until juice cooks down. Then add the flour and salt and pepper. Place in oven and simmer for one hour. Serve over rice to 4.

The Trousseau Tea turned out to be an all-day affair, and on that warm June day Anne served tall glasses of iced tea with lemon and fresh mint, very thin cucumber sandwiches, and lemon tea cookies.

Mr. and Mrs. Everette Looney gave another luncheon for all the out-of-town guests. They used a flowerpot theme — clay flowerpots of fresh flowers decorated the tables. Helen Corbitt, who planned the whole thing, had her usual fabulous food, and I'm sure she impressed all the Mississippians. She carried out the flowerpot theme in the menu by serving individual *Baked Alaskas in small flowerpots, with sweetheart roses like those used in the centerpieces.

★

Flowerpot Alaskas

Use an 8-ounce glazed ceramic flowerpot. Place a piece of plain cake in the bottom. Pile with whatever ice cream you like, to three quarters full. In the middle of each pot force a large ice cream soda straw, and cut off even with the top of the pot. Pile meringue around the inside of the pot, leaving space over the soda straw open. Bake at 400 degrees until the meringue is brown. Insert fresh flowers in the soda straw.

A luncheon I particularly remember was the one given by Mr. and Mrs. Ronald Byram. Their daughter, Carilu, was Lelia's maid of honor. The entrée was *Creamed Sweetbreads — perfectly delicious — and they should surely be served more often, especially if they are prepared like this:

★

Creamed Sweetbreads and Mushrooms

Soak sweetbreads in icy water for 1 hour. Blanch 15 minutes in salted water, in white wine, wine and water, or water with lemon juice or vinegar. Trim the tough membrane and connecting tissue. Plunge in cold water again to keep white and firm. Sauté 1 lb. mushrooms in 4 Tbs. butter until tender. Add 2 Tbs. sherry; simmer for several minutes. Combine sweetbreads and mushrooms with 3 to 4 cups rich cream sauce. Simmer until well blended; salt to taste. Serve on toast points or in patty shells.

The wedding took place in Austin's old historic St. David's Church, and of course, was perfectly beautiful. The reception was held across the street at the gracious old Driskill Hotel, which is almost like home to many of us. It was a very beautiful and gay affair.

This wedding was a good number of years ago, and Lelia and Doug have lived happily ever since in Greenville, Mississippi. I suppose one of the reasons I was thinking about them is that I recently saw Doug interviewed on TV at the 1964 National Democratic Convention. He was one of the three delegates from Mississippi who were seated. On returning home, a friend called and said, "Doug, I want to work for the Democrats here. There are so few of us that I think I'll just give a seated dinner!"

I suppose I have catered for a thousand wedding receptions during my career. My friend Gina Mezzetti had the right idea about them. She said that the ceremony should be sweet and solemn and the reception fun and festive. "It is a time for great celebration

— there should be music, champagne, dancing, food, and laughter!" Virginia Prasatik's was such a reception.

There is a sizable Czech population in Central Texas, and they have made great culinary contributions to these parts. Maybe one reason I like the Czech weddings so much is that they bring all the food! For Virginia's reception, we got Green Pastures all dolled up and baked some hams and beans. But then came her Uncle Henry from La Grange with one hundred pounds of hot Czech sausage; the Bartoshes came with large bowls of potato salad; Louis and Johnnie Struhall brought a gigantic bowl of the greatest cabbage salad (*Zelovy Salat), which Louis said his mother always took to picnics, weddings, and wakes; Martha Hill brought pans of apricot, prune, and poppy-seed *Kolaches; and the bride's grandmother, Mrs. Wychopen, brought the strudel. Green Pastures made a tall, beautiful wedding cake, but really shouldn't have bothered because Aunt Octavia brought three, Mrs. Simmicek came with two, and Lillian Struhall brought her fabulous *Banana Cake.

★

Zelovy Salat (Cabbage Salad)

½ medium cabbage, cut as for slaw
3 Tbs. apple cider vinegar
2 scant tsp. salt
3 (or more) Tbs. sugar
½ tsp. ground pepper
1 small chopped onion
2 Tbs. fresh bacon drippings

Having cut cabbage, place on fire in boiling water. Cook rapidly 5 minutes; drain. Take apple cider vinegar, salt, sugar, ground pepper and onion and bring to boiling point, then add bacon drippings. Pour this juice over the cooked cabbage and mix. Season more if desired. Serves 6.

★

Orange Layer Cake

2 cups sugar
¾ cup butter
5 eggs
1 cup milk
3 cups flour
2 heaping tsp. baking powder

Combine cake ingredients and bake in two layers.

FILLING

¾ cup sugar
2 yolks of eggs
1 whole egg
2 heaping Tbs. flour
1 Tbs. butter
1½ cups milk
1 orange rind, grated
1 lemon rind, grated
Sliced oranges

Cream sugar, eggs, flour and butter. Add this to milk and cook until thick. When cool, add the rinds. Spread between layers, adding sliced oranges on top.

★

Tutti-Frutti Cake (This was a tremendous hit)

⅔ cup butter or margarine
2 cups sugar
5 stiffly-beaten egg whites
3 cups cake flour
3 tsp. baking powder
Pinch of salt
½ cup milk
½ cup water or coconut milk
1½ tsp. vanilla

Cream together butter and sugar, add gradually to stiffly beaten egg whites. Sift flour together with baking powder and salt. Combine milk and water (or coconut milk) with vanilla. Add flour and liquid alternately, beating slowly. Bake in three layers at 350 degrees for 30 to 40 minutes.

FILLING

1 cup sugar
8 egg yolks, beaten well
½ cup melted (but not hot) butter or margarine
1½ cups chopped white raisins
2 cups chopped pecans
1 cup grated coconut
1 to 2 tsp. mixed lemon, orange and almond flavoring *or*
1 small wine glass Bourbon (2 oz.)

Add sugar to egg yolks and butter; cook in double boiler till it thickens slightly. Add raisins, pecans, coconut, mixed flavoring (or Bourbon). Let stand for a few minutes, then spread between layers. Ice with *Never-Fail White Icing.

★

Lillian's Crushed Banana Cake

1 cup butter
3 cups sugar
4 eggs, separated
6 medium bananas, very ripe, crushed
1 cup chopped nuts
8 Tbs. sour milk
2 tsp. soda
3 cups flour
Brown Sugar Nine-Minute Icing with pecans

Cream butter and sugar. Add egg yolks, crushed bananas, nuts, sour milk in which soda has been dissolved, and flour. Fold in beaten egg whites. Bake in four 8-inch layers and ice with Brown Sugar Nine-Minute Icing with pecans.

★

Kolaches

Soft yeast
2 cups lukewarm milk
¾ cup and 1 tsp. sugar
1 Tbs. salt
¾ cup shortening
2 eggs
3 cups flour, and some more
Prunes, apricots or poppy seeds

Dissolve soft yeast in milk. Add 1 tsp. sugar and let stand long enough for yeast to rise. Cream ¾ cup sugar, salt and shortening. Add eggs and beat. Add dissolved yeast and about 3 cups flour and beat well. Keep adding flour little by little until the dough comes out smooth and has some blisters on it. Let rise until more than double in size. Roll on floured board. Cut in 3-inch squares. Make slight indention, and fill with cooled prune, apricot or poppy-seed filling.

PRUNE FILLING

1 lb. prunes
Sugar
Cinnamon
Grated lemon peel
Vanilla

TOPPING

¾ cup sugar
⅓ cup flour
Soft butter

Cook prunes, drain and pit them. Then chop and gradually add sugar, cinnamon, a little grated lemon peel and a little vanilla. Top this with mixture of sugar, flour and enough butter to form crumbles. Bake in 375-degree oven for about 12 to 15 minutes.

Besides all the cakes, there was an abundance of cookies. Mrs. Zvesper brought *Listy, Mrs. Kallus brought *Cinnamon Stars, and Mrs. Micek brought *Black Hearts and *Calla Lily Cookies, which she takes to all weddings, arranged together on a tray with Black Hearts in the center and the Calla Lily Cookies around the edge. There was also a tray of delicious *Mincemeat Cookies.

★

Listy (Leaves)

3 eggs
¼ cup powdered sugar
½ cup cream
Pinch salt
About 2 cups flour

Beat eggs separately, add sugar, cream, salt, and flour enough to make stiff enough dough to roll out very thin. Roll out a small piece at a time as thinly as possible on floured board, cut into pieces about 4 by 6 inches. Make 3 or 4 slits in them and fry light brown in hot deep fat. Sprinkle with powdered sugar. Makes 3 dozen.

★

Cinnamon Stars

1 lb. grated almonds
1 lb. granulated sugar
Whites of 6 eggs
Juice of ½ lemon
⅛ oz. cinnamon
Flour

Almonds should be washed, dried and then grated with the brown skin left on. Stir the sugar into the beaten whites of eggs, add the lemon juice and continue beating for 15 minutes, then add the cinnamon. Reserve a small portion of this mixture for top of cookies. To the large portion add the almonds. Roll out about ⅛ inch in thickness, using only as much flour as necessary. Cut with star-shaped cutter, brush each cookie with the reserved egg mixture and bake slowly on well greased pans. About 50 cookies.

★

Black Hearts

½ lb. flour
½ lb. sugar
1 egg
½ lb. butter
½ lb. ground nuts
1 tsp. vanilla
½ tsp. cloves
½ tsp. cinnamon
2 Tbs. chocolate

Mix up, roll thin and cut in heart shapes. Cook 8 to 10 minutes at 325 degrees. Makes 5 to 6 doz.

★

Calla Lily Cookies

10 eggs, separated
2 cups sugar
1 cup flour
3 cups heavy cream
2 tsp. vanilla

Beat the yolks of eggs vigorously, add the sugar slowly, then add the flour and fold in the stiffly beaten whites. Drop on oiled cookie pans in round shape. Bake in a moderate oven. When slightly cooled, roll in shape of calla lily. Whip the cream, sweeten to taste, add the vanilla and fill the cold lilies. A strip of orange peel placed in the narrow end completes the lily. About 50 cookies.

★

Mincemeat Cookies

Cream 1 cup butter with 1½ cups sugar. Add 3 eggs beaten together. Dissolve 1 tsp. soda in 1½ Tbs. hot water. Add 2¾ cups flour and ½ tsp. salt. Mix ½ cup flour with 1 cup nutmeats and 1 pkg. mince meat broken in pieces. Drop from a teaspoon on buttered sheet and bake in moderate oven 10 to 15 minutes. Makes about 5 doz.

Well, I don't know why I said that food is number one — number one is actually beer. I remember the first wedding reception I planned for one of the charming Czech people. The bride-to-be, from a Czech settlement near La Grange, said that her uncle would bring the beer. "Beer?!" I exclaimed. "But, dear, I don't have enough of the right kind of glasses for beer. We usually serve punch or champagne, and I have really never served beer at a wedding reception!" "Well," she said firmly, "in La Grange, I have never been to a wedding reception where they *didn't* serve beer, and they just use paper cups!" So we set up a keg of cold beer under each of the two big oaks in the front yard, and a good time was had by all. Some of the oldtimers brought along their dominoes and had a few games in the shade, while the dancing and merrymaking went on inside.

A very popular Austin bride was pretty Diane Wilder, who was wined and dined for days before the wedding. Anne Bird Nalle, who never likes to have just a "routine" party, called and said, "Mary, the bride and groom have had every kind of party at least twice! Elaborate, elegant parties! What can George and I do?" As always, the Nalle party was a tremendous success. We sprayed pasteboard cakeboxes a variety of brilliant colors, lined them with multicolored tissue paper, and filled them with:

Corned Beef and Swiss Cheese on a French Roll
Chicken Salad Sandwich
Two little round boxes, one with fresh fruit,
one with Potato Salad
Deviled Eggs (dropped in vegetable coloring before stuffing)
A ruffled cup of olives

Each item was carefully wrapped in Saran Wrap and then in the multicolored paper. George Nalle, Jr., came driving up across the grounds in his newly painted Model T Ford, Matilda, which was decorated with streamers and tissue flowers and a big heart painted on the back. The trunk of the car was opened and everyone came and got a box lunch and took it to the tables under the shade trees. The tables were also covered with the bright paper, and in the center of each table was a spectacular bunch of brilliant tissue flowers. We passed long glasses of a cold Wine Cooler. And for dessert we had delicious *Chewy Pecan Pralines wrapped individually and placed in a piñata which swung merrily from a tree. Everyone had his turn at hitting at the piñata, and it was finally broken by the bridegroom after much tantalizing by the two young Nalle boys who pulled the piñata up and down trying to prolong the fun as well as the anticipation of its contents.

★

Chewy Pecan Pralines

This recipe was given to me by my friend Mrs. W. W. Powell. She used to make them for the St. Ignatius Church bazaars.

1 cup brown sugar
1 cup white sugar
1 cup white Karo
1 can sweetened condensed milk
½ lb. butter
3 cups pecans
1 tsp. almond extract
1 tsp. vanilla extract

Combine brown sugar, white sugar, Karo, milk and butter. Stir over low fire. Boil, stirring constantly until it forms a soft ball when dropped in a cup of cold water. Take off fire and add pecans, almond and vanilla extract. Stir until thick and drop by spoonfuls on a buttered platter.

I usually toast the pecans a few minutes in the oven before adding them to the candy.

A pretty luncheon given at Green Pastures in honor of Patricia Scott and her fiancé, John McHargue, the day before the wedding, featured:

Fresh Fruit served with Marmalade Dressing
** Shrimp Acapulco*
Heated rice on side

★

Shrimp Acapulco (for 4 persons)

4 fresh coconuts
1 lb. shrimp, cleaned and cooked
2 heaping Tbs. hot, cooked rice per coconut
Chutney
Toasted slivered almonds
Grated coconut
Chopped chives

SAUCE

3 Tbs. melted butter
3 Tbs. flour
2½ cups hot milk
½ cup coconut milk
1 Tbs. curry powder
Salt
¼ cup red wine
1 Tbs. onion juice

Cut tops off 4 fresh coconuts with a hand saw. Retain part of the milk for sauce. Make sauce with butter and flour and let simmer 5 minutes without browning. Add hot milk and coconut milk; whip till smooth. Add curry powder, a little salt, wine and onion juice and whip till smooth. Strain and add shrimp. When thoroughly heated, remove from fire. Place hot, cooked rice in coconut, fill ¾ of remaining space with curried shrimp, put a good-sized piece of chutney on top and close with coconut lid.

Place each coconut in a small aluminium foil bowl half-filled with rock salt; this will keep the coconut from tipping. Place these on a flat pan and cook in oven at 325 degrees for 30 minutes. The day before, make "hats" or covers out of heavy gold foil. On removing coconuts from oven, cover with "hats," pulled together on top with 1½-inch satin ribbon. For added flair, stick a white plume in the top. This makes a very dramatic appearance, and very happy guests once they find their "surprises" under the gold covers. Additional condiments passed include slivered toasted almonds, grated coconut, chopped chives, etc.

I'm sure no one in Acapulco ever heard of this! I got the recipe in Chicago a number of years ago when my husband, Chester, and I were attending the National Restaurant Convention.

IN AND AROUND AUSTIN I

My own, beautiful, lovely Austin! I had intended to confine my collection to right here in the heart of Texas, which well I could do, as I am sure there is no place where hospitality is projected more "in toto," where the population is made up of dearer, finer people who certainly know and prepare fine food.

Austin and the surrounding communities could well compose a fascinating library on the subject of food. There are literally thousands of fabulous cooks and, as I have said before, they have indeed been most kind and helpful to me. But for the most part, I am saving Austin for my next book.

People who were born here but moved away, people who were stationed here during the war, people who have visited here at one time or another, all want to come back to live in the Friendly City. The others of us, Austinites who were born, reared, educated and always lived here, who have spent many a summer swimming in Barton Springs, boating and waterskiing on Lake Austin, climbing to the Capitol dome with visitors, proudly watching Austin grow from a small town to a city, and who have traveled far abroad, are always glad to get home; home to our beloved Austin.

Austin is very big on clubs; there are hundreds, I am sure, and all have parties throughout the year. Both faculty and students of the University of Texas have a tremendously busy social calendar; the state officials and their families are also kept busy partying, so Austinites on the whole are very social-minded and active. Then there are just that many more parties given by individuals, so be sure and bring a long dress when you come, or a costume.

Susan Shaw and some of her schoolmates at the University gave an original party to celebrate finals being over. The invitation read:

You are invited to
EEYORE'S BIRTHDAY PARTY
on
Friday, May the 8th (a very hummy sort of day)
at
4:00 in the afternoon until ???
in
Our favorite part of the forest
That Being
Eastwoods Playground, Park Place and Harris Blvd.

There will be suitable free beverage, such as beer, for those who think young. Also EEYORE's Birthday Cake, music, *special* ENTERTAINMENT, and possibly a Maypole!

Those who wish may bring red balloons; they are EEYORE's favorite. If it is an unhummy sort of day, please bring umbrellas or suitable rain attire. Hope for sun.

Hope everyone will be able to come and make EEYORE happy.

Well, everyone *did* come! Some in tuxedos, some as children's characters, one as a nun playing the guitar. The Maypole dance was the most fun. Many brought balloons, and all had a happy, hummy, hilarious time in the forest — most of all Eeyore!

On the other hand, you may find yourself at a fun Peon Party, like the one given by the Al Williamses and P. J. Allen. P.J. — who spends most of his time flying around Texas transforming, with his great flair for decor, ballrooms into French markets and country clubs into Venetian Palaces, for debutante parties and such — put his considerable talents to work to create a good facsimile of a Mexican plaza in the Williamses' backyard. It included the thatched cantina, "La Perla," flowers in riotous bloom on the trees, and a wishing well from which the Tequila Punch was served. The guests all wore Mexican costume — and two arrived on live donkeys! An oxcart was used for the beer bar, and the tables, scattered throughout the yard, were covered with red and white checked cloths. A Mexican band played for the dancing and joined the guests (who came from many countries) in singing familiar Mexican songs. All this was very wonderful, but nothing excelled the fantastic Mexican stew called *Calabazita, on which P.J. and Polly Williams collaborated and served in Mexican pottery, with *Frijoles Borrachos and Polly's *Muy Bien Garbanzos Salad.

★

Calabazita (for about 100 people)

3 whole heads of garlic
Pure lard (olive oil will do, but is not Mexican)
30-35 lbs. lean pork, cut in bite-sized pieces
10 lbs. onion, chopped fine
3 1-gal. (No. 10) cans tomatoes with juice
2 lbs. green bell peppers
15 lbs. calabazo (green squash) cubed
50 cobs of fresh corn, or 5 lbs. (2 boxes) frozen whole kernel corn
Oregano and cumin to taste
Black pepper to taste
Fresh green chili, seeded and ground, to taste

Crush garlic and fry in just enough lard to brown. Sauté pork pieces till browned. Add onions, tomatoes and bell peppers and simmer for several hours. Add calabazo, cut corn and additional seasonings, and simmer till squash is tender, but not mushy.

★

Frijoles Borrachos (serves 100)

Boil 5 lbs. pinto beans with garlic, onions, cumin, oregano, salt pork and bacon. Add hot water from time to time. Reduce, and for last addition of liquid, use about 2 cans of beer — remember that it will froth, so watch it doesn't overflow.

★

Muy Bien Garbanzos Salad (*serves 10*)

2 cans garbanzos (Mexican beans) drained
1 cup celery
½ cup chopped onion
1 cup chopped green pepper
2 Tbs. chopped pimento
Salt and fresh ground pepper to taste
2 garlic cloves

Mix above ingredients and toss with a good oil and vinegar dressing. It is better if made the day before serving.

Nat Henderson, who, along with Al, is a distinguished member of the Austin press, made his superb *Venison Chili — without chili powder but with the real chili; and it *do* make a difference. For a smaller amount than he made for the party:

★

Venison Chili (*to serve 18 to 20*)

5 lbs. venison (*or* 3 lbs. venison, 2 lbs. beef) coarsely ground
Vegetable oil
20 dry red chili pods (chilis Colorado)
Beef stock
1 tsp. (approx.) oregano
Ground cumin
Salt
5 or 6 cloves garlic

Sauté meat in oil until light brown. Clean seeds out of chilis, rinse in cold water. Cover with a little water and bring to a boil; cook for about 30 minutes, or until they peel easily. Keep water; remove chilis, scrape pulp away from skin and mash pulp into paste. Add sautéed meat and mix together. Cover with beef stock and season to taste with oregano, cumin, salt and garlic. Let simmer slowly 5 to 6 hours.

One of the first social events of each fall is the annual Jewel Ball given by the Austin Symphony League, with private parties before or after. Then there are many gay and fun parties given during the football season; there is the bachelors' elegant Presentation Ball, when the season's debutantes are presented, who in turn inspire rounds and rounds of beautiful parties. The Junior League annual charity ball in the early spring is a major social event everyone looks forward to from year to year; the Headliners' Award dinner dance also attracts many out-of-town and out-of-state guests. The year Sonny Davis was chairman it was held in the Municipal Auditorium; Kathleen Gee did the very elaborate decor, and Green Pastures catered the food. The theme was "Around the World in 80 Days" and an exact replica of the balloon used in the movie by the same name was hanging from a star-studded sky. Movie stars John Wayne and Carol Burnett were honorees.

There were very charming and authentic-looking sets for Switzerland, France, Italy, Texas, Indonesia, Scotland, India and Spain. We had a huge wheel of Swiss cheese flown in by Swissair from Switzerland and, with a wide variety of crackers, served it as hors d'oeuvres.

For Texas, the huge hindquarters of a barbecued beef were sliced and served on buns by men in cowboy suits.

The Italian piazza, hung with grapes and flowers and the Italian colors of red, white and green, was where Victor Nardeccia and his staff, in provincial Italian costume, served *Lasagna. The Chianti was served from a wine barrel; and Joe Picandra sang Italian folksongs and played the accordion. I am sure Victor was insulted when I offered him my Lasagna recipe, and of course he used his own, which is equally delicious.

We had *Curried Chicken in enormous brass tubs, with ceramic linings, served on saffron rice for India. Six small boys were dressed in white jodhpurs and little boleros and turbans, and each held a brass bowl of condiments for the curry. This was one of the most popular "countries." Kath Gee did a golden temple effect for the set, with a live peacock on the top which spread its colorful feathers proudly throughout the party. Students from India who were attending the University came in their native dress and added to the atmosphere.

The Indonesian corner had palm trees, a real waterfall, growing plants and flowers. My friend Mr. Clark came and brought his pet monkeys to chatter and play nearby. There we served a luscious assortment of fresh fruit from *everywhere,* including baskets of those gigantic strawberries with long stems from California. We had large clam shells filled with sour cream for anyone who wanted to dip.

Ernesto, in his black Spanish pantalones elaborately embroidered in white, kept the guests laughing with his Cantinflas-type antics, as he served the barbecued cabrito and pepitas and the long loaves of Spanish bread. There was a whole carcass of cabrito turning slowly over the glowing coals, which gave an irresistible aroma! *Esta fué la mejor comida!*

The Scots were holding a meeting in Austin at that time, so the Harry Gordon clan, wearing their kilts, came with bagpipes and served the haggis which we had flown in from Glasgow and *Scotch Scones we had made from Mrs. Gordon's recipe at Green Pastures.

The French sidewalk café with a pastry shop in the background was the real conversation spot of the party, for only in Europe had anyone ever eaten such pastries. They were made by my friend Mr. Walter Koenig of San Antonio, who learned this speciality in Munich, where he was born and reared. They were so beautiful, and they just melted away with each bite. He made réligieuses, gateaux normands, croquembouches, napoleons, tarts of all kinds and many other dainties.

Dr. Silvio Sconti, well-known music teacher, critic and judge for the international piano competitions, came to Austin to help us plan our trip to Europe. He is a great enthusiast for Italian food, and loves to prepare it. There wasn't a modest bone in his body when it came to his animated reciting of just how *he* made Lasagna. With all the family and hired help assisting, Silvio prepared this great dish for us. We, however, now make it single-handed, very often, especially during the football season. This is the recipe that Victor *didn't* use for the ball, but that I use at Green Pastures:

Lasagna Romana (prepare in advance)

- 1 eggplant
- 2 Tbs. salad oil
- 2 medium-sized onions, minced
- 1 lb. chuck, ground
- 1 clove garlic, minced
- 1½ tsp. salt
- ¼ tsp. black pepper
- ¼ tsp. oregano
- ¼ cup dehydrated mushrooms
- 3 Tbs. snipped parsley
- 1 No. 2 can peeled Italian tomatoes (2½ cups)
- Tomato paste
- 1 Tbs. sugar
- ½ cup grated imported Parmesan
- ½ lb. lasagna (1½ inch wide noodles)
- ¾ lb. mozzarella cheese, thinly sliced
- 1 lb. rocotta or cottage cheese (ricotta can be purchased at Italian food stores)

Peel and slice eggplant in thin slices; sauté in oil, lightly browning on each side till tender. Drain on absorbent paper. Sauté onion and ground beef and set aside. Make sauce.

Mix garlic with salt and add pepper, sugar, oregano, mushrooms, parsley, tomatoes, tomato paste and 2 Tbs. Parmesan cheese. Simmer, covered, 40 minutes. Refrigerate until final preparation. About 45 minutes before serving, cook lasagna according to package directions. Drain and cover with cold water.

Now, Dr. Sconti's procedure was this:

Spread sauce to well cover bottom of oblong baking dish; cover with strips of drained lasagna. Spread with more sauce. Next, cover with thin slices of eggplant, a little more sauce, then lasagna, next slices of mozzarella cheese, a little sauce, ground meat, lasagna, sauce, ricotta cheese, sauce, meat, lasagna, sauce, ricotta, sauce; and finally Parmesan. In no particular order, just so that it all gets in, and end with sauce and Parmesan on top. With an Italian green salad and Chianti, you'll never forget it!

Bake 30 minutes in 350-degree oven. Serves 8.

★

Curried Chicken (serves 6)

1 3-lb. hen, boiled till tender
2 Tbs. butter
2 Tbs. flour
1 cup hot chicken stock
1 cup milk
1 Tbs. grated onion
2 Tbs. curry powder dissolved in warm water (adjust amount to taste)
2 Tbs. dry red wine

Remove chicken from bones and cut in cubes. Simmer butter and flour 5 minutes without browning. Add stock and milk; whip with wire whip till smooth. Add onion. Dissolve curry powder in warm water and add; then add wine, and last of all, 1½ cups diced chicken.

Serve on rice which has had a little saffron added for seasoning.

★

Scotch Scones

2½ cups flour
1 Tbs. baking powder
3 Tbs. sugar
¾ tsp. salt
6 Tbs. butter
⅞ cup milk
1 egg, beaten

Take flour, baking powder, sugar and salt and sift together three times. Then cut in butter and gradually add milk to make soft dough. Knead lightly on floured board till it is ½ inch thick. Cut with round cutter and brush with beaten egg. Cut each round in quarters, making

4 triangles. Sprinkle lightly with sugar and bake at 400 degrees for 12 to 15 minutes. Makes 1 doz. *Very* good.

Supper Clubs

Supper clubs are also very popular around here. They all seem to be organized for the same basic reason — just getting together with friends. Some groups may put emphasis on fancy dishes, others on cocktails, another group may meet at a member's home, then all "go out" for supper. An original and clever group of young executives and their wives call their group the "No Supper Club." They claim to be affiliated with I.P.W.T.A. (International Po' White Trash of America)! Then there are those who are real gourmets; their suppers always include exotic and original fare. I am glad these people are well established in their own professions 'cause I'd hate to have them as my competitors. Two especially talented couples in this gourmet group are Dr. and Mrs. Ralph Hanna (Ralph is a prominent pediatrician) and Mr. and Mrs. William Kay Miller (Kay is an attorney). Ralph says that on a Sunday afternoon he may be just "fooling around" with a recipe and it starts tasting pretty good, so Marie calls the Millers to come over and try it. Or vice versa, with Kay and Evelyn calling the Hannas to try out their latest discovery. After close analysis and a few suggested touches, they have the rest of the critics in for a "finished" production.

One night the Hannas had *Beef Fondue Bourguignonne, just to try out some of the sauces Ralph had concocted:

Beef to be dipped in Barbecue Sauce, Mushroom Sauce,
Whipped Cream and Horseradish Sauce, or Mustard Sauce
** Baked Eggplant*
Tossed Green Salad
French Bread
** Peppermint Pie*

★

Beef Fondue Bourguignonne

Cut filet of beef into 1-inch cubes and place on a platter by a copper kettle of hot oil (kept hot by a medium flame from an alcohol burner). Each guest has a fondue fork with a long insulated handle, and cooks his beef to his own taste — rare, medium, or well-done — and then transfers it to another fork and dips it in one or all of sauces Ralph has perfected.

BARBECUE SAUCE

¼ lb. butter
2 cloves of garlic
2 Tbs. prepared mustard
1 Tbs. chili powder
1 Tbs. Worcestershire sauce
1 can tomato sauce or catsup
8 oz. vinegar
2-3 small bottled deviled red peppers, snipped fine
Cayenne and salt to taste

Melt butter in saucepan, add garlic cut small. Cook gently 5 minutes. Mix in mustard, chili powder, Worcestershire, tomato sauce, and vinegar. Add peppers and seasoning. Simmer slowly on low fire ½ to 1 hour.

MUSHROOM SAUCE

Sauté until brown:

2 Tbs. melted butter
Add 2 onions (green and white) chopped fine

Add:

1 small can chopped mushrooms
½ tsp. salt
¼ tsp. pepper
½ cup red or white wine

Cook until reduced to about ½ the original substance. Add:

1 can Italian meat sauce
1 Tbs. tomato paste
Chopped parsley

Cook until slightly thick.

MUSTARD SAUCE

1 cup mayonnaise
½ cup mustard
1 medium dill pickle, finely chopped

Mix mayonnaise, mustard, and dill pickles, chopped fine.

★

Baked Eggplant

6 large tomatoes, peeled, seeded and chopped

Put into a saucepan with:

2 Tbs. olive oil
2 Tbs. tomato paste
Pinch of salt

Simmer uncovered for 30 minutes. Meanwhile, wash, dry, and cut into ½-inch strips:

1 medium-sized eggplant

Place in bowl, cover with hot water, and let stand for 5 minutes. Drain thoroughly and let dry on absorbent paper. (It is very important for the eggplant to be dry.) Fry in very hot olive oil 3 minutes on each side or until soft and lightly browned. Sprinkle with salt and pepper and remove from pan. Mix together:

2 cups bread crumbs
½ cup grated Parmesan cheese
1 Tbs. chopped parsley
2 cloves of garlic put through a garlic press
A pinch of salt and pepper

Blend these thoroughly. Place a layer of eggplant in a casserole. Sprinkle with breadcrumbs and tomato sauce. Alternate layers until ingredients are used, ending with eggplant on top. Cover with mozzarella cheese. Bake in 375-degree oven until cheese is slightly brown.

The Hannas' son, Hank, shakes up the salad dressing. It is an oil and vinegar base with lots of interesting herbs, and he is always called forward to make his bow. Ralph said that Marie couldn't cook a thing when they married. He once told her to put something under the broiler, and she didn't even know where the broiler was. But she has undoubtedly made great progress. Her *Peppermint Pie just about steals Ralph's thunder.

★

Peppermint Pie

PIE SHELL

Cream 6 Tbs. butter and gradually add 6 Tbs. powdered sugar. Add 1½ squares of melted unsweetened chocolate. Add 1 egg yolk and mix well. Spread in chilled 9-inch pie plate.

FILLING

1 envelope (1 Tbs.) gelatine
¼ cup cold water
2 egg yolks, unbeaten
1¼ cup milk
½ cup finely crushed peppermint stick candy
½ cup cream, whipped
2 or 3 drops of red coloring

Mix gelatine and cold water. Combine egg yolks and milk. Cook and stir over low heat until the mixture coats a metal spoon. Pour over gelatine. Add candy and stir until dissolved. Chill. Fold in whipped cream and coloring.

2 egg whites	**¼ cup sugar**
⅛ tsp. salt	

Beat egg whites and add salt and sugar. Beat into peaks, and fold into the gelatine mixture. Pour into pie shell and chill.

TOPPING

Top with whipped cream. Sprinkle slivered chocolate and crushed peppermint candy over the top.

Evelyn and Kay Miller could truly live off the land, and just about do, even making their own wine. They planted a cutting from a grapevine at Kay's mother's home. This grape is a sweet small one, and it makes a light rosé-type wine. They also (quite involuntarily) raise squabs, and in self-defense Evelyn has become expert in preparing these delicious birds. She may serve:

Jellied Black Cherry Salad
** Squab*
Wild Rice
Broccoli with Browned Butter
** Baked Meringue Shells with Ice Cream and Strawberries*

★

Squab

Clean one whole squab per person. Rub inside with salt and pepper. Put rolled-up strip of bacon in the cavity. Add breadcrumbs browned in butter, onion, a little apple, lemon juice, raisins, chopped onion and celery. Don't stuff fully. Place more bacon across breast. Put in baking pan with each bird barely touching the others. Start at 350 degrees; 20 minutes afterwards baste with mixture of half butter and half white wine, and lower the oven to 275 degrees. Bake till tender, about 1 hour.

★

Meringue Shells

2 egg whites	**6 Tbs. sugar**

Beat together until it forms high peaks and drop by large spoonfuls on greased cookie sheet; bake in 250-degree oven.

Actually, Kay doesn't spend as much time cooking as one might suspect. He just cooks in quantity and then freezes the desired portions. He says this makes cooking worth his time. For instance, since *Corned Beef and Corned Tongue take quite a bit of time to prepare, he may cook three briskets and four tongues at a time.

★

Corned Beef

Fresh, heavy brisket with all fat trimmed off
3 to 5 cups salt
Lots of water
Onions, clove, bay leaf
Salt and pepper
Garlic
Pickle chips
Beef stock
Chili powder

SAUCE FOR CORNED BEEF

2 cups basic white sauce
1 cup fresh horseradish

Marinate beef in next five ingredients for 18 to 21 days in refrigerator, turning at least three times. Drain, put in fresh cold water and bring to boil. Pour off, rewater and then add beef stock, chili powder and salt. Cook 3 to 4 hours. Put in foil and freeze. Add a little sauce to the portions before freezing and they will be moist when thawed.

Tongue can be done in the same way, except that it only need marinate for 8 days, and takes less time to cook. With the Corned Beef, Kay serves:

** Mashed Potatoes and Turnips*
**Kay's Cole Slaw*

★

Mashed Potatoes and Turnips

Boil potatoes and turnips together in salted water. Mash and season with butter.

★

Kay's Cole Slaw

Shred firm medium-sized head of cabbage. Place shredded layers in mixing bowl and salt and pepper heavily. Put ½ bell pepper and 2 crushed pimientoes on top of cabbage and toss until well mixed. Add 4

Tbs. white grain vinegar and 2 Tbs. olive oil and toss. Place in ½-gallon crock. Cool 2-4 days.

This cole slaw is delicious with *Smoked Fish.

★

Smoked Fish

Brush fish with butter and place over low coals made from oak chips.

Kay beamed, "This fish is great and made so easily. Serve it with a baked potato, and, man, you're eating!"

Kay highly recommends marinades for meats. He uses equal parts of olive oil, soy sauce (which gives a nutty flavor) and any kind of good dry wine. This marinade is very good on backstrap venison.

In true sharecropper fashion, Kay and Eve went back to the soil and gathered onions in a surplus crop. They experimented with pickling and came up with wonderful results. Somehow, pickled onions never struck my fancy, but after eating these, my attitude has changed. With the next onion crop, I'm putting up a passle.

I've discovered Kay's secret for looking so bright-eyed when he arrives at the office. Try this — it works!

★

Oatmeal and Rum

Cook oatmeal according to directions on package. Then just before serving, add 2 Tbs. brown sugar, 1 Tbs. rum and ¼ cup chopped pitted dates to 2 cups of oatmeal.

★

Kay Miller's Pasta and Bean Soup
(*Pasta e fagioli*)

1 cup dry white beans (any small dry bean may be substituted)
1 soup bone, ham bone or 2 cups chicken stock or beef stock
¼ lb. lean salt pork
2 tsp. olive oil
1 large onion, minced
2 large cloves garlic, minced
1 Tbs. chopped parsley (celery leaves may be substituted)
1 Tbs. catsup
1 cup small pasta (ditalini preferred, but any small tube-shaped pasta may be used)
Butter
Grated Romano or Parmesan cheese

Wash beans and soak overnight. Pour off soaking water and simmer beans with soup bone, ham bone or 2 cups of chicken stock or beef stock and enough water to more than cover for about 2 hours.

Cut ¼ lb. of the lean part from a piece of salt pork into thin slices, then cut slices across the grain into small squares or strips. Fry pork over very low heat until fat is rendered and meat is brown (almost crisp). Remove meat from grease.

Heat 2 Tbs. of olive oil in skillet, or substitute the grease rendered from the salt pork for the olive oil. Cook chopped onion and garlic in the oil very slowly until yellow. Add the chopped parsley or celery leaves, 1 Tbs. of catsup and cook about 5 minutes more, stirring occasionally. ¼ tsp. basil, savory, or rosemary, crushed, may be added. Stir this and the fried pork meat into the bean soup and continue simmering until beans are tender but not mushy.

Put pasta into a separate pan of deep fast-boiling salted water. Cover the pan, remove it from burner and let pasta stand 20 minutes, stirring quickly with wooden spoon at about 5-minute intervals so pasta will not stick together, and be sure to cover after each stirring. At the end of 20 minutes, pour off salted water, run cold water over pasta in a large sieve or put it through several changes of water. Drain and add to bean soup and cook about 10 minutes longer. Add water as needed and salt and pepper to taste.

Serve hot over pat of butter covered with grated cheese.

Now Kay and Ralph get a lot of publicity for their cooking, but we all know that behind every great chef there is a great woman to "hand me this, hand me that, hand me the other" and to wash mountains of pots and pans.

Harold Lawrence may be an exception. He sorta likes to cook alone, and Margaret, his wife, says she really has no objection to staying out of the kitchen while the genius is at work. One night not long ago he invited us over for *Tamale Pie. He had worked with a combination of recipes and turned out this masterpiece.

★

Harold's Tamale Pie

Sauté ½ lb. to ¾ lb. ground beef or deer meat, or combination of both, with one chopped onion and one chopped green pepper in 4 Tbs. oil or butter or a combination of the two. Then add and stir in:

8-oz. can tomato sauce
2 tsp. chili powder
Pinch of oregano and basil
1 tsp. salt
½ small clove of garlic (optional)
12 cut-up stuffed olives

Simmer for about ten minutes and set filling aside.
To prepare cornmeal mush, boil:

4 cups water

Stir in

1 cup cornmeal
1 tsp. salt

Cook and stir over low heat until the mush is thick.

Fill a flat greased baking dish with about ⅔ of the mush. Add meat filling. Top with remaining mush. Sprinkle generously with grated Parmesan cheese and paprika.

Bake in moderate 350-degree oven for about 30 minutes.

If you want top to be brown, put pie under broiler for a short time.

Another specialty of Harold's is his

★

Spicy Red Cabbage

Shred 6 cups red cabbage, after removing the hard core.

Sauté 3 Tbs. of chopped onion in 3 Tbs. bacon drippings or butter. Add:

5 Tbs. brown sugar
3 Tbs. vinegar
2 apples, cut into thin slices

Then add the red cabbage and cook it for 30 minutes, stirring frequently.

Optional: If you desire a sweet and sour taste, add a small can of sauerkraut, stir in and simmer.

Our supper club is an exclusive group of friends who try to meet at least once a month for supper, and also have an annual meeting for breakfast on the Fourth of July at Barton Springs. We meet in one another's homes, mostly because we would never get to visit unless we set aside a specific time and place to gather. The host family furnishes the main dish and the others bring vegetables, salads, desserts, etc. This is in no way a gourmet club, but we do show up with some very interesting surprises, like *Olga Bredt's Venison

Roast, *Mary Love Bailey's calorie-loaded potatoes, Sammie Reed's *Asparagus Casserole, and Frances Burcham's *Coffee Dessert. We usually suggest that Bess Jones bring the greens to toss a salad, or the potato chips. I had tried to include one of her recipes in this book, but I never succeeded in finding one. She did serve us some very delicious pimento cheese sandwiches one day, but when I asked for the recipe of the spread, she dashed my hopes by answering enthusiastically that she had bought it ready-made at the store. (After all, Bess has so many other talents, why should she try to cook?)

One night a former Supper Club member who happened to be back in town from Washington, Congressman Homer Thornberry, asked if he could bring along a friend to supper. The "friend" turned out to be Lyndon B. Johnson. After supper, he asked if he could have the floor. Now this is very hard to come by at the Supper Club, but Carl Bredt said, "All right, if you won't talk over five minutes!" I thought Carl was mighty brave to say that, but Lyndon didn't notice. He only wanted to tell us how much it meant to him to be at home among old friends. Lyndon concluded by saying if he ever got to the White House, the club should have a covered dish supper there, and he as host would furnish the meat! The evening had started with the Chrys Doughertys' *Apricot Champagne.

★

Apricot Champagne

The day before making, freeze whole, peeled, seeded apricots in ice trays. Place frozen apricots in cold champagne glasses. Add 1 jigger of Southern Comfort. Fill glasses with cold champagne.

★

Olga Bredt's Venison Roast (serves 10 to 12)

1 leg of venison, about 6-8 lbs.
Pieces of salt pork
Lard
Salt and pepper
Garlic powder
4 or 5 pieces of bacon
1 bay leaf
1 cup water
1 cup dry red wine
1 medium-size onion
Adolph's seasoning salt

Make holes in joint with a sharp knife and insert salt pork. Rub well with lard, salt, pepper and garlic powder and lay bacon across leg. Marinate overnight. Add bay leaf and water and cook in 450-degree oven for 45 minutes. Lower heat to 325 degrees and add wine; cook for approximately 1½ hrs. or till tender. Turn roast once during roasting period.

★

Sammie's Asparagus Casserole (serves 4)

Drain 1 large square can asparagus. Place in a buttered baking dish. Add 4 sliced hard-boiled eggs. Sprinkle with chopped pimento and cracker crumbs. Pour 1½ cups rich cream sauce over the asparagus and other ingredients. Put slivered almonds on top and place in 350-degree oven. Bake until piping hot.

★

Mary Love's Escalloped Potatoes

Boil potatoes in their jackets until done; peel and slice. Make a medium cream sauce. In a casserole, put a layer of potatoes, then cream sauce, then grated cheese; continue layers, finishing up with cream sauce and cheese on top. Bake slowly at 250 to 300 degrees until cheese melts.

★

Frances Burcham's Coffee Dessert

In a double boiler, melt 1 lb. marshmallows by pouring ½ cup strong coffee over them. Let cool and set. Fold in as many pecans as "you can afford," and ½ pint whipped cream. Chill. Serve in compotes and pass with sugar cookies if so desired.

★

Olga Bredt's Chocolate Fudge

3 6-oz. pkg. chocolate chips
2 sticks margarine
4½ cups sugar
1 tall, large can evaporated milk
2 cups chopped pecans
Dash of salt
1 tsp. vanilla

Soften chocolate and margarine, and put aside in a mixing bowl. Bring sugar and evaporated milk to a rolling boil over medium flame, stirring constantly. Pour over chocolate-butter mixture. Add pecans, dash of salt and vanilla. Stir mixture until creamy. Pour in large, greased Pyrex dish. Chill 2 to 3 hours. Cut in squares — and wonder where the fudge went!

One of the most distinguished organizations to which we belong is the Singing and Chowder Society, a club that requires no dues, no officers, no committee meetings — and only meets twice a year for sure. One meeting is held the day after Christmas, when members bring all sorts of dishes, exotic (like *Aunt Zella's Turkey and Barley Casserole) and not so exotic (like my cold sliced ham), made mostly from Christmas leftovers. The membership is made up of six families with all ages of children and a span of three generations, now that my and Maxine Kavanaugh's grandchildren love to come.

After we eat supper, we sing for at least two hours — old songs, new songs, fun songs. Some of the more talented members sing solos, some team up for duets, and we even have barbershop quartets. John Kavanaugh is the tireless pianist; you name 'em and he plays 'em. It's interesting how the young sophisticated college group won't miss this night of fun. Margaret Gregory's *Turkey Soup warms our vocal cords before we start singing.

★

Margaret's Turkey Soup

Break turkey carcass and cover with water, leaving on whatever meat remains.

Add 2 Tbs. chicken stock, 2 large onions, chopped fine, 6 pieces of celery (including leaves), 4 carrots, cut in small pieces, ¼ cup chopped parsley.

Simmer slowly, strain through colander, add equal quantity of tomato juice, and serve hot in cups.

Then we feast on Mrs. Harry Wise's:

★

Aunt Zella's Turkey and Barley Casserole

1 cup slivered almonds
½ cup corn oil
1 cup chopped onion
1 finely minced clove of garlic
1 cup pearled barley
1 cup finely chopped celery leaves
1 tsp. salt
Fresh ground pepper
1½ cups turkey (cut in small pieces)
6 cups chicken or beef bouillon

Sauté almonds in oil until golden brown, turning often. Remove nuts, retaining oil in pan or large skillet. Sauté onion, garlic, and dry barley in oil, stirring constantly until light brown. Add remainder of ingredients except bouillon and place in casserole. Pour hot bouillon over this mixture until completely covered. This may not take the full 6 cups. Bake at 350 degrees for 1½ hours or until barley is completely cooked. Stir about every 30 minutes and add more hot bouillon or boiling water, keeping mixture covered, since much of the liquid will be absorbed in baking. Serves 6 to 8.

The summer meeting of the Singing and Chowder Society is held on the Fourth of July at the Morton Ranch, and no one wants to miss this fun-time, either. The youngsters, oldsters, and in-betweeners would rather go to the Mortons' than any other place, and they even sing a song to that effect. There is always a game of softball for the older boys, a variety of horseback riders, with and without saddles, and the under-six-year-olds usually go wading in the creek to catch tadpoles and minnows, slipping down (on purpose) and squealing with delight. So when the dinner bell rings, appetites are sizable, but easily satisfied with the spread. Mr. Dean O. Smith, who is the game warden in the Dripping Springs area, barbecues the cabrito for us, and what a treat that is! Cabrito is a very young Spanish goat between one and a half and two years old. When properly slaughtered and cooked, cabrito is absolutely one of the best meats you could ever eat, and Mr. Smith is a past master at barbecuing. The day before the party, he selects a young stocky kid goat, slaughters it, and hangs it on the screened porch where the wind can reach it and keep it cool. Mr. Smith says that time is the secret ingredient for all good barbecues, especially cabrito. He cooks the meat over low coals for eight to ten hours, carefully turning and basting it with special sauce until the meat is tender and flavorful.

★

Barbecue Sauce

1 cup mustard
1 pt. salad oil
1 qt. vinegar
1 pt. lemon juice
1 pt. Worcestershire sauce
Black pepper
2 Tbs. red pepper
½ lb. butter (not margarine)
1 tsp. garlic salt
2 tsp. onion
2 Tbs. salt

Mix all ingredients and simmer over low flame for about one hour.

Mr. Smith never stops to eat the delicious cabrito. He says he has eaten his fill during his early days as a Texas ranger. He would chase cattle rustlers all day, and at night he would sit around a campfire, the rain running down his hat into his plate — and that just sorta spoiled his taste for barbecue. One time he had to shoot a rustler in self-defense and handcuff him to a tree while he rode to town to get the sheriff.

Early one morning just before deer season opened, Mr. Smith came to the Morton Ranch. He had promised Helen Morton he'd teach her how to shoot and show her where the deer would be running. After the lesson Helen invited him in to breakfast saying, "Mr. Smith, I was hoping you'd have breakfast with us, so I have made a big pan of hot corn bread." "No thank you, ma'm," he replied. "I ate so much of that ol' cornmeal mush out on the trail, I just somehow can't face cornmeal in any style." A few mornings later, Helen had hot biscuits, hoping this would suit her kind friend's fancy on a cold morning. "No, ma'm, I thank you, but that was the only kind of bread we had when I was riding the range — those old sourdough biscuits." "Well, Mr. Smith," Helen asked, "What kind of bread *do* you eat?" "I'll tell you, I sure do like those loaves of store-bought bread. There was an old German baker out West. Everybody said he kneaded the bread with his feet, but I didn't care. Mama would send us kids to get bread for supper, and I'd eat a whole loaf before I got home, while it was still soft and warm."

Everybody brings a basket with something to go with barbecued cabrito — a variety of salads, and cakes, and there are always at least three freezers of homemade ice cream. However, if we forgot to bring our baskets there would still be an abundance. Helen always has her tall *Three-layer Chocolate Mint Cake; Nana adds her good Arroz and Frijoles; and Helen her whole grain bread and a big bowl of butter.

★

Helen Morton's Three-layer Chocolate Mint Cake

¾ cup shortening
2½ cups sugar
2 squares unsweetened chocolate, melted
6 whole eggs
1 tsp. soda
1 Tbs. hot water
1 cup buttermilk
2 cups cake flour
2 tsp. vanilla

Mix shortening and sugar together and stir in melted chocolate. Beat eggs well and add gradually to mixture. Beat with rotary egg beater till smooth. In small bowl, dissolve soda in hot water. Add buttermilk to soda mixture and whip up with spoon until foamy. Add to first mixture. Stir in flour a little bit at a time. Add vanilla. Bake in layers at 350 degrees until done (at least 45 minutes). Cover with fudge frosting.

FUDGE MINT FROSTING

3 cups sugar
1 cup milk
2 squares unsweetened chocolate, grated
3 or 4 tsp. white syrup
Large lump butter
1 tsp. vanilla
2 or 3 drops peppermint oil
1 cup nuts

Boil sugar, milk, chocolate and syrup until it will form a soft ball in ice water. Add butter, vanilla, peppermint oil and nuts and beat until creamy.

Cliffy Kavanaugh asked, "What kind of cake *is* this? It looks chocolate, but it tastes *green*."

After a lengthy supper of Mr. Smith's cabrito and many other tasty dishes, we shoot off fireworks — everything from sparklers to the multicolored bomb bursts. Our special guests for the last several Fourths have been a beautiful family, Dr. and Mrs. Luis de Laosa, who are exiles from Cuba. They have joined in the fun and are becoming very familiar with our songs, for a singsong is always the finale to our Singing and Chowder Society meetings.

Señora Nana Barrera-Valejo is as much a part of the Morton ranch as the windmill on the west side of the ranch house. Charles Morton is a contractor by day and a rancher for the love of it, and he has added all sizes of rooms to the original rock house which was built in 1890. By popular demand, Helen serves at most of her parties antojitas, Spanish term for tidbits before supper. Nana makes a spicy delicacy called *Panecitas, which is a favorite with Helen's Shakespeare Club and the Singing and Chowder Society. I watched Nana make these — by the hundreds — and it is fascinating. When she brought them out of the oven, eager hands reached for them before she could place them in the little baskets in which she intended to pass them.

★

Panecitas

2 lbs. masa de harina
1 cup sharp cheese, grated
1 small onion, grated
Cayenne pepper
1½ tsp. salt
3 Tbs. lard

Mix above ingredients until they make a stiff dough, then roll in 2-inch balls, flatten with palm of hand and place on a lightly greased cookie sheet. Bake at 450 to 500 degrees for about 10 to 15 minutes, or until golden brown.

Masa de harina is ground from whole kernels of dried corn after it has been soaked in water then cooked very slowly in lime water almost all day. It is used in making tortillas and tamales. It would be good to cultivate the habit of eating it daily, for it contains most of our needed vitamins. Have you ever noticed the beautiful white teeth, shiny dark hair, and twinkling eyes of the children, and the longevity of our Mexican friends whose total diet is tortillas and pinto beans? Perhaps masa de harina is the reason. Another interesting fact about masa is that it is a natural repellent of strontium 90, a radioactive material found in fallout, and those people who eat masa are immune to this matter. Make mine tortillas any time, especially Nana's handsome, thick, handmade ones.

Helen says that Charles is a man of very simple tastes; all he wants for supper is bread and butter and jelly, fruit and milk. However, the bread must be homemade, the butter freshly churned, the fruit tree-ripened, and the milk fresh and raw. Does sound pretty good, doesn't it?

★

Helen's Homemade Bread

1 tsp. sugar
1 cup lukewarm water
2 pkg. dry yeast
3 Tbs. sunflower oil
3 Tbs. honey
1 Tbs. butter flavoring
1 cup powdered milk
4 cups whole wheat flour
2 cups hot water
1 Tbs. salt
4 cups unbleached white flour

Dissolve sugar in lukewarm water; then add yeast and let it "work" until it foams up to fill a 2-cup measuring pitcher. Dissolve the oil, honey, butter flavoring, powdered milk and 2 cups of whole wheat flour in the hot water. (Measure the oil first, then the honey and butter won't stick to the spoon.) Mix the powdered milk with the flour so that it won't lump. Beat well. Add dissolved yeast, beat some more. Let rise in a warm place till very bubbly. Add salt. Beat in 2 more cups of whole wheat flour; beating brings out the gluten and lets it rise, and also helps wet the flour. Whole wheat flour doesn't absorb the moisture as well as white flour. Knead in white flour and let rise till double in bulk. Knead dough until it loses its flabby feeling and becomes firm and elastic. Make out in 3 loaves. Let rise till double in bulk. Bake at 400 degrees for 10 minutes, then at 350 degrees for 30 minutes more.

No greater love has anyone than to share his *Agarita Jelly with a friend. Helen gave us some for Christmas (wonder if Charles knew she did?). Her recipe starts: "Pick, stem and wash the berries." I wonder how many people outside Texas know what this involves? The agarita grows on a little thorny shrub, an evergreen, which is usually the first to bud in spring. The berries are very small, and the leaves are stiff and spiny, so they are gathered by spreading a cloth on the ground under a bush, holding the end of a branch in the (gloved!) hand, and lightly threshing the branches one at a time. But the result is more than worth the trouble, because Agarita Jelly just can't be beaten.

★

Helen's Agarita Jelly

Pick, stem and wash the berries. Put them in a preserving kettle and cover them well with water. Bring to a quick boil and strain through a cloth; boiling too long makes a hard jelly. Do not mash or squeeze too much, as the seed is bitter. Add 1 cup of sugar to each cup of juice. Boil to the jelly stage, testing with a spoon. If the jelly sheets and two drops hang from the side of the spoon, it is done. If you use a thermometer, cook to about 220 degrees. Agaritas jell very rapidly.

We would like to have Carl Edward and Carolyn Bock as regular members of the Singing and Chowder Society. They pass all the rigid requirements: they serve delicious food and they are both very fine musicians. Carl Edward has played viola with the Austin Symphony since its beginning. He is responsible for the success of many picnics and such gatherings by his fine accordion music. Besides her numerous civic and church activities, Carolyn is president of the Texas Federation of Music Clubs. While *I* may be interested in their musical talents, *some* of the members — whom I won't mention by name — are more interested in Carolyn's culinary talents. In fact, they'll gladly settle for one of her delicious Cheese Sandwiches.

★

Cheese Filling (8 sandwiches)

1 lb. cheese
7-oz. can pimentos
4 hard-boiled eggs
1 fresh onion
Salt and pepper to taste

Grind all the above together. Then melt 1 Tbs. butter, add 1 Tbs. flour, and brown slightly. Add 1 cup milk slowly and 1 tsp. sugar. Boil well and add ½ cup vinegar. Add slowly, and if it seems a little lumpy, beat it with an egg beater. Add one beaten egg and boil a little longer. Pour over cheese mixture. If a smooth consistency is desired, pour over immediately; if a rough texture is wanted, cool dressing slightly before pouring over cheese. Season with salt and pepper to taste.

When Carolyn asks what else she should bring to the picnic, the vote is split between *Mom's Potato Cake and *Mahogany Cake.

★

Mom's Potato Cake

1 cup butter
2 cups sugar
4 eggs, separated
½ cup cocoa or semisweet grated chocolate
1 tsp. cinnamon
⅓ tsp. nutmeg
2 cups chopped pecans
1 cup mashed potatoes (cooked and mashed just before baking cake)
2¼ cups flour
2 tsp. baking powder
½ cup milk
1 tsp. vanilla

Cream butter and sugar until fluffy. Add egg yolks, then add cocoa, cinnamon, nutmeg, nuts, and potatoes. Add flour and baking powder that have been sifted together, alternately with milk; add vanilla. Last, fold in stiffly beaten egg whites. Bake in tube pan at 350 degrees until cake leaves sides of pan, approximately 1 to 1½ hours. Delicious served with or without icing.

★

Mahogany Cake

½ cup butter
1½ cups sugar
4 eggs
2 oz. bitter chocolate
5 Tbs. hot water
1¾ cups flour
2 rounded tsp. baking powder
½ cup milk
1 tsp. vanilla
1 cup pecans

Cream butter and sugar. Add yolks, beaten. Melt chocolate by pouring 5 Tbs. hot water over it after it has been chipped into a double boiler; heat this mixture until the chocolate is completely melted. Add to egg yolks. Stir in flour, baking powder, and milk. Beat egg whites until stiff and add last. Then vanilla and chopped pecans.

Carolyn's *Fruit Salad Dressing is also a recipe we have all asked for and passed around. Sally Rudd put it over fresh fruit in a compote, with a mound of whipped cream on top sprinkled with chopped pecans for a most delectable dessert.

★

Fruit Salad Dressing

2 eggs, separated
1 cup sugar
½ cup pineapple juice
Juice of one lemon
Salt

Place egg yolks in double boiler. Add sugar, pineapple juice, and lemon juice. Add pinch of salt and beat slightly. Cook until it begins to thicken a little. It does not get thick. Remove from fire and add thickly beaten egg whites. Cool and pour over fruit. Especially good over fresh oranges, apples, pineapple, fresh grapes, and banana combinations. Top with whipped cream and nuts for dessert.

Ever get to the point where it seems all your time is involved in planning meals, preparing meals, serving meals, cleaning up after meals, and buying groceries to start the routine over the next day, and the next, and the next? Well, let me tell you about Mrs. George Martin, mother of twelve. One might think she'd simply give them some porridge without any bread, spank them all soundly and put them to bed; but such is not the case with this remarkable woman. She is a good cook and lets her children know it by the interesting meals she serves. Eve and George own the ABC Shop, which sells children's toys, clothing and furniture. George says he should be in the food business, too, to completely provide for his brood.

Interesting meals or not, George complained that he just couldn't come home after a hectic day in the store and face the clamoring of the clan, and go about cutting up several portions of meat to be placed on the unbreakable plates, wiping up spilled milk from high chairs, etc. So he suggested that the children have their supper early, soon after the older ones got home from school. Eve and her gentle maid, Catherine, followed his suggestion; the children had eaten and were out playing when George made his entrance. Ah, how quiet it was! He had a leisurely drink and then declared that he was ready for supper. Alas, there was no supper left, for regardless of how much is prepared, the platters are always licked clean! "Never mind," said George, still enjoying the solitude. "I'll just cook some bacon and scramble a couple of eggs." As you know, nothing is more tantalizing than the aroma of bacon frying, and as the scent sifted out to the back yard where the children were playing, they came filing into the house one by one. They gathered around the table and watched every bite that George put in his mouth. "Are you going to eat all those eggs, Daddy?" "May I have a piece of bacon?" George gave up! The children had played up another appetite! It was resolved then and there that there would be only one setting for dinner at the Martin house.

Just before Helen and Paul White left for their trip around the world, the Martins had one in the series of farewell parties in their honor. Now that the children are older (the youngest is school age), Eve has a built-in house staff, and she entertains with the greatest of ease. Every pair of hands has its own special job, and Helen White commented that she hadn't been to a dinner with so much "back-of-the-chair" service since the 20's.

Marge and Loretta made the rounds before dinner with the hors d'oeuvres. We all held our breath when Johnny came in carrying a silver tray with thin-stemmed glasses and a frosted pitcher of *Daiquiris; but he made it safely. Young Mary had set the table, using the beautiful lace dinner cloth, Haviland china and tall crystal goblets which had belonged to her grandmother. Laura made a clever centerpiece with a globe of the world the honorees were soon to encircle. Johnny helped to clear the table between courses, Cris passed rolls, Edward refilled the water and wine glasses, and Helen and Nina served the dessert.

★

Daiquiris

Place in a gallon jar 1 16-oz. can of frozen lemonade, 1 fifth of Bacardi light rum, ½ cup fresh lemon or lime juice, 6 drops of vanilla, and ¼ cup Maraschino cherry juice. Stir well, cover tightly and place in the freezer. It freezes into a mushy state, not solid. Stir frozen mixture and scoop into champagne glasses. Serve with short straw.

Dinner that night consisted of:

Leg of Lamb, garnished with fresh pear halves broiled with Mint Jelly in the center
** Wild Rice and Sausage Casserole*
Fresh Asparagus with browned butter, lemon juice, and Parmesan cheese sprinkled on top
Green Salad with French dressing
Hot Rolls
Hot Apple Pie à la Mode.

★

Eve Martin's Wild Rice and Sausage Casserole

1 lb. sausage (or skinless link sausage)
1 lb. mushrooms
2 medium-large onions
2 cups wild rice
¼ cup flour
½ cup heavy cream
2½ cups chicken broth
1 tsp. Aćcent
Generous pinch each thyme, oregano, marjoram
1 tsp. salt
2 tsp. pepper
½ cup slivered almonds

Sauté sausage and drain on paper towel. Break in small pieces. Sauté mushrooms and chopped onions in sausage fat. Add to cooked sausage. Cook washed wild rice in boiling salted water for 10 to 12 minutes. Drain. Mix flour with cream until smooth. Add chicken broth and cook until it thickens. Season with Aćcent, oregano, thyme and marjoram, salt and pepper. Combine with rice, sausage and vegetables. Mix and toss together. Bake in a casserole for 25 to 30 minutes at 350 degrees until it bubbles. Sprinkle with slivered almonds around the rim.

With fourteen Martins around the table, Eve usually doubles the quantities for this next recipe. When she serves it, the boys come in with a "Yipee! *Shrimp Creole tonight!"

★

Shrimp Creole

2 No. 2 cans tomatoes
2 small onions, chopped
1 green pepper
3 chopped garlic cloves
¼ lb. butter
1 pinch chili powder
Dash of Tabasco
Sugar to taste (about 2 Tbs.)
1 bay leaf
Dash of red pepper
Salt and pepper
5 Tbs. flour
1 cup water
1 can tomato puree
2 lbs. shrimp
1 lemon, peel and all

Sauté vegetables in butter, add other ingredients, except shrimp and lemon, simmer 2 hours. Add shrimp the last 30 minutes, and put in lemon for last 10 minutes. Serve with rice and lemon juice. Six servings.

Eve has finally caught on, and when I ask her, "How, just *how* do you make your *German Potato Salad?" she'll just whip up a batch for me, rather than tell me *again!*

★

German Potato Salad

Boil California potatoes so that they will slice thin and not break. Allow 1 large potato per person. Peel and slice medium thin. Place a layer of potatoes in a dish, sprinkle with salt, pepper, garlic salt and place thin sliced white onions on top. Repeat.

Sauce: Take 8 slices of bacon and cut them in saucepan. Fry until crisp and remove from grease. Add 2 Tbs. sugar, 1 cup apple cider vinegar, and 2 cups water. Mix in 2 heaping Tbs. of flour, 1 tsp. dry mustard and 1 heaping Tbs. of prepared mustard. Add enough evaporated milk to make it smooth. If it is too thick, add more water. Grate 2 hard-boiled eggs into the sauce if desired. Pour over potatoes while warm.

Football weekends usually find the beautiful home of Jay and Kitty Patterson like a hotel, American plan — with the meals included. The Pattersons make an enviable team; Kitty cooks indoors and Jay outdoors, and always well in advance of their guests' arrival.

How do they manage so much for so many, and *so* delicious? We plan to send Kitty to the Olympics for her *Lemon Pie making. For a recent house party of fourteen, Kitty and Jay had prepared:

Jay's Smoked Turkey — he does them superbly, in a specially built smoker.

** Strawberry Salad*

Baked Beans

Potato Salad

Assorted breads and spreads

A wide variety of pickles, jams and relishes which Kitty puts up every year

Her delicious pimento cheese spread for sandwich-making

** Lemon Pie*

Applesauce Cake

Pound Cake Cookies

★

Lemon Pie

CRUST

⅓ cup butter	**2 Tbs. powdered sugar, sifted**
1 cup flour	

Mix together and press in pie pan; do not turn over edge of pan. Cook till light brown in 350-degree oven.

FILLING

½ cup flour	**1 cup hot water**
3 eggs, separated	**Pinch of salt**
⅓ cup evaporated milk	**Grated rind and juice of 2 lemons**
1¼ cups sugar	

Mix together, stir until thick and smooth. Pour into cooked pie shell.

MERINGUE

3 egg whites	**6 Tbs. sugar**
¼ tsp. vanilla	

Whip whites till stiff; add vanilla and sugar slowly. Put over top of pie, making swirls and little peaks. Bake in 250-degree oven, very slowly, until meringue is light brown.

★

Kitty's Strawberry and Banana Jellied Mold

3 pkgs. strawberry gelatine	**4½ cups boiling water**
1½ pkgs. plain gelatine	**5 large bananas, mashed with potato masher**
1 No. 2 can crushed pineapple with juice	**½ pt. sour cream**
2 boxes frozen strawberries	

Mix all ingredients except sour cream. Pour half into 2-qt. mold and let set slightly. Spread with sour cream, then pour on remainder of mixture. Nuts may be added. Refrigerate.

Mrs. John Rauhut, a perfectionist in many arts, gives generously of her talents and time to the cultural developments of Austin, where she has always lived. I have known Laverne all my life, and her parents, Mr. and Mrs. Fred Barge, were also friends. Laverne is a needlewoman of wide repute. The charm and beauty of her home is greatly enhanced by her exquisite works of needlepoint and petit point. However, her *Divinity is also a work of art.

Laverne was so small when she first started making Divinity she had to stand in a chair to see into the pan, and the making of Divinity was just as much a part of Christmas preparation as trimming the tree. It is no longer a seasonal item; friends enjoy it all year round. This Divinity candy can be packed and shipped or stored in candy tins for weeks. Laverne had round silver trays stacked high in a pyramid making a lovely centerpiece. This is exactly how Laverne Rauhut makes her divine

★

Divinity (*125 pieces*)

In a small pot cook quickly to 238 degrees:

½ cup sugar **½ cup water**

Pour over:

3 stiffly beaten egg whites

Beat until well mixed.

In a large pot mix and cook to 258 degrees:

3 cups sugar **1 cup water**
1 cup white Karo

When syrup reaches 258 degrees, pour immediately and slowly over the egg mixture. Add 1 teaspoon vanilla, beat at high speed until the candy resembles very thick white paint. Remove the electric blades and let the candy rest about two minutes. Add a large cup of chopped pecan pieces and drop on waxed paper. Use a silver teaspoon. If the candy grows a bit stiff dip the spoon in cold water and continue. This makes about 125 pieces of candy and lots of friends.

If the phone rings during the crucial time of dropping, let it ring!

Sewing clubs, like supper clubs, are very popular in Texas, but this time only the girls get together. They function under all sorts of titles: the Sew and Sos, the Needlers, the Sip and Sews, Stitch 'n Snip, the Knit-Wit Club and what have you. One is more reluctant to miss the sewing club than she is an appointment at the beauty shop.

Mama, for thirty-five consecutive years, went every Thursday to quilt at the Grace Methodist Church. She used to take my Gretchen before she started to school. Gretchen loved being the center of attention. She would help Gran and the other ladies thread their needles and sit on a high stool and watch as they skillfully followed the lovely designs with tiny stitches. It was Gretchen's reward for being good to get to go with Gran and have lunch with the "quilting girls with grandma faces," as she once referred to them.

The "quilting girls" were rather casual about the dishes they brought for lunch. There might be Chicken and Dumplings, Pot Roast and Vegetables, or something similar. Lunch usually consisted of a main dish or casserole, one or two salads, maybe rolls, and a dessert. All the ladies were excellent cooks, so the food was sure to be good! In fact, the quilting group was my source of recipes when I first married.

★

Mrs. W. D. Faubian's Beef-Noodle Casserole

1 lb. ground chuck
Butter
1 onion chopped fine
1 8 oz. can tomato soup
1 8 oz. pkg. cooked noodles
1 cup whole kernel corn
1 cup sliced stuffed olives
1 4 oz. can of sautéed mushrooms
1 cup slivered almonds
1 can fried onion rings

Sauté meat in a little butter, also the onion. Add remaining ingredients, except onion rings, and pour into a buttered casserole. Sprinkle with a can of crumbled fried onion rings. Put in 350-degree oven till heated thoroughly. Serves 4.

★

Mrs. Charles Weyerman's Ham Loaf (serves 6)

1½ cups well-drained crushed pineapple
1 lb. lean cured ham, ground
1 lb. lean fresh pork, ground
1½ cups crushed Rice Krispies
1 cup milk
3 eggs, beaten
Salt, and ground pepper to taste
Flour

Mix 1 cup pineapple and all the other ingredients except flour together and pack into a loaf pan (about 4 by 8 inches). Bake in 350-degree oven for approximately 30 minutes. Then reduce heat to 250 degrees and continue baking for approximately another hour. Then turn out of pan into shallow pan to allow loaf to brown slightly. Spread ½ cup pineapple mixed with 1 teaspoon flour on top.

SAUCE FOR BASTING DURING BAKING

½ cup brown sugar
½ cup water
1 tsp. dry mustard
¼ cup vinegar
Dash of Worcestershire

★

Mrs. B. F. Wright's Cherry Pie

1 2½ can sour red pitted cherries
1 cup sugar
2 Tbs. cornstarch
¼ tsp. salt
1 tsp. almond extract
Cream
Uncooked pastry shell

Drain cherries, add enough water to juice to make 1 cup. Add sugar, cornstarch and salt, and heat till sugar is dissolved. Add cherries and almond extract. Pour in pastry shell and cover with strips of dough (dampened to make them stick), crisscrossing to make a lattice. Polish with cream and sprinkle with sugar. Cook in 400-degree oven 15 to 20 minutes till strips are golden brown.

★

Mama's Osgood Pie

½ cup butter
2 cups sugar
4 eggs
2 cups chopped nuts
1 cup chopped raisins
Pie shell

Cream butter and sugar. Add beaten yolks of eggs, nuts, and raisins. Lastly, stir in beaten egg whites. Put in pie shell and bake in 350-degree oven for about 45 minutes.

When it was Mama's turn to bring "the bread," she would make her good rolls, then take them along to rise and be cooked in the little kitchen at the church.

★

Mama's Hot Rolls

- 1 2-oz. yeast cake (dissolved in 4 Tbs. lukewarm water)
- 1 cup milk, scalded
- 3 Tbs. shortening (let it melt in the hot milk)
- 1 tsp. salt
- 4 Tbs. sugar
- 1 egg, slightly beaten
- 4 cups (approximately) flour

Mix the above and add enough flour to make dough stiff enough to handle. Knead on floured board until smooth. Place in buttered bowl, cover with cup towel and let double its bulk. Roll out on slightly floured board, cut with round cutter, brush with melted shortening, fold over Parker House style and place on baking sheet. Makes about 28 to 30. When risen (about 45 minutes), bake in 350-degree oven.

These are marvelous hot rolls. Wish I had a buffalo nickel for every one eaten at our house.

In the 40's, when war broke out in Europe, Mrs. Goodall Wooten got together some friends to knit Bundles for Britain. They met in the little cottage in Mrs. Wooten's yard and, needless to say, made great contribution to this great cause and later to the American Red Cross. Through the years, many of the original group still meet together regularly at each others' houses, and while knitting and sewing are not too evident, good food is: Mrs. Fred Nagle, a founder-member, spent quite a spell in the hospital — got out, however, in time to have the Sewing Club but was not quite up to fixing the food, so asked me to help her. The card in my menu file is marked *repeat* and the next year still *repeat same menu*. So this is what Eva likes to serve them for Brunch.

** Chicken and Cranberry Ring*
Hot cheese balls, olives
Lemon Jelly Roll, mints
Coffee

★

Cranberry and Chicken Ring

CRANBERRY RING PART

1 pkg. raspberry-flavored gelatine
1 Tbs. plain gelatine
1½ cups boiling water
¼ cup sugar
1 pinch salt
1 cup fresh cranberries, washed and picked
1 medium sized orange (seeds removed)
1 cup of juice dripped from fruit when grinding
½ cup crushed pineapple (well drained; save juice)
½ cup chopped pecans

Dissolve gelatines in hot water. Add sugar and salt and stir until dissolved. Let cool. Grind cranberries and orange, including half the peel. With fine blade on food chopper "catch" the juice of the orange and cranberries and add to pineapple juice to make 1 cup of liquid. Combine all ingredients.

Oil 2-qt. ring mold by rubbing well with mayonnaise. Pour cranberry mixture to fill mold halfway. Let set till it begins to congeal. Pour cooled chicken mixture next, filling mold completely. Let set overnight or until firm. Turn out on romaine leaves. Place homemade mayonnaise in center of ring.

CHICKEN RING PART

1 3 lb. chicken
3 Tbs. plain gelatine
Seasonings: salt, white pepper, Beau Monde, cayenne
Onion juice
1 Tbs. fresh lemon juice
1 cup mayonnaise
1 cup sour cream
¾ cup celery chopped fine

Simmer chicken gently till tender (the day before is usually preferable). Let chill. Remove all fat from the broth. Cut chicken in fine pieces. Reheat 1 qt. of broth. Add gelatine, seasonings to taste, onion juice and lemon juice, mayonnaise and sour cream. Whip till smooth. Let congeal slightly, then add chopped chicken and celery.

*Cabinet Pudding is an old-time and all-time favorite dessert. Mama used to serve it during the Christmas holidays. However, I have never been able to find her recipe for it. She only had three cookbooks; *The White House Cook Book, Old Boston Cook Book,* and the Calumet Baking Powder one. In between the pages are cards, and on the blank back pages additional recipes are written in her handwriting. But I suppose this was one she just had in her head. I mentioned this to my friend Mrs. Virginia Parry, and she said she had a wonderful recipe which had been used in the White House kitchen from the time of George Washington. It was given to Mrs. Parry by Mrs. Robert Lee Henry, whose husband had served as congressman from Waco. It must be the same as Mama's, as its taste was indeed familiar:

★

Cabinet Pudding

2 Tbs. gelatine
6 eggs, separated
6 Tbs. brown sugar
½ cup wine
1½ doz. almond macaroons
1 cup pecans chopped
1 bottle Maraschino cherries

Dissolve gelatine in cup of cold water. Heat. Beat together yolks and sugar. Add wine. Boil until thick, stirring constantly. Let this cool. Beat whites until stiff. Alternately add whites and gelatine. Pour into 1-pt. mold first a layer of mixture, then macaroons sprinkled with nuts and cherries, till all is used. Serve with whipped cream.

On a pretty moonshine night try General and Mrs. John Horton's *London Fog. Virginia Roberdeau Horton has lived just about all over the world. Her Austin friends were mighty glad to have her back. They have set her and her husband busy with many civic jobs! While stationed in Merry Olde England, Virginia discovered this eye-opener. When you try it there will be no doubt as to why it was so named.

★

London Fog

1 fifth Bourbon
1 fifth strong cold coffee
3-qt. block of French vanilla ice cream

Pour the bourbon and coffee over ice cream. Serve from punch bowl.

FIRST LADIES OF TEXAS

At the time Beauford Jester was governor of Texas, his lovely wife, Mabel, very graciously took on the responsibilities of First Lady in the governor's time-worn Mansion. Mabel liked to have an abundance of food on every occasion, whether it was a dinner for one of the state committees or a morning coffee for the wives of the legislators — which would often number three hundred. Angelfood Snowballs were a great favorite at that time, and were usually served at evening receptions or afternoon teas, and we must have made a million for the Mansion. We would make long pans of a light moist angelfood cake; cut it in two-inch squares, cut off the corners of each square, and ice with a seven-minute frosting; then roll in fresh grated coconut. This was an assembly-line production when done in such quantity as these parties required. The Koock kids and Koock friends wanted to form a Coconut Graters' Union, and demand shorter hours and *more* pay!

A menu I have recorded for a morning coffee Mabel gave for the Senate ladies included:

** Chicken Amandine, served from a chafing dish on very thin*
** Wafflettes*
A large platter of fresh fruit
** Hot Cheese Sticks*
** Sour Cream Twists, small and delicious*
Coffee and Tea

★

Chicken Amandine (*for 6 to 8*)

2 Tbs. butter, melted
2 Tbs. flour
1 tsp. Beau Monde seasoned salt
1 tsp. white pepper
1 Tbs. grated onion
Salt to taste
2½ cups hot chicken stock (1 Tbs. concentrated chicken stock may be added to make richer stock if needed)
3 Tbs. heavy cream
1½ cups cooked chicken, diced
½ cup mushroom slices, sautéed and drained
Small bowl of toasted, slivered almonds

Simmer butter and flour without browning for 5 minutes. Add Beau Monde, white pepper, onion, salt, and chicken stock. Stir with wire whip until smooth. Let simmer 15 to 20 minutes. Add heavy cream; then strain and add diced chicken and mushroom slices. Place the bowl of almonds near chafing dish to sprinkle on top of chicken.

★

Wafflettes or Rosettes

1 egg, beaten
1 cup milk
1 cup flour
1 tsp. sugar
1/8 tsp. salt

Mix ingredients together to make batter. Dip a rosette iron in deep hot fat and then immerse half way (on the iron) into batter. Dip back in the hot fat until rosette floats off the iron when done. Brown to a light color; remove from fat with fork, and drain on absorbent paper. This is simple and only takes practice. They can be made several days in advance, kept in airtight containers, and run in a hot oven for only a minute when ready to serve.

★

Hot Cheese Sticks

Mrs. Few Brewster gave me this recipe when her husband was on the Texas Supreme Court.

1/2 lb. Old English cheese, grated
1/4 lb. bacon, cut in small pieces
2 eggs, beaten
1 medium onion, chopped
Dash Worcestershire sauce

Mix above ingredients and spread on rye bread cut into thirds or rounds, toasted on one side. Broil until cheese is melted and hot.

★

Sour Cream Twists

1 oz. yeast
4 cups sifted bread flour
1/2 tsp. salt
1 1/4 cups butter
3 egg yolks, beaten
1 tsp. vanilla
1 cup commercial sour cream
Powdered sugar

Crumble yeast into flour and salt. Cut in butter with pastry blender until mixture resembles meal. Add beaten egg yolks, vanilla and sour cream. Mix well. Divide into 7 balls. Roll each ball separately in powdered sugar and roll quite thin into a circle. Cut each circle into 8 pie-shaped wedges. Put 1 tsp. filling (below) on each and roll tightly, starting at the broad end. Shape as a crescent and place on ungreased cookie sheet. Bake 15 to 20 minutes in 400-degree oven. Remove, sprinkle with powdered sugar. Makes 56.

FILLING

3 egg whites, stiffly beaten
1 cup sugar
1 cup ground pecans
1 tsp. vanilla

Fold sugar, nuts and vanilla into beaten egg whites.

Allan Shivers, who was lieutenant governor, took over as governor of Texas when Governor Jester died in office. I think when Allan married he must have known one day he would be governor of Texas, and chose Marialice with that in mind. She was so adaptable to the demanding role of First Lady of Texas. Marialice also is very knowledgeable in food, and some of the best recipes I have I have gotten from her through the years. One of the first parties I catered for the Shivers was a buffet luncheon for members of the press and some out-of-town guests before the Texas–S.M.U. football game. I remember how impressed I was with the fact they had twelve dozen rock crystal glasses for double old-fashioneds and that many crystal muddlers. Old-fashioneds were made in the pantry and passed to the guests in the Green and Gold Rooms. Marialice had brought her own beautiful silver to use at the Mansion, and the long table in the state dining room was laden with her delicacies, such as:

** Hot Deviled Eggs*
Pineapple Spears wrapped with thin sliced ham and broiled
Charcoaled Sirloin Strips, carved at the table
Thin, hot, buttered biscuits
A large tray of assorted fresh fruits
A big Edam cheese, scooped out, slightly mashed, and returned to its red case, surrounded with warmed crackers
** Chicken Superb* (a casserole good on any buffet)
Bowls of colossal black and green olives
Fresh toasted almonds
Trays of stuffed celery and cherry tomatoes stuffed with cream cheese and anchovies
Hot Coffee
Pecan Cookies, Fruit Drop Cookies, Petits Fours

★

Hot Deviled Eggs (*serves 6*)

12 hard-boiled eggs
½ tsp. mustard
Salt, pepper, Lawry's seasoned salt to taste
Dash of Tabasco
1 Tbs. chicken stock
1 Tbs. heavy cream
1 Tbs. mayonnaise
½ cup chicken or ham, finely chopped

MUSHROOM SAUCE

2 cups medium white sauce
1 Tbs. onion
1 cup sautéed mushroom slices
½ tsp. dry mustard
Salt, pepper, cayenne to taste
Little heavy cream

SPRINKLE TOP WITH

½ cup toast crumbs
¼ cup imported Parmesan cheese
2 Tbs. chopped parsley

Cut eggs in halves; mash yolks well, add seasonings, stock, cream and mayonnaise and stir until smooth. Add chopped chicken or ham. Fill white of egg with mixture and press firmly together. Place in casserole and cover with Mushroom Sauce. Sprinkle top with crumb, cheese and parsley mixture. Heat in oven until it bubbles around the edges, 350 degrees. We serve this often at Green Pastures because it can be prepared the day before, then put together just before ready to serve.

★

Chicken Superb (*serves 8*)

1 large fowl, cooked until very tender
½ of 8-oz. pkg. egg noodles
6 Tbs. butter
6 Tbs. flour
1½ tsp. salt
½ tsp. pepper
½ tsp. celery salt
Beau Monde seasoned salt
Marjoram to taste
2 cups rich chicken broth
2 cups heavy cream, scalded
2 Tbs. sherry wine
1 large can mushrooms
⅓ cup toasted, slivered almonds
3 Tbs. minced parsley
½ cup grated cheddar cheese

When fowl is very tender, cut in fairly small pieces. Cook noodles in boiling salted water until tender. Drain. Melt butter, add flour and blend. Add seasonings and chicken broth. Cook over low heat until thick, stirring constantly. Remove from heat, stir in scalded cream, sherry, mushrooms, almonds, parsley, noodles and chicken. Pour into 2-quart buttered casserole, top with cheese. Bake uncovered in 350-degree oven for 35 to 45 minutes.

The governor was always the first to sample the beef with the same connoisseur's smack as a Frenchman's when tasting the wine! If given his nod of approval, the guests could proceed to the table.

It is customary for the outgoing governor to leave a hot meal on the table for the incoming governor and his family after the swearing-in ceremonies at the state capitol, which is just across the street from the Governor's Mansion. For this occasion, the main dish left for newly elected governor Price Daniel was *Beef Stroganoff on Green Noodles, something hearty to sustain them through the heavy schedule of the day and which could be eaten easily with only a fork. I have tried several recipes for Beef Stroganoff, but I like this one so much that I have used it ever since.

★

Beef Stroganoff on Green Noodles (for 4)

2 lbs. filet of beef, cut into thin strips ½ x 2½ in.
Salt and pepper
3 Tbs. butter
3 Tbs. grated onion
1 cup sautéed mushroom slices
¼ cup heavy sour cream
½ tsp. chopped chives

ROUX

1 Tbs. flour
2 Tbs. butter
2 cups beef stock

After cutting the filet of beef into thin strips, sprinkle with salt and pepper and let stand in the refrigerator. Make the roux by blending the flour with butter over gentle heat until the mixture bubbles and is smooth. Gradually stir in beef stock and whip until it thickens. Boil for 2 minutes, then strain through a fine sieve into a saucepan. Simmer very gently, without boiling.

Fry pieces of beef in butter and grated onion. When the meat is brown, pour meat, onion and butter into the roux, taste for seasoning, and simmer gently, or cook in double boiler over hot water for 10 minutes. Add mushroom slices. Just before serving, add heavy sour cream. Serve on buttered green noodles with a spoonful of heavy sour cream on top sprinkled with chopped chives.

Marialice was moving out of one Governor's Mansion into another. It was the old Governor Pease Mansion built in 1853. Restoring the place, landscaping its spacious grounds, furnishing it and making necessary additions to the original building must have been at least half as big a job as governing Texas. It is indeed one of the showplaces of the Austin area, and the scene of many social activities, for in addition to the Shiverses' personal entertaining, they very generously open Woodlawn for the benefit of various civic and charitable organizations. Regardless of what the occasion is, Marialice Shivers sees that a bountiful board is spread, such as when they had as their guests the delightful Duke and Duchess of Albercorn from Ireland:

Half Avocado filled with Fresh Gulf Shrimp which had been marinated in French dressing
Rémoulade sauce
Clear Soup
Breast of Pheasant on Ham Slice with white wine
Wild Rice
* *Eggplant Soufflé*
* *Orange and Grapefruit Salad with Pomegranate Seed Dressing*
* *Tipsy Pudding*
Brandy, Liqueurs, and Coffee (served in the library)

★

Eggplant Soufflé

2 lbs. eggplant
2 eggs
4 Tbs. butter
½ cup minced onion
Little garlic
1 cup cracker meal
½ cup milk
Salt and pepper to taste
1 cup grated American cheese

Peel and cube eggplant and cook until tender. Add remaining ingredients (except cheese) and pour into oiled baking dish. Top with cheese and bake at 350 degrees for 30 minutes.

★

Orange-Grapefruit Mold

2 Tbs. plain gelatine
1½ cup boiling water
⅛ tsp. salt
½ cup sugar
½ cup fresh lemon juice
1 cup mixed orange and grapefruit juice
Grated rind of 1 lemon
1 cup orange sections
1 cup grapefruit sections (seeds and membrane removed)

Dissolve gelatine in boiling water. Add salt and sugar and let cool. Add fruit juice and grated lemon peel; let cool and thicken slightly. Add orange and grapefruit sections and pour into individual molds. Place in refrigerator. Serve in a crisp lettuce cup with *Pomegranate Dressing.

★

Pomegranate Dressing

1½ cups sugar
2 tsp. dry mustard
2 tsp. salt
⅓ cup vinegar
3 Tbs. onion juice
2 cups salad oil (not olive oil)
3 Tbs. pomegranate seeds

Mix together sugar, mustard, salt, and vinegar. Add onion juice and stir thoroughly. Add salad oil slowly, beating constantly, and continue to beat until thick. Add pomegranate seeds and beat for a few minutes. Store in a cool place or in a refrigerator.

★

Tipsy Pudding

4 egg yolks
½ cup sugar
2 cups milk (scalded)
2 envelopes gelatine
¼ cup water
4 egg whites
1 tsp. vanilla
Pinch of salt
¾ cup whiskey
1 cup chopped dates
1 cup white raisins
1 cup chopped nuts
Whipped cream

Beat egg yolks with sugar and add to scalded milk. Cook in double boiler until thick. Dissolve gelatine in cold water and add to the hot custard, then cool. Add egg whites, beaten stiff, the vanilla, salt and whiskey. Let cool until it sets, then fold in dates, raisins, nuts, and pour into mold. When serving, cover with whipped cream.

Marialice is famous for hot hors d'oeuvre surprises such as:

★

Clam Burgers

Miniature Parker House rolls
Mixture (to each dozen rolls):
1 3-oz. pkg. cream cheese
1 tsp. mayonnaise
1 Tbs. heavy cream
1 cup minced clams, well drained
1 Tbs. clam juice
1 Tbs. onion juice
1 Tbs. lemon juice
⅛ tsp. red pepper

Mix the mixture ingredients all together. Remove the soft part of small Parker House rolls and fill the cavity with the mixture. Bake in a 350-degree oven for 5 minutes. If you are inspired to try these be sure to have *plenty!* They disappear easily and quickly!

A tasty variation is:

★

Crab Devils

Parker House rolls
Deviled ham
King crab marinated in French dressing

Remove soft part of small Parker House rolls (same as for Clam Burgers) and spread inside of roll with Deviled Ham. Place one bite-size piece of King Crab (marinated) in the center. Bake in 350-degree oven for 5 minutes and serve piping hot. *Loverly!*

Everyone went home raving about the food Marialice served one morning after the meeting of the Austin Symphony League at Woodlawn:

---

*A large silver English hot tray of * Ham Rolls*
*Individual molds of * Pickled Peach Salad, garnished with fresh flowers*
Cheese Straws
Tree-ripened olives
*Squares of hot * Nut-Gingerbread and a small tureen of * Lemon Sauce on the side*
Coffee

★

Ham Rolls

8 oz. cream cheese
4 Tbs. cream
1 small grated onion (2-3 Tbs.) or 1 Tbs. chopped chives
3 tsp. horseradish
4 Tbs. horseradish mustard
Salt to taste
¼ tsp. Beau Monde seasoned salt
¼ tsp. dry mustard
Ham, thinly sliced
Thinly sliced bread, cut in finger lengths
Canned asparagus tips

Mix cheese, cream and seasonings and spread on ham slices. Add 1 bread finger and 2 asparagus tips to each ham slice; roll up, fasten with toothpicks. Place in refrigerator overnight. Bake at 400 degrees until slightly brown.

★

Pickled Peach Salad (*serves* 10)

1 envelope unflavored gelatine
½ cup cold water
1 large can spiced peaches (chopped)
1-2 cans pineapple tidbits
1 pkg. lemon-flavored gelatine
½ cup stuffed olives, sliced thin
5 gherkins, sliced thin
1 cup pecans, chopped

Soften unflavored gelatine in cold water. Heat juice from fruit (about 2 cups) to dissolve both gelatines. When cooled slightly add all other ingredients. Pour in slightly oiled ring mold and put in refrigerator to congeal.

★

Old Fashioned Gingerbread (*with Lemon Sauce*)

½ cup butter or margarine
½ cup sugar
1 egg
1 cup dark cane syrup
2½ cups sifted flour
1½ tsp. soda
1 tsp. cinnamon
1 tsp. ginger
½ tsp. nutmeg
¼ tsp. cloves
½ tsp. salt
1 cup boiling water
3 Tbs. preserved (crystallized) ginger, chopped fine
1 cup chopped pecans (optional)

Cream butter, sugar and egg. Add syrup. Sift flour, soda, spices, and salt together and add to first mixture. Beat well. Add boiling water, crystallized ginger and nuts. Grease and lightly flour a baking pan 14 by 10 by 1¾ in. Pour in mixture and bake in 350-degree oven for about 25 minutes. When done, cut in generous squares and pour on the Lemon Sauce.

LEMON SAUCE

2 whole eggs
¾ cup sugar
2 Tbs. flour
Juice of 2 lemons
⅛ tsp. lemon rind
Pinch of salt
2 Tbs. butter
1 cup very hot water

Mix all but hot water together in saucepan. (An electric blender does this trick in an instant.) When ingredients are well mixed, add hot water. Stir well and cook until thick, but do not boil. Variation is to omit lemon juice and add a little nutmeg and cinnamon.

The Shiverses had just returned from the "Cav-oil-cade" in Port Arthur, where their daughter Marialice Sue had been one of the princesses. There were numerous parties given in her honor and beautiful food at all of them, including a brunch given by Mrs. Robert Shivers, Allan's mother, who lives in Port Arthur. Marialice said the *Banana Nut Bread was really something extra special and had written to her mother-in-law for the recipe. Here it is: Mrs. Shivers had baked it in small round fruit juice cans, filled three-fourths full, which made the pretty sandwiches she had spread with a cream cheese mixture:

★

Banana Nut Bread

1 stick (4 oz.) butter
1 cup sugar
2 cups flour
1 tsp. baking powder
½ tsp. salt
1 tsp. soda
3 Tbs. buttermilk
2 eggs, well beaten
1 cup nuts, finely cut
1 mashed banana

Cream butter and sugar well. Sift flour, baking powder, salt together. Stir into creamed mixture. Dissolve soda in buttermilk and add. Stir in banana and nuts. Bake for 30 minutes at 275 degrees if it is in the 5½-oz. fruit juice cans; 40 minutes at 275 degrees if it is in the 12-oz. fruit juice cans; 50 minutes at 300 degrees if it is baked as a loaf.

Of course one of the most famous Shivers recipes is the governor's *Arroz con Pollo. It was one of the recipes chosen by the chef at the Barbizon-Plaza Hotel in New York.

Green Pastures served it with Guacamole Salad the week after it was featured at New York. We had to keep it on the menu by popular request.

★

Arroz con Pollo

In skillet sauté six shallots, minced, and two medium onions, thinly sliced, in three or four tablespoons of hot oil. Sauté in same oil the sectioned pieces of two chickens, two pounds each, dredged slightly with Lawry's seasoned salt, salt, and freshly grated pepper.

Brown each piece delicately, turning often to prevent burning. Slice six fresh tomatoes into pan and add two cups of chicken or beef stock, and a pinch of saffron. Cover skillet and simmer chicken in this mixture.

Wash one pound of rice in several waters and drain well. Add rice and cook for about 20 to 30 minutes, until done. Cut into slivers two medium-sized sweet green peppers, and add them to the pan. When the rice and chicken are tender finish with a glass or two of dry white wine.

The Price Daniel family, who enjoyed the hot dinner left for them by the Shiverses, seemed right at home in the Mansion. Price and Jean Daniel, with their four almost-grown children, had a special interest in the Mansion, as Governor Sam Houston, the first Governor of Texas, was Jean's great-grandfather. His huge four-poster bed is still used in the guest room. Jean was gracious and relaxed as a hostess, keeping everything on the note of simplicity. The Mansion seemed very homey during the Daniels' stay, and with all the children in either high school or college it would naturally be. Young Jeanie made her debut at that time, and her parents gave a lovely brunch honoring her. Price, Jr., would bring his college friends home from Baylor University on weekends, so Jean had a rather steady stream of entertaining going on with family and official activities. Also there always seemed to be something cooking in the big kitchen at the Mansion, the glorious aroma of which would greet us as we drove in to the grounds. When the children came in after school, they would head straight for the cookie jar, which Jean usually managed to keep full. Their favorite cookies were made from a recipe she had received from her great-aunt Jennie and they are wonderful to have on hand cooked or uncooked.

★

Great-aunt Jennie's Cookie Recipe

- 2 sticks oleo or butter
- 1 cup granulated sugar
- 1 cup brown sugar
- 2 eggs
- 1 tsp. soda
- 1 tsp. salt
- 1 tsp. vanilla flavoring
- 2 cups broken pecan meats
- 4 cups flour

Let oleo or butter soften in a large mixing bowl; mix well with granulated sugar and brown sugar. Add eggs, well beaten, soda, salt, vanilla flavoring, pecan meats and mix well. Gradually stir in flour. Keep stirring or working until all is thoroughly mixed. Tear off six pieces of waxed paper about 18 inches long. Divide the dough into 6 parts. Shape each part on the sheet into a long roll, working the dough so that the roll will be round and compact. Store in the refrigerator until cold and firm. Slice in thin slices and cook on the waxed paper the dough was rolled in on a cookie sheet. Bake in oven, 350 degrees, until light brown. Remove the batch from the cookie sheet and let cookies cool on the waxed paper, when they are easily removed to cookie jar. Will keep in cookie jar indefinitely but are better fresh from the oven. Each roll should make about 3 to 4 dozen cookies.

Another aroma which used to tease the Texas Rangers on duty at the Mansion was from the *Hot Rolls baked almost daily.

★

Hot Rolls

This is from Mrs. Robert A. John, granddaughter of General Sam Houston, grandmother of Mrs. Price Daniel.

1 cake yeast
½ cup cold water
3 Tbs. sugar
1 tsp. salt
½ cup shortening or margarine
½ cup hot water
1 egg, well beaten
3 cups unsifted flour

Soak yeast in cold water. Cream sugar and salt in shortening. Add hot water. Stir until dissolved. When cool, add well-beaten egg, the yeast and unsifted flour. When well mixed, grease slightly and put in a greased bowl. Set in refrigerator about 12 hours. Make into rolls about 2 hours before baking. Let rise till double in bulk. Bake at 375 degrees for 18 to 25 minutes. Makes 24 rolls.

Jean has a delightful sense of humor and has many stories of the funny incidents which occurred at different times when they entertained distinguished guests, like President López Mateos of Mexico. Just before he was to arrive, Mrs. Daniel said to Jean Miller, her secretary, "We ought to play something appropriate for the occasion!" Jean said, "Yes, like the Mexican National Anthem," which begins, *Mexicanos, al grito de guerra . . .* but she could only remember half of it. She sang this to Jimmy Grove, who was to play the piano — they had five or six minutes to figure it out, and Jimmy ran over it once. He was getting it all right, and was ready to start again when they looked up and there stood President López in the doorway — so Jimmy struck the opening chords, the President snapped to attention and the Presidential party entered to the strains of the Himno Nacional Mexicano. Jimmy only played half of it — the half he had just learned — then hesitated, naturally, but that got them through the door okay. So then he adroitly switched to something he knew. Later on, the President thanked him for the music. Another time they had a luncheon for Chancellor Konrad Adenauer, and of course great care had to be taken about the seating and other arrangements. They worked out the protocol with Wiley Buchanan. The table was all set correctly, when just before time for serving someone told them: "You have not provided a chair for the interpreter," and very swiftly they had to adjust the other plates and chairs at the table. But it all got done in time, so there was no delay in serving the meal!

The governor and his family entertained many visiting notables during his tenure in office, like those mentioned, but one of their favorites was evangelist Billy Graham, who was the guest speaker at the Prayer Breakfast that Price established on Inaugural Day. For lunch that day, Jean served a *Texas Star Salad and Mr. Graham liked it so much he asked for the recipe to give to his wife.

★

Texas Star Salad (*Shrimp-Cheese Molded Salad*)

- 1 can undiluted tomato soup
- 3 pkg. cream cheese
- 2 envelopes gelatine dissolved in ½ cup water
- 1½ cups mayonnaise
- 1½ cups chopped celery, green pepper and onion (combined)
- 1 pkg. cooked frozen shrimp, cut up, or 1 lb. fresh shrimp, cut up

Heat soup, add cheese, and blend well. Pour over gelatine mixture in large bowl. Stir. Add mayonnaise, chopped celery, etc., and shrimp. Pour into mold that has been rinsed with cold water. Congeal. Can make day before. The Daniels use a mold in the shape of a Texas Star and serve the salad on a large tray garnished with tomatoes, avocado slices, olives, celery and carrot curls, etc.

When the Daniels left the traditional hot dinner on the table for incoming Governor John Connally and his family, we used Jean's own delicious *Curry recipe and *Chutney she had made. It was served with this menu:

** Curried Chicken with Rice and the usual condiments of Chutney, Almonds, Coconut, Shallots, Bacon, etc.*
Cold Plate of: Asparagus Spears, Tiny Whole Beets, Artichoke Hearts, marinated in French dressing.
Tray of individual Texas Star Fruit Salads
Hot Rolls
Coffee
Fudge Cake Squares with Chocolate Pecan Icing
Angelfood Squares with Lemon Cream Filling and iced with an Old-Fashioned Boiled Icing

---

★

Chicken Curry

4-5 lb. chicken
Salt to taste
¼ tsp. cayenne or several small pepper pods

SAUCE

4 cups stock
1½ cups chopped onion
1½ cups chopped celery
2 green apples, peeled and diced
3 medium sized squash
1 chopped green pepper
1 can mushrooms with liquid
Milk from 1 coconut
2 Tbs. curry powder
2 Tbs. Worcestershire sauce
4 Tbs. flour browned in chicken fat or vegetable oil

Boil chicken until tender. Add salt, cayenne or pepper pods while chicken is boiling. Let cool. Remove meat from bones and cut in large cubes. Add meat to the sauce according to instructions (turkey, lamb, beef, or seafood meat may be substituted).

For sauce: combine stock, onion, celery, apples, squash, green pepper, mushrooms, milk, curry powder, and Worcestershire sauce. Boil until vegetables are soft and well done. To thicken add flour that has been browned in chicken fat or vegetable oil. If the sauce is too thick, add a can of bouillon or celery soup. At this point, "taste for balance," as a veteran cook once advised. This means that the sauce might need a little more curry powder, a dash of cayenne, a pinch of salt, a pinch of thyme, a small portion of ginger, or a small clove of garlic chopped fine (if one is partial to that flavor).

About 30 minutes before serving (or time enough to insure that the dish will be piping hot), add the cubed meat to sauce and heat in a casserole or double boiler. Serve over fluffy rice, with a selection of condiments and relishes. The success of curry lies in the condiments or relishes that are served with it. The East Indians used to provide a boy to carry each condiment and called the dish "two-," "six-," "ten-," or even "fifteen-boy curry," depending upon the number provided in the service.

The condiments and relishes are served in individual dishes, and guests add the ones they prefer to make the meal exotic and unusual. Some condiments are considered "musts," and these have been marked with an asterisk in the following list. Others are optional with the hostess who can prepare them ahead of time. Ten to fifteen side dishes arranged around the curry and rice make a colorful and delicious whole-meal party dish:

---

* *Chutney*
* *Grated fresh coconut*
* *Crushed peanuts*
* *Crumbled crisp bacon*
* *Riced hard-boiled egg whites*
* *Riced hard-boiled egg yolks*
* *Chopped crystallized ginger*
* *Relish, either sweet or sour*
* *Boiled puffed raisins*
* *Minced green onions*
Diced bananas sprinkled with lemon juice, to keep them from turning dark
Tomatoes cut up fine
Candied chopped orange peel
Diced bell pepper
Broiled mushrooms
Thinly sliced radishes (very colorful and good)
Very small chunks of pineapple
Thin marinated avocado slices
Crumbled French-fried onions
(may be canned)
Currant jelly or the like

CHUTNEY (FOR 2 QUARTS)

1 cup juice from watermelon preserves or spiced peaches
½ cup vinegar
½ cup water
1 tsp. salt
1 Tbs. cinnamon
1 Tbs. ground cloves
1 Tbs. curry powder
1 tsp. white pepper

Boil together and then add:

1 cup watermelon preserves
1 cup pineapple chunks
1 cup seedless raisins
3/4 cup green or red peppers
2 large apples diced
1/2 cup candied orange peel

Boil until thick and seal in jars. This recipe may be kept in the deep freeze for future use, as may be the grated fresh coconut in condiment and relish list.

It was hard to say which came first, whether this was the inauguration or the homecoming for the Connallys! Ida Nell Connally grew up in Austin and was chosen sweetheart of Texas University when she and John were in school — and John was elected president of the student body. So their family and friends from all over the state were present on the great inauguration day. I'm sure it must be a great disadvantage being First Lady and returning to your own hometown, but vivacious Nellie Connally took it all in her stride and graciously hostessed the official affairs as well as the never-ceasing requests of old friends and neighbors!

The Connallys had been in the Mansion less than a year when the Governor was critically wounded at the time of President Kennedy's assassination. Naturally this was a very grim and sad period for the Connallys and for their friends. The entire First Family was most heroic and emerged from the tragedy full of plans, including building a house on their ranch near Floresville. It was completed just in time to use for the Conference of Southern Governors. This was a great occasion for all who attended, but especially for John and Nellie Connally. It was the realization of a long-time dream to have such a home on this beautiful rolling South Texas land where John had grown up. Mrs. Rosemary Kowazki from San Antonio and her efficient staff prepared the delicious dinner the Connallys gave during the Conference. The guests were served from a buffet on the terrace and then seated at small tables around the swimming pool. The out-of-state guests enjoyed the nachos and tiny cheese onion pies which were passed as they sipped their drinks or cups of gazpacho. The buffet included:

Grilled Chicken Liver Wrapped in Bacon
Tenderloin of Beef, charcoaled
Baked Fresh Corn Pudding
** Chalupas*
Heart of Artichoke in Caper Marinade
Avocado and Orange Salad
Hot Biscuits
Coffee
Snowballs and Mocha Balls (Angel food cake, iced in white and rolled in fresh coconut; and devil's food cake with mocha icing rolled in toasted pecans)

★

Chalupas

Tostados (fried tortillas)
Grated sharp cheese
Refried beans (may be canned)
Jalapeño peppers

Cut 1 tostado into 4 squares and spread each with refried beans, sprinkle with 1 tsp. grated sharp cheese and put a thin slice of jalapeño on top. Run in a hot oven until cheese melts. Serve immediately.

All the parties Governor and Mrs. Connally give or attend always have pretty fancy food, but it needn't be, as Governor Connally said his favorite supper was Corn Bread crumbled in sweet milk — which was also Mr. Sam Rayburn's number one choice, and which he called "Crummin." Or another family favorite is the first dessert Nellie made after she and John married. It was given to her by her grandmother and never ceases to win the praises of John, Jr., Sharon and Mark, the three Connally children, whenever it is served.

★

Orange Custard Pudding

2 oranges
1 cup sugar
1 qt. milk
3 Tbs. flour for thin custard (for thick custard, add another heaping Tbs. flour)
3 egg yolks
1 tsp. vanilla extract
3 egg whites (4 makes it even better)

First peel and skin the sections of the 2 oranges and marinate in a little sugar. Let set while mixing the other ingredients. Simmer the milk; don't boil. Mix the flour, egg yolks and sugar and add slowly to the milk, stirring constantly. Cook to desired thickness. (It is good either thick or thin; so just cook to individual taste). Pour into a Pyrex casserole and add vanilla extract. Finally stir in orange sections. Beat egg whites until stiff and use as topping. Brown quickly in a very hot oven. Chill and serve ice cold. If you want a plain basic custard, just leave out the oranges. It can be used for banana pudding, coconut pudding, or just plain.

The Connallys gave a lovely cocktail party before the University of Texas Distinguished Alumnus Award Dinner, which honored Mrs. Lyndon Johnson, Mr. G. B. Francis and news commentator Walter Cronkite. It was a rather elaborate menu for a before-dinner affair; however, it seems the people at the head table have to make introductions, or be introduced, and give undivided attention to the speakers, so maybe if they don't eat before they get there — they don't eat! At one end of the long table in the state dining room was a whole smoked turkey with slices of turkey around it. And at the other end was a beautiful baked and glazed ham. Trays of assorted breads cut in thin slices, buttered, were placed by the ham and turkey. Almost a standing order we make for every Connally party is Jeanne Southerland's *Liver Pâté. We had two star molds of this, one on each side of the table, with crisp thin crackers. *Broiled Stuffed Mushrooms were also served, as well as a cream cheese ring filled with thin squares of smoked salmon, split miniature bagels to spread with cheese and top with salmon; and a tray of *Marinated Artichoke Bottoms with Shrimp circled with deviled eggs.

★

Liver Pâté

1 can beef bouillon
3/4 cup water
1 Tbs. gelatine
Juice of 1 lemon
Dash Lawry's seasoned salt

1 1/2 lb. cream cheese
1 Tbs. onion juice
8 oz. liverwurst
1 Tbs. mayonnaise
1 Tbs. sour cream

Bring to boil 1 can bouillon less ¼ cup and ¾ cup water; let cool, then add to gelatine soaked in ¼ cup bouillon (left over). Add juice of 1 lemon, strained, and Lawry's Salt. Pour in bottom of wet mold and hold mold in ice water turning slowly so that mixture will coat sides of mold. Let mold set until very hard. Soften cream cheese with onion juice; and liverwurst, mayonnaise and sour cream. Whip until smooth, pour over gelatine mixture in mold.

★

Broiled Stuffed Mushrooms (*makes 12 hors d'oeuvres*)

12 large mushrooms
3 Tbs. butter
1 small onion, chopped
1 cup breadcrumbs
½ cup chopped cooked shrimp (or chicken, ham or chopped nuts)
2 Tbs. cream or sherry
Salt and pepper to taste
Sweet marjoram, rosemary or oregano to taste

Preheat broiler; remove and chop mushroom stems. Heat 1 Tbs. of the butter in a skillet and add onion and chopped mushroom stems; cook about 2 minutes. Add crumbs, shrimp, enough cream or sherry to moisten and all the seasonings. Place mushroom caps on a baking sheet and brush with remaining butter, melted. Broil, cup side down, in preheated broiler about 2 minutes. Invert and fill with the stuffing. Brush with melted butter and broil about three minutes longer.

★

Artichoke Bottoms with Shrimp (*serves 6*)

1 jar artichoke bottoms
3 Tbs. olive oil
1½ Tbs. wine vinegar
Salt and pepper to taste
1 cup cooked shrimp, cut into small pieces
½ green pepper, finely diced
⅓ cup mayonnaise
2 tsp. lemon juice
Paprika to taste
6 cooked whole shrimp

Marinate the artichoke bottoms in a mixture of olive oil, wine vinegar, salt and pepper for about 1 hour. Mix the cut-up shrimp, green pepper and mayonnaise seasoned with lemon juice and paprika. Drain the artichoke bottoms and place on serving plates. Pile the shrimp mixture on top each artichoke bottom, cover with a thin layer of mayonnaise and garnish each with a whole shrimp. Very pretty and delicious.

RECIPES OFTEN ORDERED AT GREEN PASTURES

This recipe was given to me by Mrs. S. J. Harrison of Austin. For years Mrs. Harrison has been one of the favorite cake makers in

Austin. Her angel food cakes are almost like a mirage, they are so moist, and simply melt in your mouth. Her chocolate angel foods, iced in chocolate, are too heavenly to describe. The success of an angel food cake is due to careful mixing, and the baking in a low temperature oven.

★

Mrs. Harrison's Chocolate Angel Food Cake

2 cups egg whites
2 tsp. cream of tartar
2 cups sugar
1½ cups flour
⅓ cup cocoa
2 tsp. vanilla

Beat egg whites until frothy (not too stiff) with cream of tartar. Add 1 cup of sugar, adding 2 Tbs. at a time, until all is used. Sift 1½ cups flour and 1 cup sugar together four times, adding ⅓ cup cocoa and sifting once again. Fold into the batter very carefully. Add vanilla. Pour into an angel food cake pan (ungreased) and rock until all the bubbles are gone. Bake at 225 degrees on the lower rack of the oven for 60 minutes. Let hang in the pan until cool, then turn out on a wire rack.

★

Filet de Sole Farci à la Christi

Fresh filet of Dover sole, stuffed with fresh salmon, shrimp sauce, from Harold Osborne, Columbian Club, Dallas, Texas.

12 6-oz. filets of sole
12 2-oz. fingers of salmon
Butter
Salt and fresh white pepper
6 oz. white table wine (any dry white wine will do)
2 lemons

Have fishmonger prepare 12 filets of sole, about 6 oz. each, and ask him to cut finger-size pieces of fresh salmon. Place salmon on top of filets of sole; dot with butter. Roll sole around salmon, secure with toothpicks. Put on *buttered* baking sheet. Brush fish with melted butter and season lightly with salt and freshly ground pepper. Pour approximately 6 oz. of white table wine and the juice of two lemons over entire fish. (Put hulls of lemon in pan, too, while baking.) *Preheat oven* to 350 degrees. Cook fish for 12 minutes, basting once or twice. DO NOT OVERCOOK! This is the secret, if any — not to overcook.

Mrs. Walter Fisher brought me this recipe to use for the dinner party she and Mr. Fisher gave in honor of their niece Margaret

Scarbrough and her fiancé. It was a beautiful formal dinner by candlelight; soft burning tapers glowed in the sconces on the wall and in silver candelabra on the tables. Lilies of the valley and white camellias were on all the tables in great profusion. The honoree was in exquisite white chiffon glittering with crystal bugle beads. This dessert is quite appropriate for such an elegant occasion and sparkled too.

★

Frozen Eggnog for Twelve

- 12 egg yolks
- 1 cup sugar
- ½ cup brandy
- 1 qt. whipping cream
- 1 cup whiskey

Beat yolks until light. Add sugar gradually. Add brandy slowly. Beat cream until stiff. Add yolks and whiskey. Pack in ice and ice cream salt till frozen.

★

Camptown Brownies

- 2 eggs
- 1 cup sugar
- ½ cup butter
- 2 squares unsweetened chocolate
- ½ cup semisweet chocolate bits
- 1 tsp. vanilla
- ½ cup sifted flour
- 1 cup miniature marshmallows
- ½ cup broken walnut meats

Beat eggs until thick and lemon-colored. Add sugar gradually while continuing to beat. Melt butter, unsweetened chocolate and semisweet chocolate together over hot water and add with vanilla to egg mixture. Fold in flour. Stir in marshmallows and nuts. Bake in greased 9-inch square pan in moderate oven (350 degrees) about 30 minutes.

The batter to this is very thick and has to be spread in the pan; we use an 8-inch square pan since we like them very thick.

We put pans, after cooling, in the icebox until cold. This makes it easier to cut in squares neat and nice.

Mrs. Walter Staehely served these Camptown Brownies to the Baby Home Guild when we met at her house. This too I consider a four-star (whatever that might be) recipe. They are *absolutely* dee·lish!

★

Confederate Coffee Cake

Amy whips this up on Sunday morning, it only takes a minute, and serves it warm.

1 cup sugar
½ cup butter
½ cup milk
3 eggs
1½ cups flour
¼ tsp. salt
2 tsp. baking powder
1 tsp. nutmeg
½ cup raisins

TOPPING

2 Tbs. sugar
½ tsp. cinnamon, nutmeg
2 Tbs. butter

Cream sugar, butter, add milk and then the eggs, and mix well. Sift flour with salt, baking powder and nutmeg. Stir into butter mixture; add raisins. Pour into well-greased and floured loaf pan, approximately 8 by 8 by 3 in., and sprinkle with topping; dot with butter. Bake in 350-degree oven 20 minutes.

IN AND AROUND AUSTIN II

As you will have discovered by now, very few of the recipes I use at Green Pastures originated with me. I have to stop and think, and sometimes for the life of me can't remember where I did first get certain ones. Some are written on the backs of envelopes, wrapping paper, brown paper sacks, the margin of a symphony program — and in my shorthand they really make a rare collection; and I am often surprised to find I can interpret them.

Why not copy them all off on to cards for the recipe file? Well, that's exactly what I'm *going* to do — next week! Anyway, I have tried to keep the best ones in the top drawer. This is definitely top drawer. Try to have it baking when guests arrive — the ones you want to stay, that is.

★

Olga Crawford's Orange Nut Bread

Rind of 5 oranges
¼ tsp. soda
1 cup sugar
½ cup water

BATTER

1 cup sugar
1 cup milk
3½ cups plain flour
¼ tsp. salt
½ cup shortening
2 eggs
3 tsp. baking powder
1 cup chopped nuts

Cook orange rind in water to cover, with soda, for 5 minutes. Drain and chop (not too fine), add 1 cup sugar and ½ cup water and cook *very* slowly until almost all the juice is absorbed, but not dry. *Cool.* Add rind mixture to batter last. Pour into greased loaf pans and bake 50 minutes at 350 degrees (325 if pyrex pans are used). For a more cake-like texture, use 2 cups all purpose flour and 1½ cups cake flour.

My friend and present (very young) head cook at Green Pastures, Julian Hernandez, has a talent for making crepes. We serve *Chicken Crepes for luncheon, and more than once guests have asked if I had a French chef.

★

Chicken Crepes

1½ Tbs. onion, finely chopped
½ cup sliced mushrooms
3 Tbs. butter
3 Tbs. flour
¾ cup milk
⅓ cup chicken broth
Salt to taste
Dash of nutmeg
Dash of pepper
2 tsp. chopped chives
3 Tbs. sherry
1¾ cup chopped cooked chicken
12 thin French pancakes

Sauté onion and mushrooms in butter. Blend in flour. Stir in milk and chicken broth. Cook and stir till mixture boils thoroughly. Add salt, nutmeg and pepper, chives and sherry. Lightly mix with chicken. Chill for easier handling. Divide into 12 portions and roll each in crepe. Place close together in buttered baking pan, seam side down. Cover pan closely and bake in moderate (350-degree) oven for 20 minutes. Serve 2 crepes for each portion and cover with sauce.

SUPREME SAUCE

2 Tbs. butter
2 Tbs. flour
½ cup chicken broth
½ cup half and half or light cream
Salt and pepper to taste

Melt butter and blend in flour. Cook a minute over moderate heat. Stir in chicken broth and cream. Cook and stir until mixture boils thoroughly and is thickened. Add salt and pepper to taste.

A popular menu we feature at Green Pastures is the following:

** Lobster Bisque, served from an old ironstone tureen*
Hearts of Palm Salad with French dressing
** Cornish Game Hen with White Grapes*
** Orange Rice*
** Onions with Wine and Mushroom Sauce*
Hot Rolls
** Mango Ice Cream*

★

Lobster Bisque

1 lb. lobster meat, cut and trimmed in small pieces
1 10-oz. can cream of asparagus soup
1 10-oz. can cream of mushroom soup
1 cup light cream
3 Tbs. sherry

Shred lobster. Combine all ingredients except sherry. Heat but do not boil. Add sherry just before serving.

★

Cornish Game Hen with White Grapes (*serves 6*)

6 hens (1 per person)
Oil
4 Tbs. cornstarch
8 Tbs. apple jelly
⅔ cups Sauterne wine
4 Tbs. orange juice
Salt, pepper
2 cups white seedless grapes
* Orange Rice
Avocado slices
Apple wedges

Split hens in half, remove giblets, then brown in ½ in. oil. Remove from skillet and place in baking dish. Add cornstarch to drippings and blend well; then add apple jelly, wine, orange juice and blend thoroughly. Add salt and pepper to taste, heat and stir until thick and smooth. Pour over the browned hens and bake, covered, in 350-degree oven for one hour. Then add grapes and bake uncovered about 15 minutes or until grapes are warm. Place hens on mound of Orange Rice and garnish platter with avocado slices and apple wedges. Serve *White Grape Sauce in gravy boat.

★

Orange Rice (*serves 6*)

¼ cup butter or margarine
1 cup diced celery and leaves
3 Tbs. chopped onion
3 cups water
1 cup rice
½ tsp. salt
¾ cup orange juice
2 Tbs. shredded orange peel

Melt butter, add celery and onion and cook until tender, but not brown. Bring water to boiling point, stir in rice and salt and boil until almost done. Drain off any remaining water and add orange juice and grated rind. Heat through, remove from fire; cover and keep hot until time to serve.

★

Onions with Wine and Mushroom Sauce (*serves* 6)

2 cups small white onions, simmered until tender but *not* soft
3 Tbs. butter or margarine
3 Tbs. flour
1 can condensed cream of mushroom soup
½ cup white table wine
Salt and pepper
½ cup slivered blanched almonds
½ cup grated American cheese

Drain onions. Melt butter and stir in flour. Add soup and wine and cook, stirring constantly, until mixture is thickened and smooth. Season to taste. Add drained onions and almonds. Turn into a greased casserole and sprinkle with grated cheese. Bake in a moderately hot oven, 375 degrees, for 20 minutes.

I had no idea these would go over so *big!*

★

Mango Ice Cream

This is made by the same method as the Green Pastures Peach Ice Cream (pages 113-115), only, instead of the peaches, I add 1 qt. mashed, canned mangos, ½ cup fresh orange juice and ¼ cup lemon juice. It is simply heavenly!

A number of years ago Julian, or "Junior," as he is called at Green Pastures, first came to us to help an excellent chef we had at that time, doing all the little things like peeling, chopping and so on. Junior has never missed a day at work; we can set the clock by his arrival and, what is even more remarkable, I have never seen Junior in a bad humor. His good disposition is as regular as his presence. He has become an excellent cook, and if he should ever become temperamental, we will classify him as chef. These are a few recipes he does beautifully:

★

Baked Steak Stuffed with Wild Rice

2 lbs. steak (round)
Salt, pepper
Flour
¼ cup chopped onion
2 Tbs. fat
¼ cup tomato juice or beef stock
2 cups cooked wild rice
¼ cup chopped parsley

Pound steak thoroughly. Season with salt and pepper, dredge with flour. To make stuffing, brown onion in fat, add 2 Tbs. flour, ¼ cup tomato juice or stock, and seasoning. Cook. Add rice and parsley. Spread stuffing on steak; roll it and fasten with skewers. Sear thoroughly. Add a small amount of tomato juice or water. Bake slowly for about 2 hours.

★

Filet of Red Snapper with White Grape Sauce

Marinate filets in lemon juice, season with a little white pepper and salt, brown lightly on both sides until done. Serve with sauce.

SAUCE

1 Tbs. melted butter
¼ tsp. salt
1 cup hot sweet milk
¾ cup white seedless grapes
1½ tsp. flour
⅛ tsp. white pepper
1 cup *Hollandaise Sauce

Mix flour and melted butter and let simmer 5 minutes without browning. Add salt and pepper. Whip up milk until smooth and add; then whip in Hollandaise Sauce. Add grapes, heat and serve over fish.

We keep *Hollandaise Sauce on hand and use it in many ways.

★

Hollandaise Sauce

1 cup butter
4 egg yolks
2 Tbs. lemon juice
⅛ tsp. cayenne

In top of double boiler, with hot but not boiling water in the bottom, melt ½ cup butter. Add egg yolks, beaten with a fork, and stir in lemon juice, strained. Stir with a wire whip until smooth and thick; then stir in remaining half cup butter and whip until all is blended and smooth. Add cayenne. If this mixture should separate while cooking or reheating, add a little cream and whip smooth.

After all, anyone who can cook can usually figure out what's in the sauce, but occasionally one finds oneself eating something perfectly divine but just can't detect what does it! This next is one of these. I thought it was undoubtedly the best sauce I had ever eaten when Mrs. Adriazola served it to us one cold, damp night in Washington after a concert. We had not had dinner, due to a late lunch, and this was a most welcome repast. It was interesting to watch the delighted reaction of each guest when he first tasted this concoction. Thanks to our friend Sister Rita Estelle, we got the formula:

★

Eggs Picante

2 slices white bread (cut in small pieces)
1 cup boiled milk
2 level soup spoons of yellow picante (powdered yellow pepper)
½ cup vegetable oil
2 onions, chopped small
Salt
½ lb. Muenster cheese
6 hard-boiled eggs, chopped
3 potatoes, chopped

Put bread to soak in boiling milk. Mix pepper in a little water, then fry in oil. Add onions and salt. Pass bread and milk through a strainer and add. Cook a very few minutes; add cheese. When cheese begins to melt, add hard-boiled eggs and boiled potatoes. The potatoes can be omitted at choice.

This has become a tremendous favorite at Green Pastures. Other dishes with which Junior delights our guests are:

★

Plantation Chicken Shortcake (*serves 6*)

1 cup milk
1 cup water
1 cup cornmeal
1 tsp. salt
2 eggs, separated
2 tsp. baking powder
1 Tbs. butter
1½ cups chicken, cubed

Place milk and water in saucepan. Add cornmeal and salt. Cook 5 minutes. Add beaten egg yolks, baking powder, butter and stiffly beaten egg whites. Add 1½ cups chicken cut in small cubes. Pour in greased casserole and bake in 425-degree oven for 40 minutes. Serve with chicken giblet gravy.

★

Chicken Livers en Brochette

Season with salt and pepper and dust lightly with flour. Put on skewer with squares of bacon in between each liver. Cook on grill, browning on each side. Serve on toast triangles with broiled pear filled with mint jelly, and with baked rice with mushrooms and garnish of parsley.

★

Beef Milano

Chopped sirloin steak
Salt
Lemon juice
Fresh ground pepper
Lawry's seasoned salt
Margarine
Sliced tomatoes
Sliced cheese
Cherry tomatoes
Parsley

Let steak stand for 5 minutes on each side in lemon juice with salt, pepper and seasoned salt. In heavy skillet with a little margarine, brown on each side. When medium done, place slice of tomato and slice of cheese on top. Run under broiler till cheese has melted and serve on warm plate. Garnish with cherry tomato rose and large sprig of parsley.

We serve this with Spinach Salad and a small glazed apple.

★

Broiled Tomatoes Filled with Beef and Rice (serves 6)

6 large ripe tomatoes
1 lb. ground beef
1 onion, chopped fine
1 egg
1 Tbs. cream
¼ cup grated cheese (Swiss, gruyere or mozzarella)
1 cup cream sauce
½ cup cooked brown rice

Scoop out center of tomatoes. Sauté beef, onions, mashed centers of tomatoes, beaten egg and cream. Add cheese, cream sauce and rice. Pile high in tomatoes, after mixing thoroughly. Bake at 350 degrees until heated through, about 15 minutes. Serve on hot plate with mushroom and cream sauce.

At Green Pastures we serve this with small Belgian carrots and green peas in orange butter, muffins and Myra Brewster's *Zwieback Pudding, which is delicious.

★

Zwieback Pudding

2 eggs
1 cup Zwieback, rolled into crumbs
1 cup chopped nuts
Pinch of salt
1 cup sugar

Beat eggs well. Add other ingredients and bake in a shallow pan in moderate oven. Serve crumbled in whipped cream, with a little cream and a bit of jelly on top.

★

Beets in Orange Sauce

1 tsp. grated orange peel
½ cup orange juice
2 Tbs. lemon juice
½ cup sugar
1 Tbs. cornstarch
½ tsp. salt
2 Tbs. butter
3 or 4 cups sliced beets (cooked or canned)

Cook mixture and drop in beets. Cook until it is slightly thickened.

This was given to me by Mrs. John Mahone, Dorothea, who, before her marriage, was one of the three beautiful Wattinger girls, with whom I grew up:

★

Candied Cranberries

1 lb. cranberries
2 cups sugar
½ cup water
1 cup white Karo

Wash cranberries. Put into shallow pan; pour sugar over, cover with water and syrup. Bake in 350-degree oven until tender and done.

Some of the sauces that Julian makes add a gourmet touch to what might otherwise be classified as "plain ol' food." He has become a real *saucier*.

★

Hot Tartare Sauce

¾ cup white sauce
1 cup mayonnaise
3 Tbs. finely chopped onion
3 Tbs. minced olive
3 Tbs. minced sweet pickles
2 Tbs. chopped parsley
2 Tbs. chopped capers
3 Tbs. vinegar

To the white sauce, after it has thickened, add mayonnaise and all other ingredients except vinegar, and blend well. Add vinegar last, and blend. This is suitable for any kind of fish, either baked, fried or broiled. It is also very good cold on slaw, sliced cucumbers, etc.

★

Bordelaise Sauce (about 4 cups)

4 Tbs. butter
4 Tbs. flour
4 cups beef stock
6 cloves garlic, minced
4 Tbs. onion, chopped
4 Tbs. ham, chopped
2 bay leaves
2 Tbs. Worcestershire sauce
2 Tbs. catsup
1 tsp. celery salt
Salt and paprika to taste
4 Tbs. sherry

Brown butter; stir in flour and brown. Stir in gradually all ingredients except salt, paprika and sherry. Simmer for 5 minutes. Strain the sauce and season with salt and paprika if needed. Add sherry.

★

Béarnaise Sauce

This is Dr. John Bickley's favorite sauce for beef tenderloin, and for me it is the king of all sauces.

½ cup tarragon vinegar
4 shallots, chopped fine
8-10 crushed peppercorns
½ cup white wine
6 egg yolks
1 Tbs. water
1 lb. sweet butter
Cayenne
Pepper
5 sprigs tarragon, chopped
1 Tbs. chopped parsley
1 tsp. salt

Add vinegar, shallots and peppercorns to the wine. Cook down until thick paste. Mix egg yolks with water and add to paste. Whip up sauce over low heat; when creamy, add butter gradually. Strain through cheesecloth; add a little cayenne, pepper, chopped leaves of tarragon and chervil, parsley and salt.

This is THE very best chocolate sauce I have ever eaten. It can be as chocolate-y as one wants it to be by adding more or less chocolate to the recipe. It was given to me years ago by Imogene Butler, whose husband was secretary of state during Beauford Jester's reign. We use this sauce every day at Green Pastures. It is by far the number one dessert when served over an ice cream ball (chocolate, coffee or vanilla) after the ice cream has been rolled in chocolate cookie crumbs or toasted pecans.

★

Hot Chocolate Fudge Sauce

½ cup butter
6 oz. bitter chocolate
1 tall can evaporated milk
2 cups sifted powdered sugar

Melt butter and chocolate in double boiler. Add milk and sugar alternately, stirring after each addition. Let cook 1 or 2 hours, stirring occasionally.

This sauce will be creamy — and dreamy! It can be kept covered in the refrigerator indefinitely; just heat the amount you want to use.

★

Drama of the Peach Ice Cream

This production is lovingly dedicated to Elizabeth Carpenter, appreciative spectator and participant.

TIME: In the good ol' summertime, during the wonderful Stonewall peach season.

SETTING: A one-and-a-half gallon freezer is turned upside down on the back porch to drain after the previous making.

A little milking stool is kept nearby for the cranker. Two sacks are hanging in the Cistern House — one to crush ice in, the other to be folded and placed on top of the freezer to add comfort for the one who sits on the freezer and, of course, to later cover the ice when the cream is frozen.

CHARACTERS: Big Boss Brother — Ken
Two Crushers — Bill and Tim
Two Crankers — Carl and Harry
Chorus — Karen, Gretchen, Judy and Martha

There have to be at least two medium-sized but strong boys to wield the ax to crush the ice. If the first one whams it ten times, the second must make it at least twelve — as the other characters watch and blink with each blow.

2 qts. peaches, peeled and sliced (peaches should be tree-ripened and very soft)
1½ cups white sugar (for peaches)
2 qts. light cream
10 egg yolks and 4 whole eggs
¾ cup white sugar (for custard)
1 cup brown sugar
½ tsp. salt
2 Tbs. vanilla flavoring
¼ tsp. almond extract
1 cup heavy cream (approx.)

Sprinkle 1½ cups sugar over peaches and let stand till sugar is melted.

For custard: scald light cream. To well-beaten eggs add ¾ cup white sugar, brown sugar and salt. Beat until smooth and pour into scalded cream. Stir over low fire until sugar is dissolved. Add vanilla and almond extract and cool.

Place custard in ice cream freezer, adding a cup of heavy cream or enough to fill the freezer to 2 inches from top. Turn about 15 minutes, until custard is thick. Add peaches with sugar and freeze until hard, about 10 to 15 minutes more. Makes 1½ gal.

FIRST ACT

Custard is poured in the freezer tank and Big Boss Brother orders Ice Crushers to fill the freezer one-third full of ice, then rock salt, then ice, then salt all the way to the top, while the cranker, seated firmly on the milking stool, slowly turns the crank. The slower he turns the smoother the cream will be. He turns slowly and rhythmically until his arm gets tired. Second cranker continues to turn while Big Boss Brother (BBB) keeps his eyes on the freezer and orders more ice and salt.

BBB removes the crank, wipes the lid with a cup towel brought by little sister — top is lifted, and second sister brings the bowl of peaches, which are carefully poured into partially frozen custard — stirred a little, then the lid is replaced. The crank is replaced and turning continues as before.

BBB folds one of the two sacks and places it on top of the freezer. Third little sister sits on the freezer until cream is frozen, and quips "My tale is told." THEN comes the golden moment when the dasher is to be taken out. By now, everyone who has heard the squeak of the freezer turning has appeared on the scene. Spoons are passed out by a little sister. Big Boss Brother shouts orders, clearly, precisely and fast in professional tones. Towel! Long spoon! Waxed paper! Cork! Pan to place dasher on — silence and expectation. All eyes are fixed on the slowly emerging dasher covered with velvety luscious cream. BBB solemnly pushes the cream off the dasher back into the freezer, leaving only enough on the dasher for the tantalizing licks by the six or eight spoons in various sizes of hands. Wax paper is placed over the top; lid is placed next with a cork or wad of wax paper in the hole. The water is drained from the tank by the hole in the side of the freezer, then it too is plugged up. The freezer is again packed with layers of ice and salt, each being packed firmly with a broom handle mastered only by Big Boss Brother himself. The sack is folded and placed on top of the freezer and sorta tucked in around the ice. The freezer is then placed in a cool shady corner of the back porch.

FINAL SCENE

FRONT YARD

Everyone on scene.

Freezer is moved to front yard. The cream is served in large bowls (Johnnie said he was in college before he knew ice cream was served in something other than oatmeal bowls.)

CHORUS: Ummm ummmmmmmm. This is better than the last time!

CURTAIN!

Every hostess should keep a menu file, with the menus she has served, dates, names of the guests present, and any other information pertinent to the occasion.

In the first place, it is like all "memory" books, just fun to look back over later, remembering some fascinating guest, a fallen soufflé (marked after it "Never again!"); one guest who came a day late, and the two who came a day early, all dressed in tuxedos.

I see the one here I gave for Mrs. Glover Johns when her sister, Mrs. Anita Englehorn from Munich, Germany, visited her. Erna Johns usually planned her own menus, and gave me her recipes to use, which I loved. She has a fabulous collection from all over the world where she and Colonel Johns have lived or traveled. When he retired, they returned to Austin and built the perfect home for entertaining, which they did so very often. But on this occasion, having just returned from Formosa, Erna said she would just leave the menu to me. This is what I had:

Oyster Broth
** Tenderloin of Pork in Red Wine*
** Green Apples Stuffed with Sweet Potatoes*
** Cauliflower and Pecan Salad*
** Marialice Shivers's Chocolate Nut Angel Pie*
Coffee

Penciled in the corner of the menu is, "They loved it!"

★

Tenderloin of Pork in Red Wine

5 lbs. pork tenderloin
Red wine
4 or 5 whole peppercorns
1 bay leaf
4 or 5 whole cloves
Garlic
½ cup flour
1 tsp. salt
½ tsp. dry mustard
1 tsp. sage
1 Tbs. brown sugar
Beef stock
1 Tbs. cornstarch

Let pork stand in red wine for 2 hours, seasoned with cracked peppercorns, bay leaf, cloves. Turn once during marinade. Remove and pat dry; rub with garlic well all over. Then season flour with salt, dry mustard, sage and brown sugar and rub into loin well and evenly all over. Place in roaster and brown quickly in very hot 450-degree oven for 15 minutes. Then pour marinade over roast and lower heat to 350 degrees. Baste with marinade during cooking time, approximately 1 hour, or till completely done. Add equal amount of beef stock, thicken with cornstarch and strain. Pass in gravy boat when pork is served.

★

Green Apples Stuffed with Sweet Potatoes (Apple Yams)

8-10 large, firm green apples
1 20-oz. can sweet potatoes
½ cup dark Karo syrup
¼ cup butter
1 tsp. salt
¼ tsp. cinnamon
16 miniature marshmallows
1 Tbs. lemon juice
¼ cup melted butter

Prepare apple shells by scooping out the fruit till wall of apple is ½ inch thick. Mix other ingredients and stuff apples generously. Place stuffed apples in 350-degree oven. Bake ½ hour, till soft but not mushy.

★

Cauliflower and Pecan Salad

1 cup coarsely grated carrots
¾ cup green pepper
1½ cups cauliflower flowerettes
1 cup chopped celery
1 cup toasted whole pecan halves (not chopped)

Blanch cauliflower flowers in hot, salted water for 2 minutes, then chill. Keep all ingredients separate until time to serve. Then toss together with the following dressing:

¾ cup mayonnaise
Fresh ground pepper
4 Tbs. drained horseradish
½ cup sour cream
Salt to taste
½ tsp. prepared mustard

Mix well, and correct seasoning according to taste.

Serve on a lettuce leaf and garnish with a radish rose in a thin carrot curl.

★

Marialice Shivers's Chocolate Nut Angel Pie
(serves 6 or 8)

Sift together ½ cup sugar and ⅛ tsp. cream of tartar. Beat 2 egg whites until stiff but not dry. Add sifted sugar gradually to the egg whites, beating well after each addition. Continue beating until the meringue is quite stiff and no sugar crystals are present. Fold in ½ cup almonds, chopped very fine. Butter well a 9-inch pie plate and fill with the meringue. Do not bring out to the edge of the plate. Bake in a slow oven, 270 degrees, for about 1 hour or until delicately browned. Cool thoroughly.

Chocolate filling: Melt ¾ cup semisweet chocolate bits in the top of a double boiler. Add 3 Tbs. hot water and cook until thickened. Cool slightly. The mixture will become quite thick. Then add 1 tsp. vanilla. Then whip 1 cup heavy cream and fold into the chocolate. Combine well, but do not beat. Pour into the meringue shell and chill 2 to 3 hours.

Then here is the Cocktail Buffet served at the Edward Clarks'. On the back of it is scribbled: "Don't know how they did, but they did," which referred to the Tartare Steak which every one seemed to adore.

** Chicken in a Blanket*
Small Cheese Biscuits
** Tartare Steak, Rye Bread*
Wedges of cantaloupe with Proscuitto ham garnished with purple grapes and grape leaves
Ann's Hot Pickled Artichoke Roots
Whole Deviled Eggs standing on end garnished with black and red caviar and rolled filet of anchovy

---

And for the ones who wanted their beef cooked, we had *Beef Burgundy and a bowl of sour cream by it. Coffee, miniature pecan tarts, and Divinity were on the sideboard.

★

Cold Chicken in a Blanket (*serves 10 or 12*)

2-3 lb. roasting chickens
Chicken broth or canned chicken consommé
6 whole carrots
4 stalks celery
4 white onions
1 pint cream
Peel of 1 lemon
4 Tbs. butter
4 Tbs. flour
Salt
Pepper
½ tsp. powdered mace
Juice of 1 small lemon

Place chickens in pan and cover with broth. Add whole carrots, celery and onions. Cover and simmer gently until quite tender. Remove from fire and let cool in their own juice. Take chickens from pan and skin them. Remove all meat in as large pieces as possible, arrange it on a platter with the white in the center and dark around the edges. Make cream sauce by heating cream in double boiler with lemon peel. Melt butter and blend in flour, then add hot cream gradually. Continue to cook in double boiler for 15 to 20 minutes, adding a little broth if too thick. Add salt and pepper to taste, mace, and lemon juice. Pour sauce over chicken carefully, so as to coat it evenly, and place in refrigerator. When ready to serve, decorate with whole carrots from the stock, crisp cut bacon curls and parsley. I made little designs with blanched almonds and black olives before the sauce set. This is real lemony and good as well as very pretty on a buffet.

★

Tartare Steak Log

If you have no aversion to raw meat, I know you will find this about the best Steak Tartare you ever flipped a lip over. First off, have the butcher use the leanest beef in the place, then take a deep breath and ask him to grind it three times. (How they hate this!) Try to have it ground the same day you are to use it, but it will still hold its color after 24 hours . . . if properly packed. Better yet, grind it yourself if you are lucky enough to have one of those wonderful new electric meat grinders.

1 lb. of raw, top-quality beef — filet or sirloin — ground
2 egg yolks
1 tsp. dry mustard
¼ tsp. monosodium glutamate
½ tsp. salt
⅛ tsp. freshly ground pepper
½ tsp. seasoned salt
¼ cup olive oil
1 Tbs. red wine vinegar
1 tsp. Worcestershire sauce
2 shallots run through the press

Put the finely ground beef into a bowl. Put the egg yolks into a mixing bowl and beat until lemon-colored. Add the dry ingredients, then alternate the oil and vinegar, adding slowly and stirring well. When this is smooth, add the Worcestershire sauce and shallots. Mix well, and then lightly fork into the beef. Mix well, keeping the beef lightly mixed; don't mash it against the side of the bowl. When you have finished mixing, roll out onto wax paper, and mold it into a log, again being careful not to mash it down.

I made my logs the size of party rye bread. Roll the log in masses of chopped chives, so this lovely green will add a color note to your buffet. Put it on a large platter; surround with thinly sliced French and rye bread.

★

Beef Burgundy

Melt in a Dutch oven, with a tight cover, and brown:

4 Tbs. butter
2 large onions, chopped
2 tsp. mixed herbs
4 lbs. lean beef, cut in bite-sized pieces, rolled in
4 Tbs. flour

When meat is brown, push to one side and add a mixture of 1 Tbs. flour and 1 Tbs. cornstarch, moistened with a bit of the liquid in pan. Blend thoroughly and allow to brown lightly and add:

2 tsp. salt
1 tsp. pepper
½ tsp. paprika
2 tsp. dry mustard
3 Tbs. cider vinegar
3 cups red Burgundy wine

Cover tightly and simmer over low heat at least 2 hours (longer will not hurt). Best if made the day before and allowed to stand overnight. Half an hour before serving heat. Serve with sour cream on top.

Next card: Birthday party given for Dr. Matthew Kreisle by his children, Dr. and Mrs. Matthew Kreisle, Jr., and Dr. and Mrs. Jim Kreisle.

Champagne
Crab Newburg; thin buttered toast triangles
Chopped sirloin made into miniature hamburgers, cooked rare, with small, warm, buttered hamburger buns kept hot on English warmer
Chopped pickles, chopped onions, mustard and mayonnaise nearby
Charcoaled drumsticks
Pickled black-eyed peas, small hot cornbread muffins
Tray of celery hearts, small whole beets and cherry tomatoes all filled with seasoned cream cheese and encircled with carrot sticks and colossal black olives
Large chocolate angel food cake with chocolate icing and crushed peppermint-stick candy and twenty-one red-and-white striped candles
Coffee

The grandchildren got to stay up long enough to blow out the candles and sing "Happy birthday dear Granddaddy!"

A Saturday Sundae Party given for Harriet Hahn before she started to Austin High School:

Invitations: on pink striped paper
Tablecloth: new pink-and-white striped sheet
Centerpiece: flowers arranged to resemble large ice cream sundae
Guest list: 75 very excited high school freshmen

Punch bowl at one end of table filled with large balls of vanilla ice cream (had been scooped and put in the bowl and then the freezer overnight to make serving easier). This was served to the girls in good-sized berry bowls. They then circled the table helping themselves to great combinations of:

Green Pastures Hot Chocolate Fudge Sauce (see page 113)
Butterscotch sauce
Whipped cream
Chopped pecans
Crushed pecans
Crushed peppermint candy

They also had a big tray of thin sugar cookies and iced tea. They then took their loaded plates in by the piano where Nat Williams was playing all of their tunes which were just the *most!*

When Dr. Tom Cranfill is not traveling, he is teaching at the University of Texas. His Shakespeare classes are very popular with the students, and I understand when he lectures there is standing room only! Tom called one day to say he would like to bring a few guests for dinner, including the Duke and Duchess of Bedford. I had the pleasure of visiting Woburn Abbey, the Duke's home, when I was in England, and had enjoyed his book *A Silver-Plated Spoon,* so we were pleased to have an opportunity to meet the Duke and Duchess. Tom said he'd just leave the menu to me. I decided to serve a Stuffed Tenderloin of Beef. It was the first time I had prepared it, so I kept some filets reserved in case it didn't work. It was a huge success, however, and we now serve it frequently and call it *Beef Bedford. That menu also included:

** Fresh Crab Sorrento in Shells*
Endive and Avocado Salad with French dressing
** Parsleyed New Potatoes in Sour Cream*
** Yellow Squash Stuffed with Corn and Tomatoes*
Watermelon Rind Pickles
Hot Rolls
** Frozen Coffee Mousse with Fresh Peaches*

★

Crab Sorrento

2 Tbs. onion chopped fine
2 Tbs. butter
1 medium-sized tomato, peeled and chopped fine
2 Tbs. parsley chopped very fine
4 Tbs. celery chopped very fine
1 Tbs. green bell pepper chopped very fine
1¼ cups mayonnaise
2 Tbs. chili sauce
1 lb. white crab meat
Juice of ½ lemon
Salt to taste
Pepper to taste

Sauté onion in butter; add other chopped vegetables; add mayonnaise and chili sauce. Heat through but do not let boil. Add diced crab, lemon juice, salt and pepper to taste, and serve in shells. This is also an hors d'oeuvre served from a chafing dish on small Melba toast rounds!

★

Beef Bedford

3 lbs. tenderloin beef
1 cup mushrooms, chopped
1 lb. ground veal
1 cup dry white wine
1 cup cooked smoked ham, ground
¾ cup sour cream
¼ cup breadcrumbs
Salt and pepper to taste
Garlic clove
4 Tbs. butter

SAUCE

⅓ cup Madeira
2 Tbs. sour cream
Pan juices

Split the tenderloin of beef lengthwise about ¾ through. Open it out on a board and pound it flat between sheets of wax paper. In a skillet sauté mushrooms in 3 Tbs. of butter for 3 minutes. Add veal and brown it lightly. Add ½ cup of the dry white wine and steam the mixture for 10 minutes. Stir in cooked ham, sour cream, breadcrumbs, salt and pepper to taste. Spread this mixture over the meat, roll it up lengthwise, and tie the roll securely. Rub the meat lightly with a cut garlic clove and sprinkle it with salt and pepper. Put the meat in a large baking dish and dot with butter (1 Tbs.). Add the remaining ½ cup dry white wine to the pan. Bake the meat in a moderately slow oven, 325 degrees, basting it frequently with the wine for 30 minutes. Remove the beef to a heated platter. Blend the sauce ingredients, Madeira and sour cream, into the pan juices and serve separately.

★

Parsleyed New Potatoes in Sour Cream

3 lbs. new potatoes
¼ cup butter
¼ cup sour cream
3 Tbs. finely chopped parsley
½ tsp. salt

Cook potatoes until they are just tender and slip off the skins. Keep the potatoes warm. In a saucepan melt butter and stir in sour cream. Add the potatoes, parsley and salt, and toss the potatoes lightly until they are well coated and very hot. Serve immediately.

★

Yellow Squash with Corn and Tomatoes

6 young yellow squash (uniform in size)
1 Tbs. chopped onion
1 medium-sized tomato, peeled, chopped, with seed removed
¾ cup whole kernel corn
1 egg yolk
Salt and pepper to season
Butter toast crumbs
3 very thin pimento strips
1 big sprig parsley

Parboil squash; when tender, not soft, scoop out centers and place in colander to drain. Turn squash with cut side down to drain well. In a skillet, sauté onion. Mash the centers of squash and add to onion. Add tomato, corn, and egg yolk. Season with salt and pepper. Fill cavity of squash with skillet mixture and sprinkle buttered toast crumbs on top. Bake in 350-degree oven 20 minutes. Remove and garnish with pimento strips and sprig of parsley.

This is a recipe which was given me by Marialice Shivers. It has been such a popular dessert for parties:

★

Frozen Coffee Mousse (makes 12 individual molds)

2 envelopes unflavored gelatine
½ cup cold water
3½ cups milk, scalded
4 tsp. instant coffee
½ cup sugar
½ cup white corn syrup
Pinch of salt
2 cups heavy cream, whipped
4 egg whites, beaten stiff but not dry
Fresh peaches, sliced and sugared

Soften gelatine in cold water and let stand 5 minutes. In a saucepan, scald milk and add instant coffee. Stir well. Add softened gelatine and stir until dissolved. Then add sugar, corn syrup and salt. Stir until sugar is dissolved. Chill until thick. Fold in heavy cream, whipped, and then fold in stiff egg whites. Pour into 2 1-qt. freezing trays. Set up refrigerator to coldest position and freeze about 30 minutes, until mixture is frozen ¼ inch around the edges. Scrape it into a chilled bowl. Beat quickly with rotary beater or electric beater until blended. Don't "linger longer" over this, as the old song says. Pour in individual molds and freeze until set. Serve with sliced and sugared fresh peaches.

Dalies Frantz is the inspiring professor extraordinaire of piano at the University of Texas Graduate School of Music. His former pupils and contemporaries come from all over the world, often appearing on the concert stage, and sometimes just "passing through" Texas. They never fail to stop for a visit with the maestro. One night after the pianist Leonard Pennario appeared in a concert with the Austin Symphony Orchestra, Dalies had a small supper at Green Pastures. Knowing Dalies and Mr. Pennario to be very fond of lobster, I decided to have *Lobster Newburg. The hour was very late when the guests arrived. I went to the kitchen to tell the cook, John (relief cook for late parties), to put the Newburg together, and *he was not there*. I called to Eddie, the waiter, to start passing the champagne, and he was not to be found. I called upstairs to my son Ken, who was studying for an examination, and told him to come quickly and pop the corks, and I continued my search for the two helpers, wondering what in the world had happened. What could I possibly do with twenty-four starving guests who would soon be going into the dining room for dinner? Julian had left everything partially ready, only it had to be finished! So, in my velvet dress and high-heeled shoes, I started grabbing bowls, opening the refrigerator then closing it before I got out what I needed, wondering about the missing men. Could it be double suicide? I ran to the back door and called, but no answer. John's car was still there???? I added the eggs to the sauce, ran the rolls in the oven. Someone said Dalies wanted to see me for a minute. I walked into the living room trying to look calm. Dalies made very gracious and lengthy introductions. Instead of the twenty-four there seemed to be forty, or was it one hundred? I tried to catch Ken's eye, but he was keeping it sleepily on the champagne glasses. Oh, me, did I take the sauce off the fire? If Ken would only know to put the salads on the table. Mr. Pennario stood up, bowed to me, and I smiled and said, "The concert was lovely, Lobster!"

Dalies whispered over my shoulder, "Mary, there are six more than we expected." "Oh, wonderful," I cooed — and staggered out to the kitchen. Now I was having hallucinations, for there stood John in his stiff white hat, stirring the sauce; Eddie with a tray of salads headed for the dining room. To see if they were real I said, "Eddie, there will be six more, can you set another round table for six?" "Oh, Miz Koock, I have already set up an extra six just in case." They were real! They were there! I didn't even ask where they had been, but later John said, "We almost missed the party" — as if I hadn't noticed — "Ed and me went out to the car and went plumb to sleep. Dreamed I heard you callin' so I woke up Ed and we just made it in time!"

Lobster Newburg (serves 6)

4 Tbs. butter
4 Tbs. flour
1½ tsp. salt
¼ tsp. cayenne pepper
¼ tsp. white pepper
6 cups light cream
8 egg yolks, beaten
2 lbs. lobster meat, cut in cubes
2 Tbs. butter for sautéing lobster
⅓ cup dry sherry

Melt butter, add flour, salt, cayenne and white pepper. Let cook together a few minutes, but do not allow to brown. Add heated cream and whip until smooth with wire whip. Beat egg yolks and add slowly to sauce, whipping with wire whip continuously until smooth. Sauté lobster in melted butter, add ⅓ cup dry sherry, stir well, then add lobster to sauce.

Bertha Dobie has many claims to fame besides being the wife of the late folklorist and writer J. Frank Dobie. One is her *Potato Salad and another her pie. At a recent picnic the Town and Gown Society had up at the Ralph Goethes' Toda Vista when a very fine caterer had brought the food, someone spoke up and said, "This is surely delicious potato salad." Whereupon Mody Boatright replied (so all could hear), "Yes, but it is not nearly as good as Bertha Dobie's!"

An honest observation with which we totally agree.

★

Bertha Dobie's Potato Salad

Boil 8 potatoes in jackets, in salted water till tender
Peel and dice fine
6 hard-boiled eggs, chopped
1 medium-sized onion, chopped very fine
2 Tbs. sweet pickle
2 Tbs. sour pickle
1 cup celery
2 Tbs. pimento
1 Tbs. capers
1 Tbs. ground clove

Chop all the ingredients very fine and add to the potatoes. Stir mustard and mayonnaise to bind. Mix well while potatoes are still warm.

Around here in Travis County, where the mustang grapes grow in abundance, a mighty good pie to make is the *Green Grape Pie. Bertha says always to gather the little grapes before they are ripe, about half grown, before the seeds get hard.

★

Green Grape Pie

2 cups grapes
1 Tbs. (approx.) cornstarch
¾ cup sugar
¾ cup water
2 Tbs. butter

Simmer grapes in water until tender; add butter and sugar, then thicken with cornstarch. Put in deep dish pie pan and cover with pie dough. Very, *very* good.

At a party at George and Nita Moffatt's, I was taking in their magnificent view of Lake Austin and the hills which surround it, never realizing everyone else was "taking in" Nita's canapés. Nita was kind enough to give me the recipe, and they have become quite a favorite with the college clientele at Green Pastures.

★

Swiss Canapé Pick-ups
(*makes about 40 Pick-ups; cut in half for less*)

1 lb. ground lean beef
½ lb. ground pork
¾ lb. ground ham
⅓ cup cracker meal or crumbs
1 egg
1 onion
Salt and pepper to taste
3 Tbs. cabbage stock or tomato juice (enough to moisten)
1 head cabbage
Sour cream

Mix together meat, meal, egg, onion, salt, pepper, juice or stock (just enough to moisten mixture). Simmer leaves of cabbage 1 minute; drain leaves and cut in half. Place 1 Tbs. of meat mixture on each leaf. Fold leaf around meat tightly so as to cover the mixture completely. Fasten with toothpick. Moisten bottom of pan with stock. Bake at 300 to 325 degrees for 25 to 30 minutes or until leaves turn brown. Serve with small bowl of sour cream, arranging Pick-ups around sour cream.

My search for good sourdough has ended. Gus Bunch gave me this one, which his father used on their ranch in West Texas. Yes, it was his father — he said his dad didn't want his mother "foolin' with this bread" — she didn't do it right — it was one job he liked to do himself. The elder Mr. Bunch kept a batch in a crock in back of their wood stove covered with a clean bran sack. He'd take out a cup or two of the sourdough mixture, mix it with flour, and there it would be, the best bread ever. If his Dad was going to be out on a round-up, he would put the crock in the back of the wagon, and the chuckwagon cook would mix it with the flour, cut it with a big tomato can, and they'd have hot biscuits and a slab of bacon with Mary Jane syrup out on the trail.

The Bunch family lived about twenty-five miles from Rotan, Texas; the nearest big town was Sweetwater. Gus said they raised all their food, and would come to town only once every three months and get flour, sugar, coffee and a package with fifty sticks of candy, but other than that, they raised their own pork, beef and chicken, vegetables, eggs, milk, butter; raised their corn and ground their own cornmeal. Gus said he was nine years old before he ever went to Sweetwater. That hearty diet and ranch work were perfect training for a football player, and he became a mighty good one. There was quite a contrast in his football training, working on the ranch, and that of his son, Joe Bunch, who was on the all-state football team; those boys had a *trainer* to massage their sore legs after the game.

Back to the sourdough: This makes such a good hard crust, and the longer you keep the sourdough, the better it becomes.

★

Sourdough

2 pkgs. Fleischman's yeast	Flour
2½ cups lukewarm water	

Dissolve yeast in warm water. Add enough flour to make the mixture about as thick as *thick* buttermilk. Place in a warm place out of a draft and let set overnight.

★

Sourdough Biscuits

2 Tbs. shortening
1 cup sourdough (This must be mixed at least overnight before using.)
2 tsp. baking powder
2 Tbs. sugar
Pinch of salt
Flour

Combine ingredients, using enough flour to make biscuit dough. This should be a stiffer dough than is used for regular biscuits. Knead dough and shape into biscuits. Place in a well-greased pan, set in warm place and let dough rise until biscuits are double in size. Bake in oven at 450 to 500 degrees until browned well.

Add 1 cup of warm water (or the amount of water equal to the amount of sourdough removed) to the remaining sourdough, add enough flour to make the consistency of thick buttermilk, and set in refrigerator for future use. Each time biscuits are made, add the same amount back to the sourdough mix, and it will keep ready to use.

After keeping the mix in the refrigerator, take out the amount needed for biscuit dough and set aside to warm to room temperature before using. *Be sure to add the same amount of warm water and flour back to the dough mix that you removed.*

It gets a little confusing at times, but my friend Mrs. Emmett O'Shaughnessy is French, and another, Mrs. Jacques Darrouzet, is Irish, as a one-half minute conversation with either will affirm. My charming Irish friend has her short stories published under Maurade Glennon, her maiden name, and stays very busy at her desk turning out delightful stories of her native Ireland. With the help of her young daughter, Deidre, she makes a quick *Irish Bread which is so very simple and delicious I wonder why we go through the long procedure of "letting rise" and punching down of yeast bread!

★

Irish Bread (*makes 2 loaves*)

2 cups white flour
3½ cups brown flour (stone ground)
½ cup wheat germ
1½ tsp. baking soda
3 tsp. salt
Buttermilk

Mix first 5 ingredients. Make a hole in the center of the dough and add enough buttermilk to make dough the consistency of biscuit dough. Knead on lightly floured board. It needs the heat of the hand to get the action of the soda, Maura says. Divide dough in half and place in greased 1-lb. loaf pan. Cook in hot oven, 450 degrees, until brown. Raisins or caraway seed may be added to dough, if desired.

Ken and Jane told me not to bother to get Maura's bread recipe, just find out how she makes the delicious *Irish Coffee she and Jacques serve for dessert.

★

Irish Coffee

Into a demi-tasse:

1 tsp. brown sugar
1 tsp. white sugar
1 jigger Irish whiskey

Fill the cup ¾ full with double strength coffee and top with whipped cream.

Dr. and Mrs. D. J. Sibley moved from Fort Stockton to Austin where he is engaged in propetology research at the University of Texas. They bought the very charming old Theo Davis residence, which is Spanish in design and an ideal setting for their furnishings and tastes. I first met Jane Sibley when she asked me to come over and help her plan a dinner for the world-famous English philosopher and writer Aldous Huxley, who was to be their first guest since they moved to Austin.

Jane said her specialities were Mexican dishes she had learned to make in West Texas, and was afraid that they might be too hot and spicy for her honor guest. She gave me an enchilada recipe that I had long wanted. It is like the one Clara Macias used to make at Memaw's on Fridays. (A great favorite with the Koock family.) Dolores Salas, who is my right hand at Green Pastures, helped me make these to surprise Chester one Friday. He was one happy fellow, and has been asking when are we going to have Jane's enchiladas again!

★

Jane Sibley's Sara Rosas Enchiladas (serves 6)

SAUCE

14 large, *sweet*, dried chilis
4 large, hot, dried chilis
6 Tbs. shortening
1 rounded Tbs. flour
⅓ tsp. garlic powder
1 lb. (approx.) longhorn cheese
1½ medium-sized onion, chopped
Bacon (or other) grease
12 Tortillas

Pull stems out of chilis and cover with hot water; place lid on pot and boil until soft, about 10 minutes. Pour liquid off and let chilis cool. Grind in blender or grinder and mash pulp through sieve to remove skins and seeds. Add enough water so that pulp is consistency of gravy.

Put shortening in 8-inch skillet about ¼ inch deep. Add flour and stir until smooth. When it simmers, add chili pulp and garlic powder. Pour into large skillet and keep hot over low heat.

Grate cheese and chop onion.

Heat skillet with ⅛ inch bacon grease; the fire should be from medium to hot. Dip 1 corn tortilla in hot grease for an instant. Then put into the chili sauce and lay on baking sheet. Put two dabs of cheese in the center and 1 dab of onion, then roll. Repeat process with remaining tortillas. Spoon extra sauce over all and place in oven. Set oven at 400 degrees, but turn off when you put enchiladas in. Keep warm until ready to serve. Serves 6 with some sauce left over.

For anyone who is a Mexican food-fancier, these cannot be beat!

Judge Ruel Walker returned from the Kentucky Derby with one firm resolution. No, it had nothing to do with "the horses": it was simply to make some of that terrific Kentucky Burgoo he and Virginia had enjoyed so much while in the bluegrass country. An occasion to do this presented itself when the Walkers discovered it was their turn to have the class of '34 of the University of Texas Law School before the Texas–Southern Methodist football game.

Virginia Walker is one of those rare people who add glamour to everything she touches, even if it is only her appearance in the room! She is the one who is put on the decoration committee when the-occasion-is-very-important-but-no-funds-are-available-sort-of-thing.

Ruel said, "Now, Mary, that Burgoo has to cook long enough for each ingredient to disintegrate completely. That's what makes it a success!" Virginia whispered, "But let's add a few carrots toward the end to add a little color." The guests all said, "Let's have this next time!" It was a perfect send-off to cheer for Texas!

The Burgoo was served from a handsome old copper tureen, on big squares of hot cornbread. The spiced peaches were in a huge turquoise compote, and a lovely mahogany bowl held a green salad. Virginia's chocolate fudge cupcakes with fudge icing for dessert were on a three-tier tray over by the brass samovar from which the coffee was served. Virginia arranged the centerpiece, of fruits and brilliant fall flowers, in her antique brass scales, which was the subject of much conversation.

With Burgoo, victory is assured! Even if the game is lost, the weekend won't be!

★

Kentucky Burgoo (*Mrs. Ruel Walker*)

2 lbs. pork shank
2 lbs. veal shank
2 lbs. beef shank
2 lbs. breast of lamb
1 4-lb. hen
8 qts. water
1½ lbs. Irish potatoes
½ lb. onions
1 bunch carrots
2 green peppers
2 cups chopped cabbage
1 qt. tomato puree
2 cups whole corn, fresh or canned
2 pods red pepper
2 cups diced okra
2 cups lima beans
1 cup diced celery
Salt and cayenne pepper to taste
Tabasco, A. 1. sauce, Worcestershire sauce to taste
Chopped parsley

Put all meats into cold water and bring slowly to boil. Simmer till tender enough to fall from bone. Lift meat out of stock. Cool and chop up the meat. Remove the bones, prepare potatoes and onions and dice. Return meat to stock and add potatoes, onions and all other vegetables. Allow to simmer along until thick. Burgoo should be very thick but still soupy. Season along but not too much until it is almost done. Add chopped parsley just before stew is taken up.

Stir frequently with long-handled paddle or spoon during the first part of the cooking and almost constantly after it gets thick.

We made ours in a four-gallon water bath kettle, and all in all it cooked approximately 10 hours.

I served this later at a party which the Charles Millhouses and the Bubbi Jessens gave. When Tim and Nancy Williams discovered there was Burgoo, they hurried right over. Nancy asked, "Where did you get the squirrels, Mary? And how much Bourbon did you use?" She said that both were necessary in the original recipe.

The beautiful home of Mr. and Mrs. James P. Nash is another site for Texas hospitality. It would be impossible even to try to count the number of parties that Anne and Jim have hosted during the last quarter of a century.

A party at the Nashes is almost "standard procedure" when any of their friends, or children of friends, take a trip, get married or make a debut. Well, there doesn't really have to be a reason, for both Anne and James love to entertain and are often supported by one or all of their lovely daughters, Catherine Tetens, Mary Scott and Beverley Bell. This makes the planning and executing of a party more fun.

The Nashes have all their parties at home, and serve magnificent food, which is prepared there too — whether it is a Sunday morning brunch on a football weekend for a hundred fifty, Anne's bridge club, or a dinner dance, such as the beautiful one they gave for Louise Houston and her fiancé Dick Rogers. The guests caught the air of elegance as they approached the front door, walking by the topiary trees which were fragrant with white carnations. The house was filled with striking arrangements of fresh flowers, and music floated through the rooms from the orchestra which was playing for dancing on the terrace. In the dining room, Anne used the exquisite organdy cloth which she and Jim had brought home from Agra, India. It was hand embroidered by the French nuns in a convent there. The same colors were repeated in the flowers used in her epergne in the centerpiece.

By popular demand, Anne always has her delicious *Cheese Straws passed during cocktails. She has them made by the "jillions." But this recipe makes about 3 dozen:

*

Cheese Straws

1 cup sifted all-purpose flour
½ tsp. baking powder
1 cup grated cheddar cheese
½ cup butter or margarine
3 Tbs. water

Sift flour and baking powder into bowl, cut in cheese and butter, add water and mix well. Roll and cut in strips. Place on ungreased cookie sheet, cut in desired lengths, or use cookie press to make the straws.

Also, an assortment of cold fancy olives, and caviar and sour cream to put on small toast rounds are passed. The menu for the buffet supper was:

** Crab au Gratin in Patty Shells*
Anne's Wonderful Pressed Chicken
Peas and Mushrooms
Breadsticks
Fresh Coconut Angel Food Balls
Coffee
Crème de Menthe Frappe

★

Crab au Gratin (*serves about* 4)

2 Tbs. butter
3 Tbs. green pepper
2 cups lump crabmeat
1 Tbs. cornstarch
1 cup light cream
1 egg yolk
Salt to taste
Paprika
½ cup grated cheese (half Parmesan, half American)

Melt butter and sauté crabmeat and green pepper about 3 minutes. Add cornstarch mixed with cream to egg yolk. Cook until thick. Season with salt and paprika. Serve in patty shells, or pour in buttered casserole, sprinkle cheese on top and run in oven just long enough to melt cheese.

The Nash parties are always a tremendous success. I have heard people say that Anne looks very much like Mrs. Perle Mesta! It may be because she plays the same role in these parts!

In spite of the sizzling summer weather in Austin, when most of us prefer a sandwich or watermelon at Barton Springs, there are a great many dress-up parties for brides and summer visitors. One of the *coolest* luncheons I had last August was such a favorite with all the guests that I have been besieged with requests for the recipes of the first and last courses. We served frozen daiquiris before lunch. They were made by the standard daiquiri formula in the Waring blender with fresh lime juice and light rum; except that Mitchell Mays, our official greeter and daiquiri maker, added a touch of 2 drops of vanilla into each batch. He always keeps the champagne glasses in the freezer until time to serve the daiquiris. The table (a large round one seating fourteen) was covered with a white damask cloth, the napkins were folded like fans, and a lovely arrangement of white and green caladiums was the centerpiece. The menu was:

** Frosted Tomatoes*
** Individual Salmon Soufflés with Cucumber Dressing*
Jumbo Green Asparagus Spears, marinated in French dressing
** Orange Popovers*
Iced Tea with Fresh Mint
** Fresh Fig Ice Cream*
Demitasses

★

Frosted Tomatoes (serves 6)

This is a recipe given me by my sister, Martha Stansbury, who lives in Houston. Her husband, Eddy, has a tomato garden in one of his flower beds, so this is especially good at their house.

6 large vine-ripened tomatoes, peeled and chopped fine
1 large sweet white onion, chopped very fine
½ cup mayonnaise
1 Tbs. parsley, chopped very fine
1 tsp. fresh coarse-ground black pepper
¼ cup sour cream
1 tsp. curry powder

Mix first 5 ingredients together and chill. Serve as cold soup with 1 tsp. sour cream which has been seasoned with curry powder on top of each serving.

★

Salmon Soufflé

1½ cup red salmon (canned)
1⅓ cup rich thick cream sauce
1 Tbs. lemon juice
1 tsp. onion juice
White pepper and salt to taste
⅓ cup cracker crumbs, rolled fine
2 eggs, separated

Drain off liquid from salmon; remove skin and bones and break into small pieces with fork. Mix together: cream sauce, seasonings, salmon and crumbs. Add well-beaten egg yolks and then fold in stiffly beaten egg whites. Fill individual buttered custard cups ¾ full of salmon mixture. Place in a shallow pan of hot water and bake about 30 minutes in a 325-degree oven. When done turn onto a warm plate and top with Cucumber Sauce.

CUCUMBER SAUCE

1 8-oz. pkg. cream cheese
¼ cup sour cream
1 tsp. onion juice
¼ tsp. salt
1 Tbs. wine vinegar
1 medium sized cucumber, peeled and chopped very fine
½ cup heavy cream, whipped
Cayenne pepper

Let cream cheese soften at room temperature, then beat well with next five ingredients. When well mixed, fold in whipped cream and a dash of cayenne pepper. Heat in top of double boiler until real warm, but not too long.

★

Orange Popovers

Use recipe on page 353, only substitute ½ cup orange juice; reduce milk ½ cup; and add the grated rind of 1 orange (only the orange part, none of the white part).

My father rarely ate dessert, but he "made supper" on *Fresh Fig Ice Cream.

★

Fresh Fig Ice Cream (serves 8)

18 to 20 figs
1½ cups sugar
4 eggs
4 Tbs. dry sherry
1 qt. cream, whipped
Grated rind and juice of 1 lemon

Peel and mash figs as fine as possible. Add sugar and let stand until sugar dissolves. Beat egg yolks; add sherry and beat well and add to figs. Whip cream, beat egg whites stiff and fold into figs. Freeze in a tray in the freezer. We made up 2½ gallons in the freezer, packed it in quart containers and kept it in the deep freeze. It is a refreshing dessert to serve and *so, so* good.

Avocadoes show up on many of our summer luncheon menus. I serve them filled with just about every combination imaginable. They make a tempting first course on a warm day when filled with a jellied consommé. Cut the avocado in half and sprinkle with fresh lemon or lime juice and a little bit of salt. I mold my consommé in small fancy molds just the size of the cavity left when the seed is removed. I usually top the consommé with a teaspoon of sour cream and about ½ teaspoon imported caviar in the center of the cream. A half of lemon cut with scalloped edge and centered with a sprig of parsley is also on the plate.

Chicken salad is also a favorite in a half avocado. I like the mayonnaise to be a little nippier and seasoned with onion and lemon juice, red pepper and a little chicken stock and freshly ground pepper. On the plate with this I serve a whole *Stuffed Pear prepared this way:

★

Stuffed Pear (*serves 4*)

4 whole canned cored pears (if whole ones are not available use 8 firm canned half pears)
4 oz. cream cheese
Pinch of salt
1 Tbs. mayonnaise or heavy cream
1 Tbs. candied ginger, chopped fine
Pink food coloring
Salad oil
1 pkg. lime gelatine dissolved in 1 cup hot water
½ cup ginger ale
1 pinch salt
Juice of 1 lemon, strained
2 jiggers of crème de menthe

Drain pears well on absorbent paper. Fill with cheese, salt, mayonnaise and ginger. Fill centers of pears; if halves are used, press two together firmly. Brush lightly with pink food coloring. Stand upright in muffin tins which have been rubbed lightly with a little salad oil. Glaze with the gelatine. Ladle over cold pears ginger ale, salt, lemon juice and crème de menthe, and return to refrigerator until gelatine is firm around the bottom of the pears. When time to serve, place on fresh fig or lettuce leaves; add sprigs of fresh mint to tops of pears. We add about 4 large potato chips to this plate. They look crisp and cool, too.

I usually toss the King Crab or Shrimp Salad with a rémoulade dressing — a spoonful of lemon mayonnaise on top with a large pitted black olive stuck in the mayonnaise. With this I serve a *Stuffed Tomato fixed thusly:

★

Stuffed Tomato (*serves 4*

4 large ripe but firm tomatoes, peeled
Salt
6 hard-boiled eggs
1 stick celery
¼ cup plus 4 tsp. mayonnaise
1 Tbs. chili sauce
1 Tbs. parsley, chopped very fine
Watercress
16 filets of anchovy, rolled

Scoop out tomatoes, turn upside down to drain well. Chill. Sprinkle with salt. Chop eggs, and celery. Mix mayonnaise and chili sauce and stir in eggs, celery and parsley. Correct seasoning. Place a spoonful of egg mixture in each tomato and then three anchovy filets next. Finish filling tomato with egg mixture. Top with 1 teaspoon of mayonnaise and 1 filet of anchovy in the center of the mayonnaise. Serve on a bed of watercress.

SWEETBRUSH

Standing at the front door of Sweetbrush is like looking through a stereoscope where many beautiful pictures become as one with deep multiple dimension. The wide doors at the opposite end of this spacious hall frame a magnificent view, opening out to the formal gardens and on to the grassy slope with giant live oak trees which border the peaceful blue Lake Austin and the green hills beyond. Sweetbrush is the picturesque home of Dr. and Mrs. Z. T. Scott. It is indeed synonymous with Southern hospitality in the truest form. Dr. Scott, great in Texas medical heritage, came from Virginia, and Mrs. Scott was one of the four Masterson girls, whose family for several generations has played an important role in developing the Panhandle and other parts of Texas. Probably because of the distinctive lives their three children have chosen, as well as their own diversified interests, the Scotts entertain with a great deal of versatility. It may be for a screen or stage star friend of son Zachary; or members of the Cattle Raising Association, which has always been dear to the Scotts' heart and life and which is vitalized by their daughter and son-in-law, Mr. and Mrs. Dick Kleberg, Jr., of the King Ranch. Then, of course, there is always a party when popular Ann Scott Hearon comes home for a visit.

One of the most elegant affairs ever given at Sweetbrush was when all three of the Scott children honored their parents with a beautiful garden party on the occasion of their fiftieth wedding anniversary. Zachary decided this was such a very special occasion they would shoot the works — which literally we did: fireworks over

Lake Austin, shooting out all sorts of brilliant displays, including the wedding dates and names of the honorees. The pavilion built for dancing was lighted with imported white lanterns called "happiness balls." The air was filled with the fragrance of yellow roses, which were used in great profusion. Flowers had been sent from friends from all over the country and the florists in Austin did a magnificent job of coordinating them effectively throughout the house and gardens. In true Sweetbrush tradition, the food was superb: Dr. Scott's favorite Virginia ham, done to perfection by Ethel Collins who has cooked under the tutorage of both Dr. Scott and Mrs. Scott for many, many years. She proudly displays a framed plaque for the "Best Cook in the World" presented to her by the Scott children several years ago. With the thin-sliced Virginia ham, which Dr. Scott insists must be carved with a knife as sharp as a surgical one, were warm beaten biscuits. Charcoal-broiled sirloin strips brought from the King Ranch were carved near the broiler and served on homemade bread and butter sandwiches; a round ice table was covered with fresh Gulf shrimp and wonderful sauces in which to dip them. Many kinds of yummy small canapés and hors d'oeuvres, both hot and cold, were passed, including *Rumakis, which were also cooked over the coals and kept hot in chafing dishes.

★

Rumaki (*serves 6*)

18 chicken livers
Salt and pepper
18 pieces water chestnuts
1½ cups maple syrup
9 slices lean bacon (cut in half)
1 Tbs. soy sauce

Salt and pepper livers. Soak chestnuts in maple syrup several hours. Remove from syrup and place 1 piece in center of chicken liver. Wrap with bacon and pin securely with toothpick. Place on wire rack over low coals, turning frequently. Add soy sauce to syrup and use to baste livers. Remove from fire when bacon is very crisp and place in a chafing dish.

The Champagne table was covered with snow, which was a very artistic and effective way to keep the bottles of Champagne ice cold as well as the glasses. We made an exquisite tall five-tiered wedding cake topped with a golden 50 and spun-sugar yellow rosebuds; larger roses with lilies of the valley cascaded down the cake, into large full-bloom yellow roses, also made of spun sugar around the bottom tier. This was indeed a splendid occasion and holds fondest memories for all who were present.

Zack Scott and his lovely wife Ruth Ford are almost as famous for their Texas–Mississippi–New York cuisine as for their excellent stage performances. One of the most delicious contributions to Sweetbrush is Ruth's way to cook *Fresh Black-eyed Peas with Okra.

★

Fresh Black-eyed Peas with Okra

Shell fresh black-eyed peas (or use frozen ones), cover with water and cook slowly in a heavy pot with a small piece of salt pork until tender. Wash and cut fresh okra and place on top of peas. Remove from fire; cover with lid and let okra cook in steam (off the fire) until barely tender, but still crisp! Season with salt and pepper to taste.

Whether a party at Sweetbrush is large or small, formal or informal, it always has an unequaled quality of warmth and graciousness, and just as consistent is the delicious food. A favorite Scott family occasion is a late Sunday morning Virginia breakfast to meet Dr. Scott's specifications, which include *Hot Apple Toddy, served around the fireplace in the living room; then, with all the family seated around the big table in the dining room, Dr. Scott serving the *Potomac Roe Herring from one end, and Mrs. Scott serving the Fried Apple Rings and Virginia Spoon Bread and topping it with butter from the big old-fashioned butter dish, from her end of the table. Ethel keeps the cups filled with good strong hot coffee.

★

Hot Apple Toddy (serves 4)

Wash and core 2 Winesap (hard cooking) apples; do not peel, but slice (not too thin). Into each mug put 1 scant tsp. sugar, 2 whole cloves, 3 slices of apples. Then barely cover apples with hot water. Place mugs in a pan of warm water; place in a low 200-degree oven until sugar has dissolved and apples are tender, but not mushy. Remove from oven and add 1½ oz. straight Bourbon to each mug. Place mugs on a silver tray, with 4 spoons, 4 linen napkins and nutmeg grinder and bring in by the fireplace, where a brass pot of water is very hot on a trivet. Finish filling each mug with hot water, wrap linen napkin around mug, grind a little nutmeg onto top and serve with silver spoon. Sip this heavenly toddy; slowly inhale its delightful aroma!

★

Potomac Roe Herring

This is available in wooden buckets from Fredericksburg, Virginia.

Rinse each piece of herring in cold water, then soak in cold water for 24 hours. Remove from water; rinse and place on paper towel to dry well. Dip in cornmeal; then fry slowly in hot vegetable oil until golden brown.

BEAUMONT

The Broussards' house in Beaumont stands empty and silent as the busy traffic of this thriving city in southeast Texas zips by. The blooming magnolia trees appear sad as they stand guard around it. Chessie Taylor lives in a comfortable house surrounded with big fig trees in the side yard. Chessie cooked for the Broussard family for fifty-five years, and of course this is her home.

Mr. and Mrs. Joe Broussard built this spacious home in 1909 for their family of eleven. Needless to say, it was brimming over with the activities of nine healthy children and is remembered as one of the happiest houses in this area. Papa Joe would beam broadly when his entire brood was around the big dining table. Even after the children married, this house was still the gathering place for all of them on special occasions such as birthdays, christenings, and Christmas, and the usual lively pace was even more lively with the hustle of twenty-six grandchildren and more than sixty great-grandchildren.

Joe Broussard was not only the patriarch of this fine family but a very strong force in the development and progress of the Beaumont area. When Joe was a young man, he tended cattle on his mother's homeplace. He was also the home gardener, for he loved the soil and trusted it. He decided there were big things to be done in farming in that part of Texas. Lumber had been the mainstay in Beaumont in those days, but the pine and cypress trees had pretty well been cut out, and this land, bereft of its timber, was almost abandoned.

With his marvelous foresight, Joe looked beyond his small farm to acres of new flat rice fields and herds of fine cattle. As the years slipped by, his dream became reality. He was one of the first to import purebred Brahmans to crossbreed with Texas longhorn cattle. He was also first to try new ideas in farming. In 1890 there were fewer than two hundred acres of rice sown in all of Texas whereas today nearly three hundred thousand acres are given to its cultivation. In 1892 Joe built the Beaumont Rice Mills, and this fine institution has flourished ever since. Then came the exciting year of 1902 when Old Spindle Top, the world's first oil gusher, "blew in" at Beaumont.

Rice was served in some form at practically every meal at the Broussard house! Someone asked Mr. Broussard if rice had vitamins. "Only when you put gravy on it," he grinned.

I used to love to go there to visit. There was always a round of parties: weekends down at the bay; a gay luncheon or dinner at the home of one of the younger generation. We never ran out of invitations — just time. Wherever we went, we had a wonderful time and marvelous food.

I used to try to detect what seasoning Chessie used in her cooking to make it so superb. My chance came recently when I was in Beaumont and went to visit her. She was so happy to talk about the days gone by as we sat in the stilled kitchen of the big house. She told me how she cooked many of the delicious things I had eaten around the big dining table. Like:

★

Trout and Shrimp

Mr. Broussard was a great fisherman, and when he would say, "Let's go fishing," the younger fellows in the crowd always made sure just how far he intended to go and when he intended to get back, so they wouldn't get "pooped" before the trip was over.

Take a 3 lb. trout, skin and filet, removing all bones. Place in roasting pan. Add heart of celery cut fine, 1 onion chopped, ½ lb. shrimp. Add a little water and a little salt to taste. Cover with lid and put in 350-degree oven for about twenty minutes. Remove to hot platter and cover with sauce:

1 Tbs. oil
4 egg yolks and 1 egg white
Juice of 2 lemons
2 Tbs. boiling water

Beat these ingredients over hot water till slightly thickened and pour over fish. Garnish with watercress, lemon slices, and shrimp. Absolutely divine!

With this Chessie served:

Grapefruit Salad
Green Peas
Potatoes au Gratin
* *Cashaw*
Corn Bread Muffins
* *Rice Pudding*

★

Chessie's Cashaw

Cashaw is a large squash-like vegetable native to this section. It is peeled, cut in cubes, and boiled until tender, and well-drained, then put in a buttered pan with generous amounts of sugar, nutmeg, and butter. (When I asked Chessie about the amounts here, she said it all depends on how big the cashaw is. She implied that any good cook should know how much.) Bake until there is a brown crust on top.

★

Rice Pudding

Beat 6 eggs until fluffy. Add:

1 Tbs. flour
4 Tbs. sugar
4 Tbs. cooked rice
½ cup raisins
1 qt. milk
¼ tsp. nutmeg
1 tsp. lemon extract
1 tsp. vanilla extract
1 Tbs. butter

Pour in buttered casserole and bake at 350 degrees in pan of hot water "until it quivers."

Every Tuesday morning, Chessie fixed beef patties in lemon sauce, for that seemed to be the day for visitors to "drop in." Chessie said: Cook patties (made of fresh ground beef) in a little butter in a heavy iron skillet. Take them out when done and put on a warm platter. Put one teaspoon flour in where you've cooked the patties and the juice of one lemon, one tablespoon of butter, ¼ cup of hot water, a little salt and pepper, and pour over the patties.

Chessie roasted duck often. Grandfather Broussard was an ardent duck hunter all of his life, and there were many wild ducks down in the marshes. Even in his eighties, come duck-hunting season he would be out ploughing through the icy waters in the lead. The younger men tried to keep up. There wasn't a trail through the swamps and marshes that Joe didn't know well. One day when Mr. Broussard was almost ninety, he told one of his grandsons, "You know, it's a good thing my eyes are going bad on me. There's a world of fat wild ducks down on Taylor's Bayou right now, but it's not duck season yet. If I could see to shoot, I'd be in jail, sure."

Chessie said they always had plenty of ducks, and this was one of Mr. B's favorite recipes:

Wash ducks and cut in half. Add:

Duck gizzards chopped fine
2 Tbs. parsley chopped
1 green onion chopped

Place in roasting pan and add a little water (about ¼ to ½ cup). Cook slowly at 325 degrees.

With the ducks Chessie often would serve Buttered Rice, *Fried Sweet Potatoes and *String Beans with Onion.

★

Fried Sweet Potatoes

Boil potatoes in jackets, peel, and quarter. Fry in a little hot fat in a heavy iron skillet. Sprinkle with sugar and drain on paper. Arrange around ducks.

★

String Beans with Onion

First remove all strings from every bean. Cook until tender in boiling water. Sauté 1 onion in 1 Tbs. butter. Add 1 tsp. flour, ½ cup milk, and 2 egg yolks beaten until fluffy. Beat together and cook over low fire till smooth and slightly thick. Pour over beans.

Sometimes instead of Fried Sweet Potatoes, Chessie served Green Apples, which she quartered, simmered in a little water until tender, and then seasoned with sugar and butter. She said Mr. and Mrs. Broussard also liked Fresh Mustard Greens served with the duck. To cook them, she boils ¼ pound salt pork, cut in slices down to the rind, adds ¼ teaspoon soda, then the washed mustard greens, which are cooked till tender.

Every Sunday Chessie had Fried Chicken and Rice and Gravy. I have noticed throughout southeast Texas that the principle "function" of rice is to hold gravy. Chessie does not make a cream gravy; she uses water in hers, and it is so light and delicious. She simply pours off the fat where she has fried the chicken, adds about 2 tablespoons flour, a little salt and black pepper, the chopped liver (which has been cooked), and the hot water and stirs till smooth. "I had to have lots of gravy. All the family just loved it," she said.

In addition to the Fried Chicken, Rice and Gravy, salad, and vegetables, there had to be a dish of *Chicken and Dumplings. I had never before eaten such fine thin dumplings. They seemed to just melt away. One Sunday the dumplings failed to appear on the table, and little Regina Broussard burst into tears — said she couldn't eat Sunday dinner without Chicken and Dumplin':

2 cups flour	**2 Tbs. butter**
2 egg yolks	**Salt and pepper**

These are rolled paper thin, cut in strips, and dropped in broth where the necks, gizzards, and a few wings have been boiled.

Chessie's food is simple, not too rich, but seasoned just right.

The table was always beautifully set with lovely linen and beautiful china and silver. The light, with a multicolored Tiffany glass shade, hung over the center of the table. Mr. Broussard always sat at the head of the table like a king ruling over his court. After his death Mrs. Broussard continued his procedure in serving — a set ritual.

On Friday mornings there were usually *Hot Cakes. One of the Broussard daughters, Estelle (who is now Sister Rita Estelle, head of the Music Department at Dumbarton College in Washington), came home for a visit every summer accompanied by another sister. Chessie said they always enjoyed her little Hot Cakes. I remember one Friday morning when we came in from early Mass there was a large cut-glass bowl of peeled fresh figs at the head of the table. Mrs. Broussard spooned them carefully into little individual bowls, and we were all tempted to send back for seconds but knew that the Hot Cakes would soon be coming.

I have really worked on "copying" these cakes, and my family welcomes them at *any* meal.

6 eggs, beaten separately
2 cups of buttermilk with 1 tsp. soda dissolved in it
½ cup sweet milk
Approximately 3 cups of flour sifted with:
3 tsp. baking powder
1 Tbs. melted butter

Mix everything together except the egg whites and stir till smooth. Then carefully fold in stiffly beaten egg whites and drop by tablespoonfuls into heavy iron skillet which has a little melted fat in the bottom. Brown lightly on each side, turning only once. Serve immediately with sugar cane syrup.

Papa Broussard used to send out a family newspaper to all his clan keeping them briefed on the special and blessed events occurring in the family and around Beaumont. Of course, one of the most special events was Christmas dinner. There were almost one hundred Broussards of the immediate family seated at Christmas dinner. This was a great time for Chessie and her numerous helpers. She said, "It wasn't any trouble. We all have a good time gettin' ready." They spent one day just baking, making fresh coconut cake in three layers, lots of dark fruit cake, white cake with lemon filling, and cookies galore of all kinds. On Christmas Eve they chopped the celery and onion for the dressing and stored it in jars. They also boiled the gizzards and necks to make broth. The large turkeys were dressed ready for the oven early Christmas morning. The dinner menu was usually Black Cherry Salad, White Asparagus, Petits Pois in a thin white sauce, hot rolls, and Peppermint Ice Cream for dessert — besides all those cakes! But the aroma which dominated the house most was from the turkeys, roasting with the *Rice Dressing and a big pot of giblet gravy.

★

Rice and Bread Dressing

Sauté chopped celery and onions in butter. Add:

- **Cooked rice and toasted white bread, broken in pieces**
- **3 hard-boiled eggs, mashed with a fork**
- **6 raw eggs, beaten slightly**
- **Salt and black pepper**
- **Boiled necks and gizzards, chopped fine**
- **Enough broth to hold it all together**

Sounds easy. Chessie doesn't use any other seasonings — she doesn't need to. This is perfect and is acclaimed so by all present from the youngest to the oldest.

Katie Belle Doyle, one of the third generation, says that Chessie makes the best *Patience in the world. She always had a big supply on hand during the holidays.

★

Patience (a favorite candy)

- **2 cups sugar**
- **1 cup milk**

Mix sugar and milk and cook in saucepan.

- **1 more cup sugar**

Brown in skillet and add to sugar and milk mixture and cook some more.

Total time is about 30 minutes — or when it forms soft ball in cold water. Remove from fire and add 1 Tbs. butter, 1 tsp. vanilla, 1 cup chopped nuts. Beat until smooth and creamy. Pour onto buttered platter.

Just burglarizing the Broussard recipes, I have enough to write a cookbook. Of course, there are many many other fabulous cooks in

Beaumont, but I never got around to all of them, for today we'd go to Verena and Clyde Broussard's for lunch; tonight, Ruth and I. D. Polk's for a buffet; tea in between at Annette and Doug Steinman's; the next day to Bertha and Fuzzy Roanne's; and in the evening to Edna and Joe Broussard's. Everywhere — always beautiful and delicious food and *great* fun!

Actually, in just reading the menus and recipes one might wonder what is so unusual about *Steak and Baked Potatoes. And I might say only the perfection of each dish — the exactly right amount of seasoning, not at all accidental, and the selected quality of each item.

Bobby Humphreys, who has been cooking for the Polks under Ruth's careful tutoring for a number of years, is a past master at timing — and so is Tommy Polk, who masterminds the outside grilling of steaks. The meat comes from the Broussard ranch, La Belle, nearby. Papa Broussard said the cattle get most of their vitamins from the husk polished off the rice. This mixed with bran, cottonseed meal, and a little blackstrap and fed to the cattle along with prairie hay makes mighty fine beef. Tommy has the steaks cut about 1½ inches thick and marinates them in vinegar, butter, lemon, Worcestershire, A-1, salt, and pepper for two or three hours before cooking. As soon as the meat is placed on the grill, the lid is closed, and the steaks are turned only once. The timing of the steaks is synchronized with Bobby's *Potatoes, and everything arrives at the table at the same time. I am sure this is what makes the "could-be-ordinary" menu so extra special.

★

Bobby's Potatoes

Select 8 uniform good-sized Idaho potatoes. Place on wire rack with prong stuck in each potato to hold it upright. This bakes the potatoes in less time and more uniformly. Place these in a 375-degree oven for approximately 45 minutes. Remove and split in halves. Scoop out potatoes and mash and stir in:

¼ stick of butter
1 tsp. grated onion
½ cup light cream
2 whole eggs

Then beat like a cake. Put mixture back into the shells and sprinkle a little paprika and grated American cheese on top. Return to oven. They rise up and shout glory.

Bobby served Fresh Asparagus topped with melted butter and lemon, and a Lettuce and Sliced Tomato Salad.

Ruth has "portions" of her grandchildren to visit her often. One day when the Simmie Polk children were having lunch, the youngest started early in the meal asking for jelly and bread. Trying to carry out her young daughter-in-law's wishes regarding the children's eating patterns, Ruth sweetly said, "First, Joey, you must finish your vegetables," which happened to be black-eyed peas cooked with okra. His request was repeated several times during lunch, and Ruth patiently tried to maintain discipline. Finally, Joey's six-year-old sister came to his aid.

"Why, Grandmother, you're not supposed to give children vegetables mixed up like that!"

"Well, darling, what vegetables should we have?"

"Green beans, of course." So Ruth plans green beans when the grandchildren dine with her, and *Bread Pudding is served for dessert.

★

Bobby's Bread Pudding

- 3 slices bread, crumbled
- 3 cups milk
- ½ cup sugar
- Nutmeg
- 1 tsp. vanilla
- 4 eggs
- 3 or 4 Tbs. raisins

Mix crumbled bread with milk, sugar, nutmeg, vanilla and eggs. Add raisins (which have been soaked in hot water). Place casserole in pan of hot water and bake at 325 degrees for approximately 30 minutes.

★

Bobby's Fig Preserves

- 1 gal. figs
- ½ gal. sugar
- ½ lemon, sliced

Let stand until mixture thickens and sugar is dissolved. Bring to boil. Cook syrup until it thickens. Cook slowly for approximately one hour.

Ruth drove over to Houston that morning to attend a Dior showing, and met her daughter, Sister Anne Marie, to bring her to Beaumont for a visit. There were about 40 to 50 guests assembled at the Polks' home almost by the time Ruth made it back, but Bobby and her many assistants had everything ready, and it was a mighty fine spread. Passed during cocktails were thimble-sized pastries filled with creamed chicken and caviar and anchovy cream cheese hors d'oeuvre pies cut in small wedges. Dinner consisted of:

Hot sliced barbecued beef
Tray of thin sliced breads
Tiny hot cheese biscuits
* *Ruth's Baked Ham*
Hot mustard and mayonnaise made by Bobby
Baked Cashaw (like Chessie's)
* *Ruth's Hominy in Casserole*
String beans
* *Mayhaw Jelly*
Spiced peach halves
Tray of sweet and sour beets
Hearts of palm
Marinated artichoke hearts

Dessert table (how could one make a choice?):

Compote of Pecan Fudge
Large silver bowl of vanilla ice cream and brandied walnuts for topping
Fresh Peach Cobbler
Small cups of steaming hot spiced coffee — one of Ruth's specialties

---

★

Baked Ham

Trim off excess fat from 14- or 15-lb. ham. Cover with paste made of brown sugar, ground cloves, prepared mustard, and vinegar. Place on rack in roasting pan. Add 2 cups of water and bake 3 hours in 350-degree oven.

★

Hominy in Casserole

Drain whole hominy well. Make light cream sauce using extra amount of butter. Season with paprika, salt, and pepper. Add 3 beaten eggs to 4 cups of sauce. Use buttered casserole and place in layers hominy, sauce, grated cheddar cheese, and sprinkle buttered cracker crumbs on top.

★

Mayhaw Jelly (an East Texas delight)

Wash and pick out bad berries. Place in kettle with just enough water to cover hand when placed on top of berries. Bring to boil and boil till mayhaws are tender. Place in cloth and let juice run out of berries. This makes a clear jelly. Squeeze more juice out by twisting and squeezing bag. Cook 4 cups of juice to 3 cups of sugar till it will jell when dripped on kitchen tile. Put in jars that are sterile. Pour wax on top when jelly is cool. Berries are available in spring.

At the Roanes', the only member of their family missing was daughter Theres Roddy, who had that morning given birth to her tenth child. Small delicious canapés were passed during cocktails. On buffet:

Beef Stroganoff with Wide Noodles
Vegetable Salad Ring
Chafing dish of Petit-Pois Peas
Baby Carrots with Artichoke Bottoms
Brandied Peaches
Small hot biscuits
Red wine
Lemon Tarts and Demitasses

Living so close to Louisiana, the Beaumont cooks have for generations specialized in Creole and Cajun dishes. Katie Belle Doyle said that crawfish were being raised in great quantities in the rice swamps, and there is a popular market for them in and around

Beaumont because they have such a delicate and luscious flavor. The fat that is found in the crawfish is used instead of other fats in their preparation, and it greatly enhances the flavor. We had *Crawfish Etouffée for lunch, accompanied by a constant murmur of praise.

★

Crawfish Etouffée

8 lbs. fresh crawfish
6 onions, chopped fine
½ cup celery, chopped
½ tsp. tomato paste
¼ lb. oleo or 1 cup cooking oil
½ tsp. cornstarch
½ cup cold water
Salt, black pepper, and red pepper to taste
¼ cup onion tops and parsley, minced

Boil crawfish. Peel crawfish tails. Add onions, celery and tomato paste to oleo or oil and cook over medium heat until onions are partially cooked. Add whole crawfish tails. Dissolve cornstarch in cold water. Add to fish mixture, stirring constantly. Season to taste with salt and peppers. Bring to a boil in uncovered pot over medium heat and cook for 15 minutes. Add green onions and parsley. Mix well. Serve with cooked rice. Makes 8 portions.

Home for the Christmas holidays, Susan Doyle brought a schoolmate, pretty Lu Wong. She *loved* Susan's grandmother's Jambalaya and wondered why the Chinese didn't fix rice like that.

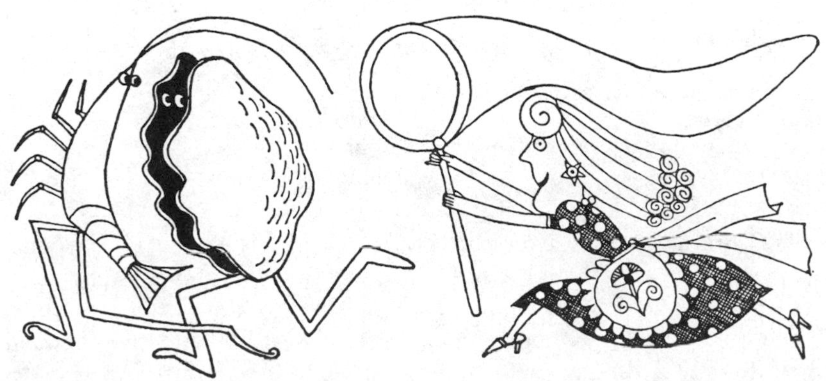

★

Jambalaya

2 Tbs. olive oil
1½ cups diced ham
3-4 cups cooked small shrimp
1½ Tbs. butter
2 large onions, finely chopped
2 or 3 cloves of garlic, minced
1 bay leaf
Salt
Pepper
1 cup uncooked brown or long-grain rice
1 qt. consommé
4 small tomatoes or 1 No. 303 can of tomatoes
1 green pepper, finely chopped
Cayenne pepper
½ cup sherry
¼ cup dry red wine

In 2 tablespoons of olive oil, sauté lightly the ham and shrimp. Then add the butter, the onions which have been finely chopped, the minced garlic, bay leaf, and salt and pepper to taste. Then add the uncooked rice. Sauté all the above until the rice is golden brown. At this point add 1 quart of consommé, which has been brought to the boiling point in a separate pan. Then add the tomatoes and green pepper, which has been finely chopped. Also sprinkle some cayenne pepper to taste.

After carefully stirring the above mixture, cover the pan and let it simmer until the rice is done, about 25 to 30 minutes. Now add the final touch, the sherry and dry red wine. Do not stir again, but let it cook through, simmering until ready to serve, at least 5 to 10 minutes.

A dish that is extremely popular in these parts is *Shrimp Gumbo, and Annette Steinman makes the best I've ever eaten.

★

Shrimp Gumbo Filé

3 lbs. shrimp
2 qts. hot water
Salt and black pepper to taste
Dash of cayenne
1 large white onion, chopped
3 sprigs of parsley
1 sprig of thyme
1 Tbs. lard
1 bay leaf, chopped
1 qt. oysters (save the liquor to put into the gumbo)
Flour
Gumbo filé powder

Shell the shrimp. Season the hot water highly with the cayenne, onion, parsley, and thyme. Cook the shrimp 3 minutes. Put the lard into an iron pot, and when hot add the flour, making a brown roux. When quite brown, without a semblance of burning, add the chopped bay leaf; pour in the hot oyster liquor and the hot water, or use the carefully strained liquor in which the shrimp have been boiled. When it comes to a good boil, and about five minutes before serving, add the shrimp and oysters to the gumbo and remove from the heat. Then add to the boiling hot liquid 1 or 2 Tbs. of the filé, thickening according to taste. Serve immediately with boiled rice.

Another memorable Beaumont dinner at noon was held when Mr. Walter Casey, husband of Loretta Broussard Casey, had just returned from a trip to Russia. We sat a long time around the dinner table listening to Walter's fascinating stories. We had *Veal Breast Piquante, *Stuffed Sweet Potatoes, Baked Cauliflower, *Coleslaw with Sour Cream Dressing, *Corn Sticks, Chessie's Cabinet Pudding, coffee, and rosé wine.

★

Veal Breast Piquante

3 lbs. veal breast
2 Tbs. fat
2 onions, chopped
1 clove garlic, minced
1½ tsp. chili powder
Dash pepper
2 tsp. salt
3 Tbs. vinegar
1 Tbs. Worcestershire
¼ cup catsup
1 cup water

Brown veal on all sides in fat in heavy kettle. Mix remaining ingredients, and pour over meat. Cover, and simmer 1½ hours, basting occasionally with the liquid. Serves 4.

★

Stuffed Sweet Potatoes

1 small can crushed pineapple
½ cup brown sugar
2 Tbs. butter
¼ cup chopped pecans
½ tsp. nutmeg
4 large sweet potatoes, boiled
8 Maraschino cherries
Salt and pepper

Drain pineapple. Mix drained pineapple, sugar, butter, nuts, and nutmeg. Scoop about 2 Tbs. of pulp from each potato half after cutting them lengthwise. Fill potato centers with the pineapple mixture. Place a cherry on top. Bake in preheated oven at 350 degrees for about 30 minutes. Serves 8.

The veal had been sliced in the kitchen and laid symmetrically on a huge platter surrounded with endive leaves and the Stuffed Sweet Potatoes.

★

Baked Cauliflower

- 1 head of cauliflower
- 2 Tbs. butter
- 2 Tbs. flour
- 1 cup milk
- ½ tsp. salt
- ¼ tsp. pepper
- 2 hard-cooked eggs, chopped
- 2 Tbs. chopped pimento
- ¾ cup chopped green onion
- ¼ cup buttered crumbs
- 2 tsp. grated cheese

Cook the whole cauliflower, covered, in one inch of boiling salted water about 10 minutes. Remove from pan and cool. Melt butter, add flour and stir in milk, cooking until smooth and thick. Add salt, pepper, eggs, pimento, and green onion to sauce. Place cauliflower in greased baking dish. Pour sauce over cauliflower and sprinkle with crumbs and cheese. Bake at 375 degrees for 10 minutes. Makes 5 servings.

★

Cole Slaw with Sour Cream Dressing

- 5 cups shredded cabbage
- 1 cup finely chopped celery
- 2 pimentoes, chopped
- ½ cup mayonnaise
- ¼ cup sour cream
- 2 Tbs. wine vinegar
- 1 Tbs. lemon juice
- 2 tsp. anchovy paste
- 1 Tbs. each of chopped parsley and scallions
- Salt and pepper

Combine cabbage, celery, and pimento in a bowl. Mix together mayonnaise, sour cream, vinegar, lemon juice, anchovy paste, parsley, and scallions and blend with salt and pepper to taste. Pour over slaw and toss together. Makes 4 to 6 servings.

★

Corn Sticks

- 1 egg
- 1½ cups buttermilk
- ½ tsp. soda
- ½ cup sifted flour
- 1½ cups corn meal
- 1 Tbs. sugar
- 1 Tbs. baking powder
- 1 tsp. salt
- ¼ cup soft shortening

Generously grease iron corn stick pans. Heat in oven while mixing batter. Beat egg, then add milk. Sift dry ingredients together and into egg. Then add softened shortening. Beat all together just until smooth. Spoon batter into hot pans until almost full and bake at 450 degrees for 10 to 15 minutes. This may also be baked in a square pan for 20 to 25 minutes and cut into squares. Makes 12 servings.

I was very impressed with some little oyster pot pies I had in Beaumont, and I can hardly wait for a month with an *r* in it to make them for the Koock crew.

★

Oyster Pot Pies

2 dozen oysters
½ tsp. salt
¼ tsp. pepper
Tarragon
⅛ tsp. cayenne
2 tsp. Worcestershire sauce
4 small onions, sliced
4 small carrots, sliced
4 medium potatoes, diced
1 cup grated sharp cheese
½ cup milk
Biscuit crust
Parsley

Drain oysters, reserving liquid. Chop oysters with scissors. Mix with salt, pepper, tarragon, cayenne, Worcestershire sauce. Place layer of onions, carrots, and potatoes in each greased, individual pie pan or casserole, then a layer of oysters, seasonings, and cheese. Repeat layers. Place 2 Tbs. milk and 2 Tbs. oyster liquid in each pan or casserole. Cover pies with biscuit crust. Bake in moderate oven, 375 degrees, for 45 minutes. Garnish with parsley. Makes 4 servings.

BISCUIT CRUST

2 cups flour
½ tsp. baking soda
½ tsp. salt
2 Tbs. shortening
1 Tbs. vinegar, plus milk to make ¾ cup

Sift then measure flour. Sift again with baking soda and salt. Cut shortening into dry ingredients with pastry blender or two knives. Add enough liquid to make a soft dough. Mix with a fork. Turn onto floured board and knead slightly. Divide dough into four parts. Roll each out ¼ inch thick; shape to fit pan or casserole. Cover each pie. Cut fish shape out of center of each pie crust.

Joe Broussard II is a fortunate young man who is following in his father's and grandfather's footsteps. He is now president of the Beaumont Rice Mills, and he's an ardent duck hunter. His lovely wife, Jeanne, is a gracious and capable hostess, and what greater compliment could come her way than that from her mother-in-law, Rena, who said, "Jeanne is such a marvelous cook!"

A favorite hors d'oeuvre of Jeanne's is *Rice Balls.

★

Jeanne's Rice Balls

2 eggs, slightly beaten
1 tsp. salt
1 tsp. dry mustard
¼ tsp. pepper
1 tsp. Worcestershire sauce
2 Tbs. horseradish
4 cups cooked rice (warm)
1½ cups grated cheddar cheese
½ cup dry breadcrumbs

Combine eggs, salt, mustard, pepper, Worcestershire sauce, horseradish in mixing bowl. Add rice and cheese. Mix well. Chill.

Roll mixture in small balls ¾ inches in diameter. Roll in bread crumbs. Fry in deep fat (hot) 375 degrees until golden brown, about 3 minutes. Drain on absorbent paper. Serve hot. Makes about 6 dozen rice balls.

Jeanne quite often has by special request of family and friends *Chicken with Sauce Piquante.

★

Chicken with Sauce Piquante

3 chickens
4 or 5 bouillon cubes or 5 cups chicken stock
Rice, spaghetti or noodles
Green onions, chopped
½ cup chopped parsley
Almonds, chopped and fried

Boil 3 chickens in 5 cups water (in which 4 or 5 bouillon cubes have been dissolved) or 5 cups chicken stock. Break chicken in small pieces. Add to cooked sauce. In a deep casserole place layers of rice, spaghetti or noodles, which have been previously cooked, layers of chicken and sauce, and top with chopped green onions, parsley and almonds. Bake.

SAUCE PIQUANTE

1 cup oil
¼ cup flour
Salt
Pepper
1 cup celery
2 cups onions
⅔ cup bell pepper
1 28-oz. can tomatoes
3 buds of garlic
2 6-oz. cans tomato sauce
½ box pickling spice

Prepare a brown roux with oil, flour, salt and pepper. When thickened, add chopped celery, onions and peppers and brown lightly. Add tomatoes, garlic, and tomato sauce along with pickling spice, and cook for 3 hours, adding additional liquid if needed.

To keep up with all the avid hunters in the family, Jeanne has many excellent ways to prepare ducks and quail. This one is superb.

★

Oak Knoll Farm Quails

Wash and dry 4 to 6 birds. Rub with salt and flour. Sauté lightly in butter in heavy skillet on top of stove. Remove and place birds in iron frying pan. In butter left in skillet lightly sauté ½ cup chopped onions, ½ cup chopped mushrooms, 1 Tbs. parsley. Pour over the birds with ½ cup white wine. Cook 30 minutes or until tender. Baste frequently. Add ½ cup heavy cream and, when thoroughly hot, serve with rice.

Jeanne's cousin, Lu Hancock, served an *Oyster Stew one night when they had all been over hunting in El Campo. Jeanne said it was undoubtedly the *most* divine. She wrote Lu an S.O.S. saying she must have the recipe for a similar occasion. Lu obliged:

★

Oyster Stew

2 stalks celery with tops
2 bunches green onions cut coarsely
4 large white onions, chopped
8 potatoes cut in 1-in. slices
1 bottle pickling spice in cheesecloth bag
½ lb. butter
½ gal. milk
1 gal. oysters
Salt, cayenne pepper, Worcestershire sauce

Clean celery, with leaves; green onions, and tops; white onions. Dice potatoes small, fix spice bag and place all in large pot with tight lid. Add water, cook slowly till all vegetables are very soft. Remove spice bag and with spatula mash vegetables as much as you can. About 10 minutes before serving, add butter and milk. Add oysters and cook until edges curl. Season well.

Jeanne modestly says that if she is a good cook it is because she is a good collector of recipes from friends — but aren't *all* good cooks just that? It was her friend Tootie Ross who generously told her how to make the *Creole Oysters which had everyone raving at the party.

★

Creole Oysters

¼ stick butter
1 qt. oysters
1 bottle catsup
¼ bottle Worcestershire (large)
1 cup chopped green onions
½ cup chopped parsley

Melt butter, add other ingredients, and heat till oysters curl. Serve from chafing dish in small pottery cups.

The girls were talking about how their husbands forgo most any other pleasure to get to go duck hunting down at La Belle on Blind Lake, about twenty miles from Beaumont. It is great sport skimming over the marshes in their air-powered boats. One cold evening as they skimmed by the hunting shack of one of the Frenchmen, they lowered their speed to get a better whiff of the appetizing aroma of the *Gumbo floating out over the swamps. They resolved to go make some as soon as they got back to the cabin.

★

Duck Gumbo (*serves* 6)

2 Tbs. bacon fat
1 whole duck (remove fat)
2 Tbs. flour
2 large onions, chopped
2 bell peppers, chopped
4 cups celery, chopped
2 cloves garlic, minced
5 cups cold chicken stock
Red pepper to taste
2 Tbs. chopped parsley
1 cup cooked rice

Heat bacon fat in heavy kettle; brown whole duck, turning on all sides, then remove from fat. Pour off all but 2 Tbs. fat. Add flour and make roux, stirring constantly until dark brown. Add onions, peppers, celery and garlic and sauté lightly. Add *cold* stock to hot roux. Return duck to this and cook slowly until duck is tender (approximately 30 minutes). Add red pepper and parsley. Take meat off bones and serve with stock in large soup bowls. These are called gumbo bowls in Beaumont. A spoonful of rice is put in the center of each serving of gumbo.

Bill Russell, who is the pretty wife of one of the hunters, and one of the town's outstanding gourmets, loves to prepare this, too. She graciously invited me for lunch to "see for myself" the rarity of this flavor. The setting for the luncheon was, I imagine, quite a contrast to the service at the cabin.

We had a *Frozen Orange Blossom before lunch to prepare our palates for the spicy Gumbo.

★

Orange Blossom Cocktail

- 1 part orange juice
- 1 part gin
- A dash of grenadine syrup

Shake well in cracked ice.

Sort of like a nursery rhyme: there was a pretty girl in a pretty house with a pretty table and pretty food. A fresh fruit salad made of melon balls, sliced peaches, plums and seedless grapes was served with the Duck Gumbo. For dessert Bill had her Aunt Jenny Chaison Hank's *Washington Pie with Eggnog Sauce. This is one of the four-star recipes of my collection:

★

Washington Pie

- 2 eggs, separated
- ½ cup cold water
- Grated rind of 1 lemon
- ¾ cup sugar
- 1 cup sifted cake flour
- 1 tsp. baking powder
- ¼ tsp. salt
- 1 tsp. lemon juice
- 2 Tbs. sugar

To egg yolks add ½ cup cold water and lemon rind. Beat with rotary beater until light and foamy. Add ¾ cup sugar gradually, beating well. Sift flour, baking powder and salt together three times. Add flour mixture in small amounts, beating enough to blend. Beat egg whites until foamy. Add lemon juice and 2 tablespoons sugar. Beat until stiff. Fold carefully into cake mixture. Pour into two 9-inch pans, ungreased, but lined with waxed paper. Bake at 300 degrees for 20 to 25 minutes.

CREAM FILLING

- 2 cups milk
- 3 egg yolks
- 1 cup sugar
- ½ cup flour
- ¼ tsp. salt
- 1 Tbs. butter
- 1 tsp. vanilla

MERINGUE

- 3 egg whites
- 3 Tbs. sugar

Heat milk in double boiler. Add the three egg yolks, which have been beaten into 1 cup sugar, ½ cup flour, and ¼ tsp. salt. Cook until very thick. Add 1 heaping Tbs. butter and 1 tsp. vanilla. Taste to be sure of flavor. Spread between cake layers and on top. Cover top and sides of cake with meringue made of 3 egg whites and 3 Tbs. sugar. Bake in 350-degree oven until brown. Cool, then refrigerate.

EGGNOG SAUCE

1 egg, separated
¼ cup sugar
1 jigger whiskey
½ pint whipping cream

Beat yolk, add ⅛ cup sugar. Beat egg white until stiff and add ⅛ cup sugar. Add jigger of whiskey to egg yolk. Add egg white and ½ pint of cream, whipped.

Here are a couple of other recipes which always please Bill's guests:

★

Cream Cheese Dip

Garlic
Mayonnaise
2 pkgs. (3 oz.) cream cheese
½ cup grated Parmesan cheese
1 tsp. Worcestershire
Salt
Dash of Tabasco
Red pepper
Small (4-oz.) can jalapeño peppers, finely chopped

Mash garlic to taste. Add about 1 cup of mayonnaise. Add to cheeses, seasonings, and peppers. This is a good dip, or, made a little thinner, it is delicious as a salad dressing on fresh tomato salad.

★

Henrietta Cookies

½ cup butter
1 cup sugar
2 egg yolks
1 cup flour
½ tsp. baking powder
⅛ tsp. salt
½ tsp. vanilla

TOPPING

2 egg whites stiffly beaten
½ cup brown sugar
1 tsp. vanilla
1 cup chopped nuts

Cream butter and sugar. Add egg yolks and beat well. Sift together flour, baking powder, and salt. Add gradually to egg mixture. Add vanilla. Press dough into two 9-inch cake pans or the equivalent and spread with topping mixture. Bake in 325-degree oven for 30 to 35 minutes. Cut in small squares.

I was delighted to have a visit with Carol Nelson while I was in Beaumont. I have known Carol since she was a small child and watched her grow up at Girl Scout camp and as a popular Tri Delt at the University of Texas. She and her husband Charles moved to Beaumont only a few years ago with their three attractive children. Carol has been chairman of some of the "Tasting Teas" sponsored by Trinity Methodist Church and Tri Delt alums, and she has thereby added some very fine recipes to her enviable collection. As Carol and I were having coffee, little Martha proudly served me her mother's latest culinary accomplishment — a most unusual oatmeal cake.

★

Oatmeal Cake

CAKE

1½ cups boiling water
1 cup quick oats
1 stick of butter
1 cup white sugar
1 cup brown sugar
2 whole eggs
1 tsp. vanilla
1 tsp. cinnamon
1⅓ cups flour
1 tsp. soda
½ tsp. salt

TOPPING

3 Tbs. melted butter
⅔ cup brown sugar
1 cup coconut
1 cup chopped pecans or walnuts
3 or 4 Tbs. heavy cream
2 egg yolks

Pour boiling water over oatmeal and let set for 20 minutes. Cream together butter, sugar. Add eggs, one at a time; add vanilla and cinnamon. Mix well and add oatmeal. Add flour sifted with soda and salt. Pour in a loaf or tube pan and bake at 350 degrees for 30 minutes. Take from the oven and spread topping over the cake; return to oven for 10 minutes.

Carol also makes a wonderful *Cranberry Nut Bread. She makes it in quantities at Christmas, wraps it gaily and gives it to her friends.

★

Cranberry Nut Bread

2 cups flour
1 cup sugar
1 tsp. salt
½ tsp. soda
1½ tsp. baking powder
¼ cup shortening
¾ cup orange juice
1 Tbs. grated orange rind
1 egg, well beaten
1 cup cranberries
½ cup nuts

Sift all dry ingredients, cut in shortening like coarse cornmeal. Combine orange and egg. Pour all at once into dry ingredients. Mix enough to dampen. Fold in coarsely chopped cranberries, orange peel and nuts. Bake in greased loaf pan at 350 degrees for 1 hour.

Carol's Aunt Bidie, who is my friend Violet Spiller, has told me about the marvelous *Chess Pie Carol makes. Everyone wants the recipe, so here it is.

★

Carol's Lemon Chess Pie

1 unbaked pie shell

Sift together:

2 cups sugar
1 Tbs. cornmeal
1 Tbs. flour
¼ tsp. salt

Add and beat until blended:

4 whole eggs
¼ cup lemon juice
Grated rind of 1 lemon
¼ cup melted butter
¼ cup milk

Pour into pie shell and bake at 375 degrees for 40 minutes.

One casserole recipe Carol got from the Trinity Methodist Church Tasting Tea she makes often for company suppers. It's called *Eggplant-Shrimp Casserole, and another good one is *Hominy Casserole.

★

Eggplant-Shrimp Casserole

1 large eggplant (2 lbs.)
2 Tbs. chopped onion
1 tsp. Worcestershire sauce
2 Tbs. chopped celery
2 Tbs. chopped bell pepper
¼ tsp. paprika
⅛ tsp. red pepper
Dash garlic salt
Dash black pepper
Salt to taste
1 lb. raw cleaned shrimp
1 can cream of mushroom soup
¼ to ½ lb. cracker-barrel cheese
1 cup cracker crumbs

Peel and cube eggplant and cook in very little salted water until soft. Drain and combine with seasonings. Put in this order in layers in casserole: (1) eggplant, (2) raw shrimp, (3) soup, (4) cheese, (5) cracker crumbs. Bake at 350 degrees for 1½ hours.

★

Hominy Casserole

2 cups canned whole hominy
1 cup canned mushroom soup
1 tsp. Worcestershire sauce
Salt to taste
Cornflakes rolled to crumbs
1 Tbs. butter

Mix hominy, soup, Worcestershire and salt, and pour into a buttered casserole. Sprinkle with the crushed cornflakes and dot with butter. Bake at 300 degrees until brown. Serves 6.

These *Shrimp Patties can be the main dish or can be made very small and served as a hot hors d'oeuvre. Either way, you'll be a success when you serve them!

★

Shrimp Patties

1 lb. shrimp
1 large green pepper
1 large raw potato
1 large onion
3 cloves garlic
Dash of salt and pepper
1 egg
3 Tbs. cracker meal
Deep fat

Grind together shrimp, green pepper, potato, onion, and garlic. Add salt and pepper. Mix all ingredients except cracker meal together with the egg. Form into patties. Roll in cracker meal and fry in deep fat.

This next recipe scored high with my gourmet friend Harold Lawrence and with my husband, Chester.

★

Corned Beef and Cabbage

4 to 5 lbs. corned beef
Water to cover
12 peppercorns
2 cloves garlic

Cover beef with water. Add spices. Bring to a boil. Boil for 10 minutes. Simmer, allowing about 25 minutes per pound. Add to the meat and broth for the last hour of cooking:

6 small peeled onions
6 medium peeled carrots
3 medium peeled, quartered potatoes

Add to this 1 head of cabbage (cut in wedges) for the last 15 minutes of cooking. (Cabbage may be cooked separately if preferred.) Serve the sliced corned beef on a platter surrounded by the vegetables with this sauce:

5 Tbs. mayonnaise or sour cream
4 tsp. horseradish
1½ tsp. prepared mustard

Especially good with the Corned Beef is Corn Bread or *Cornmeal Dumplings.

★

Cornmeal Dumplings

Sift:

1 cup cornmeal
¼ cup flour
1 tsp. baking powder
½ tsp. salt

Add:

1 egg
½ cup milk
1 Tbs. melted butter

Beat only until well blended. Then drop by tablespoonfuls into boiling corned beef stock from which the meat and vegetables have been removed. Cover and simmer for 15 minutes. Remove at once and serve with the boiled dinner.

One could spend a long time in this part of Texas and never experience boredom to any degree. There is a wide variety of what were once called "pastimes." Mrs. W. C. Gilbert, longtime Beaumonter, took us on an interesting drive out a few miles from town to one of her projects, called "the Big Thicket." She has a charming little weekend house there. It is peaceful and quiet. Most of the big timber has been cleared for lumber, but the young pines are shooting their branches skyward, and the dogwood, magnolia, and pecans are taking on a rather rapid rate of growth in the forest. While waiting for them to mature, Betty's son Buddy had the ingenious idea of using the land as a retreat for fishermen. They catch some pretty big ones in the lake there, and it's a terrific spot to find peace and quiet. Betty said she usually tries to think of something cool and quiet to have for lunch out there. In contrast, when she leaves town in the other direction and goes to the ranch, she always plans hearty, warm meals, such as charcoaled steaks, corn on the cob, fresh black-eyed peas, mustard greens, fresh tomatoes, fried onion rings, corn bread and luscious desserts all at one meal. Her friends look forward to dinner at Betty's ranch. Since I had done so much damage to my waistline while in Beaumont, I was glad she took me in the other direction, and, to quote Goldilocks, it was "just right." We had individual *Curry Rings Filled with Chicken Salad.

★

Curry Rings Filled with Chicken Salad

1½ envelopes (1½ oz.) plain gelatine
¼ cup cold water
1½ cup hot chicken broth
¼ cup mayonnaise
½ cup sour cream
1 Tbs. curry powder, dissolved in 2 Tbs. of broth
1 tsp. onion juice
Dash of salt

Soak gelatine in cold water. Add to hot broth and whip until gelatine is dissolved. Let cool, then whip in mayonnaise and sour cream and curry powder, onion juice and salt. Pour in individual ring molds. When firm turn out on crisp green romaine leaves. Fill with chicken salad. Garnish with 1 tsp. sour cream and pitted ripe olive (olive may be filled with piece of chutney). Betty passes large paper-thin round crackers with this.

The dessert would have easily fit in at the ranch.

★

Betty's Dessert

¾ cup softened butter
2½ cups sugar
6 eggs
9 Tbs. strong coffee
1 cup almonds (ground fine)
1 cup whipped heavy cream
2 dozen ladyfingers
Whipped cream for garnish
Maraschino cherries

Beat butter and sugar together. Add eggs one at a time. Add the coffee and almonds, and fold in the cream. Make layers of split lady-fingers and spread with the mixture, layer after layer, until the mixture is all used. Put in freezer overnight. Cut in small squares and serve with whipped cream and Maraschino cherry.

Beaumont is the scene of many large social events throughout the year — the Junior League's Charity Ball, the Symphony League's Venetian Ball, the Annual Horse Show, and the Neches River Festival, to mention only a few, in addition to the continuous round of private parties.

The L. W. Pitts entertain frequently at their interesting and beautiful home. Skeet, who was his own architect, must have had fun working out the little unusual touches, such as a mirrored ceiling in the powder room. The house projects comfort and hospitality and is a place one shouldn't visit unless he can "stay longer." It is tastefully done, with many antique pieces which the Pitts inherited combined with interesting contemporary furnishings. There is nothing Garnette possesses which she treasures more than a collection of recipes which belonged to her mother, who was renowned for her fine cuisine. She was a teetotaler, and one of the boys remarked, "She wouldn't drink liquor, but she sure would eat it." A Sunday dessert:

★

Almond Macaroon Dessert

2 cups crumbled almond macaroons
1 cup chopped nuts
4 oz. bottle Maraschino cherries
½ cup Bourbon
½ pt. whipped cream

Break macaroons in small pieces, then add Bourbon. Let stand a few minutes and add cut-up cherries and nuts. Fold in whipped cream and chill. Serve in compote.

The Reverend Billy Sunday, celebrated evangelist, was a guest at dinner when Garnette's mother served her famous brandied peaches. The number he consumed indicated that he was a teetotaler to about the same extent she was!

★

Frozen Chocolate Pie

1½ sticks butter
¾ cup sugar
4 oz. melted unsweetened chocolate
4 whole eggs, added one at a time
1 cup nuts
Graham cracker crumbs

Beat for 5 minutes. Add nuts. Line spring mold with graham cracker crumbs. Pour in mixture and place in freezer.

★

Scalloped Oysters (*Frances Weir*)

12 stale or day-old biscuits, rolled into crumbs
1 stick (¼ lb.) butter
1 qt. oysters
Salt and freshly ground black pepper
1 cup heavy cream
4 Tbs. oyster juice

Alternate layers of biscuit crumbs, dotted with butter, with oysters, seasoned very lightly with salt and pepper, in a buttered casserole. Then pour cream mixed with oyster juice over casserole and bake in 325-degree oven until heated through thoroughly and bubbling around the edge (approximately 25 minutes). The biscuit crumbs give this casserole a distinctive flavor.

Scalloped Oysters are truly great, and Garnette's friend Frances Weir says its sumptious flavor is due to the biscuit crumbs.

We have sorta worn out Poppy-seed Dressing as a complement to fresh fruit salad. For a change here's an awfully good dressing:

★

Fruit Salad Dressing

1 8-oz. pkg. cream cheese
Juice of 2 lemons
1 6-oz. jar of currant jelly
1 tsp. Worcestershire

Soften cream cheese with lemon juice. Melt jelly over hot water and add to the cream cheese. Add Worcestershire. Whip till smooth and serve on fresh fruit salad.

★

Amazetta's Cheese Muffins

2 cups flour
4 tsp. baking powder
Cayenne pepper, salt to taste
2 eggs
1 pt. milk
½ cup melted butter
1 cup grated cheese

Mix dry ingredients. Beat eggs and add them to the dry ingredients. Then stir in milk. Add melted butter and most of grated cheese. Pour into greased muffin pans. Make a hole in the center of each muffin, and place a little grated cheese in it. Cook for 15 minutes at 350 degrees.

★

Spinach Stuffed Eggs (*serves 6*)

½ pkg. frozen chopped spinach
6 hard-boiled eggs
½ tsp. prepared mustard
Dash of Worcestershire
Dash of Tabasco
1 tsp. vinegar
Salt to taste
1 Tbs. horseradish
1 cup rich cream sauce
¼ cup buttered cracker crumbs
2 Tbs. Parmesan cheese

Thaw spinach and blanch in hot water; drain well. Cut eggs lengthwise; remove yolks and mash with mustard, Worcestershire, Tabasco, vinegar, salt, horseradish. Add chopped spinach and fill the cavity of eggs with this mixture. Press 2 halves firmly together and place in a small buttered casserole. Cover with rich cream sauce and sprinkle with cracker crumbs and Parmesan cheese. This is a very good Lenten casserole. I served it with a large ripe peeled tomato filled with a white tuna salad and *Amazetta's Cheese Muffins on Friday. 'Twas a splendid combination of tastes.

One of the most "talked about" recipes in superlative terms was Georgia Singleton's *Avocado Bisque.

★

Avocado Bisque

1 cup cream of chicken soup
½ cup milk
½ can beef broth
1 scraped onion
½ tsp. chili powder
Ground black pepper
Avocado, cubed

Mix and let simmer. Add cubed avocado shortly before serving. Cover until heated through, then serve and listen smugly.

Mirliton is a large *vegetable* pear. It is grown in southeast Texas and Louisiana. It is similar to a cashaw, yet it has a distinctive flavor all its own. Mrs. Samuel Lyons reportedly fixes it best with shrimp in a casserole. I brought two mirlitons home and gave them to Amy with this recipe. She said it looked too complicated, but it really isn't at all. She agreed that it was one of the most "worthwhile" dishes I'd come up with.

★

Lucille Lyons's Mirliton

5 large mirlitons (about 3½ cups of pulp)
Toasted buttered breadcrumbs
3 Tbs. bacon drippings or other fat
¼ cup minced celery
¼ cup green onion
¼ cup green pepper
Salt
Pepper
1 lb. uncooked, cleaned shrimp
2 whole eggs

Cover mirlitons with water. Cook covered 1 hour or until tender. Remove seed, skin, and fibrous tissue. Roll toasted breadcrumbs. Heat fat in heavy skillet. Add celery, onion, green pepper, salt, and pepper. Fry gently until the vegetables are limp. Add mirlitons and shrimp.

Remove from fire. Add well-beaten eggs. Put in buttered casserole and add buttered crumbs. Bake 45 minutes in 375-degree oven. Serves 8.

We had cocktails at the Lyonses'. No mirliton at this occasion, but some very "choice" surprises. Among them *Avocado Crunchies, and *Golden Gate Cocktail Sauce with King Crabmeat. Lucille had a big bowl of this, and right beside it a tray of paper-thin crackers and Melba toast rounds. Bravo!

Everyone admired her *Cheese Mold Frosted with Caviar. It looked too pretty to cut into, but thank goodness some brave soul did! Absolutely fabulous!

★

Avocado Crunchies

2 large avocados
Juice of 2 lemons
Large bag of potato chips

Halve 2 avocados with no blemishes on fruit after they are skinned, and cut in cubes. Dip cubes into lemon juice. Place in refrigerator. A short while before serving, roll in crushed potato chips. Put on picks. Makes about 3 dozen cubes if the avocados are large.

★

Golden Gate Cocktail Sauce with Crabmeat (for dip)

1 cup chili sauce
¼ cup mayonnaise or French dressing
1 Tbs. horseradish
Dash of Tabasco
Salt and pepper to taste
1 Tbs. Worcestershire sauce
2 Tbs. minced green pepper
2 Tbs. minced parsley
2 Tbs. chives
2 Tbs. minced celery
1 lb. crabmeat

Mix all together, adding the crabmeat last. Serve with crisp vegetables, crackers, or Melba toast.

★

Frosted Caviar Cheese Mold

4 jars imported caviar
Dash of Tabasco
Juice of ½ lemon
1 Tbs. soy sauce
1 Tbs. Lawry's seasoned salt
1 cup sour cream
1 cup cottage cheese
1 drop garlic juice
1½ Tbs. gelatine
2 Tbs. sherry

In blender mix all seasonings, sour cream, and cottage cheese. Mix gelatine and sherry and put over hot water to melt. Then add to cream and cheese mixture and blend again. Put in lightly greased mold in refrigerator 24 hours before serving. Unmold on platter or round tray. Frost with imported black caviar. If red caviar is used, surround the cheese mold instead of frosting it. Serve with unsalted (preferably) thin wafer crackers or Melba toast. Serves 12 or more.

SOUTH MIDDLE EAST

It was difficult to get off the Broussard circuit to visit my niece Peggy, who is married to a native Beaumonter, Arthur Greenspan. Peggy agreed with me that Beaumont has some of the finest cooks to be found *anywhere*. Peggy is pretty good herself; I wheedled a recipe out of her that I have wanted for a long time:

★

Christmas Cake

1 cup butter or margarine
2 cups sugar
6 eggs
3 cups flour
1 lb. white raisins — soak in whiskey to cover overnight
1 qt. shelled pecans
1 tsp. salt
1½ tsp. nutmeg

Cream butter and sugar thoroughly. Add eggs one at a time, beating alternately with the flour (½ cup at a time). Add raisins and remaining liquid, then pecans, salt, and nutmeg. Bake for 2 to 2½ hours in medium to slow oven (275 to 350 degrees.)

The Greenspans with their four adorable children were in the throes of moving into their new contemporary house, but they took time to have me for lunch at the handsome Beaumont Club. Here they introduced me to Mrs. Elliott Jacobs and her mother-in-law, Mrs. M. L. Jacobs, who can call off fascinating recipes like a trainmaster calling the trains. And she delights in preparing them, too!

I was highly honored to be invited to dinner at the home of Zelda and Elliott Jacobs. They are perfectionists where food is concerned, and every detail of the dinner revealed this. Dinner was indeed a family affair; their son Barry, a pre-med student, had done many of the preliminary chores, like starting the charcoal and assembling ingredients for his father's custom-made Old-Fashioneds. His sister Patsy had set the table to a T, and as is the custom in many Jewish homes on Friday night, two candles were lighted before sundown; Debra, twelve years old and the youngest Jacobs child, said the blessing, first in Hebrew, then in English: "Blessed art thou, O Lord our God, King of the Universe, who has sanctified us with Thy commandments and commanded us to kindle the Sabbath lights."

The candles are lighted fifteen minutes before sunset in accordance with the Bible, which prohibits fire to be kindled on the Sabbath. Debra covered her eyes with her hands after lighting the candles and before pronouncing the prayer because, according to regulations, she may not enjoy the light of the Sabbath candles before she speaks the blessing over them.

The senior Jacobses and Zelda's mother joined us for dessert and coffee after dinner. The delectable dessert was:

★

Lime Light Pie

CRUST

¾ cup flour
¼ tsp. salt
2 Tbs. sugar
¼ cup shortening
½ square melted chocolate
1-2 Tbs. cold water

Combine dry ingredients. Cut in shortening and melted chocolate. Add cold water to the proper consistency for rolling. Make a single crust and bake at 400 degrees for 10 to 12 minutes.

FILLING

1 can sweetened condensed milk
¼ cup lime juice
¼ tsp. salt
1 cup crushed pineapple, *well* drained
Green food coloring

Stir milk, lime juice and salt together. Add *well-drained* crushed pineapple and green coloring. Stir well. Pour into baked crust.

TOPPING

¾ cup heavy cream
1 Tbs. powdered sugar
2 tsp. vanilla

Whip heavy cream until stiff, add powdered sugar, beat until peaks are formed and add vanilla.

Spread topping over pie filling. Trim with chocolate curls. Place in freezer until set. Keep in freezer until ready to serve.

Elliott recommended these recipes of Zelda's very highly:

★

Chicken in Orange Sauce

2½-lb. fryer, cut in serving pieces
1 tsp. Accent
Salt, pepper, and seasoned salt, to taste
⅓ cup butter or margarine
1 large onion, chopped
2 Tbs. flour
1 cup orange juice
2 Tbs. sherry

Sauté seasoned chicken until light brown. Remove from pan; keep warm. Cook onion in drippings. Blend in flour. Add orange juice. Cook and stir constantly until mixture boils and thickens. Season sauce and pour over chicken. Cook very gently 45 minutes, or until tender. Add sherry just before serving.

★

Date and Nut Bread

1½ cups boiling water
1 cup chopped dates
1½ cups sugar
1 egg, beaten
2½ cups sifted flour
½ tsp. baking powder
½ tsp. salt
2 Tbs. baking soda
1 cup chopped nuts
1 Tbs. melted shortening
1 tsp. vanilla
1 tsp. almond extract

Pour boiling water over dates and let stand. Add sugar to beaten egg. Sift dry ingredients and stir nuts into flour mixture. Add date mixture alternately with flour to sugar and egg. Stir in shortening, vanilla, and almond extract. Pour into greased loaf pan and bake at 350 degrees for 1½ hours.

Mrs. Jacobs's *Chinese Meat Casserole has gained the approval of the Koock family as well as of our summer house guests.

★

Chinese Meat Casserole

2 lbs. ground meat
2 large onions
2 Tbs. oil
Salt, pepper, garlic, and soy sauce to taste
½ green pepper
1 cup cooked rice
1 can tomato soup (no water)
1 can bean sprouts, drained
1 large can of sliced mushrooms
1 can Chinese noodles

Sauté meat and onion until light brown. Season, cover, and simmer until tender. Add rest of vegetables. Mix well. Place in large greased casserole and top with noodles. Bake at 350 degrees for 1 hour.

Mrs. Jacobs says that *Hot Water Chocolate Cake will stay moist for days. There was not any left to experiment with at our house.

★

Hot Water Chocolate Cake

4 squares unsweetened chocolate
2 cups boiling water

Drop chocolate in water. Let stand until tepid, room temperature.

2½ cups sifted cake flour
2 tsp. soda
2 tsp. baking powder
⅔ cup margarine
2 cups sugar
2 eggs
2 tsp. vanilla

Grease and flour a 10- x 14-inch pan. Sift flour, baking soda, and baking powder together. Cream shortening. Add sugar gradually. Add eggs, one at a time. Beat well. Pour water off chocolate, but reserve the water. Add chocolate to creamed mixture. Beat well. Add vanilla at lowest speed on mixer. Add flour and water alternately. Bake at 350 degrees for 40 to 50 minutes. Cool 15 minutes before removing from pan. Ice with dark fudge frosting.

After dinner the Jacobs family and I began talking about the beautiful Bar Mitzvah service, the occasion when a Jewish boy becomes thirteen and officially becomes a man, ready to assume responsibilities and more adult privileges. He recites his part of the Torah in Hebrew as well as in English. It is a very impressive ceremony held in the synagogue and is followed by a reception, at which a bountiful table is spread with just about every delicacy you can name. I remember when my friends the Sam Glossermans of Lockhart asked me to cater the food for their son's Bar Mitzvah. I shook in my boots until Elsia explained that her mother and sisters would bring most of the food. They had been preparing special delicacies for this occasion for months, and Sam teased that he was going to have to transport it all in one of his big Chevrolet trucks!

The very long table was skirted in a white organdy cloth embroidered in blue. Several elaborate arrangements of white carnations and blue delphiniums were arranged down the center of the table, and in between were silver candelabra holding blue candles. The traditional large double loaf of challah was on a silver tray. Challah, or Sabbath bread, is a braided loaf used to commemorate the double portion of manna which was collected on Fridays by the Israelites in the desert in order to have enough food for the Sabbath. The two challahs are covered with a special Sabbath cloth that symbolizes the manna covered with dew. A luscious white cake with the Star of David crest was on a separate table, as was the ceremonial sweet wine. Fathers and sons recite the kiddush (blessing over the wine) in order to consecrate the Sabbath. Long ago every festive meal began with a cup of wine; thus, the Friday evening meal at the beginning of the Sabbath began that way with the recitation of the prayer announcing the Holy Sabbath. Later, the symbol of wine became known as a cup of joy appropriate for welcome to the joyful Sabbath.

Besides the challah and the white cake, the following foods were arranged like a picture on the table:

BAR MITZVAH TABLE

Chocolate and vanilla pinwheels
Brown Drops
* *Sand Dabs*
* *Holiday Sandies*
Dark Brown Sugar Squares
* *Italian Pastry*
* *Bittersweet Cookies*
* *S.J. Cake Fingers*
* *Chinese Noodle Cookies*

** Fruitcake Cookies*
** Cinnamon sticks*
** Jelly Dabs*
** Cheese Cake, Sour Cream Topping*
** Fresh Plum Cake*
Sunshine Sponge Cake
Sand Tarts
Brownies with Fudge Icing
** Lox and Cream Cheese Mold*
** Chopped Chicken Liver Mold*
** Herring in Sour Cream*
Rye Bread Rounds
Chicken Sandwiches
Cream Cheese and Marmalade Rolled Sandwiches
Olives
Salted Nuts
Cheese Straws
Ribbon Sandwiches
Little Round Cucumber Sandwiches
Butter and Watercress Sandwiches
Star-Shaped Cheese Bread spread with Egg Salad
Olive and Pecan Sandwiches
*Pastrami on thin slices of * Dill Bread*

Most of these cookies were made by Elsia's mother, Mrs. Klein of Beaumont.

★

Sand Dabs

¾ cup butter
4 Tbs. granulated sugar
2 cups flour (sifted)
2 tsp. vanilla
2 Tbs. cold water
1 cup fine chopped nuts

Cream butter, sugar; add rest of ingredients. Mix well. Pinch off bits of dough, roll size of finger. Bake at 350 degrees for 30 to 40 minutes. While still warm, roll in granulated sugar.

Variation: When cool, instead of rolling in granulated sugar, dip ends in melted chocolate and then crushed pecans, leaving center of strip plain.

★

Holiday Sandies

½ lb. butter
1 cup sugar
1 egg
1 tsp. baking powder
1 12-oz. pkg. potato flour
1 cup regular flour
1 tsp. vanilla

Mix, roll into small balls in palm of hand. Flatten with fork. Place small piece of glazed red cherry in center. Bake in 325-degree oven about 20 minutes or until done but not brown.

★

Italian Pastry (makes 12 dozen cookies)

1 lb. oleomargarine
1 lb. vegetable shortening
10 cups sifted flour
1 tsp. salt
1 cup warm milk
1 Tbs. sugar
1 Tbs. vanilla
2 yeast cakes
4 eggs, beaten
2 lbs. confectioner's sugar

Cut margarine and shortening into flour and salt mixture until it is as fine as cornmeal. Combine milk, sugar and vanilla. Stir in yeast until dissolved. Add yeast mixture to flour mixture. Beat in eggs. Add more flour if necessary. Knead slightly. Let rise until double in bulk (about 1 hour). Cover bread board with powdered sugar. Break off *small* pieces of dough. Roll into sugar and shape in crescents or knots. Place on greased baking sheets. Bake at 375 degrees for 12 to 15 minutes.

This recipe can be cut in half if desired.

★

Bittersweet Cookies

½ cup shortening
½ cup brown sugar
¼ cup granulated sugar
1 egg, well beaten
½ tsp. soda
1 Tbs. hot water
1¼ cups flour
⅛ tsp. salt
½ cup broken nuts
1 7-oz. bar unsweetened chocolate
½ tsp. vanilla

Cream shortening, add sugar and egg. Add soda, which has been dissolved in 1 Tbs. hot water. Add flour, salt and mix well. Add broken nutmeats and melted chocolate. Flavor with vanilla. Drop by teaspoonfuls on greased tin. Bake at 350 degrees for 10 minutes.

★

S.J. Cake Fingers

½ cup butter
1 cup sugar
1 egg yolk
1 tsp. cinnamon
Salt
Vanilla
2 cups flour
2 Tbs. brandy or Bourbon
1 egg white
2 cups crushed pecans or walnuts

Cream butter and sugar. Add egg yolk and flavorings. Beat in flour alternating with liquid.

Grease pan. Spread dough, press with fingers. Brush with egg white. Sprinkle with crushed nuts. Bake in moderate oven at 350 degrees for 45 to 50 minutes until light brown.

Cut while hot into strips, finger size, and remove from pan.

★

Chinese Noodle Cookies (makes about 3 dozen)

1 8-oz. can chow mein noodles
½ cup chopped pecans
1 pkg. Nestle's chocolate chips, semisweet
1 pkg. caramel chips or butterscotch

Warm noodles. Melt chips together in double boiler. Let simmer. Mix noodles and nuts in mixture. Drop from spoon onto waxed paper and allow to dry.

★

Fruitcake Cookies

Cream:

½ cup butter
1 cup brown sugar
4 eggs beaten

Add:

2 to 3 cups flour (use ½ to dredge fruit and raisins)
2 to 3 Tbs. milk
Fruit juice glass of whiskey
½ lb. pecans, chopped
½ lb. candied pineapple
½ lb. candied cherries
1 box raisins
1 scant tsp. soda
1 tsp. each: cinnamon, cloves, nutmeg

Mix and drop from spoon and shape. Bake in moderate oven for about 25 minutes.

★

Cinnamon Sticks

1 cup margarine
1 cup sugar
2 cups flour
1 egg yolk
2 tsp. vanilla
1 tsp. cinnamon
Pecans

Mix all except pecans well and press into greased cookie sheet. Rub unbeaten egg white over mixture. Press 1 cup chopped pecans in well. Bake about 50 minutes at 300 degrees. Cut into strips while still hot.

★

Jelly Dabs

½ lb. butter (1 cup)
3 heaping tsp. sugar
2⅓ cups flour
1 tsp. vanilla

Cream butter. Add sugar and mix well. Add flour and vanilla. Form into round cookies about ¼ inch thick. Add jelly in the center. Bake at 375 degrees about 15 minutes.

★

Cheese Cake with Sour Cream Topping

CRUST

1 pkg. zwieback, graham, or vanilla wafers (crush until powder fine)
½ cup flour
¼ cup sugar
1 tsp. cinnamon
½ cup pecans, chopped fine
1 cup butter

Mix well and reserve ¾ cup for topping. Grease spring mold and pat mixture well on sides and bottom of mold.

FILLING

Combine:
1 lb. finely creamed cottage cheese
1 lb. cream cheese
1 cup sugar
6 eggs, added one at a time as you beat mixture
1 Tbs. vanilla wafer crumbs
1 heaping tsp. cornstarch (make a paste with 2 Tbs. milk)
1 pt. whipping cream, folded in by hand
Juice of ½ lemon

Pour in shell. Bake at 300 degrees for one hour. When cool top with sour cream and place in refrigerator.

★

Fresh Plum Cake

½ cup sugar
¾ stick margarine
2 cups flour
1 Tbs. red wine
1 egg
Lemon rind
3 lbs. blue plums
Cinnamon and sugar
¼ stick oleo

Cream sugar and ¾ stick margarine. Add flour, 1 cup at a time, with wine. Add egg. Pat dough onto *ungreased* cookie sheet. Grate lemon rind over dough. Wash, dry and pit plums. Place plum halves upon dough, skin side down. Sprinkle with cinnamon and sugar. Dot with rest of margarine. Bake at 400 degrees for 40 minutes. Cut in squares with a plum in the center of each square.

★

Lox and Cream Cheese Mold (really delish)

1 or 2 lbs. lox, drained of oil (depending upon how much is desired — unsalted lox gives a milder taste)
3 pkgs. cream cheese
4 hard-boiled eggs

Grind lox, removing strings. Blend cheese with small amount of sour cream if it is too stiff. Add eggs, which have been put through ricer. Blend all with beater, or in blender. Use a bit of the oil to grease mold. Pack tight. Mixture will spread after refrigeration. Particularly good as an hors d'oeuvre.

★

Chopped Chicken Liver Mold (2 qt. party size)

10 to 15 lbs. chicken livers
Chicken fat
6 to 8 bunches of onions (fresh green ones)
1 or 2 large white onions
3 or 4 dozen hard-boiled eggs
Salt
White pepper

Drain livers in colander. Use chicken fat to sauté livers. Fry onions in fat, after livers are done. Use fresh green onions when possible and supplement with regular onions. Grind liver, eggs, and onions alternately. Season with salt, white pepper and remaining chicken fat (after frying). If mixture is too dry, add a small amount of chicken fat or cooking oil. Try not to use any more chicken fat than necessary (it makes it too heavy and too rich). In a "pinch" use a very small amount of salad dressing or mayonnaise to blend. This depends upon the amount you are preparing and gives an added flavor. Pack *firmly* in ring molds (1 qt. each) which have been rubbed with mayonnaise. Turn out on round tray — garnish with parsley, radish roses, and rounds of rye bread.

★

Herring in Sour Cream

16-oz. jar herring tidbits, boned and skinned, in wine sauce

Slice thin into bowl:

2 medium sweet onions
1 peeled and cored apple, sliced and cut in thin strips
1 lemon
1 pt. sour cream

Blend sour cream mixture with herring that has been drained of jar juices and spices. Let stand in refrigerator, covered, until ready to serve. (Mixture will keep several days in a large covered jar.)

★

Dill Bread

1 pkg. dry yeast
1/4 cup warm water
1 cup lukewarm creamed cottage cheese
2 Tbs. sugar
1 Tbs. butter
1 Tbs. finely chopped onion
2 tsp. dill seed
1 tsp. salt
1/4 tsp. soda
1 egg
2 1/4 to 2 1/2 cups flour

Dissolve dry yeast in water. In a large bowl combine lukewarm creamed cottage cheese with sugar, butter, onion, dill seed, salt, soda, egg and yeast mixture. Add gradually to flour, beating well after each addition. Cover the bowl with a light towel and let the dough rise in a warm place (85 to 90 degrees) for 50 to 60 minutes, or until the dough doubles in bulk. Punch down the dough, turn it into a well-buttered 1 1/2- to 2-quart round casserole, and let it rise for 30 to 40 minutes, or until it is light. Bake the bread in a moderate oven (350 degrees) for 40 to 50 minutes. Brush the bread with soft butter and sprinkle it with salt.

The Saturday morning following the Bar Mitzvah there is another service in the temple, or shul. This is usually followed by a seated luncheon or dinner at a hotel or club. The occasion brings many friends and relatives from far and near. A brunch is often given on the following Sunday morning to wind up the festivities.

After her grandson's Bar Mitzvah, Mrs. M. L. Jacobs had a beautiful brunch for the out-of-town friends and relatives at her home. She served:

Fresh Melon Wedges — watermelon, honeydew, and cantaloupe
— around a mound of cottage cheese, the tray garnished with white grapes
*Tray after tray of * Blintzes with Sour Cream and Cherry Preserves*
** Miniature Bagels and Lox with Cream Cheese*
Small Raisin Rolls
Egg Salad
Herring Salad
Party Rye Bread
Small Cakes
** Chopped Liver*
Pound Cake
Cheese Cake
** Tayglech*
** Finck Brod*
Tea and Coffee

★

Blintzes

1 cup flour
½ tsp. salt
4 eggs
1 cup water or milk
½ tsp. sugar
Cherry preserve
Butter
Sour cream

Sift together flour, sugar and salt. Beat eggs. Add liquid. Beat again. Gradually add flour to eggs, stirring constantly to make a thin, smooth batter. Lightly grease a 6-inch skillet with butter. Place skillet over a moderately high flame. Fill a cup with batter. Pour about ½ cupful batter into the skillet. As soon as the batter sticks to the skillet, pour the excess back into the cup. Fry until the blintze begins to "blister" and the edges curl away from the skillet. The top of the blintze may still be slightly moist. Turn out, fried side up, by inverting the skillet over a wooden board. It may be necessary to tap the edge of the skillet against the board. The skillet should be greased at about every third blintze. When blintzes are all fried, fill with sour cream and cherry preserves. Place 1 Tbs. filling in the center of each blintze (on the browned side). Raise the bottom flap of dough to cover the filling, then overlap with the top flap of dough. Tuck both sides under so that they almost meet at the back center. Fry in a liberal amount of butter until lightly browned on both sides. Serve hot with sour cream. Serves 6.

★

Bagels and Lox

3 lb. block cream cheese
Cream
Mayonnaise
Lox (smoked salmon)
Vegetable coloring
Miniature bagels

Get a 3 lb. block of cream cheese and scoop out the center. Mash this portion of the cheese with a little cream and mayonnaise. Cut lox in small squares (use scissors) after it has been well-drained on paper towels. Then place them in scooped-out cheese block. Tint the softened cheese mixture with vegetable coloring and pipe it around the edge of the cheese block. Place on silver sandwich tray and surround it with split miniature bagels. Place a spreader close by for the cheese and a fork to remove the lox and place on top of cheese for fabulous eating.

Mr. and Mrs. Nat Goodfriend gave me this recipe to use for their son Gary's Bar Mitzvah. It was the recipe of Rosalie Goodfriend's mother. It is marvelous.

★

Chopped Liver

1 lb. liver
4 hard-boiled eggs
1 onion, sautéed
Salt and pepper to taste
2 Tbs. schmaltz (rendered chicken fat)

Place liver in warm water for 5 minutes and remove the membranes and skin. Place liver under broiler and broil until well done (about 10 minutes), turning once. Remove from broiler and cool. Put liver, eggs and onion through a food grinder, using the fine blade. Season with salt and pepper. Add schmaltz, working it through the liver with a fork. The liver should be moist enough to hold together; if necessary, add more schmaltz. Grease a small mold with schmaltz and pack chopped liver in firm. Chill. When ready to serve, dip mold in hot water for 30 seconds and turn out on tray. Garnish with fresh parsley and serve with thin sliced party rye bread.

★

Tayglech

½ cup oil
8 eggs, beaten
4½ cups flour (scant)
2 tsp. baking powder
⅛ tsp. cinnamon
⅛ tsp. ginger
2 lbs. honey
1 lb. brown sugar
2 tsp. ginger
1 cup walnuts, broken into rather large pieces

Stir oil into beaten eggs. Sift together flour, baking powder, cinnamon, and ⅛ tsp. ginger. Then add the flour mixture to the egg and oil mixture. Knead thoroughly. This makes a dough soft but firm enough to roll. Take pieces of dough and roll them in the hands to make ropes about ½ inch thick. Cut ropes at ½-inch intervals. Place these pieces of dough on a floured cookie sheet. Bake in a moderate oven (350 degrees) about 20 minutes or until slightly brown. Place honey, brown sugar, and 2 tsp. ginger in a large, deep kettle and bring to a rapid boil. Drop browned tayglech into the honey mixture, stirring constantly with a wooden spoon. When tayglech begin to get reddish brown, drop in the walnuts. Continue to stir for about 30 minutes. Test by dropping one "taygle" into cold water; it is done when the honey forms a hard crust on the outside. Turn out onto a wet wooden board and let cool just a few minutes. Dip hands in ice water and roll into 2-inch balls.

★

Finck Brod

1 stick margarine
¼ cup sugar
1¼ cups sifted flour
1 tsp. vanilla

Cream margarine, add sugar and flour and blend. Add vanilla. Shape dough into 2½ by 2½ round sticks. Make long sticks and cut.

1 egg, beaten
¾ cup finely chopped pecans

Dip sticks in egg, roll in nuts. Place sticks on ungreased baking sheet. Bake at 350 degrees for 20 to 25 minutes, depending on the thickness of the sticks.

Mrs. Fania Kruger is one of Austin's most beloved citizens. She spent her early childhood in Russia where she was born. In 1910, she came with her husband to Wichita Falls, which was then a rugged little North Texas town. There Mr. Kruger was a jeweler for forty-two years. Mrs. Kruger made a great contribution to the cultural advancement of the community with her Russian background and Jewish education. She moved to Austin after the death of her husband to be near her children and grandchildren. She has been awarded many national honors for her beautiful poetry and delightful stories, which have been widely published. She is still creative and active at the age of seventy-three.

Aside from her literary achievements, Mrs. Kruger is a wonderful cook, and she always keeps choice treats on hand for her grandchildren and friends.

★

Matzo Meal Pudding

2 cups grated apples
4 egg yolks, beaten
⅔ cup powdered sugar
½ lemon rind
½ cup matzo meal
4 eggs, well beaten

Bake in hot oven (375 degrees).

★

Strudel

About 3 cups flour
4 eggs
½ cup shortening
½ cup sugar
1 tsp. vanilla

Make a cookie dough of the above ingredients. Mix the following well to make the filling:

¼ lb. pecans
½ can Angel Flake coconut
8-oz. jar cherry preserves
Lemon rind
½ tsp. almond extract
Cinnamon sugar for topping

Cut the dough in four parts, roll each part separately, put the above filling in each one, and shape into a roll. Put a small amount of shortening into a pan large enough to hold the four long rolls. Brush top well with vegetable oil, sprinkle freely with cinnamon sugar over the oiled top. Bake in 375-degree oven.

Each year, the University of Texas attracts around six hundred foreign students. Many of Austin's families "adopt" a student for a year and act as his particular host while he is attending the university. This is indeed a pleasant experience for both student and host. There is also a broad representation of nationalities on the faculty, and in the Austin business world. These charming people of various backgrounds have made contributions to the culture, business and industry, as well as to the cuisine of the city, and because of them Austin is far more cosmopolitan than many other cities its size.

The A. Anthony Topracs are such a family. Tony came from Greece about fifteen years ago, and now teaches in the Department of Civil Engineering at the university. Dena is native born. They have three sons, Dennis, Anthony, and Paul. The family lives in a comfortable home near the campus. In furnishing their home, Dena has tastefully combined contemporary furniture and Greek objets d'art. She is a typical Grecian beauty with a lovely olive complexion, dark shining hair, and eyes as blue as the Mediterranean. She is a gracious hostess who adjusts her Greek recipes to the tastes of her guests, sometimes using less rich oil and spicy seasonings than the Greeks do. She has given me several tasty recipes. One of my favorites is *Baklava, an original Greek dessert. I discovered that the phyllo (ready-made pastry sheets) is available in most of the fancy food departments in better grocery stores. It gives one an opportunity to achieve greatness with little effort.

★

Baklava

10 to 15 sheets of phyllo (ready-made pastry sheets)
2 cups blanched almonds (or pecans)
1 cup sweet butter

For the syrup:

1 cup honey
2 cups sugar
2 cups water
A few lemon or orange rinds and a few cinnamon sticks

Blanch and chop the almonds. Line a rectangular or square buttered baking pan with a sheet of phyllo. Sprinkle with melted butter and spread with 2 to 3 Tbs. chopped almonds. Place 1 to 2 more phyllo on top, sprinkle with melted butter and proceed as above, using alternate layers of almonds. Use 3 sheets of phyllo on top without a filling. The last sheet of phyllo or pastry should be whole and not broken. Any broken sheets may be placed in between with the almonds. Baste with melted butter, and with a pointed knife score the top sheets in square or diamond shapes. At first bake in a moderate oven and then increase heat until pastry becomes golden brown. Bake for one hour. Let cool. In the meantime, boil syrup ingredients together, removing rinds after boiling a few minutes. Pour hot syrup over the Baklava. Let it cool, cut the pieces through and let them absorb the syrup before serving.

The Topracs often serve this before dinner:

★

Mavrodaphne Frappe

½ wine glass Imperial Mavrodaphne
Soda water
Cracked ice

Shake well in a cocktail shaker and serve.

★

Vine Leaves Stuffed with Chopped Meat

1 lb. chopped beef or lamb
½ cup rice
½ cup chopped parsley and anise
¼ tsp. pepper
2 tsp. salt
2 chopped onions
50 vine leaves
3 Tbs. butter

Combine meat, rice, parsley, anise, pepper, salt, and chopped onions. Stuff vine leaves. Take each leaf with the smooth, shiny surface on the outside. If the leaves are too small, use two at a time. Place a teaspoon of filling in the center of each leaf. Fold like an envelope and roll lightly to allow for the puffing of the rice. Place leaf balls side by side in layers in a covered saucepan. Add 2 cups water, butter and salt. Press with a plate and simmer for 30 to 40 minutes. Serve hot with *Egg and Lemon Sauce.

The vine leaves also can be found in fancy food departments of grocery stores.

EGG AND LEMON SAUCE

3 eggs
1 tsp. cornstarch
Juice of 1 lemon
Salt and pepper

Beat eggs. Add cornstarch diluted with a little water. Add lemon juice, pepper and salt. Gradually add to it the meat stock from stuffed vine leaves and return to saucepan containing the leaf balls. Or, cook sauce separately in a small saucepan stirring constantly for a few minutes until sauce thickens. Carefully serve the leaf balls on a platter and pour the hot sauce on top.

This is a main course dish. Grapevine leaves are traditionally used, but the stuffing may be used for cabbage, tomatoes, or peppers.

When the ladies from St. Jude's Ladies Auxiliary in Austin give their annual Lebanese Benefit Luncheon for St. Jude's Hospital for Leukemia Research founded by Danny Thomas, tickets are much in demand. It has snowballed from year to year, for anyone who ever goes and tastes of these delicacies wants to go for sure the next time and take a friend. In fact, this food has become so popular that Harry Joseph and other food importers enlarged their stock of such special items as pine nuts and burghul (wheat), and everybody is keeping his mint bed growing. Mrs. Fred Ferris gave me the recipes for the dishes we all had and enjoyed so much at the luncheon.

★

Stuffed Cabbage

1 lb. raw lamb (no fat or gristle)
1 cup raw rice
1 can tomatoes, drained (adjust quantity; not too much required)
Salt and pepper
Cabbage leaves (if large, tear in two)
4 whole cloves of garlic
1 Tbs. mint, chopped fine
Juice of 1 lemon

Chop lamb into small pieces. Wash rice. Drain tomatoes. Mix all three together and season with salt and pepper. Plunge cabbage leaves into boiling water. Do not overcook. Remove and drain well. Put about 1 Tbs. meat mixture on each leaf. Roll up and *squeeze*. Lay in baking dish and put plate on top to weight and to prevent leaves' unfolding. Then add water to cover, salt and garlic cloves, and boil on top of stove for about 30 minutes. Just before serving sprinkle with mint chopped fine and a squeeze of lemon juice.

★

String Beans and Lamb

½ lb. lean lamb, cut in bite-sized pieces
1 onion
1 lb. (2 cups) green beans, *must* be fresh, broken in small lengths)
Salt to taste
2 medium-sized tomatoes
1 cup rice
½ cup vermicelli noodles
Sweet butter

Brown lamb, onion and beans in butter. Salt, when onions are half cooked (about 15 minutes before end of process). Add tomatoes. Wash rice well in separate pan; sauté rice and vermicelli until golden brown in butter. Add boiling water and cook for 20 minutes or until water is absorbed. Serve lamb and beans with rice-noodle mixture.

★

Kibbe

1 good Tbs. mint
1 medium onion, chopped
Salt and pepper
1 cup burghul (wheat)
1 lb. lamb, finely ground
Pine nuts

Grind together with mortar and pestle mint, onion and salt and pepper. Ice will be necessary in summer to achive the correct pasty consistency. Wash the wheat, drain it and let stand for 30 minutes. Then mix by hand with the meat. Place a layer of the meat, slightly cooked, and wheat mixture flat in a baking tin. Cover with a layer of mint-onion mixture and sprinkle with pine nuts. Then repeat with a thin layer of the wheat and meat mixture and cut the top in diamond shapes. Cook in oven. This can be used also for stuffing squash, etc.

DALLAS

For me Dallas has always been a very special place, which I associate with very special occasions and people who were important in my life. As long as I live I will never forget my first visit to Dallas. My brother Hamilton agreed to take my sister Martha, our two cousins, Catherine and Lucy, and me to Dallas to visit our Aunt Pearl and Uncle Jim and our beloved bachelor uncle Amos. We spent days getting ready. Mama carefully packed our Dallas clothes between sheets of tissue paper, made sure we had the right color hair ribbons and socks, and gave multiple instructions on how to be "good company." We left Austin in Hamilton's T Model Ford before sunrise. Seems like whenever we took a trip in those days we would always leave before daylight, which added to the mystery and excitement and I am sure caused us to wake up much earlier than was necessary. Mama had also packed us a big lunch, and Ham said we would stop at the park in Waco to picnic, but as it turned out we were a long way from Waco at lunchtime and a long way from Dallas by dark. We had seventeen blowouts and flat tires! Yes, sir, seventeen! Now while we perish the thought today, at that time this seemed only to add to the merriment and did not dampen our spirits one bit!

We met all sorts of interesting and kind people who would stop and visit, tell jokes and help Ham fix the tires. Ham was the essence of good humor and patience — he still is — as we arrived in Dallas on three tires and a rim (rather noisily as we bumped across the brick viaduct), much to the relief of our parents and relatives, who had been phoning wildly trying to find our whereabouts. Why can't children today have aunts and uncles and cousins like we had! They spent the entire time of our visit showing us the wonderful sights of the big city. North Dallas High School, which was just across the street from Aunt Pearl's, had just been completed with an indoor swimming pool. Our cousin Jimmie Faulk got special permission to take his country cousins over for a swim.

Fair Park was an all-day excursion. Uncle Jim tirelesly explained all the amazing exhibits, loaded us with all sorts of souvenirs, such as whistling birds on a stick, lizards that changed colors, pennants and cotton candy.

Uncle Amos took us over to ride on the roller-coaster. I can still hear the rumbling of its wheels and the ceaseless screeching of the passengers. I held on so tight as we swerved the curves and made the breathtaking dips that I rubbed blisters on my thumbs.

Another highlight of our visit was the afternoon matinee at the Palace Theater, and a palace it was indeed! Catherine and I both said we wanted a house like the Palace when we grew up and married. Lew White played the organ between films and the audience sang. The words were flashed on a screen and a little ball would bounce along to direct the tempo. We were absolutely fascinated. After the movie we all went to a nearby ice cream parlor and had our first banana split. No wonder we thought Uncle Amos was the richest man in the world.

Dallas is still a place of great excitement and big-time events — a wonderful city which has kept a good balance in its rapid growth between educational facilities, the industrial area, cultural achievements, scientific and medical developments, the elegant residential section and the skyscrapers thrusting into the blue. Millions of dollars earned in private enterprise have been poured into philanthropies to help boost Dallas to the forefront in these endeavors. There is a magnificent sense of responsibility to the city by an endless number of men and women who have given tirelessly of their time to help this city reach its present top-ranking status in so many fields. There is always something big going on there and the city extends its arms in helpful and hospitable tradition.

Dallas is the only place west of the Mississippi where the Metropolitan Opera performs. This attracts people from all over the Southwest. During the past season the huge State Fair Music Hall was sold out for each of the three operas. In true Dallas style, the stars, members of the cast and out-of-town guests were entertained lavishly throughout their stay. Sally Rudd and I drove up from Austin to attend and took enough of our best "bibs and tuckers" to enjoy all the fringe benefits! Opening night was very gala. Champagne was served in the lobby to the elegantly dressed assembly before curtain time.

The opening opera was *Manon,* with lovely Anna Moffo singing the title role. We had an opportunity to meet Miss Moffo at the ball and dinner given after the opera in the Grand Ballroom of the Sheraton Hotel. She is beautiful and very gracious and a most interesting conversationalist. She was also quite realistic about being hungry, so with Mr. Rudolf Bing, manager of the Met, she went straight to the buffet table, which was bountifully spread with a great array of luscious foods, such as Roast Beef, Crab au Gratin, Chicken and Mushrooms, a wide assortment of beautiful salads and vegetables of all kinds. A circular table around the lighted fountain held a treasure of desserts. So between dances we'd circle around that!

The Ballroom was spectacular. Mr. J. O. Lambert, Jr., had been in charge of the decorations, and used huge colorful Chinese kites in shapes of fish, butterflies and flowers and multicolored balloons in profusion throughout the Ballroom. It was such a congenial party not a soul left until Joe Reichman's orchestra let go the final note!

The second night we heard the ever popular *Aida,* with Leontyne Price. It seemed fantastic to be sitting practically in the heart of Texas and have the entire Metropolian Opera at our feet, the stars, the conductors, orchestra, stagecrafters, and the exquisite new sets. It was also like homecoming seeing so many people I knew from all parts of the state. All this — and another heavenly party afterwards at the home of Mr. and Mrs. W. W. Overton, Jr. The Overtons are a very strong motivating force behind the Met's appearance in Dallas and work hard the year round on this and many other cultural projects.

The *Aida* theme was continued at the party. A brilliant satin-striped canopy covered the terrace and led to the spacious grounds, which were all a-glitter with hurricane lights. Round tables covered in bright pink cloths, each centered with an exotic arrangement of red roses, shiny satin balls and pink candles, were arranged under an enormous party tent. The poles around the tent held lavish arrangements of red-, purple-, and orange-colored plumes. In another spot under the trees a dance floor had been erected, and the men in the dance orchestra said they loved playing for the Metropolian Opera!

The food that night was just perfect for the occasion. There were several identical buffet tables, arranged so the food was easily accessible and there was no waiting in line, which is an accomplishment when one has two hundred hungry guests for a midnight supper.

The menu was:

---

*Delicious * Chicken Cannelloni*
Assorted Melon Wedges: watermelon, honeydew and cantaloupe
Small peeled Cherry Tomatoes and Avocado Wedges, marinated in French dressing with a bowl of sour cream and Russian caviar to put on top
Lovely little cakes and sweets were passed later with coffee

★

Chicken Cannelloni

4 cans chicken broth (7 cups)
¾ cup butter
16-oz. pkg. tufoli macaroni
3 whole chicken breasts (boned)
3 shallots, chopped
3 cloves garlic
5 celery stalks
2 small onions
¾ cup chopped raw spinach
Salt and pepper
3 bay leaves
¾ tsp. oregano
½ tsp. thyme
4 egg yolks
Parmesan cheese

In boiling chicken broth and ¼ cup butter, cook tufoli, covered, 20 to 30 minutes. Cool. Cut chicken into chunks. Then, in butter in skillet, sauté shallots and garlic. Add chicken, celery, onions, spinach, salt and pepper, bay leaves, oregano, thyme. Simmer covered until tender. Quickly stir in egg yolks. Remove from heat. Discard bay leaf. Chop fine. Stuff tufoli. Heat in buttered casserole at 375 degrees. Top with Bolognese Sauce and sprinkle with cheese. (To eliminate extra trouble, this can be stacked using Lasagna noodles instead of stuffing.)

BOLOGNESE SAUCE

6 Tbs. butter
¼ cup finely diced ham or prosciutto
1 small onion
¼ cup grated raw carrot
¼ lb. ground meat

Brown above ingredients and add:

1 thin lemon rind
⅛ tsp. nutmeg
2 Tbs. tomato paste
2 cups beef bouillon
Salt and pepper

Simmer covered 1 hour. Remove rind; add ¼ cup heavy cream. Simmer 2 minutes.

As I have said before, Dallas does everything up so superbly! The next day, some of the Dallas girls took us on an official tour of the city, which included the antique shops, art galleries and Dallas's very lovely residential area, and then to a beautiful lunch at Brook Hollow Country Club. It was my idea of what ladies on a busy partying schedule should have for lunch:

** Cold Cucumber Soup*
Cheese Soufflé
Stuffed Broiled Tomatoes
Fresh Asparagus
Orange Popovers
Raspberry Ice
Coffee

When I returned to Green Pastures I used this menu often during the warm summer months, and everyone is ecstatic about the Cold Cucumber Soup.

★

Cold Cucumber Soup (*serves 4*)

2 Tbs. butter
¼ cup chopped onion, or one leek, sliced and cubed
2 cups diced, unpeeled cucumber
1 cup watercress leaves
½ cup finely diced raw potato
2 cups chicken broth
2 sprigs parsley
½ tsp. salt
¼ tsp. freshly ground black pepper
¼ tsp. dry mustard
1 cup heavy cream
Chopped chives, cucumber and radishes

In a saucepan melt the butter and cook the onion in it until it is transparent. Add the remaining ingredients except the cream and vegetables for garnish, and bring to a boil. Simmer fifteen minutes, or until the potatoes are tender.

Puree in an electric blender or put the mixture through a food mill and, if desired, through a sieve or cheesecloth. Correct the seasonings and chill. Before serving, stir in the cream. Garnish with chopped chives, cucumber and radishes.

Our delightful day ended with tea at the Penthouse on Twenty-five Thirty Turtle Creek, the home of Mr. and Mrs. J. O. Lambert, Jr. I have saved the timeworn phrase "out of this world" for now. It truly is out of this world, housing a sizable art collection and showing Mr. Lambert's own artistic hand in the stunning planting in the spacious solarium quietly overlooking Big Busy Beautiful Dallas.

A few hours later the evening started just as excitingly as the previous two, with the fresh gay rendition of Verdi's comic opera *Falstaff*. We were especially looking forward to hearing Luigi Alva sing the role of Fenton. Formerly of Peru but now living in Austin is his cousin the attractive Señora Luz Arauzo. She and her husband, Dr. Arauzo, and friends of ours came to Dallas for this great occasion. It was most thrilling for all of us as Luigi delivered his inspiring arioso and received a thunderous applause! After the performance we met Luigi and his wife and had a small, quiet, but delightful party, listening to all the thrilling tales of his climb up the ladder to fame.

A few months before the opera season opened, Mr. Rudolf Bing came to Dallas to make plans for the forthcoming operas. It was at a luncheon in Mr. Bing's honor that I met Lily Pons. What a charming mignonne she is! On a later visit to Dallas, I had the delightful experience of visiting her at her apartment, or I should say her villa!

Miss Pons has a house in Palm Springs, California, where she spends part of each year, but she loves Dallas. She has brought most of her luxurious furnishings and her treasured collection of paintings from her native France. In the library are mementos of her colorful and glorious career, informal pictures with other famous personalities, honors and citations she has received for her tireless contributions. She always has fresh flowers throughout the house and blooming on the terrace, which is enlivened by small splashes from a fountain. "I love nature," said Miss Pons. "I love to take walks. I always discover something new, some little bird or something. I need nature, it inspires me!" We discussed our families, and the contrast of the American and European way of life.

"Here," she said, "people don't like to take a long time to eat. They seem to just gobble lunch." In France, her brother-in-law, the president of a large garment factory, comes home every day at twelve-thirty for lunch with the family. "The pleasure of the table is enlightening and relaxing," she said. "In Cannes, we were always ten and twelve around the table at every meal and we would eat and visit until two-thirty. No one ever has a nervous breakdown there!"

When the young prima donna Joan Sutherland made her debut in Dallas, Miss Pons gave a lovely buffet supper in Miss Sutherland's honor, which was attended by the entire Italian Opera Company. For this, Miss Pons had a caterer. But for a small dinner for six or eight, she enjoys nothing more than preparing dinner herself with perhaps the help of one maid. She arranges her own centerpiece of fresh flowers, always serves wine, as she points out, "It is not only digestive but also contains vitamins, and if two glasses are taken slowly with dinner it is most agreeable." This is one of the menus Miss Pons enjoys preparing:

Clam Bisque
** Poulet Chasseur*
** Salad with Artichoke and Palm Hearts*
Fresh strawberries in season with whipped cream or Tangerine Dessert
Coffee

★

Poulet Chasseur (*serves 6 to 8*)

2 chickens cut up (do not salt)
Mixture of half olive oil, half margarine (better than butter, according to Miss Pons)
3 slices bacon
½ lb. fresh mushrooms, sliced
1 large onion, sliced
2 cups celery, chopped
1 6-oz. can tomato paste
1 28-oz. can tomatoes, drained
Bouquet of: parsley, bay leaf, garlic, oregano, pepper
2 cups beef bouillon
3 Tbs. flour
1 cup red wine
1 eggplant, peeled and cubed
5 to 6 zucchini, cut in finger strips
Parmesan cheese

Brown chicken in oil and margarine, and place in baking dish. Cook bacon till crisp. Remove bacon and drain on paper. Sauté mushrooms, onion, celery in bacon grease. Add tomato paste and tomatoes. Simmer bouquet in bouillon, then add bouillon to above. Thicken with flour, made into a paste. Add wine and eggplant and zucchini. Place in baking dish on top of the chicken. Sprinkle with Parmesan cheese and cook in 350-degree oven for 20 to 30 minutes.

★

Salad with Artichoke and Palm Hearts

Place artichoke and palm hearts on endive and crisp lettuce leaf. The dressing is four parts oil to one part vinegar, seasoned with salt, pepper and chopped parsley.

There have been innumerable books, editorials and stories written and told about the fabulous Neiman-Marcus store, such as the story a friend of ours, who lives on a ranch in West Texas, told us. She said they always look forward to getting their Sears Roebuck catalog and their Neiman-Marcus catalog. They do quite a bit of shopping from both. One time when she and her husband were leaving for a trip to Dallas her five-year-old said, "Be sure to bring me back something from Neiman-Roebuck's!" Our friend was laughing about it when she met Mr. Stanley Marcus in the store. Later he handed her a beautiful Neiman-Marcus wrapped gift and said, "Take this to Patty and tell her it is from Neiman-Roebuck's!"

One can hardly think of Dallas without the name of this "great institution" popping up, as it and its owners play such a vital role in many facets of the life of this city. The wide variety of its publications will substantiate this: *Retailing and Economic Growth, America Is Fashion, Dallas Wonderland, Texas Store, Life Goes to a Fashion Show, The First Fifty Years, Taste of Texas, Neiman-Marcus — a State of Mind, Fashion Is My Business, That's How Fashion Is Born, Dazzling Dallas, Neiman-Marcus Looks at London, Chic in the Heart of Texas, That Special Neiman-Marcus Magic, Santa Among the Millionaires, Our Good Neighbor Policies,* to mention only a *very few. But* there is one relatively new field that is not registered with the store but is instead a private enterprise of the executive vice president, Mr. Edward Marcus — Black Mark Ranch.

Edward Marcus has always been an outdoors enthusiast. His mother, Mrs. Herbert Marcus, told me that he had always loved animals. On weekends he and his wife Betty, who shares this interest, started looking around for a farm not too far from "the store" where he might work a "split shift." They were successful in finding such a place only twenty miles from Dallas toward Grapevine and near Lewisville, and like all other ranchers they wanted only one thing, the adjoining land, which after a few years they were fortunate enough to acquire.

At first, Edward and Betty had commercial cattle, black chickens and palomino horses. Betty laughingly says they thought these would make such a pretty color scheme on the green landscape. However, Edward Marcus, being brought up on the Marcus philosophy of "only top quality," and having attended cattle sales around the globe, could not be satisfied with anything less than a pedigree herd.

We were in Dallas at the time of the fall sale at Black Mark Farm. Buyers had come from Scotland, England, Ireland, Mexico and South America as well as from all over the United States and Canada to see one of the most outstanding herds of Black Angus in existence. The night before the sale the Marcuses had a lovely cocktail-buffet supper in the Zodiac Room atop their swank store. The tables were centered with ceramic Black Angus filled with yellow chrysanthemums. The buffet featured rib eye of beef from the Black Mark Farm, the delicious flavor of which was an impressive selling point. Beautiful models walked in and around the tables for the guests to see how the latest in white minks compared to the greatest in Black Angus! It was indeed a delightful evening, with food and wine, lots of good continental conversation: staccatos of the English broad A, the soft Spanish accents intermingled with Scottish burrs, the Irish brogue and Texas drawls.

My friend Patricia Farquharson, from London, who was with me, was happily surprised to meet her friends the Corrigans, from England. The next morning we drove out to Black Mark Farm. It was a brilliant Texas fall day, perfect for driving out in the country. Mrs. Herbert Marcus, Sr., told us the night before that Eddie's farm was in no way a hobby, but a real business at which he worked very hard. We drove through the sweet-smelling fields waving with soft green Coastal Bermuda grass and into the pasture, where the auction had already started. In the first pen we passed stood Elegance of Charterhouse, called "the Round-the-World Bull." I do not claim to know anything about cattle or the cattle business, but I do know that this was the most magnificent animal! He was from Scotland and was the 1958 Perth Supreme Champion, and his first twenty-four sons sold for $100,000.

There is a small farmhouse, painted yellow. The barn, scientifically designed by the international architect O'Neil Ford, is also yellow. For this occasion, two large tents had been stretched, one with bleachers for the prospective buyers and the auctioneers, and the other for the food and tables. The waiters passed through the tent serving drinks and coffee as the auctioneers rumbled on. I waved at someone coming in and it almost cost me a calf.

There really isn't any emphasis put on the food. It is simply there to accommodate the four or five hundred guests whenever they should get hungry. But emphasized or not, have hamburgers made from a Black Mark Angus steer, and Helen Corbitt to see to the serving of it, you can depend on mighty fine victuals!

Two electric griddles were set up under the tent. Two cooks grilled the hamburgers and knockwurst as the guests came by. There were also homemade buns, buttered and grilled, a big crock bowl of cole slaw and a big bowl of bean salad, coffee and iced tea. Because it happened to be Mr. Edward's birthday, Helen had made a tall three-tiered devil's food cake, frosted with mocha and topped with a small Black Angus steer. Not a live one of course! The sale had been set up to go two days but Mr. Edward hung up the "sold out" sign at the end of the first day.

It is a treat to see Betty and Edward Marcus in this setting because it is so obvious how much they love the farm. Betty tried her hand with the land a few years ago and planted some of the fields in miniature watermelons. It was a bumper crop. She and a friend loaded them in a truck and started to market. Her first thought was Neiman-Marcus. However, the buyer there would not pay her asking price, so she took them to Simon David's Dallas fancy food store and they sold "like hot cakes."

There isn't the slightest chance of even a moment's boredom in the lives of these two active people. Their interests are vital and wide. They may attend a committee meeting of the State Fair Pan-American Livestock Exposition by day and the Dallas Museum of Contemporary Arts by night. Their interest in art is very keen, as is depicted in their important and valuable collection of paintings which hang in the Dutch Colonial house. The paintings range from Piet Mondrian's early twentieth-century works down to present-day artists such as Ben Nicholson. The interior of the house is contemporary, done with grays, yellows and white, and accents of brass.

The Marcuses do most of their entertaining at home, which must be a happy experience for their distinguished guests. Betty prefers to have only eight persons for dinner in order to enjoy the full pleasure of her guests. I am sure their guest register reads like a *Who's Who.*

When "the store" recently presented Dorothy Rodgers's remarkable book *My Favorite Things,* she and her famous husband, Richard Rodgers, were guests of the Edward Marcuses one evening for dinner. The menu was:

Shad Roe in a Tomato
Squab cooked with oranges and currant jelly
Tiny Artichoke Hearts
Wild Rice
Bibb Lettuce with French dressing
Croissants
Chocolate Cups which Betty makes. They are filled with her homemade *Coffee Ice Cream* and topped with *Chocolate Sauce,* which she also makes.
The wine was a Mercurey.

There has been no one who has done more to promote the reputation for fine food in Texas than Helen Corbitt. She is a Texan by choice twice — hers and Texas's! However, her fame far outreaches the borders of the state; she was the first woman ever to receive the National Golden Plate Award, which is the greatest honor anyone in the food service industry can achieve. Helen's superlative flair for the extraordinary and her original combination of complementary flavors has caused her to be dubbed "the greatest cook in Texas." Her friends are constantly amazed at "how she does it!" Besides her demanding role as director of the Neiman-Marcus restaurants, where patrons stand in line daily waiting to be served in the Zodiac Room, she occasionally even gets around to having a party for herself.

Like many busy people, Helen has had little opportunity to know the neighbors on her block, so she put an invitation in each mail box which read:

> I live on your street and being a small town girl would like to know you better. Won't you come by for a drink and a snack on Saturday, August 8 from 7 till — ?
>
> Helen Corbitt
> 4684 N. Versailles
>
> Most Informal
> Back Yard

She had white director's chairs with blue canvas seats and backs; outdoor candelabra with blue flowers at the base were on each of the two large round tables, which were covered with hot pink cloths. A bar was set up on the barbecue fireplace. All kinds of drinks from snappy Toms to beer, whiskey and so forth. Everyone sat around and talked and got acquainted and reveled in:

Beef Fondue Bourguignonne
Party Barquettes filled with Chicken Hash au Gratin
Cold Curried Cooked Vegetables
Cold Baked Ham, sliced and jellied with Cumberland Sauce
Salt Rising Bread and Butter Sandwiches
Iced Olives and Pickled Okra with lime juice sprinkled over

ON THE SECOND TABLE

Coffee Angel Food Squares rolled in coffee butter icing and toasted almonds
Coffee

TYLER

We just returned from the Texas Rose Festival in Tyler. It is something one has to experience to really fully realize the grandeur of this annual event. Tyler, now known as the Rose Capital of the World, is a beautiful, small city in East Texas, recognized for many years as the center of aristocratic culture and later as the oil capital of East Texas. Tyler claims also to be the home of the prettiest girls in the world, and this becomes very evident during the Rose Festival, when they are all on hand, not only beautiful but charming and gracious, seeing that all the visitors become a part of these gala festivities. Showers of rose petals constantly flutter down from low-flying airplanes onto the streets, which are already festooned with literally millions of roses. Pretty Tyler girls throw bouquets of roses into the cars of startled visitors arriving in town for the festival.

This year Lucy Ross was the Duchess from Austin. Lucy had been presented at the International Debutante Ball in New York. The parties there were quite lush, but actually nothing can quite compare to the Tyler Rose Festival. She and her mother, Mrs. Ellen Steck Ross, received the design for her fabulous royal robe, invitations to parties, luncheons, dinners and dances, and all pertinent information in advance, with every detail of the arrangements outlined for them. So when they, as well as some twenty other attendants from all parts of the state and country, arrived, all they had to do was to enjoy the elaborately planned affairs on the agenda booked solid for the three-day celebration. The Queen's Coronation and the Rose Parade, with their inspiring beauty and pageantry, are events none of us will soon forget.

There was also the Queen's Tea, given in the Municipal Rose Garden, the Rose Show, Fiesta Night, the Rose Vesper Service, the Queen's Luncheon, cocktail parties, beautiful buffets, and dinners. Every detail, from the beautifully engraved and gold embossed invitations to the demitasses and cordials, was absolute perfection.

In 1951, fifteen couples, all good friends, began to gather for Sunday evening steak supper get-togethers. The steaks were cooked outdoors on charcoal broilers — thus the name of the group — the Charcoal Club — came into being. The host couple rotated, and the gatherings were held at the various homes.

In 1953, the group decided to build a clubhouse at Lake Tyler. This house was completed in 1954 and is the setting for our regular meetings as well as our annual Rose Festival luncheon.

The First Festival party was in 1954, after the Parade on Saturday. This custom has continued through the years. Our guests have been out-of-town visitors — we do not include our Tyler friends. From this annual affair our parody of the Rose Festival Coronation evolved — and is known as the "Stinkweed Festival Coronation." A visitor is chosen at the end of the presentation to be our Queen for the coming year. All participants, including the King, Duchesses and special entertainers in the Coronation, are Charcoal Club members. Our one rule is — *we never rehearse* — it all is spontaneous!

From the beginning, we have served a substantial luncheon, because most everyone has got up early to get to the parade without a good breakfast, and by the time the party begins, food is essential. A typical menu is:

Prime Rib Roast
Potatoes with Cheese Sauce
** Tamale Pie*
Marinated Green Beans
*Pound Cake — * Fudge Squares*
Coffee

Of course the menu varies from time to time, but they *always* try to have it include Mozelle Huffstutler's Fudge Squares.

★

Mrs. Joe Huffstutler's Fudge Squares

Melt 1 cup butter (oleo will not do), and 2 squares Baker's chocolate in double boiler. Beat 4 eggs until very thick, then add 2 cups sugar gradually, pinch of salt, 2 teaspoons vanilla, then fold in the chocolate mixture. Blend well; add 1 cup flour, and 1 cup toasted pecans, chopped fine.

Pour into two 9-inch-square pans that have been greased and floured. Put pan of water in bottom of oven and cook at 325 degrees for 40 to 45 minutes. Let cool thoroughly and ice while still in the pans with any good powdered sugar chocolate icing. I use cocoa in mine. These might rightfully be called "Willis, Texas, Fudge Squares!"

★

Tamale Pie (also by Mozelle Huffstutler and just wonderful)

1 can cream-style corn
1 can tamales
1 can chili
2 cups grated New York cheddar cheese (or any good sharp cheese).
2 Tbs. flour (approx.)

Cut tamales into small pieces, take grease off can of chili, mix all ingredients, and blend well. Bake in casserole at 325 degrees about 45 minutes or until bubbly.

Judge and Mrs. Joe Fisher, of nearby Jasper, are frequent visitors in Tyler. Katheleen Fisher is considered one of the best cooks in East Texas. Her friends and family prevailed upon her to write down her recipes and memoirs of the many wonderful dinners and luncheons served around the Fisher table. Served at the Charcoal Club on special occasions have been her Apricot Glazed Spareribs. I heartily recommend that you try these at once.

★

Apricot Glazed Spareribs

4-5 pounds pork spareribs
1 12-oz. jar apricot preserves
1 4-oz bottle soy sauce

Wash, then wipe ribs dry. Cut in desired portions and place in shallow pan. Pour the soy sauce over the ribs and then spread with preserves. Cook in 300-degree oven 2 to 3 hours, basting frequently with the sauce.

★

Katheleen's Texas Goulash
(*the Hungarians want her recipe*)

1 small onion, chopped
4 buttons minced garlic
1 Tbs. bacon drippings
1½ lb. ground steak
Salt and pepper to taste
1 Tbs. chili powder
1 8-oz. can tomatoes
¾ cup uncooked rice

Sauté onion and garlic in bacon drippings. Add ground meat and brown. Then add seasonings, tomatoes, and lastly, rice that has been washed. Put in casserole, cover and bake at 350 degrees for 40 minutes.

★

Katheleen's Surprise Potatoes
(*quick, easy and so delicious with roast beef*)

6 large Idaho potatoes
1½ cans frozen shrimp soup
2 ounces butter
Salt and pepper

Bake potatoes in medium oven. When done, cut a thin slice off the top to make a nice, deep shell, and scoop out potatoes carefully. Put potatoes, defrosted soup and butter into mixer. Beat until smooth. Salt and pepper to taste. Refill the 6 shells, piling high. Place in medium oven for twenty minutes; serve piping hot.

In East Texas so many good fresh vegetables are grown and they know so many exciting ways of serving them; they are a very important part of every meal. So often I am asked, "What vegetables can I serve besides green beans and peas?" I want to answer, "Thousands." Just get Katheleen's *Justice in the Kitchen* and try each recipe in her chapter on vegetables for real treats in vegetable eating.

*Tuna Casserole has long been a family Friday favorite — and especially since I've perked it up with Katheleen's version:

★

Tuna Dinner

3 onions
½ green pepper
1 can mushrooms

Sauté above ingredients in four tablespoons bacon drippings.

2 eggs, hard boiled and chopped
1 8-oz. can tunafish, flaked
5 oz. noodles boiled in salted water, then drained
2 cups cream sauce with ½ cup Velveeta cheese added

Mix all ingredients together. Put crushed potato chips on top, and bake twenty minutes.

BROWNSVILLE

I really wish I could set my lines on Brownsville to music like a spirited tango. Brownsville is lush and lavish with brilliant blooming plants such as bougainvillaeas, exotic hibiscus, poincianas, palm and papaya trees. In the spring the air is fragrant with the blossoms on the citrus trees.

Bienvenidos amigos is not only the friendly greeting in border lingo for saying "Welcome friends"; it is the real atmosphere which is prevalent among the populace. I am certain this is one of the reasons Brownsville is becoming such a popular resort for visitors from all over the country, a few of the others being: the very desirable year-round climate, the outstanding fishing opportunities, along with hunting at its best for the famous white wing dove, wild turkey, quail and lots of deer which are plentiful in this region. It is the consensus of those who live or visit in Brownsville that the food there is also quite superior and has its own distinctive flavor.

It was a delightful experience being the guest of Leefe and Peyton Sweeney who have always lived in Brownsville, and Peyton is quick to declare he just would not live anywhere else. I wouldn't either with a home like theirs. It is a lovely contemporary white brick on the grassy sloping banks of one of the pretty little lakes which are interspread through the residential sections of the city. The house is beautifully designed for entertaining, which is one of the Sweeneys' chief occupations.

Leefe introduced me to what has become my favorite dish at a brunch one morning. It is called *Chilaquiles. The amazing thing about this dish is it can be served almost at any time, brunch, lunch, or dinner, or after the theater, as was the case the last time I served it. That morning, along with the Chilaquiles, Leefe had fresh valley fruits beautifully arranged in a scooped-out melon on a large tray garnished with hibiscus blooms, coffee and *Leche Quemada. One thing for certain, everyone forgot about his diet!

★

Chilaquiles

2 onions, chopped
1 clove garlic, minced
Fat
2 large cans tomatoes
Salt, pepper
1 can green chili peppers
1 dozen tortillas
2 lbs. grated cheese — preferably Monterey jack
1 pt. sour cream

Sauté onions and garlic in 2 Tbs. of fat until clear. Add tomatoes, salt and pepper, and simmer until tomatoes are cooked. Add peppers that have been cut in strips. Cut tortillas in fourths and dip in hot fat. Remove immediately and drain on paper towels. Put layer of tortillas in baking dish, layer of sauce, layer of grated cheese. Continue until dish is filled; top with grated cheese. Heat in oven until cheese melts. Just before serving top with sour cream, and watch this dish disappear.

★

Leche Quemada

2 qts. milk
1 lb. granulated sugar

Boil, stirring frequently, until mixture leaves side of pan, about 2 hours. Pour in greased pan and, when cool, cut in squares. Pecan halves may be put on top.

Peyton says he and his friends go more for Leefe's *plain* food after a day in the office, or half-day, I should say, followed by eighteen holes of golf. He is joined by Peyton, Jr., in these sentiments, and Leefe has a wonderful assortment of stick-to-your-ribs foods, such as the following:

** Hot Chicken Salad*
** Creamy Chicken-Rice Casserole*
Casserole for the Crowd
** Tuna Tetrazzini*
** Family Style Beef Stew*

★

Hot Chicken Salad

4 cups cooked chicken
4 cups celery, chopped
1 cup slivered almonds
2 cups mayonnaise
1 tsp. monosodium glutamate
4 tsp. lemon juice
4 tsp. chopped onion
Salt to taste

Mix and put in baking dish. Refrigerate for several hours. Cover top with the following:

2 cups rolled potato chips
1 cup grated cheese

Bake at 350 degrees 10 to 20 minutes or until salad is warm through and cheese has melted.

★

Creamy Chicken-Rice Casserole (8 servings)

1 cup wild rice
½ cup chopped onion
½ cup butter or margarine
¼ cup enriched flour
6-oz. can broiled sliced mushrooms
Chicken broth
1½ cup light cream
3 cups diced chicken
¼ cup diced pimento
2 Tbs. snipped parsley
1½ tsp. salt
¼ tsp. pepper
½ cup slivered blanched almonds

Prepare wild rice according to directions on package. Cook onion in butter until tender, but not brown. Remove from heat; stir in enriched flour. Drain mushrooms, reserving liquid. Add enough chicken broth to liquid to measure 1½ cups; gradually stir into flour mixture. Add cream. Cook and stir until mixture thickens. Add rice, mushrooms, chicken, pimento, parsley, salt and pepper. Place in 2-qt. casserole. Sprinkle with almonds. Bake in moderate oven (350 degrees) 25 to 30 minutes or until hot.

★

Tuna Tetrazzini

¼ cup butter
¼ cup chopped onion
¼ cup green pepper
¾ cup diced celery
1 cup coffee cream
1½ cup grated sharp cheese
¼ cup chopped pimento
1 cup pitted ripe olives
2 7-oz. cans tuna, drained and flaked
1 7-oz. pkg. thin spaghetti

Melt butter, add onion, green pepper and celery. Cook until tender. Add cream, 1 cup cheese, pimento and olives. Heat slowly until cheese melts. Add tuna. Pour mixture over cooked spaghetti and mix lightly. Season with salt and pepper to taste. Put mixture into buttered 1½-qt. casserole. Top with remaining ½ cup of cheese. Bake at 350 degrees for 30 minutes, or until hot through and through. (I add 1 can of mushrooms to the above.)

★

Family Style Beef Stew

2 Tbs. fat
3 lbs. stewing meat, cubed
2 large onions, sliced
2 garlic cloves, minced
1 cup chopped celery
¼ cup chopped parsley
2½ cups canned tomatoes
1 bay leaf, crumbled
½ tsp. thyme
1 Tbs. salt
Freshly ground pepper
2½ cups water
1 cup green peas
12 small carrots
12 small onions
6 potatoes, quartered
½ cup flour

Melt fat in saucepan and brown meat. Add sliced onions, garlic, celery, parsley, tomatoes, bay leaf, thyme, salt, pepper and 2½ cups water. Bring to a boil, reduce heat; cover and simmer for 2 hours. Add remaining vegetables and simmer for 1 hour. Just before removing, stir in flour.

Her *Baked Beans were *terribly* good.

★

Baked Beans

2 tall cans pork and beans
½ cup chopped celery
½ cup chopped onion
Chopped bacon or chopped baked ham

Season with:

Catsup
Chili sauce
Brown sugar
Cracked black pepper
Salt

Add celery and onion to beans. Add seasoning. Sprinkle top with bacon or pieces of baked ham. Bake at 325 degrees for 2 or 3 hours. Chopped green pepper may also be added if desired.

The dinner that got the most superlative description, with which I quite concur, was:

Barbecued Ham
Candied Yams
Black-eyed Peas
Tossed Green Salad with Garlic Dressing
Corn Bread (Sometimes she serves hot buttered French bread)
* *Applesauce Cake*

★

Applesauce Cake

1 cup butter
2 cups sugar
3 cups flour
1 cup hot water
2 eggs
2 cups applesauce
2 tsp. soda
1 cup raisins
1 cup nuts
1 tsp. nutmeg
1 tsp. cinnamon
1 tsp. cloves

Cream butter and sugar. Add flour, hot water, eggs, applesauce and other ingredients. Pour into 1 or 2 buttered loaf pans. Bake at 350 degrees for approximately 1 hour. The nice thing about this recipe is that all ingredients can be mixed quickly together.

Ice with this icing:

Cook until thick:

2 cups sugar
1 cup butter
1 cup milk
1 cup raisins
1 cup nuts

Another delicacy of Leefe's is her recipe for *Lizzies:

★

Lizzies

1 cup brown sugar
1 cup butter
2 cups flour
4 eggs, beaten
3 tsp. soda
3 Tbs. milk
⅔ cup whiskey
1 tsp. nutmeg, allspice, cinnamon
1 lb. seeded raisins or dates
1½ cups broken pecans
½ lb. candied cherries
1 lb. candied pineapple

Combine ingredients. Drop by spoonfuls onto greased baking sheet and bake at 250 degrees for 20 minutes. Makes about 5 dozen.

The International Bridge at Brownsville is indeed a modern and dramatic entrance to Old Mexico, with colorful flags of all nations fluttering from tall standards. The illuminated fountains rhythmically splashing and the blooming tropical plants compose an inviting picture! The overhead serpentine walkways are very popular for the pedestrian commuters, and it is an ever present temptation to cross the border for a Margarita and a quail dinner or to see a cockfight or just browse in the charming and interesting shops of Matamoros.

Mary Yturria joined Leefe and me for a delightful lunch in Matamoros. Mary is another reason Brownsville has gained such fame for fine foods. Mary, a soft-spoken and beautiful girl whose home was Alabama before she married Frank Yturria, is a few chilaquiles ahead of most of us, as she has spent as many hours in cooking schools around the world as she has in college and considers cooking one of her very favorite recreations! A few nights before Frank and Mary left for a vacation in Spain, some of their friends got together for what may be known as a "covered dish supper" in the Yturria patio — but I would call it more of a gathering of gourmets. Hot from the charcoal broiler in the yard, they served *Shrimp Sate Babi (Mary Jo and Jimmie George brought these). On the table were the following:

---

* *Barbecued Pork Ribs* (Martha and Ben Brite)
Green Salad and Onion Bread (brought by Peggy and Linwood Bland)
* *Gnocchi* (made by Mary and Frank, and fabulous)
* *Chocolate Refrigerator Cake* (Leefe and Peyton)

★

Barbecued Pork Ribs

10 lbs. small pork ribs
Brown sugar
Salt
Java cracked pepper
Small bottle soy sauce and/or lime juice or red wine vinegar
2 cloves garlic

Rub ribs lightly with brown sugar and sprinkle with salt and cracked pepper. Marinate in small bottle of soy sauce and/or fresh lime juice or red wine vinegar and sprinkle with cut cloves of garlic. Cook and smoke slowly in covered barbecue for at least 1½ hours, basting frequently with marinade.

★

Gnocchi

This recipe was given to Mary by the countess with whom she stayed in Paris.

1 cup and 1 Tbs. water
Pinch salt
5 Tbs. butter
1 cup flour
6 eggs

Put water, salt and butter in a pan. Bring to boil and add flour all at once; remove from fire while stirring with a wooden spoon until it forms a ball. Add two eggs and stir some more. Add the remaining four eggs and mix well. Put a cloth over the top of the pan and let rest for at least 2 hours. In a large pan put plenty of water and bring to the simmering point (not a hard boil). Work with 2 teaspoons, filling one with the dough and pushing it out of the spoon with the other into the simmering water. When the dumpling-like balls come to the top (takes 10 minutes) lift them out and drain. When dry, put in a buttered casserole. Make a rich, thin cream sauce with lots of grated Swiss cheese and pour over the Gnocchi. The sauce should be the consistency of pancake batter, that is, *it must not be too thick.* Run in the oven for about 20 minutes until lightly browned on top.

★

Chocolate Refrigerator Cake

1 pkg. semisweet chocolate
1 Tbs. instant coffee
3 eggs
1 cup heavy cream
Dash of salt
2 doz. lady fingers

Melt chocolate in top of double boiler; stir in coffee and cool. Beat yolks in chocolate (one at a time). Beat egg whites until they stand in peaks. Mix in chocolate carefully. Whip cream and fold in mixture. Put in casserole over lady fingers. Chill in refrigerator.

Mary and Frank also do a great deal of bird hunting and are often asked to join Tom and Henrietta Armstrong at their nearby ranch. Mary says a hunting trip with the Armstrongs is a very delightful experience. The Armstrongs are followed by a well-equipped pick-up truck which carries folding chairs, and table, linen and complete bar along with well-qualified members of their household staff. After the hunt, in the middle of the pasture, "dinner is served."

The birds are cooked in a charcoal-fired earthen oven, basted with wine and seasoned to perfection and "washed down" with cold Champagne!

Mary said on one such occasion the Armstrongs also had as their guests Vic and Helen Bergeron, renowned restaurateurs of Chicago, San Francisco, London and other faraway places. Mary said that afternoon they had been shooting up at the King Ranch and having so much fun swapping stories and recipes she just got carried away and issued a very enthusiastic invitation to all. She would prepare an Indonesian lunch the next day. When she got back to the ranch house that evening, after the shoot, she thought to herself, "Vic will go back to California and split his sides laughing at the Texas girl who made a fool of herself." The more she thought about cooking for one of the world's greatest gourmets the more uneasy she got. But, luckily, she put her mind to doing something about it. She sent into Brownsville, eighty miles away, to get all of her equipment, which consisted of wooden plates in the shape of big leaves, wooden serving bowls, real coconut shells to drink from, etc. Mary said she had always believed that she has the most wonderful guardian angel in the whole world. That day the angel must have been Indonesian — and one who could cook — as the lunch was a howling success, and she and Vic have been steadfast friends ever since! As a matter of fact, a few weeks later, she had a long-distance call from Trader Vic in San Francisco and he wondered if she would give him the recipe for *Shrimp she had served for that glorious and inspired dinner! Mary explained she had promised it to the Espiscopal Church in Brownsville for their cookbook. Vic sent a very generous donation to the church and got the recipe he wanted.

★

Sate Babi Shrimp Sauce

For every 1 lb. cooked shrimp use the following measurements for the sauce:

5 cloves garlic, grated
Small piece ginger
½ cup soy sauce
1 cup water
⅓ cup peanut butter
1½ cup brown sugar
Juice of 1 lemon
3 Cerano chilis, ground

Mix garlic, ginger, soy sauce and water. Simmer about 10 minutes. Add peanut butter, sugar and lemon juice. Add chilis at the end. Cook on very low heat for 25 minutes. (The peanut butter is the subtle flavor that no one is able to detect.)

Brownsville is the acknowledged "shrimp capital of the world," and the king of this world, I would say, is Jimmie George, who owns and operates a fleet of shrimp boats. Jimmie does a complete job of shrimping. He calculates, catches, cooks, consumes, and capitalizes. He and Mary Jo have built the most beautiful, fascinating home in the country a short distance from Brownsville. It is both elegant and casual with a great deal of individuality. The Georges planned every detail to suit their own particular need and taste, and to follow the contour of the land along the picturesque lagoon. Much thought and emphasis was put into the large kitchen, as they both enjoy entertaining on a very informal note and doing most of the cooking themselves. Shrimp and Mexican food are their specialities. The night Chester and I went with the Sweeneys and Yturrias, Mary Jo served delicious little hot hors d'oeuvres right from the stove as we all stood around with our drinks trying to see what Jimmie was putting into the kettle of shrimp. Mary Jo had broiled little pig sausages and drained them well. Then she rolled a quarter of a tortilla around each sausage, held it together with a toothpick and then dipped it in hot vegetable oil. They were crisp in about 15 seconds. Even so, that was hardly fast enough for the eager guests standing *very* close by! Another yummie is *Shrimp Dollars.

★

Shrimp Dollars (makes 12 to 15 balls)

1 lb. uncooked shrimp
1 Tbs. cornstarch
½ tsp. salt
10 water chestnuts, chopped
1 tsp. sherry
1 egg, slightly beaten

Shell, clean and chop the shrimp up fine. Mix chestnuts well with shrimp. Add cornstarch, sherry, salt and egg. Mix well and form into balls, then flatten with spatula. Fry in deep oil until golden brown. Serve hot.

The shrimp dish that evening was *Jalapeño Shrimp with potatoes. They couldn't be anything but delicious. The shrimp were so beautiful! Fresh limes gave this an indescribable flavor.

★

Jalapeño Shrimp

1 small can jalapeños (seedless)
1 box crab boil
7 cloves garlic, minced
Salt and pepper
1 bottle of beer
2 onions, finely chopped
6 limes (juice and slivered rinds)
6 medium potatoes, peeled and quartered
1 lb. peeled, deveined shrimp

Place all ingredients except potatoes and shrimp in pan of boiling water and cook for 40 minutes. Add potatoes and let boil for 20 minutes. Add shrimp and cook 5 minutes.

*Nachos show up at many cocktail parties in Texas. They are easy to make and go away with about the same amount of effort!

★

Nachos

1 dozen tortillas
Sliced cheese
1 can jalapeño peppers

Cut tortillas into 8 wedge-shaped pieces. Fry in hot fat until golden brown. Cut wedge-shaped pieces of cheese just a little bit narrower than tortilla wedge and place on top of tortilla. Put thin sliver of jalapeño pepper on top of wedges. Place under broiler until cheese melts. Serve hot.

Since my friend and houseguest from England, Patricia Farquharson, has been so enthusiastic over Mexican food, we have tried just about every recipe we know on her. She likes this one from Brownsville very much.

★

Laguna Madre Envueltos

1 lb. ground beef
2 Tbs. butter or oleo
Salt and pepper
2 dozen tortillas
1 onion, chopped
½ green pepper, chopped
2 pieces celery
1 clove garlic, minced
1 No. 2 can tomatoes
1 large bottle pitted green olives
2 pimentos
Grated cheese

Brown meat in small amount of fat. Salt and pepper to taste. Place cooked meat in center of tortillas and roll tightly. Place in baking dish. Sauté onion, green pepper, celery and garlic in butter. Add tomatoes and simmer for 30 minutes. Add chopped olives and pimentos. Pour sauce over rolled tortillas. Top with grated cheese. Cover and bake for 30 minutes in 300-degree oven.

*Border Buttermilk makes a wonderful innocent-sounding drink. With an electric blender, a bottle of Tequila, crushed ice and a can of frozen lemonade you are in business. Put the can of lemonade in the blender. Then fill the can with Tequila and pour it in the blender. Fill the blender with ice. Let it spin half a minute, and it is foamy, white and ready to sip. (This is much faster than churning!)

I recommend that you have a good supply of *Turcos on hand to go with this Border Buttermilk. They are simply divine. Mrs. William Long, who is another Brownsville gourmet, gave me this recipe. We have made large quantities and put them in the freezer. Come party time, Dolores drops them in the hot fat, drains them and smiles while everyone says *Muy bien!*

★

Turcos (fried meat pies)

PASTRY

2 cups flour
½ cup shortening (or a little less)
Water

FILLING

3 Tbs. lard
1 lb. lean beef or pork, coarse or chili grind (or half of each)
2 tomatoes, diced
1 onion, diced
2 cloves garlic
1 tsp. cumin
½ cup celery, finely diced
1 Tbs. sugar
1 bell pepper, finely diced
Salt, pepper
½ cup pecans, chopped
½ cup raisins
Chile pequins or jalapeños (optional)

Simmer all ingredients except nuts and raisins in melted lard until quite dry. Add nuts and raisins when nearly done. If you add the hot peppers use very little black pepper.

Roll out pastry and cut in 2-inch rounds. Place 1 tsp. meat mixture on each. Pinch edges together well. Fry in deep fat (370 degrees) till golden brown.

The names Dr. and Mrs. C. W. Smith on the mailbox a few doors up the street didn't mean a thing until I discovered from the Sweeneys that Mrs. Smith was my good friend Mary Lasswell.

Mary is well known for her delightful stories *Suds in Your Eye, Mrs. Rasmussen's Book of One-Arm Cookery, High Time,* and the book she finished while living in Austin a few years ago, *I'll Take Texas.* We had all missed Mary in Austin. It was she who had put many a sit-down party on its feet with her rollicking, swinging and singing piano playing and her effervescent personality.

I should have known when she left, if she went anywhere it would be to her native Brownsville, as she always spoke of it in warm glowing terms. So, with the additional bonus of a charming husband she is living happily on Calle Cenizo.

Besides being a successful writer and businesswoman, Mary is a fine cook, and I used her *One-Arm Cookery* book often. As one of her characters, Mrs. Rasmussen, says, "You can stir up most of the dishes with one arm an' hold a beer in the other . . . but if you're lookin' for pink and green whipped cream or a salad made out of a canned pear with a girl's face painted on it, and a head of curly hair made outta cream cheese squoze thru a pastry tube you sure come through the wrong swinging doors!" For most of her food is hearty and substantial.

When we have duck, I very often use Mary's recipe for *Roast Duck with Orange and Guava Sauce.

★

Roast Duck with Orange and Guava Sauce

1 duck, about 4 lbs.
Salt, ginger and pepper
1 whole raw onion
1 cup orange juice
Rind of 1 orange, cut into slivers
1 small jar guava jelly

Sprinkle duck with salt, ginger and pepper, inside and out. Place the peeled raw onion inside of the duck and place duck in a pan in a very hot oven for 20 minutes. Remove and pour off the fat. Reduce heat and finish roasting the duck in a moderate oven, basting frequently with a sauce made of the orange juice, rind, and guava jelly. Be sure that all the white membrane is removed from the orange rind before cutting into slivers with kitchen shears. The duck may be roasted to any stage desired, but should be well done, like most fowl. It will not be dry if the basting is kept up steadily, and should be roasted a full hour after the heat of the oven is reduced.

Also her *Guacamole and her *Salsa Brava:

★

Guacamole

3 large very ripe avocados
2 Tbs. very ripe fresh tomato pulp
1 Tbs. onion juice
1 tsp. garlic vinegar
Salt to taste
Black pepper
1 tsp. chili powder

Rub all through a coarse sieve; serve very cold with hot tortillas. Make the puree into a mound the shape of an old-fashioned sugar loaf. Place the avocado pits on top of it to keep it from discoloring while in the icebox.

★

Salsa Brava (Ferocious Sauce)

8 large dry Mexican chilis, ancho, grueso, or redondo
1 cup boiling water
2 Tbs. Tabasco sauce
1 Tbs. vinegar
Salt

Clean the peppers thoroughly, discard seeds, membrane, and stems, handling only when thoroughly dry. Pour boiling water and salt over them and let stand an hour or two, but do not cook or boil them. Press through the vegetable puree cone. Add Tabasco and vinegar; taste for salt. Serve in a small pottery olla with a wooden spoon for a ladle.

— with which she gives the following suggestion: "Don't hold a lighted match near your face — you'll think you're a flame-thrower if you do!"

I also love to do *Stuffed Broiled Mushrooms.

★

Stuffed Broiled Mushrooms

6 large mushrooms per person
Dry breadcrumbs
Chopped parsley
Chopped chives
Anchovy paste
Butter
Lemon juice
Black pepper
Toast

Clean mushrooms and remove stems. Mix dry breadcrumbs with chopped parsley and chives. Add a very small quantity of anchovy paste, not more than ½ tsp. to six mushrooms. Work into the breadcrumbs along with a little soft butter and lemon juice. Season with pepper. Fill the mushrooms with the crumb mixture and dot the tops with butter. Broil quickly under a medium hot broiler and serve on buttered toast.

In her chapter titled "Something for Your Cavities" everything is great, but I have particularly used *Complexion Candy and *Spiced Pecans.

★

Complexion Candy

1 pkg. (8 oz.) dried figs
1 pkg. (8 oz.) seeded dates
1 Tbs. walnut meats
1 cup seedless raisins
1 Tbs. grated orange rind

Put all ingredients through food chopper, using fine blade. Mix well. Place in square cake pan and flatten. Cut in strips and roll in confectioner's sugar.

★

Spiced Pecans

½ cup light brown sugar
½ cup white sugar
½ tsp. powdered cinnamon
½-inch stick whole cinnamon
¼ tsp. powdered cloves
Pinch of salt
½ cup water
1 cup shelled pecan halves (jumbo)

Mix all ingredients except pecans. Boil until a few drops of syrup harden as soon as dropped in a little ice water. Remove from fire and add nuts. Stir fast until the mixture begins to sugar. Try to coat all the nuts evenly. Pour out on wax paper and break apart into individual nuts when cool. Discard the stick cinnamon.

The bit of Mrs. Rasmussen's philosophy Mary has injected into her book we all might well note: "If we buy ten cents' worth o' somethin' — don't enjoy it an' thrown some of it out — it was extravagant. If it costs two dollars an' we eat every crumb an' lick the dish — it was a bargain!"

Here are two more recipes from Brownsville cooks:

★

Empanadas Dulces

1 qt. canned sweet potatoes, drained
1 qt. canned crushed pineapple
2½ cups sugar
Grated orange and lemon rind

Mix all ingredients; cook and stir constantly till thick. Cool.

PASTRY

2½ cups flour	1 tsp. baking powder
½ tsp. salt	¾ cup shortening
3 Tbs. sugar	4 to 5 Tbs. water

Mix as pie crust. Pull off balls the size of marbles. Roll in circles about the size of a teacup. Prick with fork. Place a heaping tsp. of potato mixture in each and press edges together with fork. Sprinkle with sugar and bake in oven at 350 degrees. This makes 3 dozen Empanadas.

★

Pots de Crème

6 egg yolks	2 cups heavy cream, scalded
½ cup sugar	1 tsp. vanilla extract

Preheat oven to 300 degrees. Beat egg yolks until thick. Beat in sugar; gradually add cream, stirring constantly. Stir in vanilla. Pour into six custard cups and place in a pan of warm water. Bake 15 minutes or until a knife inserted in the middle of the custard comes out clean. Chill.

(A bit of strawberry preserves in the bottom of the cup before pouring in the custard adds for a pleasant little surprise when you get to the bottom. A simple, easy dessert that can be made ahead of time—so delicious!)

THE KING RANCH

If there were to be named an eighth wonder of the world, the King Ranch would spring forward as one of the magnificent marvels of nature. Even if this were to happen, I agree with Tom Lea that no mere facts or statistics could convey the final meaning of this largest ranch in the world. The wonder and marvel lives in the land itself, in the growing grass and the grazing herds. All the beautiful, exciting stories I had heard all my life about this spectacular piece of land in South Texas are true. Only did I begin to catch the real spirit of its beauty when I drove through the big, white gates with the sentry boxes on each side, and started along the winding road that stretched out with the contours of the land.

The ranch headquarters standing grandly on the left farther down the road is perhaps one of the few marks of mankind on the ranch; everything else blends into unmarred landscape. If the walls of this old house could speak, they would tell an unequaled story. Tom Lea relates many of the tales in his books, but his sketches are perhaps more poignant. One room of the house is filled with Lea's drawings and paintings of the ranch. The big house is really like a small hotel. When guests come for the cattle sale it is like a three-day house party; they always look forward to staying in this grand ol' ranch house. When I visited the ranch it was Easter week, and throughout the house were hundreds of tall, blooming Easter lilies in clay pots, large arrangements of bells of Ireland and deep-blue larkspurs grown in the ranch gardens.

In contrast to the old Ranch House is a beautiful sprawling pink brick house where Dick Kleberg and his charming wife, Mary Lewis, and their family live. Dick is the grandson of Captain Richard King, founder of the ranch; Mary Lewis is the daughter of Dr. and Mrs. Z. T. Scott of Austin, and the sister of Zachary Scott. Mary Lewis is a remarkable young woman — calm and efficient. She takes the job of being number one hostess of the ranch in her stride but, in reality, is never casual about her responsibilities. As she and Dick point out, this isn't a showplace full of marvelous wonders, it's primarily a working ranch. To shake hands with Dick, to see him in action, one knows he is a working individual on the ranch. He was, of course, born there and grew up there; in a saddle by the time he was able to sit up. They have four lovely children, three in college and little Scott, whom Mary Lewis refers to as her dividend. Mary Lewis carefully plans the activities of her family, of her own life and of the very active social life there on the ranch. There is a well-seasoned staff at the big house to provide for each meal so that it is a perfect event when it takes place. Beef is always served and also a great deal of wild game in season; wild turkey, plenty of venison, quail and doves. The deer, like the beef, are very well fed and therefore the venison, too, is very fine. They often use the recipe for *Venison Roast of Alice Reynolds, Dick's sister who lives in Austin.

★

Venison Roast

Take meat out of the freezer and soak in water 24 hours. The next day, pour the water off and cover again with water, adding 2 Tbs. vinegar to every 4 cups water, and soak another 24 hours.

The third day, pour off water, wipe the meat off well and score about 1 inch deep all over. Season with lots of salt and pepper and completely cover with butter, pushing it down into the cuts. Top with brown sugar. Pour red wine over the meat to make about an inch of liquid in the pan. Cook very slowly in a 325-degree oven until black. Baste every 15 minutes for the first two or three hours of cooking.

This is the Klebergs' favorite way of cooking quail:

★

Naomi's Superb Quail Supreme

10 quail
Salt and pepper to taste
Flour for frying
1 cup onions
½ cup celery
1 clove garlic
2 green peppers, cut
Worcestershire sauce to taste
1½ cups water

Wash the quail well. Salt and pepper and roll in flour; fry in deep fat until golden brown. Place in roasting pan and pour other seasonings and water over birds. Placc in oven set at 200 degrees and cook three hours. Add more water to make plenty of gravy, if necessary.

The first night the guests arrive for the sale they may enjoy a game dinner; the next night charcoaled steaks; and the last evening, perhaps a large prime rib. Dinner is served in the big, handsome dining room. Here is the complete menu featuring the prime rib:

Fresh Crab au Gratin served in shells
Onion Soup
*Prime Rib carved on a side table and served with * Yorkshire Pudding*
Red wine
Green salad
Green vegetables grown in the ranch vegetable garden
Fresh fruit

The ladies sometimes have their demitasses in one of the parlors and the men continue their conversation with brandy and cigars in another.

★

Yorkshire Pudding (*serves 12*)

1 cup all-purpose flour, sifted
1 tsp. salt
1 Tbs. shortening
1 cup milk
2 eggs, well beaten
¼ cup melted shortening or roast drippings

Sift flour and salt into bowl of electric mixer; cut in 1 Tbs. shortening and cream well. Add milk and eggs, and beat on high speed for 10 minutes. Chill thoroughly in refrigerator. When ready to prepare for serving, place empty popover or muffin tins in oven until very hot. Pour about a tsp. of shortening in each and fill only half full with batter. Bake in a 425-degree preheated oven for 30 minutes. Serve at once.

One night during a sale Mary Lewis had an Italian buffet everybody loved. The dining room was decorated with very tall Italian bottles of wine and baskets of fresh flowers. The menu was:

Prime Rib Santa Gertrudis
Lasagna
** Spinach Strudel*
** Zucchini Salad*
Italian bread, dry wine
Fresh fruit, cheese

★

Spinach Strudel

1 medium onion, chopped
½ cup olive oil
2 lbs. chopped spinach
7 eggs
Salt and pepper
Phyllo sheets (thin Greek pastry)
3 Tbs. olive oil
3 Tbs. butter

Brown chopped onion in oil. Combine with spinach, eggs, salt, and pepper. Grease a shallow baking pan with oil and line with 4 or 5 phyllo sheets. Brush each sheet with mixture of oil and butter (melted) to prevent sticking. If phyllo sheet is not available, use half pastry shell for undercrust (as for pie) and other half for top crust. Put filling over bottom layer, spreading evenly. Cover with remaining sheets or pie crust. Brush top with oil. With point of knife, trace crust in squares. Bake in moderate oven, 350 degrees, for 40 minutes.

★

Zucchini Salad

Slice small zucchini in finger strips. Cook 3 minutes in boiling water, slightly salted. Drain. Coat with garlic dressing and sprinkle with chopped parsley and grated Parmesan cheese.

The dining room opens out onto a large patio and is terraced down to the swimming pool and a playground which has swings and seesaws for the children. There is a pool house furnished with white wrought-iron furniture; often at noonday, hamburgers will be served there for guests. This, of course, is quite informal and light, because everyone looks forward to the lovely dinner in the evening. Dinner is the principal meal, but breakfast is also very hearty, since everyone gets up early to "get on the trail" and see the beauties of the ranch. Whatever the occasion, hot sauce, *Salsa Piquante, is always on the table. The chili pequins (very small peppers) are grown in abundance and put with a pod of garlic, chopped onions and tomatoes mashed in a mocajete, which is a little rock piston sort of thing similar to a mortar that the Mexicans use a great deal to make guacamole and chili sauce, sometimes referred to as the Mexican Mixmaster. This sauce is put on eggs, vegetables, or meats.

The day I was at the ranch, Javiel, a faithful worker who was also born and raised on the ranch, drove Mary Lewis, Mrs. Scott, little Scott and me about twenty miles to a camp house where the cowboys working in that section would be having lunch from the chuck wagon. By King Ranch standards, this is a very short distance to go for lunch. On the way, we passed by one of the game preserves, and Mary Lewis told me more about the Santa Gertrudis cattle. These cattle originated at the King Ranch from tedious cross-breeding of the shorthorn or Hereford blood with the Brahman blood. The new breed resulted from the necessity of finding a beef-type animal that was better suited to the climate and range conditions of South Texas. The cattle are a deep, mellow red color and all wear the swinging W brand used at the King Ranch. When we arrived at the camp house, the chuck wagon was there; it is no longer a wagon but a well equipped pick-up truck, furnished with stainless steel utensils which I'm sure weren't on the original chuck wagons. The cowboys were waiting on the porch when we drove up. This, I understand, was a regular everyday dinner. I don't know of anything that could have been added if the Queen of England had been expected. We had rib roast, cooked over the coals; a big heavy beef, which is always superb; and the most delicious beef stew. You can always depend on the good beef from the Santa Gertrudis, fed and fattened so scientifically. I asked the cook what made this stew so delicious, and much to our amazement he said he added a little mayonnaise just before he took it off the fire! They also served barbecued ham. The hogs on the ranch run wild and are rather thin and lean. The hams had been cured and smoked at one of the smokehouses and were also extra special in flavor. We also had sausage, Mexican rice and the inevitable ranch-style beans cooked in a heavy iron pot. Little Scott and I both could have made the meal on the *Camp Bread. I was so fascinated by this bread cooked over an open fire in a Dutch oven I asked Mary Lewis if I could get the recipe. Everyone who eats it asks her for the recipe, so she said she had written it down as close as she could: the cook "cooks by gum and by gosh!" But she measured the ingredients as the cook picked them up by the handfuls. Bill Koock and I tried this recipe in our Dutch oven and it was heavenly!

★

Camp Bread

10 cups flour
3 tsp. salt
4 tsp. black pepper
2 tsp. sugar
5 Tbs. lard and add:
4¼ cups water (Mary uses ¼ cup evaporated milk)

Sift and mix ingredients together. Have water lukewarm (dough is rather dry). Allow dough to sit 15 or 20 minutes before cooking. Roll out in thin rounds and cook in a hot greased skillet, pricking with a fork and turning.

On the way back to the house, Mary Lewis, Scott and Javiel told us about different grasses they grow there, and the seasons for each. There is also a great variety of wildflowers, which Scott can readily identify. All of a sudden, Javiel stopped the station wagon and said, "Pardon *un momento*, let me get that rattlesnake." Now as long as I have lived in Texas, I don't think I had ever seen a rattlesnake killed. Javiel has killed hundreds in his time, for down in South Texas they are plentiful. He got out, pulled off a mesquite branch, more like a big switch, and started switching the big rattlesnake.

I hastily said, "Javiel, you'll never kill him with that," me telling him, you know! The snake's tongue was going back and forth full speed, and his rattlers were up high, rattling like mad, but Javiel just kept switching it with the mesquite limb. Finally he whipped the snake down, and then finished him off by putting the heel of his heavy boot on the back of the ol' boy's subdued head, pulled off the rattles, and handed them to me.

The regular ranch staff gets pretty swamped taking care of "routine business" when the sale is in progress. So often Mary Lewis has to call on Tillford Collins and Joe Stivers from San Antonio to give a hand. They are so well qualified, Tillford being a very talented florist and decorator and Stivers quite an expert on fabulous food. Together they put on parties of true King Ranch quality and tradition, such as the one when Sally Kleberg made her debut.

It was one of the most colorful parties Dick and Mary Lewis have ever given. Friends came from all over the country. The party was held at the main house, on the terrace, and out on the grounds. What a gay fiesta! The old cannons on each side of the steps were shooting out red and orange plumes like fire and were manned by life-size papier-mâché soldiers in the old Mexican Army uniforms. Brightly colored lanterns with streamers and amusing piñatas hung from the trees. The bougainvillaea and hibiscus were in full bloom, and an esplanade of Mexican flowers and birds was along the walkways. A clear plastic canopy covered the long terrace where the dancing took place and was festooned with thousands of balloons and green garlands. Barrels of cold beer stood under the ancient palm trees, a gaily painted donkey cart held the hot tamales, and there was a clay pot of fire underneath the metal bottom of the cart to keep the tamales hot.

The dining room was also a blaze of splendor and color. A brilliant rose sateen cloth with jauntily deep scallops around the borders covered the table, which was centered with arrangements of tissue paper poppies in red, pinks, orange and purple intermingled with a variety of colored votive lights. The food was delicious and abundant. The menu:

** Turkey Mole*
Shrimp on ice
Charcoaled sirloin strip carved at the table
Hot Tamales
Chili con Queso with Tostados
Guacamole
Relish tray
Dulce Mexicana

★

Turkey or Chicken Mole

There are thousands of interpretations of Turkey or Chicken Mole. I like this one, as it does not have the usual sweet chocolate or cinnamon seasoning. However, it can be added if this taste is preferred. Serves 6.

¾ cup cornmeal
1 cup milk
1 small green pepper (chopped fine)
1 clove garlic, minced
½ tsp. salt
¼ cup cooking oil
1 cup chopped green olives
1 4-oz. can of tomato sauce

Soak cornmeal in milk for one hour. Add remaining ingredients and mix well. Put in greased loaf pan and bake 35 minutes. Then serve with Chicken Mole Sauce.

CHICKEN MOLE SAUCE

3- to 4-lb. chicken (turkey may be used if you are making a large quantity)
Salt, pepper
½ cup raisins
½ cup pecans
½ cup peanuts
3 Tbs. shortening or butter
1 small can (2 oz.) Mexican mole powder

Cut up chicken as for frying. Simmer in enough water to cover until tender. Season with salt and pepper. Simmer until about half done and then turn off fire.

Sauté in 3 Tbs. shortening, separately, raisins, then pecans and peanuts. Remove from pan and chop fine. Then mash with approximately 1 cup chicken stock to make a paste, and add the mole powder. Pour into pot with chicken and broth and cook together very slowly until chicken is done and sauce is thick. Serve over the cornmeal loaf above. It is also delicious served on Mexican Rice.

Through the years, ever since Captain King made this first purchase of land, it has been visited by many members of royalty, heads of state, world celebrities, other cattlemen and ranchers; but whoever it has been, they all look back on their visit at the King Ranch as a most privileged experience long to be remembered. Will Rogers, who used to visit the ranch frequently, said that the hospitality there was as big as the ranch, and "it's a million and a half acres!"

AMARILLO

We have all been brought up on stories from the "Panhandle," the northern part of Texas that is truly the shape and just as flat as the handle of an old pot iron skillet. Perhaps the most famous tale is the myth that in winter there is nothing between Amarillo and the North Pole but a barbed wire fence — very often the fence gets blown down.

Somehow none of the trips we had made through Texas had ever taken us to the Panhandle; we were always turning up in the middle of the skillet, so to speak. Five hundred miles from Austin to Amarillo is a fer piece, unless, of course, there is some special occasion. Indeed such an opportunity arose when our oldest son, Ken, announced that he and Jane were to be married June 22, at her home in Amarillo! This caused a great flurry of excitement in our household. We held the traditional Sunday morning brunch to make the announcement to all of our family. There were twenty-four of us seated around the long family dining table. We were fortunate to have as guests Jane's parents, Judge and Mrs. Carl Periman. They had come down primarily to attend Jane's graduation at Texas University and to hear President Lyndon B. Johnson give the address — but academic "triumph" soon became of secondary interest. At breakfast, we tried to keep the conversation centered around the young prospective bride and groom, drinking toasts intermittently with *Milk Punch, followed by this menu:

** Smoked Pork Chops and Baked Apple Rings*
** Cheese Soufflé*
Hot Biscuits
Wild Plum Jelly
Fig and Peach Preserves
Coffee
** Patricia's Coffee Cake*

★

Milk Punch

2 cups vanilla ice cream
1 cup sweet milk
½ cup Bourbon
¼ cup white rum
1 jigger dry brandy
Nutmeg

In a blender mix and blend the ingredients 5 or 6 seconds and pour into a cold pitcher. Continue until you have desired amount. Serve in Old-Fashioned glasses with a dash of nutmeg on top.

★

Smoked Pork Chops and Baked Apple Rings

Pork chops 1 inch thick
Lawry's seasoned salt
Winesap cooking apples
Butter
Brown sugar
½ cup rosé wine
¼ cup water
Chopped parsley

In a heavy skillet, brown chops lightly on each side. Place in a heavy baking pan and season with a little Lawry salt. Place thick-sliced Winesap apples around the edge of the pan and cover. Cook at 350 degrees for 30 minutes. Remove apple slices to a lightly buttered cookie sheet; brush with butter, sprinkle with brown sugar and return to the oven for about 5 minutes. To the chops add the wine and water and return them to the oven for 5 minutes. Place chops on the center of a hot platter and arrange apple rings, slightly overlapping, around the chops. Cook down water and wine and drippings from the chops just a little and pour over chops. Sprinkle with chopped parsley.

★

Never-Fail-or-Fall Cheese Soufflé

I usually use this recipe of Helen Corbitt's.

3 Tbs. butter
¼ cup flour
⅞ cup milk
1 tsp. salt
Dash of cayenne pepper
1 tsp. prepared mustard
2 drops Worcestershire sauce
1 packed cup grated American cheese
6 eggs

Make a cream sauce by melting the butter and blending in the flour; cook until it bubbles. Add the milk, salt, cayenne, mustard and Worcestershire sauce and bring to a boil, stirring constantly. Boil 1 minute: time it! Remove from heat and cool slightly. Add the cheese. Beat the egg yolks until thick and add the cheese mixture, stirring constantly. Beat the egg whites until stiff. Fold into the cheese mixture carefully; pour into a well-buttered baking dish (three-fourths full). Bake at 300 degrees in a hot-water bath for 2 hours, or until a silver knife inserted into the center comes out clean. This soufflé keeps a day in the icebox after baking, so it can be left over successfully.

I am so proud of my family additions in terms of in-laws. Bill's wife, Patricia, is a marvel getting the baby ready to come for a visit to Austin and then to find time to make her mother's *Coffee Cake to bring along too! It looks like a pretty picture.

★

Coffee Cake

⅓ cup sugar
¾ cup shortening
1 tsp. salt
1 cup scalded milk

Dissolve sugar, shortening and salt in hot milk and cool. When cool, combine with:

2 oz. (1 cake) yeast
2 Tbs. warm water

Add to milk-yeast mixture:

1 tsp. sugar
2 beaten eggs
3½ cups flour

Turn into greased bowl. Cover bowl and chill in refrigerator for one hour. Remove, knead lightly for a few minutes; let dough rest for approximately five minutes. Divide dough in half; flatten ball of dough and roll out to form a long narrow sheet about 6 inches wide and ¼ inch thick.

FILLING

¼ stick (1 oz.) butter
Cinnamon
Sugar
¼ cup brown sugar
¼ cup slivered almonds or chopped pecans

Spread with melted butter. Sprinkle with sugar-cinnamon mixture and brown sugar; add almonds or pecans. Roll up to make a long slender roll; seal edge by pressing firmly. Twist roll; tuck ends under to keep from untwisting. Cut ¾ through ring with scissors every 4 to 5 inches. Cover; let rise for about 1 hour. Bake at 350 degrees for 30 to 40 minutes. When done and still warm, spread with powdered sugar icing.

ICING

1 cup powdered sugar
½ stick butter
Enough cream or milk to make smooth icing
Cherries and nuts to garnish

This tea ring may be prepared well in advance, frozen, covered with foil. When ready for use, heat in 400-degree oven for 45 minutes. Add the icing after heating.

Soon it was evident that our family was just about as excited over getting to go to Amarillo as we were with the wedding! The Perimans asked us to come as early as possible since there would be at least a week of prenuptial festivities. Excitement grew when the announcement with Jane's picture appeared in the papers. Our Amarillo friends all wrote with invitations for Chester and me or any of the children to stay in their homes and asked might they help. Amarillo hospitality was shining through the five hundred miles 'tween us. Friends of the Perimans insisted on "putting up" out-of-town guests, bridesmaids . . . and Koocks. The red carpet was rolled out and it was hard to tell who were the honorees.

Most of us have a great uncle older than this young city's seventy-seven years! Our arrival was just as delightful as that of the early cattle herders as they circled their thirsty steers around Wild Horse Lake and the "Yellow Creek" for water. The name Amarillo Creek goes back to Spanish days. It became the origin of the town's name, meaning yellow, the color of the subsoil in its channel. In early days during the 1890's, most of the houses were painted yellow to commemorate the name. Also, in those times, it was reported that a steer could be raised on the open range for the cost of a chicken.

The parties for the big event were numerous and gay! The day before the wedding, Mrs. Periman invited our whole flock over to have lunch at her house. Her neighbors and other friends had brought over a beautiful cold buffet. The salads were especially delicious, and when Ken and Jane went back for seconds, I knew I would have to get the recipes, if not for myself, for them!

★

Chicken or Turkey Loaf (*serves 20*)

6-lb. hen (or 2 canned 3-lb. hens)
1 cup blanched almonds
1½ cups celery, chopped fine
1 large can pimentos, chopped
Chopped parsley
Salt and pepper to taste
2 envelopes plain gelatine
1 cup mayonnaise
Lemon juice

Boil and then grind the chicken with almonds, celery, pimentos, parsley and salt and pepper. Heat 4 cups of broth and add gelatine soaked in cold broth or water. When cool, add other ingredients with mayonnaise and a little lemon juice. Mold and congeal.

★

Cucumber Salad

1 pkg. lime-flavored gelatine
1 pkg. lemon-flavored gelatine
1½ cups hot water
2 to 3 tsp. lemon juice
1½ to 2 fairly large cucumbers (grind or chop fine and drain)
1 large onion (grated or ground)
1 pt. cottage cheese (drained)
2 cups mayonnaise
Sugar to taste
Salt and pepper to taste
1 cup slivered almonds

Mix all and jell. Serves 15.

For dessert, Mrs. Periman served us homemade ice cream with strawberries, and the Judge's favorite:

★

Oatmeal Cookies

1 cup sugar
1 cup shortening
3 eggs
2 cups flour
2 cups oatmeal
½ tsp. each: allspice, cloves, nutmeg, soda
1 tsp. cinnamon
1 cup raisins, chopped or whole
½ cup dates, chopped
½ cup nuts, chopped
6 Tbs. raisin juice (boil raisins in water to cover 5 minutes for juice)

Cream sugar and shortening; add eggs one by one and continue beating. Sift all dry ingredients and add to shortening mixture. Simmer raisins 5 minutes; retain juice. Chop raisins, dates and nuts; dredge with flour and add to mixture. Drop by teaspoonfuls on greased cookie sheet. Bake 15 to 20 minutes at 350 degrees.

We stayed for a few days after the wedding to "rest up," but most of our intended naps were replaced with more Amarillo hospitality. Much to my surprise, I found my friend Frances Bauman's backyard next to the Perimans'. She had called over the fence offering a room to the prospective groom so he could be closer to his bride, and also invited him to have breakfast the morning of the big day. Ken told her he was too nervous to eat, but strangely enough, he managed to get down three stacks of Frances's pancakes, and later asked me to be sure and get her recipe! This recipe belonged to Frances's grandmother, Mrs. Carl Sundberg of Austin. For the best results, Frances says you must be willing to chance the "old-fashioned" method of using a teacup and a silver teaspoon, like her grandmother did.

★

Pancake Recipe

1 cup flour (teacup)
½ tsp. salt
2 eggs (slightly beaten)
1½ cups milk

Mix flour and salt with a fork. Add eggs and milk and stir well. Fry on a hot skillet with a little shortening.

Frances's mother-in-law, Christine Bauman, is reputedly one of the most gracious hostesses in Amarillo. Christine had us all over for dinner and we agreed that her reputation as a fine cook was well justified. She served us:

Grapefruit and Avocado Salad
Baked Rice
Green Peas
Hot Rolls
* *Shrimp with Sour Cream*
* *Fudge "to make Amarillo famous"*

★

Shrimp with Sour Cream

5 lbs. shrimp
10 Tbs. chopped onion
1¼ cups butter
2½ lbs. fresh mushrooms
5 Tbs. flour
2½ tsp. salt
Freshly ground pepper
15 Tbs. sherry
7½ cups sour cream

Sauté shrimp and onion in butter until shrimp is pink. (If canned or frozen shrimps are used, sauté onion till transparent and add shrimp to warm through.) Add mushrooms and cook 5 minutes. Sprinkle with flour, salt and pepper. Add sherry and sour cream. Cook over low heat till hot. Serve with rice.

★

Fudge

3 cups sugar
1 tsp. salt
3 Tbs. cocoa
1½ cups half and half cream
1 tsp. vanilla
2 Tbs. butter
2 cups pecans

Before cooking, mix thoroughly sugar, salt, cocoa, half and half. Cook in a heavy skillet until a soft ball is formed when dropped in cold water. Add vanilla, butter and pecans and beat a long time. Set aside and let cool for the finger test (touch it without burning the finger). Pour in a buttered pan and cut in squares.

Christine and her husband, Rudy, both love to cook. Christine manages the food cooked inside, and Rudy takes charge of all outdoor cooking. Part of the "inside" job includes a special treat for her grandchildren. When the grandchildren come over, Christine makes *Taffy so they may enjoy an old-fashioned taffy pull. The night we were there the phone rang, and on the other end of the line a small, sweet voice asked, "Grandmother, may we come see you 'morrow?"

★

Salt-Water Taffy for Grandchildren

2 cups sugar
1 pinch salt
¾ cup water
¼ cup vinegar
Hunk of butter (⅛ lb.)
½ tsp. vanilla

Stir well and cook sugar, salt, water and vinegar until a firm (not hard) ball forms when dropped in cold water. Put the hunk of butter and vanilla in the center of each of 2 buttered platters. Work taffy in this and give pieces to the little waiting hands. Let them pull on it until the candy turns white, providing they have "minded" their grandmother and washed their hands!

Here are some additional recipes for which Christine is highly recommended:

★

Baked Chicken and Dumplings

DUMPLINGS

1 cup milk
1 egg-size hunk of butter
1 pinch of salt
1 cup flour
5 eggs

CHICKEN

6-lb. hen
Flour
3 hard-boiled eggs (chopped)
1 pkg. frozen peas

In a pot, boil the hen and cut bite-sized. Make quite a bit of gravy with the stock, adding flour to thicken. Add eggs and peas and cook while making dumplings.

For dumplings: heat to boiling point milk, butter and salt. As the mixture starts to boil, add flour and whip until stiff. Add 1 egg, beaten, continue to whip and whip. Repeat for remaining eggs, adding one at a time. Drop by teaspoonfuls into chicken-and-gravy mixture. Bake in a hot oven (350 degrees) until brown.

★

Rolled Asparagus Sandwiches

1 can green asparagus spears
1 bottle French dressing
Cottage cheese
Mayonnaise
1 clove garlic
Onion juice
Salt
Paprika
1 loaf fresh, thin-sliced sandwich bread
Melted butter

Marinate asparagus in French dressing for 20 minutes. Put cottage cheese, a small amount of mayonnaise, garlic, onion juice, salt and paprika in blender for 5 minutes. Cut crusts from bread and place 3 asparagus spears in center of each slice, brush with butter on each side, spread generously with cottage cheese mixture and roll up firmly; pin with a toothpick. Wrap in foil and refrigerate overnight. When ready to serve, brown on all sides in 350-degree oven.

This is such a wonderful luncheon dish — with Shrimp Salad it makes an entire meal!

We were the house guests of Ed and Lois Shaw. I met Lois years ago in Phoenix at the National Symphony League meeting. We have continued our friendship through the years, but this was my first visit. Lois is one of those miraculous persons who cook painlessly. She plans everything in advance and does quite a bit for the freezer. As a result, she can pull a meal out at the ring of the doorbell! While it is thawing, Lois will be making an appearance, unruffled and lovely, at a morning coffee, attending a committee meeting, or teaching her classes in antiquing furniture! One evening for dessert she served a *Dobosch Torte that I would have bet money was flown in from Bavaria, but this was her secret:

★

Lois Shaw's Mock Dobosch Torte

1 frozen all-butter pound cake
2 4-oz. pkgs. German sweet chocolate
¼ cup brewed coffee
2 Tbs. Cognac
1½ cups heavy cream

With serrated knife, while cake is still frozen, cut the cake lengthwise into 6 layers. Melt the chocolate in the coffee. Mix until very smooth; then stir in Cognac. Cool. Whip the cream and fold in the chocolate mix. Spread between the layers; put cake together and cover tops and sides with remaining chocolate mixture. Chill well before serving.

A hearty dish Lois can pull out of the freezer to have ready for her sons Hoot and Steve when they come in from the lake is a very delicious *Lasagna.

★

Lasagna Napoli

1 medium onion (chopped fine)
1 clove minced garlic
2 Tbs. olive oil or salad oil
1 lb. trimmed ground chuck
1 3-oz. can sliced mushrooms
1 8-oz. can tomato sauce
1 3-oz. can tomato paste
2 tsp. salt
1 tsp. oregano
¾ cup water
2 eggs
1 pkg. frozen chopped spinach, thawed
1 cup cream style cottage cheese, drained
½ cup Parmesan cheese, grated
1 12-oz. pkg. lasagna cooked in boiling salt water and drained
1 8-oz. pkg. American cheese, cut in strips

In medium-sized skillet, lightly brown onion and garlic in 1 Tbs. oil. Add chuck and brown. Blend in mushrooms and mushroom liquid. Add tomato sauce and paste, 1 tsp. salt, oregano and water. Simmer 15 minutes. Meanwhile, mix 1 egg with spinach, cottage cheese, Parmesan cheese, 1 Tbs. oil and 1 tsp. salt. Beat second egg slightly and toss with lasagna. Pour one-half sauce in 9- by 12-inch baking dish and cover with layer of ½ lasagna. Spread spinach mixture over lasagna. Repeat. Cover and bake in moderate oven, 350 degrees, for 45 minutes. Remove cover and place cheese strips on top and bake for 15 more minutes.

We drove to the beautiful Weymouth Ranch on the outskirts of town for a visit with Chanslor and Fanny Fern Weymouth. Part of their land is of the old XIT Ranch and is the "beauty spot" of the Panhandle. The grant for the original XIT Ranch was in payment for granite to build the Texas State Capitol Building. The stately ranch house sets back in the large mesquite and cottonwood trees. Under the shade of these tress on the grounds near the house, once each year the Weymouths hold a Communion Service for members of the family, the people who live on the ranch and members from different parishes of the towns nearby. The outdoor service is most impressive in the quiet countryside. Little activity is planned in order not to detract from the quiet reverence created there. The Weymouths are hosts for many other occasions, one of the most delightful ones being the annual Junior League Garden Club Picnic. Visiting ranchers help Chanslor carve and serve the barbecue after he has personally supervised its cooking. A half-carcass of beef is cooked over the coals in a long wide pit. The traditional barbecue menu is served with all the trimmings, but the extra-special and unique trim is a *Squash Casserole.

★

Weymouth Ranch Squash and Cheese Casserole

4 lbs. yellow squash
2 lbs. zucchini squash
1 large onion
2 Tbs. sugar
1 tsp. salt
2 cups water
1 cup New York cheese (grated)
1 cup Velveeta cheese (grated)
1 cup half and half cream
1 stick butter

Slice squash; peel and chop onion. Add sugar, salt and water and simmer until tender, about 20 minutes. Drain and mash. Make 4 layers squash and mixed cheeses in buttered casserole. Dot with butter. Pour half and half cream over the top and cook for 15 minutes at 300 degrees.

Another favorite at the ranch is the wonderful pancake recipe of Fanny Fern's sister, Mary Fain.

★

Silver Dollar Pancake Recipe

1 egg	1½ tsp. sugar
2 cups buttermilk	1 heaping tsp. baking powder
1 tsp. soda	2 Tbs. bacon fat
1 tsp. salt	2½ cups flour (approx.)

Beat egg in buttermilk. Add soda, salt, sugar and baking powder, and mix thoroughly. Fry bacon for breakfast and add 2 Tbs. hot grease to this batter. Sift enough flour in to make the batter fluffy.

One afternoon I was privileged to have "high tea" with Immie Taylor. Out on their shady brick terrace by the pool, she served a light fruit bread and fresh plum jelly with piping hot spiced tea and nippy cheese dip.

Immie's husband, Jay, is an independent oil operator and rancher who loves to have parties as much as Immie just as long as beef is on the menu. Jay has done much work with and for the cattle industry, and often he brings home dinner guests from all parts of the world. One night the Taylors had as a guest a Welshman who was collaborating with Jay on some cattle business. With cocktails, Immie served guacamole dip with Fritos. The Welshman was unaccustomed to the Texas "dip" idea, but finally he decided to step in line and try a Frito with the guacamole. He took one bite and quickly spat it out! Immie was saved, however, when he proceeded to serve his plate generously from the buffet, and polished it off with compliments and Welsh praise!

On one end of the table:

Rib Eye of Beef, cooked pink, sliced thin
** Cattle King Potatoes*
** Eggplant Casserole*
** Green Tomato Relish*
** Whole Wheat Biscuits*

On the other end of the table:

Large Roasted Turkey
** Rice Pilaf*
*Vine-ripened tomatoes with * Crisp Onion Rings*
Chocolate Potato Cake
Hazel's Cake

★

Cattle King Potatoes

3 lbs. Idaho potatoes
Garlic clove
⅓ cup butter
2 egg yolks, beaten
½ cup cream
Salt and pepper to taste
½ lb. sliced mushrooms, sautéed
¼ cup minced parsley

Peel potatoes and boil with salt and garlic clove until tender. Remove garlic, drain and mash well with butter. Add egg yolks, cream, more salt if needed, pepper, mushrooms and parsley. Pour into a baking dish and brown in the oven at 375 degrees about 20 minutes. This can be made ahead and reheated at the last minute.

Eggplant Casserole

Everyone wonders what this is, and no one guesses right!

1 medium-sized eggplant
1 cup fine crumbs (unsalted soda crackers)
½ stick butter
½ cup or more light cream
Salt, freshly ground black pepper

Peel eggplant and cut into small cubes. Soak cubes in cold salted water for at least one hour. Drain and put in saucepan with enough boiling water to cover. Simmer until very tender and mash with a fork. Add ¾ cup cracker crumbs, butter, cream, salt and pepper to taste. The mixture should be soft and fluffy. Place in a baking dish, sprinkle with remaining crumbs and dot generously with butter. Bake in 350-degree oven until golden brown.

★

Green Tomato Relish

2 cups salt
½ bushel green tomatoes, chopped
1 dozen green peppers, chopped
24 large onions, chopped
2 heads cabbage, chopped
1 2-oz. box celery seed
1 2-oz. box black pepper
1 2-oz. box white mustard seed
2 cups brown sugar
1 gallon cider vinegar
1 Tbs. each cinnamon, allspice

Sprinkle salt through mixture of tomatoes, peppers, onions and cabbage and let stand overnight. The next morning, drain through a flour sack and press as dry as possible. Season with remaining ingredients. Divide into several pans and cook on top of the stove about 45 minutes. This should make 12 quarts.

★

Whole Wheat Biscuits

Use regular biscuit recipe, only use half whole wheat or graham flour. Make large and thin and cook in small quantities so as to come out piping hot.

★

Rice Pilaf

2 cups rice
⅔ stick butter
4 cups chicken stock
¾ cup carrots (chopped)
¾ cup celery, finely chopped
¾ cup parsley, chopped
½ cup green onions, chopped
1 cup almonds, chopped

Place casserole in oven to have hot before setting rice in it. Sauté rice in butter about 5 minutes or until delicately brown. Pour in hot casserole and cover with boiling hot chicken stock. (If not highly seasoned, add 1 Tbs. chicken concentrate.) Cover and bake in 375-degree oven for 30 minutes. Remove from oven and add remaining ingredients. Mix well with a fork, cover and bake another 30 minutes.

★

Crisp Onion Rings

Onions
Chopped parsley

Slice desired amount of onions very thin. Cover with boiling water and let stand 3 to 4 minutes before draining. Place in a quart jar with the lid screwed tight. To serve, sprinkle with chopped parsley. These will stay crisp and are so handy to have on hand.

★

Cinnamon Cookies

1 cup butter
1 cup sugar
2 eggs
3 cups flour
1 cup seeded raisins
1 tsp. soda
5 Tbs. raisin water
1 tsp. cinnamon
1 tsp. vanilla
1 cup chopped nuts

Cream butter with sugar. Add eggs, flour, and raisins (which have been cooked about 10 minutes). Add soda, dissolved in raisin water, cinnamon, vanilla and chopped nuts. Drop by teaspoonfuls on buttered baking sheet. Bake at 300 degrees for 20 minutes.

★

Delaware Crybabies

1 cup brown sugar
1 cup melted shortening
1 cup molasses
2 well-beaten eggs
4 cups sifted flour
½ tsp. salt
2 tsp. soda
1 cup boiling water
1 tsp. cinnamon
1 tsp. nutmeg
1 tsp. vanilla
Nuts (optional)

Mix together brown sugar and melted shortening. Stir in molasses and eggs. Sift flour with salt. Dissolve soda in boiling water and add to first mixture alternately with second mixture. Lastly, add cinnamon, nutmeg and vanilla; nuts if you wish. Cook 20 minutes in 300-degree oven. Makes approximately 12 dozen.

Immie is active in her own particular, feminine "business." She told me that in Amarillo, the men, in their spare time, play bridge; and the women, in their financial endeavors, play poker! For her poker club that day she served Shrimp Salad. The girls were wondering what made it taste so special. Immie simply adds toasted Ritz cracker crumbs when she tosses it, sprinkling some on top, too. It is surely good! Immie taught her daughters to cook one or two things to "fall back on," such as baking a ham . . . what's more versatile? One of the most delicious by-products is *Ham Spaghetti, and Penny's, Jane's and Sally's young friends have all asked for this recipe:

★

Ham Spaghetti

1 stick butter
2 cans mushrooms, drained
1 minced garlic clove
2 Tbs. flour
½ lb. cheddar cheese, diced
2 cups milk
2 lbs. diced cooked ham
1 No. 2 can tomatoes, or 6 fresh tomatoes, peeled and quartered
16 oz. spaghetti

Melt butter and in it sauté mushrooms and garlic. Add, slowly, flour, cheese and milk. Add ham and tomatoes. Add this to spaghetti, which has cooked for only a few minutes and is well drained. Heat and serve.

A very special favorite dessert of all the Taylors is Lemon Lotus Cream served in cold cantaloupe.

★

Lemon Lotus Cream

4 lemons
2 cups sugar
4 cups (2 pts.) medium cream
2 cups milk

Trim off and discard the ends of the lemons. Cut one lemon into thin slices. Remove the seeds from the slices and cut slices in half, resembling half moons. Squeeze the remaining three lemons and combine the juice with the sugar in a mixing bowl. Add the lemon slices and refrigerate 1 or 2 hours, preferably overnight. Stir until all the sugar is dissolved. Combine the cream and milk in the churn of an ice cream freezer, after having chilled thoroughly in refrigerator. When very cold, add lemon and sugar mixture to the cold cream mixture and freeze according to standard directions. Serve this and see your friends go wild!

The Taylor family has many unique and fascinating traditions. On New Year's Day, Immie boils silver dollars (to kill germs) and places one at each place for good luck. Circling the Birthday Cake with English ivy is her symbol for good health and prosperity, something the Taylors surely have and share abundantly!

We were sitting in the Amarillo Club having lunch one day with Babette Green and Toinette Seay discussing recipes when a bright-eyed boy passing by the table said, "Lady, if you want a recipe to make everybody sit up and take notice, let me tell you how I barbecue my turkeys!" Well, he told us in great length. When I got home, Ken and I decided to give it a try. It has now become a big hit number! It's so easy to do and perfectly delightful to eat! Of course, everybody tried to figure out what kind of dressing that was!

★

John Best, Jr.'s, Barbecued Turkey Stuffed with Hot Tamales

Take a young turkey, 6 to 8 lbs., and wash and dry. Fill the cavity with hot tamales (remove shucks first). I used 3 dozen. Then pin the turkey closed. Put this on a spit and turn slowly over low heat, brushing regularly with your favorite barbecue sauce. It takes about 3 to 4 hours cooking. This is a real treat and a "surprise" for your guest and yourself.

Somewhere in between hops, we stopped by to meet Mrs. John Fullingham and to see her beautiful house. She gave me this quick good dessert; Amy has made it several times (it only takes five minutes!) and gets thanked heartily for it each time.

★

Cobbler Pie

¼ lb. butter
2 tsp. baking powder
Pinch salt
1 cup sugar
¾ cup milk
3 to 4 cups fruit
1 cup flour

Melt butter in large casserole. Mix rest of ingredients except fruit and beat well. Pour into melted butter. Pour fruit over batter. Bake 45 minutes in moderate oven, 350 degrees.

Someone asked me if I had ever eaten Vinegar Pie, and I was quick to say I never had and it was fine with me if I never did — sounds terrible! Well it just goes to show we never know until we try! There are lots of apples grown in the Panhandle, and in the early days, folks made their own apple vinegar. Citrus fruits were very hard to come by, maybe a few oranges around Christmas, but lemons, never. So these ingenious people used apple cider vinegar instead of lemon juice, and this pie tastes very much like a lemon meringue pie, but more subtle in flavor. This and Wild Plum Cobbler were two of the most popular desserts on the plains!

★

Vinegar Pie

2 cups boiling water

Add slowly, stirring constantly:

¼ cup cider vinegar
1 cup sugar
3 Tbs. flour
3 egg yolks, added separately

Cook in double boiler until done. Put in pastry shell and cover with this meringue:

3 egg whites, put in separately
1 tsp. lemon flavoring
⅓ tsp. salt
3 Tbs. sugar

Here it was the end of June. We were visiting the Lee Bivinses' home and being invited to their annual Christmas Open House. From all I heard it would surely merit any distance of travel to attend. Lee and Betty Bivins have continued a Christmas night tradition started by their parents, when a few of their friends would come over to "pick the turkey bones." Then it was a very informal, sit-around-the-table affair. When the group began to increase and the turkey disappear quicker, Lee originated a supplement, his present-day specialty, a marvelous chili. It wasn't long before generations began to expand until finally the traditional turkey-picking turned into an elaborate open house, "featuring" Lee's chili.

★

Lee's Chili

½ lb. beef suet
½ lb. lamb suet
6 medium onions, chopped
Flour
6 lbs. beef round steak, cut coarsely
2 lbs. lean pork, cut coarsely
Salt and pepper
4 to 6 cups brown beans

Melt suet thoroughly in large skillet or two skillets. Flour onions lightly; put in skillet to cook until transparent. Do not brown. Flour meat lightly, add salt and pepper. Add to skillet and simmer until brown. This requires much stirring to avoid hard browning. Butter may be added to avoid sticking. When done, combine in large skillet or pan with 4 to 6 cups brown beans, which have been cooked half done with salt pork or suet. Add:

2 cans tomatoes
4 cloves garlic
4 Tbs. cumin seed tied securely in cloth bag
¾ cup chili powder mixed well with water

Fill kettle with water. Add:

Cayenne pepper
Black pepper
Tabasco sauce
Salt

Betty has professional talent in decorating her beautiful English mansion–type home for the holidays. Garlands of fresh spruce are dropped over doors and mantels. A lovely Madonna in a Della Robbia wreath is over one of the mantels, which is banked with fresh holly. Choir boys in red cassocks stand up the stairway holding candles. It is so festive and tastefully done that this occasion makes the Christmas season one to be remembered and to look forward to by all who attend the party. Lee looks after the bar and Betty takes care of the large selection of food. People who live on the Bivins ranch, such as the foreman's wife, bring a variety of delicious cakes, including fruitcakes, layer cakes and this wonderful

★

Orange Pound Cake

- 1 cup butter
- 2 cups sugar
- 4 eggs
- 1 cup buttermilk
- ½ tsp. soda
- ½ tsp. salt
- 3 cups flour
- 2 tsp. vanilla
- 1 cup fresh orange juice
- 1 cup sugar

Mix and bake at 350 degrees for about 45 minutes. When cake is done take out of pan and pour mixture of 1 cup orange juice and 1 cup sugar over it. Let it cool. This does keep the cake nice and moist.

There is also a vast assortment of cookies — this one seemed so original, and Betty says it is very popular.

★

Carrot Cookies

- 1½ cups salad oil
- 2 cups flour
- 2 cups sugar
- 3 cups grated carrots
- ½ cup chopped nuts
- 1 tsp. salt
- 4 eggs
- 2 tsp. soda
- 2 tsp. cinnamon

Mix and bake in deep cookie pan at 300 degrees for 30 minutes. Ice with the following in pan and cut into 1½-inch squares. This freezes well in pan before being cut.

ICING

- 2½ cups powdered sugar
- 8 oz. cream cheese
- ½ stick butter
- 2 tsp. vanilla
- 1 cup finely chopped nuts

Lee makes four hundred to five hundred pounds of sausage every year and presents it for gifts. Wonder how one gets on his list!

The chili takes an important place on the oval buffet at the big bay window in the dining room. It is served from a huge silver tureen into chili bowls.

On the long table:

A chafing dish of eggs in a delicate Lemon-Cream Sauce

Another chafing dish of Creamed Chipped Beef served on toasted salt-rising bread triangles

A beautiful whole smoked salmon, flown from New York (one Christmas it came a day late and got flown back! Another Christmas someone sent the Bivinses a barrel of fresh oysters. So rare are these in the Panhandle that no one knew how to open the shells — finally one of the guests from England arrived and came to the rescue).

SOB's — and that's what they are, they are so good. Betty makes worlds of these.

Cheese Ball covered with Red Caviar

Cheese and guacamole dips

Swedish Bread

Spanish Melon with Prosciutto

Hot Biscuits; bowls of mayonnaise and mustard

Trays with a variety of eight kinds of homemade candies and a very "ambitious" dessert on another side table, Profiteroles au Chocolat filled with ice cream and topped with chocolate sauce — served from a large silver bowl placed in another large bowl of ice

Coffee

★

Swedish Bread

Scald 2 cups milk. Add 1 cup cold water. When lukewarm dissolve 1 yeast cake in 1/4 cup lukewarm water. Add:

9 tsp. sugar
4 cups flour

Beat well and let rise double. Add:

2 eggs, well beaten
12 Tbs. sugar (3/4 cup)
1 Tbs. salt
1 tsp. almond extract
1 cup melted shortening

Beat well and work in and knead until smooth 4 cups flour or more if possible to get it to take up. Let rise double. Knead air out and let rise again. Knead a final time and divide into 3 equal portions, put in greased loaf pans, and let rise. Brush tops of loaves with unbeaten egg white and sprinkle with sugar. Bake in moderate oven, 400 degrees, about 45 minutes.

★

SOB's

Cut tops off small finger rolls; scoop out and brush with butter. (You can do this early in the morning and make the filling, leaving the egg until you get ready to fill rolls.)

1 No. 2 can tomatoes
1 glass jar chipped beef
1 whole bottle Tabasco sauce
4 Tbs. Worcestershire sauce
½ lb. sharp cheese
½ dozen eggs, beaten whole

Cook tomatoes and chipped beef until thick. Add Tabasco sauce and Worcestershire and set aside. Grate cheese, using large size. When ready to serve, heat rolls in oven. Now reheat sauce, adding cheese slowly, then fold in beaten eggs. Put a small amount in rolls and place in oven. Add more as this sets, but don't let it run over.

Lee showed me an old picture of the original Bivins house, with Hereford cattle grazing in what is now Main Street but was then grassy pasture. It was given to the city by his grandmother and is now the Mary E. Bivins Library. I asked them if they ever entertained outdoors on their beautiful grounds. Lee said that he and Betty, his mother, Mrs. Ernest Thompson, and his sister, Betty Childers, decided to join forces and have a great big party on the grounds. They had scattered gaily colored lanterns on bamboo poles, and six hundred whistling Chinese birds hung in the trees. A circular bar was built around a huge, weeping willow on which they tied multicolored helium-filled balloons. Betty had borrowed life-sized Chinese manikins, dressed them in brilliant brocade mandarin coats she had brought back from the Orient, and placed them on the terrace to create the atmosphere of a tea garden. A dance floor was also set up near the terrace for the dance band. The long barbecue pits were radiant with lighted coals, waiting for the especially selected filets. Miniature cherry tarts were arranged on dessert trays.

Suddenly, as the festivities were about to begin, the notorious crackling and howling noise started. The Chinese birds began to whistle in screeching tones, the lanterns stretched down to the grass, filling with water, and mannekins fell over on one another to be soaked. The wavering willow brushed its branches against the ground and the darkening sky was momentarily brightened with multicolored balls before they, too, popped and fell to the ground with the uninvited guest — the rain! Just a deluge of rain!

On my way to Amarillo I stopped in Vernon to see my friend Mrs. Robert Wright. Anna was getting ready to have a shower for a young bride-to-be (Anna quipped that the bridal showers were the only showers they could really depend on out there!). Anna and her co-hostess had made the invitations and envelopes from kitchen wallpaper with a spice design. Each guest was to bring a jar of spices or seasonings of the brand and kind specified on his invitation. The hostesses provided the walnut spice rack for them to be presented to the honoree.

In the large informal game room, Hot Apple Cider was served from an antique German cider crock into mugs and mulled with stick cinnamon. The entire occasion was delightful. For instance, each guest ground some fresh coffee beans in Anna's very old coffee mill for the bride's coffee canister.

The thing that took my eye was the beautiful shiny loaf of *Brioche on a breadboard with homemade wild plum jam and butter to spread on it as it was sliced. I was sure this had been flown in from some New York bakery, but not at *all*. Anna had made loaf after loaf for the party. She was kind enough to write down how she did it step by step, and when Amy and I made it, it also turned out looking "sto'-bought," but tasting even better.

★

Brioche

- 1 envelope of dry yeast
- ¼ cup lukewarm water
- 2 cups all-purpose flour
- 3 eggs
- ½ tsp. salt
- 1 Tbs. sugar
- ¾ cup butter
- 1 egg yolk
- 1 tsp. water

Soften yeast in lukewarm water. Mix in ½ cup all-purpose flour, adding, if necessary, a little more lukewarm water to make a soft dough. Roll the dough into a ball and put it in a bowl of lukewarm water to rise while you make the brioche paste.

Sift 1½ cups flour onto a pastry board and make a well in the center. Break 2 eggs into the well and begin to knead the paste, adding, little by little, a third egg, to make a soft dough. A good brioche dough is very elastic. Scoop the paste up in the hand and knead thoroughly about 10 minutes or until the dough becomes very elastic.

Knead into the beaten dough ½ tsp. salt and 1 Tbs. sugar. Knead ¾ cup butter until soft and mix it in gently but thoroughly, being careful that the dough does not lose its elasticity.

By this time the yeast dough will have doubled its bulk and will be floating. Remove it carefully from the water to a towel and sponge off the excess moisture. Mix the two doughs together well. Shape the dough into a ball and put it in a floured bowl. Cover and let it rise in a warm place for about 3 hours or until double in bulk. Turn the dough onto a lightly floured board and punch it down to its normal size. Return the dough to the bowl, cover it, and put it in the refrigerator for 6 hours or overnight.

During the chilling it will rise a little. In the morning punch it down and it will be ready to shape and bake.

Cut off ¼ of the dough for the "head," roll the rest into a large ball and put it in a buttered fluted brioche mold. Roll the remaining dough into the shape of a pear and push the pointed end well into the center of the large ball. Cover and let it rise for about 30 minutes or until double in bulk. Cut around the base of the head with a sharp pointed knife to keep it separate from the body of the brioche during the baking, and brush the brioche with 1 egg yolk beaten with a little water. Bake the brioche in a hot oven (425 degrees) for about 45 minutes, until it tests done.

ABILENE

Perhaps more than most towns — or cities, if you prefer so to call a population of more than 100,000 — Abilene is a comunity of contrasts. Within the city limits of this dry West Texas spot are three church-supported colleges. Incongruously, within these same city limits, indeed, right in the heart of Abilene itself, is the recently founded "town" of Impact, whose forty-odd taxpaying residents voted, in contrast to those of the city of Abilene itself, to sell liquor and beer to anyone who wanted to visit their dusty street — which is now handsomely paved from the profits of this independent venture!

Another of the noticeable contrasts is perhaps no different from that of any city with a few decades to its heritage; but Abilene is full of the "old" families that have lived there since before Grandma's day, and today in increasing numbers the newcomers are joining them in the community. Dyess Air Force Base, especially, has brought many young people to Abilene from all over the country. The contrast becomes most apparent when these two groups merge, as they frequently do at social affairs.

One such occasion was the fabulous "Circus" party, at which the old, established residents entertained the commanding officer and members of the Air Force base at the Country Club. "Clowns" helped with car parking and serving, and both decorations and refreshments were typical of a circus visit, including popcorn, hamburgers and candied apples; and both service and civilian guests had a wonderful time under the "Big Top."

Abilene has many "big city" ways, such as its own Symphony Orchestra, which is partially sustained by the annual Symphony Ball, one of the principal social events of the year.

Also, Abilene presents its debutantes, which also adds to its social whirl and world. Debs from larger cities such as Dallas and Fort Worth always love to come to the Abilene parties!

But even without the big affairs there is a lot of entertaining that goes on practically round the clock and the year round. Mr. and Mrs. Hal Sayles had a tree-trimming party at Christmas — a wonderful way to get the tree trimmed, as well as get the Christmas spirit. Nancy carefully unpacked the lovely collection of antique ornaments; the children also helped with this, and unwrapping each ornament was almost as much fun as opening Christmas gifts. Then, just before supper, there was the blessing of the crèche, as the little figures were placed under the fresh pine branches and lighted with the flicker from the votive candles. Nancy served:

** Roasted Whole Canadian Bacon*
** Brandied Apricots*
** Baked Stuffed Tomatoes*
** Spinach Supreme*
** Christmas Green Salad*
** Strawberry Ice with * Black Magic Cookies and*
** Chocolate Snowballs*

★

Roast Canadian Bacon

Remove wrapping from a 6- to 8-lb. piece of Canadian bacon. Place in roasting pan, pour pineapple juice over it; pack brown sugar on top. Bake at 350 degrees for 1 hour, spooning juice over it occasionally. Garnish with *Brandied Apricots.

★

Brandied Apricots

Drain 2 No. 2½ cans whole unpeeled apricots. Boil syrup about 30 minutes, until there is about 1¾ cups. Stir in ½ cup brandy. Pour over apricots and place in refrigerator. Cover bowl with foil. Let set 24 hours before serving.

★

Baked Stuffed Tomatoes

Scoop out large, firm tomatoes. Put a canned artichoke heart in each tomato with salt and pepper. Crush 1 garlic clove and add buttered toast crumbs. Add a little grated onion and tomato pieces to toasted crumbs. Mix well and fill tomato shells round the artichoke hearts. Brush with melted butter. Bake in hot oven about 15 minutes. Serve hot.

★

Spinach Supreme

- 2 lbs. spinach
- 2 onions, 1 whole and 1 chopped fine
- ½ cup imported Parmesan cheese
- 2 cups warm milk
- 2 Tbs. butter
- 2 Tbs. flour
- 3 eggs
- 2 bouillon cubes dissolved in hot water
- 1 can mushrooms
- Juice of 1 lemon
- Breadcrumbs

Boil spinach in a very little water with whole onion and put through colander. Make cream sauce with cheese, milk, butter and flour in double boiler. When cool, add chopped onion cooked slowly in butter. Add other ingredients except breadcrumbs. Put in buttered dish and cover with breadcrumbs. Bake in moderate (350-degree) oven until brown.

★

Christmas Green Salad

Crush together in a mortar 1 green onion, 1 tsp. monosodium glutamate, ½ tsp. sugar, ½ tsp. dry mustard, ½ tsp. Beau Monde salt. Add ¼ cup red wine vinegar. Let stand for a while, then slowly add ½ cup olive oil. Use over lettuces and watercress; sprinkle with herbs, as parsley and chives.

★

Strawberry Ice (serves 8)

1½ cups crushed strawberries
2 cups water
⅛ tsp. salt
1 Tbs. lemon juice
1 cup sugar

Make a syrup of the sugar and water (boil 12 minutes). Add lemon juice, salt and crushed strawberries. Freeze in pudding tray, stirring occasionally. If frozen strawberries are used, get the whole, unsweetened berries.

★

Black Magic Cookies (makes 24)

⅓ cup melted butter
2 cups oatmeal (uncooked)
½ cup brown sugar
¼ cup dark corn syrup
½ tsp. salt
1½ tsp. vanilla
1 6-oz. pkg. chocolate chips
¼ cup chopped pecans

Grease small muffin tins. Pour melted butter over oats; mix well. Add sugar, corn syrup, salt and vanilla. Fill small muffin tins half full; press down to smooth tops. Bake at 450 degrees from 5 to 7 minutes or until cookies are rich brown on top. Let stand until cool. Run sharp knife around cookies to remove from pan. Melt chocolate chips and spread over top of cookies, then sprinkle with pecans.

★

Chocolate Snowballs (makes 6 dozen)

⅔ cup sugar
1¼ cups butter
1 tsp. vanilla
2 cups flour
⅛ tsp. salt
½ cup cocoa
2 cups chopped pecans

Cream sugar and butter until fluffy; add vanilla. Sift together flour, salt and cocoa. Gradually add to butter and sugar mixture. Blend the chopped pecans. Mix thoroughly. Refrigerate for 6 hours. Roll into balls about 1 inch in size and place on ungreased cookie sheet. Place about ½ inch apart, as these cookies do not spread. Bake in 350-degree oven for 20 minutes. Roll in powdered sugar. Store in freezer in airtight container.

Two of the young girls brought guitars, and after supper they played, and everyone sang Christmas carols — a wonderful way to start the season.

Mr. and Mrs. Elbert Hall decided that since the trimming of the Christmas tree took on such a festive air, the holidays should likewise close with a ceremony, so they had a Twelfth Night party for their neighborhood and asked everyone to bring along the dismantled Christmas trees for burning. Mary even took the precaution of asking the Fire Department to stand by while the trees burnt. It was a gay evening and a delightful climax to the holiday season, and has now become a tradition.

Their menu on that first occasion was:

** Darjeeling Tea*
** Gladys Hall's wonderful Eggnog*
** Cheese Soufflé sandwiches*
** Hot crabmeat Lorenzo Toasties*
** Twelfth Night Cake*

★

Darjeeling Tea (for 40 to 50 cups)

Save time by making a tea concentrate beforehand. Bring 1½ qts. cold fresh water to a full rolling boil. Remove from heat and immediately add ¼ lb. loose tea. Stir to immerse leaves. Cover. Let stand 5 minutes. Strain into teapot and leave until tea time. At the table, pour about 1 oz. concentrate into each cup, and add fresh boiling water from the teakettle. Serve with a choice of lemon slices, rum, sugar and cream.

★

Gladys Hall's Eggnog

8 egg yolks
1¼ cups sugar
½ pt. whiskey
¼ cup water
⅛ tsp. salt
8 egg whites
1 qt. whipped cream

Whip egg yolks with ¾ cup sugar until *very* light. Pour whiskey over yolks and set aside. Make a syrup of ½ cup sugar and water. Cook to threading stage. Pour the hot syrup over the stiffly beaten egg whites, to which salt has been added. Now gently fold yolks and whites together, and fold the whipped cream into the mixture.

The flavor improves if it is allowed to set an hour before serving.

★

Cheese Soufflé Sandwiches (makes 60)

1 lb. butter
1 lb. brick of processed American cheese
1 to 1½ large loaves of sandwich bread, extra thin

Allow butter and cheese to warm to room temperature. Whip for 5 minutes in electric mixer.

Decrust bread. Stack 3 slices together and cut stacks into 4 sections. Ice each layer and frost top and sides like small 3-layer cakes. Bake at 350 degrees for about 15 minutes. Insert toothpick into each sandwich while baking to prevent slipping of layers. These can be frozen or stored in refrigerator until ready for baking.

★

Hot Crabmeat Lorenzo Squares

4 egg yolks
¼ cup lemon juice
¼ tsp. white pepper
1 cup melted butter
½ tsp. salt

Make a sauce of these ingredients, adding lemon juice gradually. Stir over hot water until thickened. Remove from fire and add:

1 lb. white crabmeat, free from bones
⅓ cup chopped mushrooms
3 tsp. chopped green onions
1 jigger sherry wine

Fold all this into the sauce gently till well mixed. Have ready:

50 small (2-inch) squares of bread, crisply toasted and buttered, and some imported Parmesan cheese

Put a teaspoon of the crabmeat mixture on each toast square. Then sprinkle a little Parmesan cheese and a dash of paprika on each. Put these in a hot oven or under a flame until lightly browned. Serve at once. Alternatively, they can be served on bite-sized rusks.

★

Twelfth Night Cake

Once a cake made of flour, honey, ginger and pepper, this is now any kind of cake with a coin — perhaps a rare one — or other favors hidden in it. Pound cake seems now to have become traditional; make it in a Bundt pan and dust with powdered sugar, or after cake is cooked, cool in pan until lukewarm, gently poke holes all over top surface, inserting fork tines as far as possible. Make an orange syrup by combining ⅓ cup sherry, ⅓ cup orange juice, ½ cup sugar and ½ tsp. grated orange rind. Bring to boil, lower heat and simmer about 10 minutes; cool and spoon the syrup carefully over the cake top.

· I am so very grateful to Mrs. George B. Hall for two wonderful recipes that are sending me on to fame. The *Coconut Cake is a Must for the Christmas parties out at the Herman Heeps', and Zachary Scott always wants one to take back to New York.

★

Old Fashioned Coconut Cake

1 cup butter
2 cups sugar
5 eggs
1 scant tsp. soda
Dash of salt
2¾ cups cake flour
1 tsp. baking powder
1 cup buttermilk
2 tsp. vanilla

Cream butter and sugar *really* well. Add eggs, beating well after each addition. Add dry ingredients alternately with buttermilk. Add vanilla. Bake at 350 degrees until done.

ICING

2½ cups sugar
1¼ cups evaporated milk
Dash salt
1 tsp. vanilla
1 cup fresh coconut, grated

Cook sugar, milk and salt to soft ball stage. Add, when ready, vanilla and coconut. Beat until of right consistency to spread. Put icing between cooled layers and all over outside of cake.

This improves with time — and is good to the last bite.

I thought I had tried just about all the Peach Pies in captivity during the Peach Festival at Stonewall; but Gladys Hall's *Cream-Kist Peach Pie was something new. We presented it at Green Pastures at Sunday dinner in June, and served it throughout the peach season.

★

Cream-Kist Peach Pie

8 freestone peaches
1 unbaked pie shell
2/3 cup sugar
3 Tbs. cornstarch or flour
1/8 tsp. salt
1/4 tsp. nutmeg
2/3 cup whipping cream
1/2 tsp. vanilla
3 Tbs. chopped almonds

Peel peaches and cut in halves. Arrange them, cut side up, in pie shell. Combine sugar, cornstarch, salt, nutmeg, whipping cream and vanilla and pour over peaches. Sprinkle with chopped almonds and bake in 400-degree oven for 45 to 55 minutes.

This is especially good when served warm.

What to serve on a West Texas summer afternoon for tea? Gladys had the perfect answer in the refreshing *Peppermint Punch she served at the tea honoring the former Carol Herring of Austin, now Mrs. Warren Weir, and with it served:

---

*Thin orange butter sandwiches on * Honey Walnut bread*
** Cheese Wafers*
Thin sliced smoked chicken on buttered rye bread, cut in little rounds
Trays of assorted cookies — all divine! — including:
** Chocolate Macaroons*
** Date and almond dainties*
** Daiquiri Balls*

★

Peppermint Punch

1 pt. peppermint ice cream
1 qt. ginger ale
1 qt. milk
A few drops of red coloring

If a more distinct peppermint flavor is desired, add a few drops of peppermint flavoring. The ice cream should be broken up into chunks and the ingredients blended in an electric blender.

★

Honey Walnut Bread

1 cup milk
1 cup honey
½ cup sugar
2 egg yolks
2½ cups sifted flour
1 tsp. salt
1 tsp. baking soda
½ cup walnuts

Scald milk, add honey and sugar; stir over medium heat until the sugar is dissolved. Cool. Beat egg yolks. Sift together sifted flour, salt and baking soda and stir into the batter. Beat well. Add walnuts, coarsely chopped. Pour the batter into a buttered and floured loaf pan and bake in a moderately slow oven (325 degrees) for about an hour, or until it tests done. Cool for 15 minutes in the pan and turn out on a wire rack to cool.

★

Cheese Wafers (makes 200 to 250 small ones)

1 lb. sharp cheddar cheese
1 lb. butter
4 cups flour (sifted once)
¼ tsp. salt
⅛ to ¼ tsp. cayenne
Pecan halves

Grate cheese and mix with butter at room temperature. Add flour, salt and cayenne. Mix well, using hands. Make small balls by rolling in palms of hands. Place on ungreased baking sheet. Press half a pecan in center of each ball, mashing in well. Bake at 325 degrees for 20 to 25 minutes; they do not really brown. Do not overbake as they become bitter.

★

Chocolate Macaroons (makes 5 to 6 dozen)

½ cup vegetable shortening
4 squares unsweetened chocolate
2 cups sifted flour
2 tsp. baking powder
½ tsp. salt
2 cups sugar
4 eggs, unbeaten
2 tsp. vanilla
Powdered sugar

Melt together shortening and chocolate. Sift together flour, baking powder and salt. Add sugar to chocolate, stirring until smooth. Add eggs one at a time, beating well after each; add vanilla. Add the flour mixture and blend thoroughly. Chill the dough 2 to 3 hours. Dip out rounded teaspoons of dough, form into small balls, roll each in powdered sugar. Bake in a moderate oven (375 degrees) about 10 minutes.

(Do not overbake. Cookies should be soft when taken from the oven.) Cool on rack.

★

Date and Almond Dainties

½ lb. almonds
1 lb. dates, cut fine
½ lb. granulated sugar
2 egg whites, unbeaten
1 tsp. vanilla
Candied cherries

Blanch almonds and cut into shreds lengthwise. Mix dates, almonds, sugar, egg whites and vanilla. Place in refrigerator for one hour. Form into small cones and top each with half a cherry. Place on a buttered sheet and bake in a slow oven for 15 to 20 minutes.

★

Daiquiri Balls (*makes* 54)

1 6-oz. pkg. semisweet chocolate bits
½ cup sour cream
½ lb. vanilla wafers
1 cup powdered sugar
¼ tsp. salt
3 Tbs. cocoa
1 Tbs. each of lemon and orange rind, grated
2½ Tbs. lemon juice
1½ Tbs. white corn syrup
¼ cup rum
1 cup pecans, finely chopped

Melt chocolate over hot water. Cool. Add sour cream; mix and refrigerate overnight. Form into 54 balls, using ½ tsp. mixture for each. Crush wafers, add powdered sugar, salt, cocoa and fruit rind. Blend in lemon juice, syrup, rum and pecans. Form balls the size of walnuts around the chocolate centers. Roll in powdered sugar. Store in airtight containers. Freeze.

In character with the town are the contrasts found in entertaining, which range from the most formal events to the stand-around-in-the kitchen type of socializing which many Abilenians prefer. Obviously there's not much that can be said about this perhaps more popular and certainly more frequent type of party. But one new trick I learned in Abilene was how to charcoal a steak indoors without a cuss, muss, or fuss. W. D. "Windy" Watkins has the system down pretty pat.

1. Windy lines the hibachi with foil.

2. He lights the charcoal by placing it on the burners of the electric stove, turned up to high; and before you have time to refill the glasses, the charcoal is turning white around the edges.
3. With tongs, he places hot coals in the bottom of the hibachi. Meanwhile, he marinates the steaks in lemon juice and cracked peppercorns, but *never* salt.
4. He turns off burners.
5. He places hibachi on top of stove, under vent.
6. He places steaks on the hibachi; about 4 minutes on each side and they are ready.

Lillian Watkins brings forth the baked potatoes and green salad and dinner is served!

Anne Smart says that when anyone thinks of Abilene food, they think of Windy's steaks.

And if anyone in Abilene would know about the food in town, it would be Anne. She is famous for such things as her elegant soufflés, unusual casseroles and heavenly desserts. It is a real treat to eat at Anne's house, and even more of one to watch her in the kitchen. With no apparent fuss or effort she waves her wand and there it is — Presto! a magnificent cake. She calls it *Angel Food Silhouette.

★

Angel Food Silhouette Cake

Angel food cake
1 pt. whipping cream
1 tsp. vanilla
¼ cup sugar (approx.)
1 cup slivered almonds

Cut cake carefully into three layers. Whip the cream stiff and flavor it with vanilla and sugar to taste. Add slivered almonds. Spread this filling over the cake layers, putting the cake back together. Ice cake with the following icing:

BOILED ICING

¾ cup water
1½ cups sugar
1 Tbs. corn syrup
2 egg whites
3 drops oil of peppermint flavoring
2 bars bitter chocolate

Put water, sugar and corn syrup in saucepan and cook to a medium syrup. Beat egg whites stiff in electric mixer, and slowly add half the medium thick syrup, while you continue to beat the whites. Allow remaining half of the syrup to cook until it reaches a thick stage. Add the thick syrup gradually to whites, and continue beating till icing is thick and fluffy. Add oil of peppermint flavoring, and spread on cake. Melt the chocolate over boiling water and with a teaspoon drip chocolate over icing.

Here are three more among the many other delicious recipes I collected in Abilene:

Anne Smart says serving this has almost become a habit. It is extra good.

★

Sweet and Sour Asparagus (*prepare 24 hours ahead*)

- 2/3 cup white vinegar
- 1/2 cup sugar
- 1/2 tsp. salt
- 1 tsp. whole cloves
- 3 sticks cinnamon
- 1 Tbs. celery seed
- 1/2 cup water
- 2 large cans all-green asparagus or 3 lbs. cooked asparagus
- Hard-boiled egg

Mix vinegar, sugar, salt and spices in a saucepan with 1/2 cup water; bring to a boil. Place asparagus in a flat oven baking dish and pour the boiling hot liquid over it. Cover and store in the refrigerator for 24 hours. To serve, pour off liquid and sprinkle with grated hard-boiled egg.

Gladys Hall said the *men* all want this recipe.

★

Mexican Corn Bread

1 cup cornmeal
½ tsp. salt
1 cup cream-style corn
2 eggs
1 small can chili peppers (green)
⅔ cup buttermilk
½ tsp. soda
⅓ cup shortening
1 cup grated sharp cheese

Drain and chop chilis. Mix other ingredients except cheese and pour one-half of the mixture into a hot skillet. Sprinkle cheese and green chilis over it. Pour the remaining mixture over it and bake in 375-degree oven for 30 to 40 minutes.

★

Ambrette's Sauce for Ice Cream

Cook until it spins a thread:

1 cup brown sugar
1 cup water

Add:

1 cup strawberry preserves
Juice of 1 lemon
Juice of 1 orange
½ cup Bourbon
1 cup chopped nuts

Then you will know you're in the South!

ROCKDALE

The University of Texas in Austin and Texas A&M in College Station have always played the traditional Thanksgiving football game. The loyal alumni from each institution travel from almost the corners of the globe to see the arch rivals clash! Alternate years, when the game is played on Kyle Field in College Station, there is a general exodus of Austinites, by plane, car or special train. Many of the fans take picnic lunches, as eating facilities are not available for all the masses who throng A&M on this day. We usually join our friends, the Malcolm Gregorys, the Raymond Gregorys, Dr. and Mrs. Edgar Poth from Galveston, and some of the Lloyd Gregorys, I think; it's hard to tell just who is who reaching into the fried chicken there on the grassy mall near the stadium. It really doesn't matter because spirits are high and deviled eggs are pretty much gulped as Malcolm reminds us we gotta go see the teams warm up — not be late for the kick-off, etc., but never mind, he won't miss a thing!

I sat next to an ardent (I understand there isn't any other kind) Aggie alumnus, Frank Litten, at the Texas A&M game. The score was seesawing at each quarter: first A&M in the lead, and then Texas would get the ball. A&M scored and Texas followed suit. Frank played the entire game from the stands. He was in on every scrimmage, and in true Aggie tradition stood, stomped and coached during the entire game. Finally in the last few minutes of play, the score tied. He pulled his Stetson down over his eyes and moaned in a low, husky voice, "Why didn't I go to Southwest Teachers College or someplace where I would not give a —— who won!"

Our family has to go in a caravan to accommodate all the members, in-laws, dates and such. None of them would miss this game for anything short of death or the big Thanksgiving dinner which follows the game at the home of our friends the George Bredts in Rockdale. Lady Jane and George Bredt have been lifelong friends, and we hope to keep them so. They are two of our few brave friends who say, "Now come and bring *all* the family," and mean it! In addition to us are the Jay Pattersons, the Carl Bredts and the Pat Pattersons from Texarkana plus several of their Rockdale friends.

When the Aggies win, the Bruno Schroeders will stop by, too! Now, mind you, the Bredts always go to the game, but dinner is awaiting the hungry mob as if by magic, but really by Mozelle's and Lady Jane's careful planning. George serves his delicious Old-fashioneds to the husky-voiced guests as they arrive. His daughter Jan brings in a delicious *Jalapeño Cheese Spread with crackers. Neither victory nor defeat dulls the appetite for this "team," and all the guests delight in it. Here is the menu for the buffet dinner:

Roasted Baby Beef Turkey
** Grandmother Bredt's Turkey Dressing*
Giblet Gravy
** Cranberry Jelly Ring*
Waldorf Salad, Whipped Cream Dressing

Fresh Green Beans Almondine
Rockdale home grown tomatoes
*Lady Jane's * Ripe Tomato Relish, specialty of the Bredt House*
** Angel Biscuits, hot and buttered*
Coffee
Pies and Cakes (from Heaven, I think)
*Candy dishes full of Lady Jane's * Pralines on all the small tables*

★

Jalapeño Spread

5 jalapeño peppers
1 lb. sharp cheddar cheese
1 large onion
8 cloves garlic
1¼ cup mayonnaise

Remove tops and seed from peppers. Put first four ingredients through food grinder. Mix in mayonnaise. Store in covered crock in refrigerator until ready to serve.

★

Grandmother Bredt's Turkey Dressing

Bony turkey pieces
Turkey giblets
4 cups corn bread crumbs
12 slices bread, crumbled
6 cups cooked rice
Leftover biscuits, crumbled
Celery, onions, salt and pepper, ground meat
4 raw whole eggs
8 boiled eggs, chopped (put in last)

Boil bony pieces of turkey and use stock in mixing dry ingredients. Add cooked onions, celery, sautéed ground meat, salt and pepper, and giblets. Add eggs. Does not require much cooking as all ingredients are cooked prior to mixing.

★

Cranberry Jelly Ring

1 lb. fresh cranberries
2 cups water
2 cups sugar

Boil cranberries in water until most of them pop. Take from fire and mash through sieve. Put back on fire and reheat. Add sugar and stir until sugar is dissolved. Pour into glasses or molds.

★

Ripe Tomato Relish

- 1 gal. ripe tomatoes; peel, core, remove juice before measuring
- 2 cups chopped white onion
- 1½ cups green pepper, chopped
- 2 Tbs. brown sugar
- 1½ cups sugar
- 1 tsp. nutmeg
- 1 tsp. cinnamon
- ¾ tsp. red pepper
- ½ tsp. curry powder
- 2 cups vinegar
- 5 tsp. salt
- 2 tsp. ginger
- 1 tsp. mustard

Prepare tomatoes and onion; add all other ingredients and boil approximately two hours until thick in an electric oven at 500 degrees without lid. Stir to prevent sticking.

★

Angel Biscuits

- 5 cups unsifted flour
- ¼ cup sugar
- 3 tsp. baking powder
- 1 tsp. soda
- 1½ tsp. salt
- 1 cup shortening
- 1 pkg. dry yeast
- 2 Tbs. warm water
- 2 cups buttermilk

Sift dry ingredients together, then cut in shortening. Dissolve yeast in warm water and add to buttermilk. Then add to dry ingredients. Cover and refrigerate. Will keep several weeks. Makes 3 dozen. Take amount to be baked and roll on slightly floured board to ½ inch thick. Cut and place on greased sheet; grease top. Let stand 1 to 2 hours to rise. Bake at 400 degrees for 15 minutes.

★

Pralines

- 1 cup white sugar
- ½ cup brown sugar
- ¼ cup milk
- 1 Tbs. butter
- 1 cup pecan pieces
- 1 tsp. vanilla

Mix first 5 ingredients and bring to a boil. Boil by clock 1½ minutes. Remove from stove, add vanilla and beat until creamy. Drop by spoon onto wax paper.

The Bredts moved from Austin to Rockdale in 1937. Rockdale was just a small country town then, but George wanted to be near his Brazos Bottom Farm. In 1952, Alcoa (the Aluminum Company of America) began operating a huge smelting plant there. It is powered by the largest deposit of lignite found in the nation. Alcoa personnel number over twelve hundred. George was afraid its coming would only ruin the pleasant atmosphere of this quiet little town, but indeed it has made a good balance between farming and industry and added much to the civic endeavors, as well as stepping up the social activities considerably.

Bea and Henry Johnston came to Rockdale from Louisiana with Alcoa. They are both great cooks and love to have parties, if for no other reason than to try out or show off some new concoction or some old one they brought over from Louisiana! Friends say sometimes you don't know *what* you're eating at the Johnstons but whatever it is, it's always good. We had been asked to drive over and have dinner at the Johnstons' and to meet Dr. George Patterson, a neurosurgeon from Los Angeles. He was in Rockdale for a very exciting occasion, the dedication of the beautiful new Lucy Hill Patterson Memorial Library. Right out of the clear blue sky, our friend Linwood Mehaffey, who is the mayor of Rockdale, received a letter from Dr. Patterson stating that his mother, Lucy Hill, who was born in Rockdale eighty-one years ago, had recently died. She was a remarkable woman of great courage and judgment, and he wanted to set up a memorial for her in Rockdale! So Dr. Patterson was here to participate in the dedication of this library. Afterwards there was a reception and then dinner at the Johnstons'.

The only hors d'oeuvre served with the drinks was a tray of small slices of tender — what? — we all wondered. Was it lamb? elk? It was so tender and juicy. Weezie Perry said, "Well, I know it isn't rattlesnake because Bea had that one night and it tasted more like frog legs!" Bea spoke up, "You silly people, don't you know, this is armadillo!" Eeeeeeak!! About that time, Henry passed a tray of *Crawfish Bisque in small cups. Bea was practically brought up on this luscious soup, and now fresh crawfish are available in Rockdale. Some enterprising farmer brought in a starter crop from Louisiana and raises them in his rice fields. The demand gets greater after one of Bea's parties when she serves her Bisque. This is what she served on the buffet:

Tenderloin of Beef encased and baked in a flaky tender pie crust and cooked rare
Boiled Rice with ½ stick butter and 2 6-oz. cans of cashew nuts
* *Cold Sauerkraut Ring*
* *Oven-Toasted Rolls*
* *Dessert Grapes*

★

Sauerkraut Ring

Drain one tall can of kraut. Stir in dehydrated dill *weed* (not to be confused with dill *seed*) and not too much. Chill:

¼ cup sour cream
2 Tbs. mayonnaise
A little red pepper
Juice from 1 clove of garlic

Make ring of kraut. Put dressing in compote in center.

★

Oven-Toasted Rolls

Cut hot dog buns into fourths. Brush with butter and sprinkle with sesame seed. Bake in hot oven until lightly browned.

★

Dessert Grapes

2 cups pickled seedless grapes

Pick grapes off one bunch. Wash and put in a bowl. Marinate about 2 hours in refrigerator in ½ cup brandy and ½ cup Cointreau. Whip:

2 cups sour cream
1 cup whipping cream

Add:

¼ cup powdered sugar

Fold into marinated grapes. Cover with ¼ cup brown sugar. Sprinkle with candied ginger.

Bea served this from an antique silver bowl on the sideboard into lovely little berry bowls (imports from old Louisiana!).

Some of my readers may not be interested in trying *Crawfish Bisque, but anyone who has ever eaten it would surely want to know how it is made. All crawfish recipes use the "crawfish fat" for flavor. It is delicate and tantalizing. When Bea serves this as a first course or main course at a seafood dinner she stuffs the heads true Louisiana fashion, and places them around the edge of the bowls. Here is the complete recipe.

★

Crawfish Bisque

18 lbs. crawfish

GRAVY

1 cup shortening
1 cup flour
2 Tbs. tomato paste
3 medium onions
4 ribs celery
4 large cloves garlic
1 medium bell pepper
½ cup crawfish fat or amount you have
Salt and pepper to taste
1 Tbs. Worcestershire sauce
2 qts. water
2 qts. hot water
1 bay leaf
1 lemon, sliced
⅓ of crawfish tails

Cook crawfish in almost boiling salted water for 20 minutes. Remove and drain. Peel tails and clean heads, saving any yellow fat that clings to them in a separate container. Save "head" shells to stuff. (These shells are actually the thorax or body.) Make a roux, stirring constantly until golden brown. Add tomato paste. Grind onions, celery, garlic and bell pepper. Cook in roux until tender. Add crawfish fat and seasonings. Slowly stir in 2 qts. water. Add 2 qts. hot water, stir and let boil up. Add bay leaf, lower heat and cook 30 to 40 minutes. Drop in lemon slices, crawfish tails.

STUFFING FOR HEADS

2 ribs celery
8 cloves garlic
½ bunch parsley
2 large onions
1 medium bell pepper
⅔ cup butter or bacon fat
⅔ of crawfish tails
½ bunch green onion tops
1 tsp. black pepper
1 tsp. red pepper
1 tsp. thyme
Juice of 1 lemon
1 Tbs. Worcestershire sauce
1 tsp. monosodium glutamate
1 Tbs. salt
1 box breadcrumbs
½ of crawfish fat

Grind celery, garlic, parsley, onions, and bell pepper and cook in fat until tender. Remove from heat. Grind ⅔ crawfish tails and green onions and add to above. Stir in all seasonings, mixing well. Add breadcrumbs (reserve ½ cup to roll heads in.) Use crawfish fat and enough warm water to make stuffing the proper consistency for handling. Stuff heads, roll in breadcrumbs, and bake in 400-degree oven for 20 minutes. Add remaining crawfish tails and all of stuffed heads to gravy and simmer ½ hour. Serve over rice.

Dr. Patterson, the thoughtful man that he is, sent me an extraordinary dressing for green salad. I may put this on the market! It is called *Dubbins Salad Dressing.

★

Dubbins Salad Dressing

- **½ cup olive oil**
- **½ cup salad oil**
- **¼ cup wine vinegar**
- **1 Tbs. fresh lemon juice**
- **2 cloves garlic**
- **1 Tbs. sugar**
- **1 tsp. dry mustard**
- **½ tsp. tarragon leaves**
- **1 Tbs. horseradish**
- **½ tsp. onion salt**
- **½ tsp. white pepper**
- **½ tsp. Worcestershire sauce**

Shake well! Add 1 whole egg and shake or beat with rotary beater until all ingredients are well mixed. Season to taste. The egg may be omitted. However, the egg keeps the dressing from separating.

Linwood asked, "Bea, when are we going to have some more of your Deviled Oysters? I wanna know because I don't want to be out of town or hunting or somewhere else." Here is Bea's popular recipe:

★

Deviled Oysters

- **1 cup white part of green onions**
- **½ cup celery**
- **3 Tbs. olive oil**
- **1 qt. oysters**
- **1 cup green onion tops**
- **1 cup parsley**
- **½ cup breadcrumbs**

Sauté white onion and celery in oil. Cook well. Add drained oysters, onion tops, parsley, and breadcrumbs. Spoon into buttered shells or ramekins. Sprinkle with crumbs and dot with butter. Bake at 375 degrees for 10 minutes. Serve at once.

For take-home presents, Bea had wrapped individual packages of delicious *Grape-Nut Bread with the recipe enclosed in each package.

★

Grape-Nut Bread

Soak for 6 to 8 hours:

1 cup Grape-Nuts
2 cups sour milk
2 cups cane sugar

Add:

2 well-beaten eggs
1 tsp. salt
2 tsp. baking powder
1 tsp. soda dissolved in ¼ cup hot water
4 to 5 cups flour

Bake 1 hour at 350 degrees in greased loaf pans. Makes two loaves.

From Lady Jane's *Aunt Babette's Cook Book* (1889):

We may live without poetry, music and art;
We may live without conscience, and live without heart;
We may live without friends, we may live without books;
But civilized man can not live without cooks.

He may live without books — what is knowledge but giving?
He may live without hope — what is hope but deceiving?
He may live without love — what is passion but pining?
But where is the man that can live without dining?

Lord Lytton

SAN ANTONIO

San Antonio, Texas, has a distinct personality, perhaps more than any other city in the country with the exception of San Francisco and New Orleans. Long years before the American Colonists threw off the English yoke, Franciscan padres from Spain were building their missions in and about old San Antonio, and there they are today — the missions — dozing in the Texas sunshine and dreaming of days when only the musical sound of Spanish was heard about their walls. In addition to the missions, many other landmarks from San Antonio's past remain to this day, preserved for all to enjoy. Much of this is due to the heroic efforts of a remarkable group of San Antonio ladies called the Conservation Society. The Conservation Society has made it their business over the years to protect the old city's historical homes, missions, and other landmarks from destruction at the hands of eager builders and developers. The society's membership boasts of many of the oldest and best established families in San Antonio. Its members are alert, tireless, and as militant as soldiers when any of the old shrines are threatened (as the city fathers have learned time and again).

One of the moving spirits in the Conservation Society has for many years been Mrs. Elizabeth Graham. Now well into her seventies, she is still alert and vital in all matters relating to the preservation of historic landmarks. Her daughter, Wanda, who is married to O'Neil Ford, one of the country's most original architects, is as enthusiastic a worker as her mother is in the matter of conservation. Many years ago Mrs. Graham bought a huge tract of land in the bend of the San Antonio River very near where the old mission, San José, now stands. There under huge pecan trees Mrs. Graham and the Fords maintain their home, Willow Way. Their beautiful grounds, adorned with flower beds and great shade trees and inhabited by peacocks and exotic birds and a monkey named Ho Ho Ho, has been the scene of some of the most original and exciting parties ever held in Texas. Both Mrs. Graham and Wanda are expert cooks and have huge files of remarkable recipes. Their kitchen is presided over by a Mexican cook, Luis Resendes-Espinosa. Luis has brought with him from his native Mexico some rare and delightful recipes. Perhaps the most exciting and certainly the most colorful one is his recipe for barbecued lamb. The preparation for this unbelievably delicious item is a remarkable ritual in itself. The Grahams and Fords are close friends of my brother John Henry, and recently gave a birthday party for him. Luis prepared his barbecued lamb.

This necessitated his going out several days before and cutting the wide leaves of a maguey plant (called the century plant in North America). He trimmed the points and the thorns from each of the leaves, then heated and beat them until they were as pliable as a piece of silk. Next he prepared his barbecue hole. This was done by digging a large hole the size of a fifty-gallon oil drum in the ground. It was bell-shaped at the bottom, a smaller hole at the top. This he filled with big sticks from mesquite trees and started his fire, which burned all night. At dawn of the day of the party, Luis repaired to his barbecue hole, where the coals glowed a bright, bright red with such intensity that the clay walls of the hole fairly glowed with heat, too. The Ford sons, Michael and John, were his assistants in the preparation. Luis laid out the wide maguey leaves, washed one side clean, then he lined the hole with the maguey leaves and placed over the coals, down in the hole, a huge earthen pot, across the top of which he laid boards to support the meat. Into the pot he had put one-half cup of rice and one-half pound of a remarkable Mexican bean called the garbanzo. He then lined the entire interior over the coals with the maguey leaves and started nestling large chunks of lamb in it. He put two large-sized lambs, cut up and quartered, into the hole, then folded the tops of the

maguey leaves over this all. He then placed a tin can top over the hole itself and covered it with a great mound of mud, so that no air whatever could get in nor even a wisp of the smoke escape. Incidentally, the meat had been only slightly salted. The sun had only just risen as Luis and Michael put the finishing touches on the mound of mud and then checked carefully to make sure that no smoke was escaping anywhere. He asked us to check the time. It was six o'clock exactly. He announced that the meat would be ready at exactly six o'clock that evening. It must cook precisely twelve hours. Luis explained that he had learned this cooking method from his father and did not know where his father had learned it many, many years ago in Mexico. While it might seem to be a highly complicated way to cook lamb, it is not at all, since the hole once dug can be used over and over again. Luis explained that his father would cook lamb this way and then on Sundays carry it to market for sale on the plaza.

Wanda had invited some seventy-five guests to the feast, which was held outside on the patio under the great trees. The ceremony of uncovering the meat was a ritual indeed. Luis's four small children had joined him, as well as his wife, and the guests all gathered around to watch him remove the now hardened mud dome from the hole. He had several vessels of water sitting around and he would wash his hands each time he touched the hot mud to cool them off. Having removed the mud dome and the tin lid from the top of the hole, he began to flip back the folded maguey leaves.

There arose from the hole an aroma that sent us all dizzy with hunger. Reaching into the hole, he removed one large succulent chunk of lamb after another and placed it on a huge platter. Having removed all of the lamb and set it beside him in a great stack on the platter, he reached into the steaming hole and removed the great earthen vessel which was brimming with a broth of such rare delicacy that it is literally indescribable. The seventy-five guests collectively and individually pronounced the lamb the best they had ever tasted, and I quite concur. The rest of the menu was:

Consommé
Hot Handmade Tortillas with Goat Cheese and Butter
Frijoles
Arroz
*Broccoli with * Fernando Dressing*
Birthday Cake
** Pecan Candy*
Beer
Coffee

★

Fernando Dressing

1 cup homemade mayonnaise (blended with 2 Tbs. wine vinegar)
1 Tbs. chopped parsley
1 Tbs. chopped onion
1 Tbs. chopped capers
1 tsp. whole dill seed, mashed

Blend seasonings with mayonnaise. Let stand overnight or for several hours. Recipe may be doubled or tripled.

Wanda's aunt, Mrs. Leonard Orynski, brought some lovely *Pecan Candy which is made from a recipe that her husband worked out himself years ago as a young man in Mexico. Everyone loves it.

★

Pecan Candy

2 lbs. brown sugar, light or dark; can use half and half
½ tsp. salt
1 cup really hot water
1 lb. pecans (preferably small)

Put the sugar and salt in a large saucepan; add the hot water and stir over low fire until sugar is dissolved. Cover the saucepan and bring syrup to a boil over low fire. This is to dissolve any crystals on the side of the saucepan.

Pick pecans carefully and when syrup starts to boil add the pecans. Boil until a soft ball stage is reached. Do not underboil. Remove from fire and when slightly cool start beating with a strong spoon. When you see candy is getting somewhat thick pour by spoonfuls on waxed paper and let cool. You can make the pieces any size.

This is a wonderful candy for Christmas. The reason it is better than the usual praline is that the pecans are boiled in the syrup, which extracts some of the pecan oil and gives it the wonderful flavor it has. No vanilla is added, just the pecan flavor.

The tables were set on the wide screened porch opening onto the patio. They were covered in bright Mexican cloths and lighted by candles held in Mexican-crafted tin and ceramics. Mexican women were making tortillas out on the patio. Their hands patted the masa at a very fast rhythm — they would flip them over onto the grill for a moment to cook, then a second señora would pick them up, fill them with cheese and Salsa Piquante! There are no words to describe these delicious handmade tortillas. I suppose their instant disappearance said the most. The luscious consommé was served into Mexican mugs and bowls; next the lamb which was too good to be true, the frijoles; arroz; and two huge Mexican trays of broccoli with *Fernando Dressing — I suggest never to serve broccoli without it. Wanda's aunt, Mrs. Jim Ada Orynski, came over from Comfort, Texas, to make this dressing for the party. The broccoli was a frozen brand and cooked only five minutes — beautiful green and crisp spears!

After all of the August birthday people had been toasted with *cerveza,* in came the big Birthday Cake, iced in white and marked off with chocolate lines to look like a calendar leaf of the month of August, a candle in the noted date of each of the honorees.

The party moved gaily on into the morning hours, with the "moon hanging low on the Alamo" and the mariachis' spirited *canciones.* No one really wanted to say "*Buenas Noches!*"

Another colorful fiesta took place at Willow Way when three of the season's lovely debutantes were honored at a Sunday brunch. These girls' mothers had made their debutante affairs together, and their grandmothers had been friends through the years. Large, hot pink invitations with a little *mulita* in the corner were received, reading:

Where the cactus and the rattlesnakes and gray cenizos grow
Near the Villa San Fernando, which is San Antonio,
An ancient Mexicano on a mule as white as snow
Sat and spoke an ancient formula to make his mula go!
"Arre Mulita!"

Now we send you this mulita, which is blanca as can be
And the mount, though muy chiquita, carries two quite easily;
So choose a caballero, y venga por alli
Take this chart in hand to guide the way, and cry out heartily;
"Arre Mulita!"

The posada that is open on this glad December day
Is the happy hacienda which is known as Willow Way,
There to honor tres bonitas, and when you find The Inn,
With lighted hearts and candles, our holidays begin.
"Alto Mulita!"

COMIDA DOMINGO:
A MEDIA DIA (12:00) — 15TH DE DICIEMBRE, AÑO 1963

En Honor: JOAN BROWNING
MOLLY DENMAN
MARTITA RICE

Posada keepers: Mr. and Mrs. O'Neil Ford
Mr. and Mrs. Henry J. Graham
Mr. and Mrs. Henry A. Guerra, Jr.

On either side of the long driveway were colored streamers, and Mexican and American flags waving a cheery welcome. A statue of Our Lady of Guadalupe stood beside the gate, and each guest lit a votive candle and placed them around the Lady. As soon as the guests arrived they were served a hot spiced rum-cider in colorful Mexican glasses. The tables were centered with little white ceramic mulitas, their "saddle bags" laden with the native bloom Seneca. There were Mexican music and the same noble tortilla makers, patting and cooking, buttering while hot, filling with goat cheese and hot sauce, and handing to the eager company. Charcoal burners were placed around the patio where each person cooked his own *Anticuchos, which were marvelous.

★

Anticuchos (*makes* 20)

- 30 lbs. backstrap strips or tenderloin
- 1 qt. red wine vinegar
- ¾ cup salt
- ½ cup peppercorns
- 50 jalapeño peppers
- 4 garlic cloves, mashed
- 1 Tbs. oregano
- 1 Tbs. cumin
- 1 Tbs. paprika

Cut tenderloin into small pieces, about 1-inch to 1½-inch squares. Place in large, deep bowl, cover with marinade. Let stand overnight. String on green cane skewer. Broil and serve en brochette. Baste as it cooks with marinade and olive oil with little red chilis added.

Also, this feast included guacamole, homemade hot tamales, garbanzo beans, and Chili con Queso; coffee and Crystallized Pumpkin Candy. Instead of flowers, the host presented each of the honorees with a handsome white rebozo.

We went down to San Antonio the night before the big party to see if we could be of some assistance in the preparations. This was so much fun it was hard to tell when the *real* party began! However, twenty-four hours before the hour of the party, all seemed very quiet at Willow Way. We had a leisurely swim followed by a long pleasant hour or so of visiting and sipping our drinks. The men all ordered the usual highball, but I adventured Mrs. Graham's *Lemon-Rum Drink, and am so glad I did. It is a delicious drink on a warm summer's evening. Mrs. Graham gave me the recipe out of her 1945 diary; it was entitled Marie Urzbach's Lemon-Rum Punch. Mrs. Graham has served this often at big parties. It is stored in a large jar in the refrigerator and very nice to have on hand.

★

Lemon-Rum Punch (*serves 60*)

24 lemons
4 lbs. sugar
2 gallons water
2 Tbs. orange pekoe tea
2 cups New England rum
4 oz. apricot brandy
4 oz. yellow chartreuse
2 oz. orange Curaçao

Cut peel off lemons; cut very thin with no white of lemon rind. Put in a large bowl with the sugar, then squeeze the lemons and pour the juice over the sugar and lemon peel. Bring the 2 gallons of water to a boil, and while bubbling and boiling, toss in the two tablespoons of tea and let boil exactly one minute. Then remove from fire and strain *hot* tea over lemon peel, juice and sugar. Stir well until sugar is dissolved. Then add all the various liquors and put aside in a cool place to blend and ripen (covered). Later, bottle in jugs for easier handling and pour a little rum on top of liquid in each jug. Serve from punch bowl to which ice has been added, and garnish with pineapple chunks, mint, and cherries.

Dinner was a real gourmet experience. The night before we arrived, Jewell, the Fords' housekeeper, said she looked out the window when she thought she saw a man climbing on the roof. She was just about to call her husband when she discovered it was Wanda in her pajamas out catching sleeping squabs! And this was what she served so magnificiently for dinner — *Squab Oostendaise.

★

Squab Oostendaise

4 spring onions
12 fresh mushrooms
1 small carrot
18 juniper berries
1 tsp. fennel seed
2 tangerines
6 squabs
¼ lb. butter
1 Tbs. flour
½ cup Marsala
Salt and pepper

Chop the onion, including some of the green tops, small. Slice the mushrooms; slice carrots very thin. Crush the juniper berries and fennel seed together in a mortar. Peel and separate the tangerines into sections. Wash the squabs inside and out with warm water. Stuff each squab inside with four tangerine sections. Melt 4 Tbs. butter in a heavy skillet or pot and sauté the squabs over a high flame (turning frequently to brown all sides) for about 20 minutes. Place squabs in casserole. Sauté mushrooms and pour them and butter over squabs. Melt remaining butter in same pan, sauté onion until soft. Add flour and wine. Stir well and pour over squabs. Sprinkle with salt, pepper, crushed juniper berries and fennel. Cover casserole. Bake at 400 degrees for ½ hour. Remove from oven and garnish with carrot. Serve at once.

With this she served wild rice, plain spinach (barely cooked and seasoned with a little lemon and butter), baby onions (also simply boiled and buttered), *Persimmon Salad (off her persimmon trees). We drank claret (St. Julien) and for desert had *Chocolate Whiffle, one of Wanda's specialties.

★

Persimmon Salad (*serves* 4)

4 persimmons
2 bunches land cress (or watercress)
French dressing

Skin the persimmons by dousing each for a few moments in rapidly boiling water and peeling off the skin against a knife blade as you peel tomatoes. Remove the thicker stems from the cress. Wash it well in cold water, and dry between towels. Arrange the cress in a salad bowl. Cut the peeled persimmons into quarters. Place them in the bowl on the bed of cress. Just before serving add the French dressing, and toss the salad well.

★

Chocolate Whiffle (*serves* 4)

1 pt. whipping cream
1 pkg. thin chocolate wafers
1 Tbs. chocolate shot
1 Maraschino cherry

Beat the cream in a glass serving bowl or other suitable container until it is quite stiff. Insert the chocolate wafers edgewise into the cream, very close together and standing on end. Cover the wafers completely with cream. Using your fingers or a serving spoon, smooth the top and sprinkle it with the chocolate shot or crumbled cookies — if you are out of shot at the moment. Place in the refrigerator to chill for at least six hours. Just before serving, garnish with a single Maraschino cherry in the center.

★

Hot Buttered Rum (for our Christmastime party)

Heat 1 cup of apple cider for each person with a stick of cinnamon and a clove. In a warm mug, pour in a jigger of rum, and over this the hot, hot apple cider. A dab of butter will melt over the top, and dash powdered cinnamon on top. Yum, yum!

The atmosphere of San Antonio seems to demand fiesta-type parties, but they do not necessarily have to have a Mexican or Texas theme. Mr. and Mrs. Louis Kocurek set out to prove this when they gave a Texas-style Luau honoring their son David and his fiancée Sharon Martin. The Kocureks entertain a great deal in their palatial home in Terrell Hills, located in northeast San Antonio. Their meticulously landscaped grounds were a perfect setting for this type of party. Millie Kocurek usually propels her parties by her own power, but she was so busy with pre-wedding chores that she asked me to cater this one.

I had short eighteen-inch legs made for our round tables. These were placed out in an irregular semicircle under the trees, each with six bright multicolored pillows around it as seats. Over near the swimming pool we placed a long buffet table covered with straw matting. An extravagant centerpiece was made of birds of paradise, tai and camphor leaves, huge brilliant-colored astors, fresh pineapples and clusters of grapes. Multicolored votive lights were also used in with the flowers and fruit. Smaller arrangements using the same flowers and lights were on each of the smaller tables. Bright-feathered birds looked very realistic in the trees.

As the guests arrived, they were given leis of fresh flowers and served daiquiris in small-sized, scraped-out pineapples — the top put back on and a hole cut in each big enough for the straw used to sip the daiquiri. An orchestra in Hawaiian attire played authentic music during cocktails and dinner, then hung up their guitars and switched to dance music after dinner. The guests were asked to find their places and be seated at the tables as the food was brought in a procession. The waiters and younger boys who helped carry in the food were barefooted and dressed in white duck pants and bright floral shirts. Leading the procession were two young boys carrying long lighted torches. Next came two carrying between them a huge tray bearing a whole roasted suckling pig with an apple in his mouth, a lei around his neck and a flower in his curled tail. He was surrounded with charcoaled spare ribs. All the big trays were carried by two boys, held low so that the guests could not only inspect the food but also get a good whiff of it as it went by. The smaller dishes were carried by only one waiter. As they completed encircling the tables, each placed his dish on the buffet. All were decorated with fresh flowers, fruit or leaves. Bringing up the rear of the procession was an old man with two monkeys, also with a lei — this added much color and fun! When the procession was completed, the guests came and served themselves to this feast:

Whole Suckling Pig Roasted with Apple in his mouth
Charcoaled Ribs
Sweet 'n Sour Sauce
** Sukiyaki on Fried Noodles*
** Chicken with Pineapple*
*Miniature Egg Rolls with * Hot Mustard Sauce*
Watermelon Bowl with Fresh Fruit
Tray lavished with grapes
Crisp Green Beans with Almonds
** Lamb Shish Kebabs*
** Cucumbers in Sour Cream*
** Rice Pilaf*
** Cold Marinated Eggplant*
Baked Red Fish

★

Sukiyaki (*makes 4 servings*)

Ezra Rachlin, who is the eminent conductor of our Austin Symphony, goes to Houston every summer to conduct a series of summer outdoor concerts. During this time, he "batches" in an apartment. So as not to get too homesick for his wife, Carmen, he spends some of his time cooking up something exotic. This is the Sukiyaki he made so successfully. I always use this recipe — it is delicious.

1 medium onion, thinly sliced (½ cup)
¼ cup butter
1 lb. beef sirloin, cut in thin narrow strips
Salt and pepper
½ lb. fresh mushrooms, thinly sliced, or 1 can (4 oz.) sliced mushrooms
½ cup sliced celery
1 can (16- or 17-oz.) bean sprouts, drained
¼ cup water chestnuts, thinly sliced (optional)
2 Tbs. soy sauce
1 cup beef stock
1⅓ cups cooked rice
½ cup chopped green onions
1½ cups hot water, if needed

Sauté onion in butter in a large skillet until transparent. Season beef with salt and pepper. Add to onion and cook until browned on all sides. Stir in mushrooms, celery, bean sprouts, water chestnuts, and soy sauce. Cook 5 to 10 minutes. Meanwhile, add the stock to a saucepan. Stir in rice and pour into center of ingredients in skillet. Sprinkle scallions over other ingredients. Cover and let simmer over low heat 5 minutes. Add water if needed. *Do not overcook!* Serve with additional soy sauce, if desired.

★

Cucumbers in Sour Cream (serves 6)

½ clove garlic
¾ tsp. salt
1½ cups sour cream
2 Tbs. vinegar
¼ tsp. pepper
2 medium cucumbers, pared and sliced (about 2 cups)

Finely chop the garlic in salt. Combine in bowl with sour cream, vinegar, and pepper. Mix well. Add cucumbers and toss lightly. Chill.

★

Cold Marinated Eggplant (makes 6 servings)

1 small eggplant
½ cup chopped celery
⅓ cup chopped pimento
1 small clove garlic, minced
2 Tbs. chopped capers
⅛ tsp. powdered dill
¼ tsp. oregano
½ tsp. salt
⅛ tsp. pepper
⅓ cup salad oil
⅓ cup vinegar

Cook eggplant in boiling salted water about 20 minutes, or until tender. Drain. Cool, peel, and cut in 2-inch lengths — about 2 cups. Add remaining ingredients to the eggplant and mix well. Cover tightly and store in refrigerator. Serve cold.

For dessert, we had fresh coconuts sawed in half (sawed on a hand saw). Each half was filled with *Fresh Coconut Ice Cream —

which is divine as is — but we went a step further and topped it with one of the best ice cream toppings I know of, and served them flambéed. Virginia Robinson gave me the recipe a long time ago and I have used it over almost every kind of ice cream.

★

Fresh Coconut Ice Cream

1 large fresh coconut
4 eggs
1 cup sugar
1 qt. milk
Pinch of salt
1½ pt. cream, whipped
½ tsp. vanilla
¼ cup coconut milk

Grate the coconut, retaining ¼ cup of the milk. Make a custard of the eggs, sugar, milk (1 qt.) and salt, and cook until it coats a spoon. Let the custard cool; then add the cream, vanilla, and coconut milk. Freeze until mushy, then add 1 cup grated fresh coconut (more if desired).

★

Ice Cream Topping

1 pt. apricot preserves
1 pt. pineapple preserves
2 cups fresh pineapple, slivered
1 cup fresh coconut, grated
½ cup slivered, toasted almonds
¾ cup rum

In chafing dish, mix ingredients together; heat, and add rum last and light. Serve over ice cream.

(To stand upright, the coconut shells can be placed in small aluminum foil cups holding rock salt. However, for the luau, we had the guests just hold them in their hands.)

THE ARGYLE

The name of Miss Alice O'Grady is almost as much a part of the history of San Antonio as many of the Texas heroes who fought at the Alamo — and her family's hotel, the Argyle, is a landmark still standing high on a hill in Alamo Heights, where for many more years than a half-century, its name has been known and the artistry of its cooking fabled. The Argyle had a heritage of rich living even before it became a hotel. It was built before the War Between the States by Charles Anderson. It is a Southern Colonial type of architecture and was the headquarters for his horse ranch where he raised horses for the United States Cavalry with a ready market at nearby Fort Sam Houston. Mr. Anderson also entertained very lavishly many notables of the time, such as Robert E. Lee and Albert Sidney Johnston.

A number of years and two or three owners later (one owner being a Scotsman who gave it the name of Argyle because this section of land reminded him of the rolling hills of Scotland), the ranch was bought by the O'Gradys, who kept the same name, of Argyle. It was a happy circumstance when Miss Alice took over the food preparation at the Argyle. She had always loved to cook. She was constantly experimenting for only one goal, which she achieved, and that was perfection, both to the palate and to the eye. Her luscious cakes with delicate spun-sugar flowers are still remembered by those who were so fortunate as to have partaken of her treats. A bowl of fresh black-eyed peas came to the table garnished with perfect facsimiles of the Black-eyed Susans — steaming platters, each a perfection, were brought to the tables in endless processions, which made dining at the Argyle a real experience. Miss Alice's *Soup Pot was famous not only to the guests at the Argyle but to her sick friends and neighbors. Her Pot seemed to have some magic source, as there was always enough for any demand. It was not only very palatable, but had great food value. She always used lots of bone.

★

Miss Alice's Soup Pot

Many bones — raw ones and any other meat bones on hand, chicken or turkey carcasses, ham or lamb bones or scraps; any leftover cooked vegetables or fresh ones as the case may be; all palatable juices from cooking vegetables, such as string beans, carrots, peas, etc., celery tops, tomato and potato peeling, asparagus juice, turnips, squash, butter beans, corn. She always added a clove of garlic and plenty of onions. She would cook this all day long, using enough water to "have enough to go around." She always had a few eggshells floating around, which she said added to the nutrition of the soup and also cleared it up. About an hour before dinner, she would pour this conglomerate mixture through a sieve and strain it into a large kettle, thickening it, if it were too thin, with tapioca or flour. With this stock she would make a variety of soups. (If she wanted to have Tomato Soup she added tomatoes; if

Okra Gumbo she'd add thinly sliced tender pods of okra and simmer long enough to cook it.) Miss Alice used little salt, leaving that addition to the individual. She always served soup for dinner, regardless of the time of year.

This was the way Miss Alice did her *Southern Style Fried Chicken:

★

Southern Style Fried Chicken

Cut the chicken into desired pieces and have thoroughly chilled before cooking. Salt and pepper each piece, then carefully roll in flour. Have the frying fat very hot and drop a few pieces into it at a time — do not cook too many pieces at a time. After each piece has been turned, lower the heat and cook until golden brown. Drain on brown paper. To make a delicious creamed gravy, you drain off the surplus fat when the chicken is fried, leaving all the crumbs in the frying pan; these must not be burnt. Add a little flour and stir while browning, then add ¼ cup of hot water and stir until smooth. As this is very thick, thin it to the desired thickness of gravy with milk or cream. Season to taste with salt and black pepper.

A typical Texas dinner might consist of Fried Chicken, Butter Beans, Spinach Ring with Hard-boiled Eggs, green salad of mixed vegetables, Lemon Pie or a cobbler of fresh peaches or berries. Oh, yes, don't forget to have plenty of mint for your tea, and no bread could take the place of hot biscuits. Have an extra pound of butter and a dish of preserves for the biscuits.

One of the Argyle recipes I have used often is for what Miss Alice called *Bride's Pie — probably because it is so simple to make, delicious to eat and will surely impress one's husband. Amy has impressed our company with this many times.

★

Bride's Pie

1 medium-sized chicken
5 cups of broth
1 cup cream
3 Tbs. butter or chicken fat
2 cups and 3 Tbs. flour
3 Tbs. shortening
2 Tbs. baking powder
1 tsp. salt
Milk to mix

Boil chicken until very tender, bone and break into pieces. Use broth, skimming off most of the fat. Mix the cream, butter or chicken fat, 3 Tbs. flour, and add to the liquid to make a thin sauce. Make a soft dough of 2 cups flour, shortening, baking powder, salt and enough milk to mix. Put chicken in a baking dish, cover with the sauce, drop the dough by spoonfuls over it, and bake 30 minutes.

The molded gelatine salads, so much a part of Texas cuisine which Miss Alice would concoct, would indeed set the style for a luncheon. She had an interesting collection of molds, and would fill them with many combinations of fruits. The gelatine was rich in flavor, which is the secret of the success of jellied salads, because she used syrups from a variety of drained fruits, fresh lemon juice, etc. Miss Alice would turn out these beautiful salads on a bed of very, very fine shredded *pink* cabbage (soak finely shredded cabbage in ice water that is colored with rose food coloring) decorated with sprays of blue morning glories around the edge. Miss Alice would cut the morning glories before the sun shone on them and put them in her icebox until needed; then, when exposed to the air, they opened quickly. Sometimes she would top them with the *Famous Argyle Whipped Cream Salad Dressing.

★

The Famous Argyle Salad Dressing

4 egg yolks, well beaten
4 Tbs. tarragon vinegar
1 Tbs. sugar
1 Tbs. butter
1 tsp. salt
1 tsp. dry mustard mixed with a little water
Dash of red pepper
1 pt. whipping cream

Cook all except whipping cream in a double boiler, stirring constantly until thick; cool. Whip 1 pt. cream and fold in the cooked mixture just before serving. Serve with fruit salads.

I suppose Miss Alice's *Sugar Cookie recipe is an all-time favorite with all ages.

★

Plain Sugar Cookies

1 cup powdered sugar
1 lb. fresh butter
3 egg whites
5 cups flour
1 tsp. baking powder
Pinch of salt
Grated rind, juice of ½ lemon
1 tsp. vanilla

Beat sugar and butter to a cream and add eggs, one at a time, then flour, baking powder and pinch of salt, and lemon and vanilla. Chill in icebox and drop by spoonfuls on baking sheet; sprinkle with sugar and bake in moderate oven.

EL PASO

About two hundred miles before we got to El Paso, we came to Pecos, the center of the agriculturally rich Pecos Valley and land of "the world's *best* cantaloupes." It was easy to visualize the past and the year 1883 with dusty cowboys and worn spectators leaving the arena of the world's first Rodeo and hastening to the pavilion for the juicy melon as a prelude to the evening with its festive square dances. It was even more enjoyable to actually be in this county where the "law of the West" and the seat of vigilante Judge Roy Bean were established, and to partake of this famous Pecos cantaloupe. It was dark by the time we left the old pioneer ranching center. We saw not a flicker of light along the way except for an occasional passing truck. Suddenly, the darkness was broken by a splendorous sight of twinkling lights and stars. Over the sprawling mesa of El Paso, the stars and lights on the mountains seemed to merge into one luminous expanse of glitter.

El Paso del Norte, once a gateway for the Spanish conquistadores, was named by Don Juan de Oñate on May 4, 1598. The proximity of metropolitan El Paso and its sister city in Mexico, Juárez, allows for the flow of the peoples and the products of two republics. The best views of the city itself are from the surrounding mountaintops or from one of the tall buildings within the city, which have been scarce in the past but are now slowly beginning to shoot up. Bessie Simpson of the El Paso *Post* took me to lunch at the beautiful El Paso Club on top of the El Paso National Bank Building — one of those new and few "lookout" buildings which tower over the city. The club is quite stunning, done in rich golds, blacks, and reds. Bessie offered me not only the good view and pleasant atmosphere, but also a very tasty recipe that our family has particularly enjoyed.

★

Chicken and Dumplings

Have one large and fat hen cut up for frying. Season and boil in a large kettle, making sure the chicken is covered with water. Cook until tender. Remove meat from bones, leaving in large pieces.

DUMPLINGS

1 cup sifted flour — **½ tsp. salt**
1½ tsp. baking powder

Sift dry ingredients, then add:

1 egg, slightly mixed with 2 Tbs. oil — **¼ cup plus 1 Tbs. milk**

Drop this mixture by a teaspoon into the simmering broth. Cook 10 minutes and return chicken to broth. Cook covered 10 minutes longer.

High up on the rim of one of the mountains which overlook El Paso live Mr. and Mrs. Richard Miller, who planned their home specifically with all sizes of parties and types of entertaining in mind. From the terrace, we watched the lights come on at night over the pass, and viewed historic landmarks such as the Rio Grande and the mountain La Cruz de Juárez. La Cruz is the site where faithful pilgrims still wind their way to the top for worship, only today they are not plagued by the ruthless bandits who once roamed the mountain. The Millers' party room can seat sixty for dinner, easily serve three hundred for tea or cocktails, and yet offer an intimate setting for small family dinners.

The Miller parties, like the hostess and the house, are dressy, pretty, and gay. The artistic setting and stimulating guests plus many splendid menus would seem to suffice for a successful evening, but Mrs. Miller — Deane — makes use of an additional attraction not all hostesses are fortunate enough to come by. There is Mike, age thirteen, and Marcy, age ten. Marcy, clothed in a frilly white party dress, passed chilled *Shrimp Deluxes and piping hot *Parmesan Crowns with the drinks before dinner.

★

Shrimp Deluxes

Cook 2-3 lbs. shrimp, the bigger the better, in salted water the day before serving and marinate in this sauce for at least 24 hours:

1 cup chili sauce
2 Tbs. lemon juice
1 Tbs. grated onion
1 Tbs. Worcestershire
Several drops Tabasco
1 Tbs. olive oil
1 Tbs. vinegar
¼ tsp. salt
2 tsp. paprika

Add shrimp and chill.

★

Parmesan Crowns

Mix together:

¾ cup mayonnaise
1 cup Parmesan cheese
1 Tbs. chopped chives

Spread on small toast rounds and run under the broiler until very hot.

Mike helped José pass drinks, and he entertained the guests by making delightful observations in an unobtrusive way. The buffet dinner was served from the long marble-top dining room table. After the guests served their plates, they found their names on decorative place cards. The tables were covered with crisp linen, gleaming silver, tall crystal goblets, and wine glasses. The centerpieces were of fresh hawthorne. Here is the menu, with recipes for two of the dishes:

Round tray of roast beef, rib eye, with the choice of well-done, medium, or rare (Deane's secret for offering a choice is to cook several roasts for different lengths of time and serve them on one tray)

French Beans Amandine

** Chilis Stuffed with Guacamole*

** Cranberry Mold*

Creamed Rice Casserole

Pickled Onions

Rolls

Coffee

Angel Food Cake with Strawberry Filling

★

Green Chilis Stuffed with Guacamole (*serves 6*)

6 chilis (fresh preferred; canned may be used)
Guacamole salad
½ pt. sour cream
Paprika (optional)

Peel 6 long green chili peppers and remove seeds. To clean: chilis should be placed in heavy skillet in a very hot oven until the outer skin scorches. (They can be stuck under the broiler if they are watched.) Remove from oven immediately and place in a damp clean towel or dish towel. Fold dish towel over chilis and rub gently until skin slips off. Split down the middle and remove seeds.

Stuff chilis with guacamole and top with sour cream. If you like, you can sprinkle paprika on the sour cream.

★

Cranberry Mold (*serves 24 to 28*)

3 1-lb. cans jellied cranberry sauce
8 Tbs. lemon juice
2 large pkgs. cream cheese whipped with ¾ cup mayonnaise (more if it is not creamy)
¾ cup powdered sugar
2 cups toasted walnuts
3 cups heavy cream, whipped

Mash cranberry sauce with fork and add lemon juice. Using small size paper cups, pour cranberry sauce to halfway mark of paper cup. Combine cream cheese, mayonnaise and sugar in mixer. Add walnuts and fold in whipped cream. Fill upper half of cup with cheese mixture and place cups in freezer. When ready to serve, slit cups and peel away. When removed from paper cup, the cream cheese will be on bottom and the cranberries on top. These should be removed from freezer approximately 20 minutes before serving. Can be served on lettuce leaf.

One of the fascinating guests at this dinner was Katus Hunyadi Walton, wife of retired Colonel Joseph Walton, who was born and raised in Budapest. After Joe and Katus married, they literally lived all over the world. When they were stationed at Fort Bliss, both of them fell in love with the people of El Paso. Army people play an important part in the city's society, and there are many interesting couples, like the Waltons, who have lived all over the world but choose to retire among the "cordial and friendly" gentry of El Paso. Katus particularly likes the food served in this part of the country.

When I asked her if her family enjoyed Hungarian food or food flavored El Paso style, she quickly replied, "Oh, zay luvf ze food *here!* I always prepare it. Ze children even like ze squash." Here is Katus's squash recipe, and we hope you like it as much as the Hungarians do!

★

El Paso Squash

Cook and drain 2 lbs. yellow squash. Sauté one chopped onion and place it in the bottom of a buttered quart casserole. On top of the onion, place layers of squash, canned green chilis, and grated longhorn cheddar cheese. Repeat layers in this order, ending with cheese.

Another guest at the party and friend of the Millers was Judge Alan Fraser, judge of the Court of Civil Appeals. He broke in on all the "ohs and ahs" complimenting Deane's delectable dinner to say, well, Deane was a good cook, but she never could make barbecued chicken as good as his. "Why, Alan, what do you *mean?* I taught you how to barbecue that chicken!" Alan went into great detail on the recipe and just exactly how it was done, but we said we didn't quite understand; when could he demonstrate? After a little more pressure, he agreed to oblige Saturday night. Now I sorta thought he'd been braggin', but actually he'd been quite modest. Dick and Deane invite the guests saying Alan will cook, and he is enthralled because he is going to be featured and fussed over. The fun begins when Deane goes to the store, buys the groceries, then gets the house polished, sets up the tables, drags out the barbecue equipment, cleans it (or rather has the maid clean it), and puts the charcoal in it. Then she makes the barbecue sauce, pre-cooks the chickens, prepares a vegetable, rolls, tossed salad, and dessert and gets out Alan's chef hat and apron. After a shower, she lights the fire in the barbecue thirty minutes before the guests arrive. With the fire ready, she dips the chickens in the sauce and has the maid take the chickens and sauce and place them on the barbecue pit. At this point, the hat and apron are brought forth and Alan is dressed for the part. He is now ready to approach the chickens and turn them, and by that time, they are *ready* to be turned. When they are

done, Alan calls the maid, who removes them from the fire onto a platter, and dinner is ready to eat. Everybody chirps over how delightful the chickens are and how wonderful it would be if all men were handy around the house, etc. Deane says that this drama has become such fun that Alan calls her about once a week and says, "Let's barbecue!" But Deane says that she is not up to one of these easy barbecue sessions except about once a month. It is, she says, rather the same idea as asking a man to repair something!

★

Judge Fraser's Chicken Barbecue Sublime

- 6 chickens, halved or quartered
- 1 lb. margarine
- 1 medium-sized jar of prepared mustard
- 1 large bottle Worcestershire
- 1 large bottle catsup
- 1 cup sugar

Melt margarine. Add other ingredients and mix well. Dip chickens in sauce and place on grill. Brush chickens with sauce while barbecuing. Alan prefers chickens not over 2 lbs., which is sometimes impossible. Fatter chickens can be precooked and nobody knows the difference.

Another dish for which Deane has a culinary reputation is her *El Paso Sopa. She simply serves this with hot handmade tortillas, a green salad, and dessert.

★

Sopa de Gallina

Boil 4- or 5-lb. hen until very tender and remove bones and cut into small pieces. Sauté 2 large onions, chopped, in butter. Add:

4 cups tomato juice
2 cups chopped green chili
1 tsp. salt
Black pepper to taste

Simmer 30 minutes; set aside.

2 large packages of tostados (or Fritos)
4 cups grated cheddar cheese
2 cups cream (half and half)

Place layer of tostados in casserole, then layer of grated cheese, then layer of chicken, and add the above prepared sauce. Continue until all ingredients are used up. Put grated cheese on top. Then pour cream and some of the chicken broth to make sufficient liquid (almost to top). Cook in 350-degree oven about 25 to 30 minutes. Serves 10 to 12.

FOR A LARGER QUANTITY, SERVES 46

14-lb. turkey
3 lbs. tostados
2 lbs. onions
4 cans tomatoes
4 lbs. cheddar cheese
4 pts. half and half cream

There are countless numbers of interesting old-timers and new-timers who wouldn't want to live anywhere but El Paso. One of these families and perhaps the most renowned is the Tom Lea family. Tom Lea was born in El Paso and for years has been known primarily as a painter. In 1949 he published his first book, *The Brave Bulls*, and in 1957 he published his famous work in two volumes, *The King Ranch*. He has not only written about this renowned ranch, but also painted and sketched a fabulous collection of the characters and scenes on the ranch. In addition to painting many popular murals for public buildings in El Paso (including the new library), he has illustrated books for J. Frank Dobie. Tom is loved and admired, his books and paintings read and appreciated, because he has a genuine sympathy and intimacy with the life in West Texas. When he was recently honored at a testimonial dinner in El Paso, he was presented with a magnificent Steuben glass bowl on which was etched a copy of one of his King Ranch sketches.

The Lea residence sits on a mountainside overlooking El Paso town. The interior meticulously blends with the vivid browns, reds, and golds of the Southwest. The rooms are both softened and intensified with choice paintings done by Tom in all parts of the world. The house has a charm that seems to lure and to hold its guests. Entertainment in the Lea home is usually small and informal. The guest list numbers no more than six or eight people, for the purpose of being able to enjoy each personality. Invitees are certain to arrive early, or at least on schedule, for the wonderful privilege of hearing Tom's stories. This particular night, Tom told us the story behind his canvas hanging over the mantel at the Millers'. It's called "The Unfinished Shadow." Tom had a tender feeling for the brave bull who refused to die though the lance had already struck him fatally. The bull was trying to keep himself up on his feet, and the sympathic-looking matador was standing with his cape over the bull with a look of pity on his face, even in victory.

When Tom speaks about the cuisine of his pretty wife, Sarah, he refuses to grant her any speciality. Instead, he says, "*Everything* Sarah cooks is good." Tom himself displays talent in the art of making martinis, which he serves before dinner. The recipe is seven to one. The Vermouth goes in first. Tom says this is most important. The Leas frequently serve:

Prime Rib of Beef, rare
** Wild Rice with Creamed Mushrooms*
*Tossed Salad with Avocado Slices and a special * Dressing originated by Sarah's grandmother*
** Frozen Lemon Pie*

★

Wild Rice with Creamed Mushrooms

1 cup wild rice
1 tsp. salt
½ clove garlic, minced
4 cups boiling water
¼ cup butter
½ tsp. poultry seasoning
1 cup sautéed onion

Combine rice, salt, garlic, and boiling water in double boiler; steam until tender (about ¾ hour). Stir frequently. Melt butter, add seasoning and onions. Put in buttered 8-inch ring mold. Set in pan of hot water and bake in moderate oven, 350 degrees, for 20 minutes. Loosen edges with knife. Invert on serving dish and fill with creamed mushrooms.

1 lb. mushrooms
2 Tbs. butter
¼ tsp. salt
2 Tbs. flour
1 cup cream or chicken stock
Pinch of marjoram
Paprika

Quickly sauté mushrooms in butter until done. Add salt and sprinkle with flour. Gradually stir in cream or stock and bring to boil. Add seasonings.

★

Grandmother's Green Salad Dressing

2 or 3 thin slivers of garlic
¼ tsp. coarsely ground black pepper
A little dry mustard

Mash all together in a wooden salad bowl. Add:

1 Tbs. tarragon vinegar
½ cup salad oil

Mix well and pour over salad.

And the dessert Tom thinks is a must for the perfect ending to a dinner:

★

Frozen Lemon Pie

3 egg yolks
½ cup sugar
5 Tbs. lemon juice
¼ cup rind of lemon
3 egg whites
3 Tbs. sugar
1 cup whipped cream
2 cups crushed vanilla wafers (reserve some for top)

Beat egg yolks, add sugar, and cook over a low heat until thick or coats a spoon. Add lemon juice and rind. Fold beaten egg whites and sweetened whipped cream into cooked mixture. Pour over most of the crumbled cookies, which have been placed in the bottom of the pie pan. Sprinkle the remaining cookie crumbs on top. Freeze and serve immediately after removing from freezer.

Here are some more of Sarah's recipes. We particularly use and like:

★

Poppyseed Cake

¾ cup poppy seeds
¾ cup butter
1½ cups sugar
¾ cup milk
2 tsp. baking powder
2 cups all-purpose flour
4 egg whites, stiffly beaten
1 tsp. vanilla

Soak poppy seeds in milk about 4 hours or overnight. Cream butter and sugar; add poppy seeds, milk, and beat. Sift dry ingredients and add small amount at a time. Beat thoroughly; it will be quite stiff. Fold in egg whites, vanilla. Bake in 3 round 9-inch pans, 1 inch deep, in a 350-degree oven for 20 to 25 minutes. Fill the three layers with the following filling:

1 cup sugar
¼ tsp. salt
3 Tbs. cornstarch
4 egg yolks
2 cups milk
1 tsp. vanilla
1 cup broken pecans

Mix dry ingredients; add egg yolks and milk, which have been mixed together. Cook until thick. Add vanilla and nuts and spread between layers. Ice with:

3 cups powdered sugar
¼ tsp. salt
3 squares bitter chocolate
¼ cup butter
½ tsp. vanilla
Enough cream or cold water to make it just right to spread

★

Sour Cream Enchiladas

Eloise Thornberry said this was one of her favorite El Paso dishes.

SAUCE

2 cups chopped fresh or canned green chilis
2 cups tomatoes with juice drained off

Put on stove and let simmer 30 to 40 minutes or until all juice is gone. Add a little cream and 2 cups grated longhorn cheese. Allow it to melt. Add 2 to 4 cups cream (sweet or sour). Don't let boil — just simmer.

Fry 12 tortillas and drain. Dip one at a time into sauce until limber. Lay in long flat dish a layer of tortillas, a sprinkle of onion (chopped and soaked in vinegar for 2 hours and drained), cheese, layer of sauce, etc., until 2 or 3 layers of tortillas. Put rest of sauce over until covered.

Sarah gave me another good dessert:

★

Orange-Banana-Lemon Ice

Juice of 1 lemon
Juice of 2 oranges
2 bananas rubbed through a sieve or food mill
1 scant cup sugar stirred into the fruit until dissolved
1 cup milk

Freeze in a refrigerator tray or Pyrex dish and beat it well 2 or 3 times before it freezes solidly, and it won't get icy.

Tom Lea's work intrigued me, and I looked forward to seeing his paintings at the King Ranch, where I planned to visit in a few days.

By the way, on this same trip we stopped at Winters, Texas, to see our friend Ruth Little. She served us the most delicious *Applesauce Cake, better known in the W. E. Little family as Special Day Cake. The recipe originally came from Germany and was brought to South Texas by early residents almost a century ago. Ruth says that her boys expect this cake to be on hand on Thanksgiving and Christmas and welcome it anytime in between. One time a very strict old lady, who detested the thought of liquor so much that she would not buy a magazine containing liquor ads, came for dinner. Ruth served this cake, and she even ate a second piece of it. She asked for the recipe, and the kind hostess substituted grape juice for the whiskey when she gave it to her. The lady was always puzzled because her cake never tasted as good as Ruth's.

★

Holiday Applesauce Cake

Cream well 2 cups sugar and 1 cup shortening. Beat in 4 eggs, one at a time. Dissolve 1 tsp. soda in ¼ cup cold water and add it to the batter. Add 1 tsp. each of cinnamon, cloves, allspice, nutmeg, and vanilla. Stir in 3 medium-sized apples, chopped fine. Sift 3 cups of all-purpose flour into the batter. Stir in 3 Tbs. Bourbon whiskey. Put cake batter into two rectangular pans and cook slowly (at about 325 degrees) for about 1 hour. Altitude and stoves may cause some variance, so watch the cake from 40 minutes on.

FILLING

1 pt. milk
2 eggs
3 Tbs. flour
1 cup sugar
1 cup nuts
1 tsp. vanilla

Let 1⅓ cups of the milk come to a boil. In the meantime mix ⅔ cup milk and two beaten eggs with the flour and sugar. Pour hot milk into this, add nuts and vanilla, then cook until thick, stirring constantly. Cool.

When cake is baked, put cold filling on hot cake — between layers and on top.

LULING

We were standing on Main Street, Luling, Texas, waving at the young beautiful belles atop the flower-bedecked floats as they cruised by in parade celebrating the Eleventh Annual Watermelon Thump. The spectators stood under the shade of umbrellas or large straw hats, or huddled under the shady fronts of the stores as the gay caravan interspersed with high school and veteran bands moved along in the hundred-degree summer sun. In the background along Main Street, the pumps on the oilwells were busily going about their business.

In 1922, when oil was first discovered in this area, Luling was a sleepy little town with only about fourteen hundred people, who were principally engaged in farming, railroading, or cattle raising. The arrival of Mr. Edgar B. Davis from his home in Massachusetts stirred this town from its drowsy inactivity.

Six attempts to find the elusive oil in Luling brought Mr. Davis down to the last dollar of his shoe and rubber fortune; but he succeeded in striking oil on the seventh try. From the day this oil well, called Rios No. 1., came in as a great gusher, the city of Luling has steadily progressed.

Edgar B. Davis believed, without any doubt whatsoever, that he was an instrument of the Lord, and that his success in finding oil had been foreordained by God. He will always be revered by the town as its first citizen, for in addition to discovering oil there, he endowed a million-dollar experimental and research farm called the Luling Foundation, which is internationally known and has been host to people from all over the world and from all walks of life.

This great man from Yankee country, fifty-six years old and with no family and no dependents, could easily have sat back and enjoyed all the money any man could use; but he recognized something that not many men do: an obligation to help those who had helped him to make his fortune. Unusually benevolent and a man of vision, he went about helping his adopted home in an even more unusual way. He invited everybody to a big barbecue — all the people from Caldwell and Guadalupe counties, all of his former employees and friends who were scattered all over the world — and they all came! He bought a herd of beef to be barbecued, all the soda water and ice cream in Central Texas, and brought in entertainers from New York. One hundred acres of land (which was white with fully opened cotton) was bought at full production price and cleared for this big jubilee, and he said, "Come one, come all!" The most conservative estimate of those attending was fifteen thousand, but to look over the sea of faces, it looked like there were twice that many. Everyone who had ever worked for Mr. Davis was given a gift. Those who had been employed for one year received 25 per cent of their total salary; for two years 50 per cent; for three years' service 75 per cent; and those with four or more years' service drew 100 per cent. His managers received checks for $200,000. The youngest clerk and the toughest roughneck were made rich overnight. This generous benefactor gave Luling two beautiful country clubs with swimming pools and golf courses, plus a generous endowment for permanent maintenance. These are still used daily by Negro and white citizens alike as a living monument to the memory of this man who transformed Luling into the thriving oil, cattle, and watermelon center that it is today.

Through the Foundation, an analysis of the soil was made that proved the sandy farm land in Luling was perfect for producing watermelons. In recent years, the watermelon industry has grown to such proportions as to rival the cattle and oil industries — and Luling has become nationally known as the watermelon capital of Texas. For the past eleven years it has held an annual celebration at harvest time known far and wide as the Luling Watermelon

Thump — "thump" because watermelons are tested for ripeness by thumping them till the correct note is heard. The three-day celebration, with a variety of activities, honors the Queen of the Thump and her court. There are parties, such as the Presentation Ball, which is held in the High School gymnasium and is a very elaborate and beautiful affair; and an afternoon tea is held, at which the pretty girls who are sent to represent their towns and industries (such as the Strawberry Festival of Poteet, Texas, the Turkey Trot of Cuero, the Peach Jamboree of Stonewall) are named honorees. In 1964, the tea was held at the home of Mrs. Tom Blackwell. On the terrace of the Blackwell home, a table covered in a watermelon-pink cloth was the setting for a large scooped-out watermelon holding a most refreshing watermelon fruit punch. The melon bowl with the punch in it had been placed in the freezer overnight, and so the punch was kept icy cold throughout the party.

★

Watermelon Fresh Fruit Punch

3 qts. diced watermelon
1⅓ cups fresh lime juice
1⅓ cups fresh lemon juice
1½ cups sugar
2 cups orange juice
½ tsp. salt
6 drops red food coloring

Combine first four ingredients. Refrigerate 1 hour or more. Press mixture through sieve or colander. Add orange juice, salt, and food coloring. Chill and serve. Yield: About 1 gallon.

As part of the activities a very interesting Arts and Crafts Exhibition is held in one of the buildings on Main Street, displaying items such as beautifully intricate needlework and oil and watercolor paintings by local artists. Of course, the exhibit which fascinated me most was the food — the wonderful preserves, which I fortunately got to taste. It was easy to see why the first prize winner was Mrs. Frank Williams, Jr., of Luling.

★

Watermelon Rind Preserves

(PRIZEWINNING RECIPE — 1964 LULING WATERMELON THUMP)

4 lbs. watermelon rind, cubed
8 qts. water
8 Tbs. lime (calcium oxide)
8 cups sugar
4 qts. water
2 lemons, sliced
Cherries (optional)

Select thick-rind melons. Trim outer green skin and pink meat. Use only greenish-white parts of rind. Cut rind into ½-inch cubes (larger if desired) and weigh. Soak cubes overnight in limewater (8 quarts of water mixed with the lime). Drain and place cubes in clear water for 1 hour. Drain again and boil for 4 hours after fresh water has been added. Drain again.

Make syrup of 8 cups of sugar and 4 quarts water. Add rind and boil for 1 hour. As the syrup thickens add lemon, thinly sliced (½ lemon for each pound of fruit). When syrup begins to thicken and melon is clear, preserves are ready for packing. Place in hot sterile jars, add enough syrup to cover, and seal. (A few cherries may be added to each jar for decoration.)

Another blue ribbon winner was *Watermelon Cake, baked by Mrs. Eunice Clay. She was generous enough to give us this unique recipe which has never before been published.

★

Orange-Watermelon Loaf Cake

1 cup shortening
2 cups sugar

Cream and add:

4 eggs (one at a time)
3 Tbs. grated orange rind

Add alternately:

4 Tbs. all-purpose flour
1 tsp. soda
½ tsp. salt
1⅓ cups buttermilk

Add:

1 tsp. orange extract
1 6-oz. pkg. diced dates
1 cup pecans
½ cup candied watermelon rind — red
½ cup candied watermelon rind — green

Place batter in greased and floured loaf pan, bake in 350-degree oven for approximately one hour. Sprinkle cake with coconut. Make sauce:

SAUCE FOR WATERMELON CAKE

2 cups sugar
1 cup orange juice
3 Tbs. lemon juice
3 Tbs. orange rind

Bring to boil and pour over cake while it is still in loaf pan. Allow to cool before serving.

WATERMELON CANDIED FOR CAKE IN THE FOLLOWING MANNER

Chip rind in small squares. Soak for 2 hours in lime solution (2 Tbs. lime to 2 qts. water). Rinse well, bring to boil, let simmer for 1½ hours in plain water. Drain. Add 1 cup sugar per cup of rind, lemon to taste and food coloring (red and green). Simmer for 1 hour (or until syrup thickens). Place rind in strainer and rinse syrup off before using in cake.

President Johnson not only wants a Luling watermelon at the ranch when he is there — but now asks for that Watermelon cake, too!

An entry in the foods exhibit was a cleverly made cake — someone had made a delicious *Red Velvet Cake, had added to the dough raisins which had been rolled in flour to look like watermelon seeds — and had iced the cake in a brilliant green frosting.

★

Red Velvet Cake

½ cup shortening
1½ cups sugar
2 eggs
1 Tbs. cocoa
2 oz. red food coloring
½ tsp. salt
2½ cups flour
1 cup buttermilk
1 tsp. soda
1½ tsp. vinegar

Cream shortening and sugar, add beaten eggs. Make a paste of cocoa and coloring and add to creamed mixture. Sift salt and flour together. Add to mixture alternately with buttermilk, flour first and last. Mix soda and vinegar together and add last. Bake at 350 degrees in two greased and floured cake pans until done. This really has a velvety texture — one of the best cakes I've ever eaten.

ICING

5 Tbs. flour
1 cup sugar
1 cup canned milk
1 cup butter
1 tsp. vanilla

Mix flour and sugar; add milk gradually and mix well. Drop in butter. Cook and stir until thick. Add vanilla. Cool and ice cake.

Guess this wasn't too new an idea though, for I was thumbing through an old cookbook published in 1885, and it gave this recipe:

★

Watermelon Cake

WHITE PART

2 cups white sugar
1 cup butter
1 cup sweet milk
3½ cups flour
8 egg whites
2 tsp. cream of tartar
1 tsp. soda, dissolved in 1 Tbs. warm water

RED PART

1 cup sugar with red coloring added
½ cup butter
⅓ cup sweet milk
2 cups flour
4 egg whites
1 tsp. cream of tartar
½ tsp. soda
1 teacup of raisins

Be careful to keep red part of cake around tube of greased and floured tube pan, and white part around edge. This takes two people to fill pan with batter. Bake in slow to moderate oven for approximately 1 hour.

In this old cookbook there is an interesting chapter devoted to cake making, and I was fascinated by the advice given as to the proper way to test the temperature of the oven. It states: "Many test their ovens in this way: if the hand can be held in from twenty to thirty-five seconds it is a 'quick' oven, from thirty-five to forty-five seconds is 'moderate,' and from forty-five to sixty seconds is 'slow.' Sixty seconds is a good oven to begin with for large fruitcakes. Any systematic housekeeper will hail the day some enterprising Yankee or Buckeye girl shall invent a stove or range with a thermometer attached to the oven, so that the heat may be regulated accurately and intelligently!"

The Luling Veterans of Foreign Wars served Dinner-on-the-ground after the parade, under big white tents furnished by the local funeral homes. The hosts were still in a jovial mood after having served over one thousand persons! I looked about for the chef to get the extraordinary recipe for Barbecued Chicken, but it was hard to tell who was the head man, since they all seemed to be slapping each other on the back and congratulating themselves on the wonderful success of the affair. Finally I asked Mr. Max Benefiel, who seemed to be the head cook, and he gladly obliged. He said that he started his fire before dawn in a great big long pit, using post oak and blackjack wood because these made the best coals; he always cooks over coals, never over a flame. He had to barbecue the chickens in relays because there were so many, cooking them slowly, basting, and turning them often to give a very crisp and juicy finished product. He said the recipe called for beer in the sauce, but he and the other cooks decided that would be a waste, so they just drank it as they tackled their enormous task!

★

Mr. Benefiel's Barbecue Sauce

With equal portions of distilled malt vinegar and salad oil, marinate chicken, and use same sauce for basting. When chicken is almost done, sprinkle with salt, black and red pepper.

With the chickens serve crisp onion rings, pickles, and big slices of light bread.

After more than doing justice to this delicious dinner, we walked across to the City Square, where the Air Force Band from Randolph Field was giving a concert. It was pleasant to sit on the park bench under the big pecan trees which made such cool shade and where a thin little breeze would quiver the leaves every now and then.

Pretty soon it was time to start one of the biggest events of the day, the Watermelon Auction. Here came General Ainsworth, the banker, who has long been an outstanding civic and business leader in the community and throughout the state. He wore a big Panama hat and a silk suit, and was ready to get on with the business of bidding. The competition was stiff, the auctioneer amusing, the bidding lively; and finally, the largest watermelon went to General Ainsworth and his brother. The beautiful prize melon was very appropriately sent to the general's longtime friend and fellow Texan, President Lyndon B. Johnson, to grace the table of the White House.

There were several melons that afternoon that went for a very fancy price, and of course this is a great encouragement to the farmers who raise them. There are eighty thousand acres of land planted in watermelons in Luling, with an average yield of about 12,000 pounds per acre. The Watermelon Thump has become such a part of Luling that the culinary artists in this vicinity experiment in their kitchens with a variety of unusual recipes, and today, they utilize all parts of King Melon in delectable and tantalizing dishes. This is the contribution of the womenfolk of Luling to the Watermelon Festival.

As we sat on the terrace with our shoes off, recounting the gay events of the Thump and listening to the music and laughter along Main Street where the Thumpers' final event — The Street Dance — was taking place, our host served us a cold roast beef sandwich and passed *Hot Pepper Jelly for us to try on the beef. We did, and we loved it! It is very unusual. Bet you'll like it too! It's Mrs. John D. Janca's recipe for:

★

Hot Pepper Jelly (makes 7 cups)

⅓ cup hot red peppers
⅔ cup bell pepper
6½ cups sugar
1½ cups vinegar
1 small bottle pectin

Seed peppers and chop. Mix peppers, sugar, and vinegar. Bring to boil for 1 minute. Cool 5 minutes. Add pectin.

Quite appropriately, our choice for dessert was a cold slice of watermelon and *Watermelon Sherbet. I took both.

★

Watermelon Sherbet

1 envelope unflavored gelatine
¼ cup cold water
1 cup sugar
3 Tbs. lemon juice
4 cups diced watermelon
⅛ tsp. salt
1 cup cream

Soften gelatine in cold water in custard cup. Place in pan of hot water (not boiling) to melt. Mix sugar, lemon juice, watermelon and salt. Refrigerate for 30 minutes. Rub mixture through sieve or mix in blender. Stir in melted gelatine. Add cream and beat in mixer until fluffy. Freeze. (This may be frozen in freezer of refrigerator, but is better if made in hand freezer.)

The menfolk were swapping "watermelon stories," and Tom Blackwell remembered the lines written by his friend Robert Lee Brothers, a well-known poet in these parts. It's called:

WATERMELON THUMPERS

We went straight to the heart of things, then
In watermelon time, in the cool fields
At early morning.
We selected with care
Our choice among melons.
We lifted and weighed it
By the tug of young muscles.
We caressed its green symmetry
With grimy hands.
We thumped it with practiced fingers,
Listening for the full sound of ripeness.
Kneeling in a ceremonial circle,
We broke the melon and ate of its heart.

We savored the sweet and airy taste
Of the red pulp's sunny texture,
And the sugary juice that dribbled
Between bright lips

Skilled in the spewing
Out of the bright black seed.

I have resigned my membership
With the back slappers;
The fellowship of drum beaters
Will see me no more.
I herewith make my plea for reinstatement
In that select and enchanted circle
Of watermelon thumpers.
Do they meet there still
In the cool fields,
In the remembered dews?
Could I find them, now, this late
In a waning season?

WACO

The name Waco came from the Waco Indians who settled there because of the fertility of the soil along the beautiful Brazos River.

Baylor University, the oldest Baptist university in the state, is located in Waco and has gained national recognition for its outstanding theater and the Robert Browning Library, which houses the largest collection of Robert and Elizabeth Browning's works in the world.

In the fashionable suburban section of Waco stands Stanton Hall, the home of Mr. and Mrs. Stanton Brown. The house was designed after the Browns' plantation home in Meridian, Mississippi, which they left in 1920 to come to Waco, which was then the largest cotton market in the world. They brought with them the South, in its truest meaning of gracious hospitality, and they have never forsaken this style in favor of the easier or more modern way of entertaining.

Gone, except for a few memories, are the days of "banqueting." No more can one lounge leisurely on a low couch while a slave girl slowly drops sugared grapes into the mouth before the main course begins. Few persons have managed to hang onto even a portion of this delightful way of life, and no matter when or where you find it, it is indeed something to cherish.

To banquet at Stanton Hall is an experience in relaxation and gracious living. When guests first arrive, they are met by Jasper, the long-in-attendance butler, who ushers them into the hall, where they are greeted by Mr. and Mrs. Brown. Next they go through the beautiful drawing room and into the library for cocktails. Following a leisurely time for drinking and nibbling delicious hot hors d'oeuvres, dinner is announced. The guests go into the formal dining room, where they are seated around the long table in handsome walnut chairs brought from Mississippi. A glance in the long pier mirrors in ornate gold leaf frames reveals in duplicate the ten-piece silver tea service which belonged to Mrs. Brown's great-grandmother. It was buried during the Civil War for safekeeping and then given to Mrs. Brown by her grandmother when she married.

When Mrs. Brown plans a party and has help she has not trained, she has a rehearsal beforehand; she sits at the table while each course is served until it meets with her approval. Then she sits down and carefully writes out the details of everything to be done. She selects the china, silver, and exquisite stemware to be used. It must be nice to have a choice, especially when it's a five-stemmed affair: water, white wine, red wine, champagne, and brandy. With her cook she makes out the menu and discusses each recipe. One of her favorite dinner menus is:

Clear Onion and Tomato Soup
White wine
Fish course
Rosé wine
* *Mississippi Breast of Chicken on Ham or * Eye of Lamb Chop with Dressing*
Petit pois peas in a thin pastry cup
Spinach Soufflé or Eggplant Soufflé or Corn Pudding
Hot dinner rolls
* *Tipsy Cake*
Champagne
Coffee
Brandy

The soup is made with a vegetable and beef stock. The vegetables are strained out, tomato juice is added, and the soup simmered for about 15 minutes. It is served with whipped cream on top, and warm soda crackers are passed. White wine is served with the soup and fish. A fresh white fish or filet of sole is served in small portions with a cream sauce with white wine in it and pieces of toast alongside. Sometimes just a touch of Parmesan cheese is added to give a little flavor to the cream sauce. When having fish, Mrs. Brown prefers to serve a red meat, but here is her superb Mississippi *Breast of Chicken on Ham recipe:

★

Breast of Chicken on Ham

Bone chicken breasts. Pour a cup of sherry over the raw breasts and rub with seasoned salt. Make a very highly seasoned corn bread dressing and stuff the breasts.

Place the chicken on a slice of cooked ham (not boiled), barbecued if possible, and not too thick or it will separate. Pin the chicken and the ham securely (tie it or use skewers) so they adhere to each other. Pour a cup of wine over the chicken and ham. Bake uncovered at 350 degrees, basting with juice until done, about 45 minutes.

Serve on fried toast. Use the gravy that makes itself during the cooking, but serve it in a separate bowl.

With this delicacy, Mrs. Brown also serves a small mold of boiled rice cooked with a little curry. She puts the chicken on the plates with a broiled tomato. For dessert she uses this recipe and serves it with Champagne:

★

Tipsy Cake

Make a sheet of *Silver Cake (white cake). Sprinkle a cup of wine over it while still warm. Before serving, spread the cake with fresh peaches or any fresh fruit, which has been pureed with sugar and lemon; black walnuts; and fresh shredded coconut on top. Then spread whipped cream on it. Pour rum or Cointreau over the cake and light it. Bring to the table on a silver tray while the sauce is burning.

The grated coconut on top burns a little and gives a caramel-like taste.

SILVER WHITE CAKE

1 cup butter
2 cups sifted sugar
3 tsp. baking powder
3½ cups sifted cake flour
½ tsp. salt
1 cup milk
1 tsp. vanilla
6 egg whites

Beat butter until creamy, add sugar, gradually beating constantly. Mix and sift dry ingredients, then add alternately with milk into butter mixture. Beat in vanilla and fold in stiffly beaten egg whites. Fold over and over, then beat vigorously until the batter is a smooth consistancy (no large pores). Bake in two 9-inch layer cake pans which have been greased and floured at 375 degrees for approximately 30 minutes. This is usually beaten by hand. It is a beautifully textured moist cake.

Fingerbowls are placed on the table and used before dessert is served. The demitasses and brandy are sometimes served at the table and sometimes in the drawing room or library. The other delightful dish that Mrs. Brown often alternates with this same menu is *Filet of Lamb Chop:

★

Filet of Lamb Chop

Take the bone out of the lamb chop which is 1½ inches thick. Place a serving of highly seasoned dressing on top and add a little grated toast crumbs.

Smother broil the lamb with the dressing. This means to broil in the oven with a little liquid, uncovered.

We visited in the Sun Room, which overlooks the formal gardens where lovely pink lilies were blooming. The bulbs had been brought from Mississippi. Jasper brought in some rum coffee — coffee with rum and whipped cream mixed in it — and a heart-shaped white cake with walnuts on a luscious chocolate icing. This is a favorite recipe in the Brown family; Mrs. Brown uses walnuts in many of her recipes. She said in Mississippi their home had a beautiful black walnut plantation, and the Negroes there were the only ones who really knew how to open the walnuts. They would hold the handle of a flat iron firmly between their knees, place the walnut on the flatiron, and break it with one quick blow of the hammer. It was easy then to remove the walnut meat. Mrs. Brown has to buy her walnuts in a can, now, but they are still a delicious touch to any dish.

While we were enjoying our delicious cake and coffee, Mrs. Brown told us a great deal about her early life in Waco. Waco was really the center of society in Texas. The Cotton Palace was founded by some of the enterprising citizens to promote the cotton industry and to stimulate exciting social activities. The annual Cotton Festival and Ball drew dignitaries from all over the South. Lovely Southern belles were presented to the King and Queen of the Cotton Palace. To be invited to be a princess was an honor greatly coveted by the young ladies of the state, and these balls were always very elaborate affairs with much time and money spent to make them so. They were discontinued during the depression, and they never started up again. It was the end of a very charming and colorful era in Waco society.

One of the most festive occasions at Stanton Hall is the traditional Christmas Night open house, which the Browns started thirty-five years ago for all their friends of three generations. Luscious Della Robbia wreaths are hung on the front door and in the library, where red and green predominate. Soft pastel-colored ornaments, accented with gold, bring the yuletide spirit to the other rooms and bobble merrily from the snow-white Christmas tree which tips the high ceiling in the drawing room. Friends send literally dozens of pink carnations for the Christmas party, and in the elegant setting, hospitality flows. The menu is traditional, too:

** Mississippi Dark Fruit Cake*
** Mississippi Light Fruit Cake*
Pretty ribbon sandwiches of sliced turkey and ham
Tiny cheese apples, tinted red
Toasted walnuts and pecans
Large cold red and green olives
*Coffee, tea, and * Plantation Christmas Punch*

★

Mrs. Brown's Mississippi Black Fruit Cake

First make an ordinary fruit cake:

- 1 lb. dark brown sugar
- 1 lb. butter
- 1 lb. flour with every kind of spice you can imagine in the flour
- 6 whole eggs
- 1 lb. black seedless raisins
- 1 lb. apricots (that will not turn dark; soak and cook with sugar. Make a jam out of them.)
- 1 lb. currants
- 1 lb. black walnuts
- 1 lb. pecans
- ½ lb. slivered almonds
- ½ lb. green pineapple
- ½ lb. red crystallized pineapple
- 1 lb. red cherries, cut
- 1 cup sherry
- ½ cup whiskey

If necessary, use milk to make a fairly soft dough. Cook in regular pans, but put a big pan of water to make steam underneath. Bake at 275 to 300 degrees for about 3 hours. When baked, pour liquor over it, and it will keep for months. This makes about 20 lbs. of cake.

★

Mississippi Light Fruit Cake

Make a *Silver White Cake (see page 321). Add slivered almonds, pecans, white raisins, regular pineapple, red crystallized pineapple, green pineapple, cherries, light apricots, sweetened and mashed almost puree, a lot of flavoring (orange, almond, banana . . .). Use the same measurements as above and the same cooking instructions.

★

Plantation Christmas Punch

- 2 lbs. white sugar dissolved in 1 qt. boiling water, but let this cool before mixing it with other ingredients
- 4 qts. of Champagne (not dry), or substitute sweet Sauterne, Moselle, Rhine, or nectar rosé
- 2½ qts. of sparkling water (Mrs. Brown calls it Apollinaris water)
- 1 qt. *light* rum
- ½ pt. of Maraschino cherries with syrup juice
- 1 qt. of medium-strength tea made with jasmine or orange pekoe tea
- ½ pt. of chartreuse
- ½ pt. of good brandy
- 1 pt. *fresh* lemon juice (1 dozen lemons)
- 1 qt. fresh orange juice (1 dozen large oranges)

Mix all ingredients in a large stone or china crock. Keep it cool until ready to serve. Place 2 lbs. of crushed ice in a large punch bowl and pour 1½ gals. of punch over it and garnish with a very thin-sliced green lime or other fruit. The recipe makes about 3 gals. of punch. When serving, be sure to add 2 lbs. of crushed ice to every 1 or 1½ gals., or the punch will be too strong. It is a very subtle drink and must have the crushed ice in order to be good.

Margaret, Mrs. Spencer Brown, Jr., treasures the happy experience of the elegant dinners at Stanton Hall. She, too, is a gracious hostess and excellent cook — but in a more contemporary style. No doubt she inherited her flair for fine food from her mother, Mrs. Boyce, of Amarillo. Mrs. Boyce generously sends enormous boxes of the candies for which she is famous to Margaret for the Christmas party and other occasions. She also fixes delicious beaten biscuits from an old Kentucky recipe.

★

Beaten Biscuits

- 4 cups flour (this *must* be Kentucky soft wheat flour, which may be ordered from: Ward Bros. Model Mill Royal Spring Flour, Georgetown, Kentucky)
- 1 tsp. salt
- 4 Tbs. sugar
- 1 tsp. baking powder
- 1 cup shortening
- 1 cup plus 3 Tbs. milk

Mix flour, salt, sugar, and baking powder. Cut in shortening and milk. Knead. Then put through a beaten biscuit machine until dough stops "popping" and all air is removed. Cut in desired shape. Pierce with fork. Bake at 400 degrees for 15 minutes, then 300 degrees about 30 minutes. They should not be brown.

I am going to try these on Ann Clark's old beaten biscuit machine. If they turn out like Mrs. Boyce's, they will be worth any effort I might extend. Margaret served them one day when I had lunch at her house and they simply melted in my mouth. They were cut in small heart shapes and served warm with a cold salad plate consisting of:

Crab salad
Brandied peach
A delicious aspic

She also passed Orange Nut Bread and had fresh Peach Ice Cream for dessert.

★

Tomato Aspic

- 1 can tomato soup
- 1 envelope gelatine, dissolved in ¼ cup water
- 1 8-oz. package cream cheese
- 1 green pepper, cut fine
- ½ cup celery
- 1 cup mayonnaise
- 1 small onion, cut fine

Heat the soup. Add the gelatine and cream cheese, then add the other ingredients. Chill and serve.

This Egg-Shrimp Creole is a wonderful buffet dish. It has been passed around in the Boyce family and used on special occasions. Margaret served it for a buffet she and Spencer gave honoring Marialice and Allan Shivers before the Junior League Charity Ball. Governor Shivers was in Waco to M.C. the ball. This amount serves sixty.

★

Egg-Shrimp Creole

WHITE SAUCE

- 2½ cups butter
- 2½ cups flour
- 10 cups milk (2½ qts.)
- Salt, pepper

Make in usual way by melting butter, adding flour gradually, then milk. Cook until thick. Salt and pepper to taste.

CREOLE MIXTURE

2½ cups chopped onion
2½ cups green peppers
13 cups canned tomatoes
20 small cans tomatoes with green chilis
10 cloves garlic (optional)
2½ tsp. chili powder
Salt
Tabasco
Lawry's seasoned salt
Accent

Cook onions and green peppers in 10 Tbs. fat until soft but not brown. Add tomatoes, mashed garlic, and chili powder. Cook until thick. Then add prepared white sauce, and salt, Tabasco, Lawry's seasoned salt, and Accent to taste. Set aside.

Before serving, add 5 cups cheddar cheese, grated, 40 hard-boiled eggs, sliced or chopped, and 15 lbs. prepared jumbo shrimp. Serve in chafing dish with crisp buttered toast triangles.

That night, over by the coffee service, she had a large three-tiered silver bon-bon tray with the heavenly candies and *Ginger Brownies made from her mother's recipes.

★

Brown Sugar Fudge

½ lb. butter
1 box dark brown sugar
2½ cups white sugar
1 tall can evaporated milk
Marshmallow cream
2 cups nuts (optional)

Heat butter in a *heavy* aluminum pan over low fire. Add brown sugar. Blend thoroughly. Add white sugar and milk. Cook over moderate heat, stirring constantly. When it reaches a complete boil, begin timing. Boil gently at same heat for 15 minutes. Remove from fire. Add 1 pt. jar of marshmallow cream. Beat well until it becomes creamy. Pour into buttered jelly roll pan. You may add 2 cups nuts before pouring, if desired.

★

Butter Toffee

1 lb. butter (cold from refrigerator)
2½ cups sugar
¼ tsp. cream of tartar
1 pkg. chocolate chips
2 cups slivered almonds (grated almonds for top)

Use heavy aluminum pan. Add butter and sugar. Place on high heat. Break up butter. Stir vigorously at all times during cooking. As mixture starts to bubble along sides, add cream of tartar. Stir vigorously. Add almonds when mixture bubbles all over. Keep stirring until mixture turns to color of penuche (a tan color). Pour in lightly greased cookie sheet with sides. Drop chocolate chips over top of toffee, and as they melt, spread and sprinkle grated almonds on top. Break off to serve.

★

Kentucky Colonels

½ cup butter
2 lbs. powdered sugar
½ cup nuts, soaked in 7 Tbs. Bourbon whiskey overnight

Cream butter and sugar, as for cake. Add whiskey and nuts. Shape into little balls. Chill in refrigerator. Take aluminum cup, grease well with butter. Add 5 squares bitter chocolate and ⅓ cake paraffin. Melt completely, blending well. Dip fondant balls. Yield: about 70.

I've known some fine Kentucky colonels in my day, but these win the medal!

★

Ginger Brownies

Take 2 pkgs. candied ginger (be sure to get the kind cut in small pieces and tender). Add 1 cup coffee cream and let sugar dissolve. Then drain well, reserving cream for icing.

BROWNIES

2 cups or 1 pkg. light brown sugar
1 cup butter
4 eggs
2 cups flour
Pinch of salt
2 tsp. vanilla

Dissolve brown sugar in butter which has been softened or gently melted. Then cream well in electric mixer. Add eggs, one at a time. Add flour, a little at a time, then salt and vanilla. Mix well. Remove from mixer. Fold in well-drained ginger and pour into well-greased and floured jelly roll pan. Cook at 350 degrees with pan of water directly underneath for about 25 minutes or until toothpick comes clean when stuck in the center. Remove from oven and ice.

BROWN SUGAR ICING

1 cup cream (reserved from ginger)
3 cups light brown sugar
½ stick butter
Vanilla

Cook to soft ball. Then spread on brownies.

There are many aunts, uncles, and cousins in the Boyce-Brown family, and when they all gather for a picnic down on the Brazos, Margaret tries to think of one thing everyone will enjoy. One of her standbys is *Chili Spaghetti.

★

Chili Spaghetti

1-lb. box spaghetti, cooked 6 minutes
1 can chili
1 can tomato soup
1 lb. Château cheese
1 chopped onion, raw
1 cup chopped celery, raw
Consommé for extra liquid

Combine ingredients in a casserole. Sprinkle top with cheese and bake in a 350-degree oven for 30 minutes.

As you can see, this recipe is for four to six servings. Margaret makes a big roaster pan full to serve fifty. Another of her quick and very delicious dishes is *Crab Newburg, which she served for a buffet luncheon before the Baylor-Texas football game.

★

Crab Newburg

10 8-oz. cans frozen cream of shrimp soup
10 8-oz. cans fancy white crabmeat
3 lbs. shrimp
¾ cup lemon juice
¾ cup sherry or white wine

Heat together until flavors meld. Serve over crisp Chinese fried noodles. One 3-oz. can noodles serves 4 people.

With this, she served *Frozen Pineapple Salad — a dessert which sent everyone cheering.

★

Frozen Pineapple Salad

2 cups sour cream
2 Tbs. lemon juice
¾ cup sugar
⅛ tsp. salt
9 oz. crushed pineapple

Mix these, then add:

¼ cup green grapes or Maraschino cherries
¼ cup chopped pecans
1 sliced banana (optional)

Freeze in muffin tins, greased with oil. Serves 6 to 8.

Over on the next street from the Browns live our dear friends the William Templars, who grew up in Austin. It was such fun visiting with Maxine in her very charming Early American home. It is furnished with many lovely old pieces which belonged to William's mother, to whose home I used to go with my mother for Missionary Society meetings. So, sitting in Mrs. Templar's big rocker, having tea with Maxine, we reminisced about our happy childhood days in Austin. Maxine served a square of *Prune Cake. She said she had made it the day before for a company dinner. It tasted as if it had just come out of the oven, so moist and fresh.

★

Prune Cake

1 cup sugar
½ cup shortening
2 eggs
¾ cup buttermilk
2 cups flour
1 tsp. soda
1 tsp. ground cloves
1 tsp. cinnamon
⅔ cup prunes, cooked, drained, and cut in pieces

Cream sugar and shortening and add eggs. Beat well and add milk. Sift in the dry ingredients. Add prunes last and mix well. Bake in loaf pan 45 minutes to an hour at 350 degrees and serve iced or un-iced.

ICING

1 cup brown sugar
1 Tbs. Karo
¼ tsp. cream of tartar
1 egg white
3 Tbs. water

Whip these over hot water until the sugar is dissolved and it stands in a peak (about 6 or 7 minutes). Add:

1 tsp. vanilla
½ cup chopped pecans

Spread on cake.

Maxine said this is almost standard dessert when friends come for dinner, because it is so simple to prepare and always successful.

COLUMBUS

I stopped off in Columbus on my way home from Houston to see Rosanne Harrison for a few minutes, but ended up spending the day! A number of the girls were over having coffee and making plans for next year's Magnolia Arts and Homes Tour Festival. It was so successful this year. People came from far and wide and just loved the band concert on the courthouse square, consumed gallons and gallons of hand-turned ice cream, and drank ten thousand gallons of cold, fresh homemade lemonade at the sidewalk café while they watched the buggies and wagons start for the tours of old Columbus homes and the Old Opera House where Houdini once appeared. In the late 1880's, this was the only place between New Orleans and El Paso where opera was performed. The builder, R. E. Stafford, millionaire, cattleman and banker, built his own two-story home adjacent to the Opera House at an angle where he could watch the performances from his own bedroom! Liza McMahan, who, with her husband, is editor of the hundred-and-five-year-old newspaper, was acting as chairman of the Festival. The girls were also talking about the party they had been to the night before down at the Taits' place. It was El and Alice Tait's thirtieth wedding anniversary, and their two daughters had sent out invitations simply saying, "A Special Occasion," with the time and the place. Special it was indeed! The guests danced on the wide front porch, which was added to the log cabin built in 1847. The music was furnished by one of those good Schulenberg bands, the Telstars. Lil Stallman started a long serpentine procession to the shed behind the house, where an enormous white-satin-tied box held a "special gift" for Alice and El. Suddenly the top of the box flew open, and amid colorful balloons, Rita Tait and her fiancé emerged to announce their engagement. Rita was wearing her mother's wedding gown and John was wearing El's wedding suit. Toasts were exchanged by Rita and her father, and later all the guests offered toasts to both couples. May West, who is reportedly one of the "best cooks" in Columbus, had made the traditional Wedding Cake she makes for her special friends on such occasions. May is a wonderful friend to have, as she has the largest deep freeze in town and keeps it loaded with all kinds of goodies she loves to cook.

★

Chocolate Wedding Cake

1 cup butter
2 cups sugar
1 cup buttermilk
1 tsp. soda
2¼ cups cake flour
5 eggs
3 squares unsweetened chocolate
1 tsp. vanilla

Cream butter and sugar; add milk, to which soda has been added, and flour alternately. Add eggs one at a time, beating well. Then add melted chocolate and vanilla. Bake in a buttered, floured tube pan at 350 degrees, 25 to 30 minutes. Make icing with:

½ cup butter
1 cup cocoa
1 egg yolk
1 tsp. vanilla
1 box of powdered sugar

The girls assembled at Rosanne's this morning were all the fourth or fifth generations living in Columbus.

Hattie Mae Dick asked us to go home with her for lunch. Their cook, Mayetta, always prepares enough dinner for a few drop-ins, and this particular day the main dish was short ribs. She flours and browns the meat in a skillet, cooks it in a medium oven, adding salt and black pepper. The meat cooks slowly until well done, making its own natural gravy. A big pan of hot corn bread, cole slaw with cooked dressing, mustard greens and *Fresh Baked Corn were also on the menu.

★

Fresh Baked Corn

6 ears of corn
1 stick butter
Salt to season
¼ cup water
1 tsp. sugar, if cooking like Hattie Mae
Bacon crumbs to season, if cooking like Hattie Mae

Hold corn upright and cut off ends of the grains with sharp knife. Then scrape the cob, getting the remainder of the grain. Pour this in a heavy iron skillet. Melt ½ stick butter and season to taste with a little salt, and ¼ cup water. Stir well and place in 350-degree oven. Stir occasionally and add more water as it cooks, and the other ½ stick butter. Cook 30 to 40 minutes, until it becomes creamy and thick and is delicious! It can also be prepared on top of the stove in a skillet the same way if it is stirred continuously.

When Hattie Mae does this, she usually fries a few strips of bacon crisply; removes the bacon to drain on a paper towel and fries the corn in the bacon dripping instead of butter. She also adds 1 tsp. sugar to this while it is cooking. Then crumbles the bacon and stirs it in the cooked corn when it is ready to be served.

Mayetta says the mustard greens have to cook longer than other greens, at least an hour, and are cooked with a little piece of salt pork.

We were told dessert today was *Dewberry Cobbler. Someone asked, "What? No Pecan and Molasses Pie?"

"You mean *Duration Pie," answered Mayetta. Mayetta names this Duration Pie because they made it often during the duration of the war when sugar was not available.

To make pastry for a one-crust pie, Mayetta says, "Ah takes fo' fingers of flour and three fingers of lard and mix it together lak this. Then jest drops in anuf cold water to holt togeather. Rolls out and puts in a pie pan. Then Ah maks the fillin':

1 pint cup full of pure cane molasses
2 Tbs. brown sugar
Butter the size of a hen's egg
Pinch of salt
2 cups of pecan halves

"Puts on the stove, lets it bile. Adds 4 eggs, beaten, and pours in this pie shell and cooks in the oven at 375 degrees. When you sticks in a silver knife and it comes out reel clean — it's dun!"

It was the *Dewberry Cobbler, however, that almost moved us to Hattie Mae Dick's. There are lots of dewberries in and around Columbus. They put up a lot, to have on hand for cobblers in the winter and of course to make worlds of Dewberry Jelly. For the Cobbler, Mayetta washes the berries. For two cups of berries she uses three-fourths cup sugar, one-half cup water and a good lump of butter. She heats these until sugar is dissolved. The berries are then placed in a two-inch-deep pan, and sometimes she drops little strips of the crust into the juice like dumplings and then tenderly covers this with pie crust, rolled thin, brushes with butter and sprinkles with sugar. It is baked at 375 degrees till brown and crisp. Mayetta serves it up in good-sized berry bowls and passes a pitcher of sweet cream for "dem dat laks it!"

The menfolks love living in Columbus for many reasons, one being that they get to come home every day when the siren blows twelve o'clock, for a feast! May's husband owns the drugstore which has served the community since 1844, and was closed only during the Civil War. Today he was coming home to fried chicken, cream gravy, fruit salad, hot biscuits, buttered rice, leaf lettuce, vine-ripened tomatoes and fresh green beans, and one of his favorite desserts, Pecan Pound Cake with *Antebellum Fruit on top. This batch of fruit has been going continuously since before the Civil War. It is not kept in refrigeration, just in a jar in the pantry. Every two weeks, two cups of any kind of drained canned or fresh fruit and two cups of sugar is added. As this stands, it sorta ferments. It's good on ice cream or cake or by itself.

Columbus is the second beef-producing county in Texas. Beef is on the daily menu for at least one of the meals because the men who raise it like to eat it. The varieties of eating beef are numerous, but the most popular are charcoal steaks, prime rib, meat loaf and beef stew. Needless to say, this magnificient beef is often barbecued down by the river. May said that instead of the traditional Potato Salad, they often serve this:

★

Green Rice Salad

4 cups cold cooked rice
2 Tbs. green pepper, grated
1 small can pimento, cut fine
3-4 Tbs. grated onion and juice
⅓ cup finely cut celery
4 Tbs. sweet relish
French dressing
Mayonnaise
Cayenne pepper to taste
Salt to taste

All ingredients should be no larger than the grains of rice. Add all ingredients except onion. Use 3-4 Tbs. French dressing — if not moist enough, use mayonnaise. Be careful not to get too much — it is better "dry." It is also better if you let it season for a day. Add onion just before serving.

If Gallup should come to Columbus and take a poll from the men about their favorite dishes, beef would be first, but a close second would be *Chicken Stew served on Corn Bread. Chicken Stew used to be made in huge wash pots, but here is a somewhat smaller recipe:

★

Chicken Stew

One hen or fowl
Onion to season
Salt and pepper to season
1 tsp. chili powder
Few thin slices lemon
2 potatoes, cut in cubes
1 onion, chopped medium
1 can cream corn
1 can tomatoes
1 can peas

Cook an old hen or fowl until tender. Cut up as for frying and season with onion, salt, black pepper, chili powder and a few thin slices lemon. Add potatoes, chopped onion, corn, tomatoes and peas. Heat until well mixed.

Serve the stew with cole slaw and *Cooked Dressing:

★

Cooked Dressing

Beat one whole egg. Add:

1 Tbs. sugar
¼ tsp. salt
¼ tsp. dry mustard
¼ cup vinegar
¼ cup water

Stir in top of double boiler until smooth and thick

For dessert serve:

★

Apple Pie

Uncooked pie crust
8-10 apples
½ cup sugar
Dash nutmeg
Dash cinnamon
Juice of 1 lemon

Make one good rich pie crust. Core, peel and slice apples; place in uncooked pie crust. Sprinkle over with sugar, and rest of ingredients (nutmeg, cinnamon, lemon juice). Cover with strips of pie dough to make a lattice top. Brush with butter and sprinkle with sugar. Put in 400-degree oven for 20 minutes. Reduce heat to 325 degrees and bake for about 30 minutes.

We stayed at Rosanne's for lunch even though the other invitations were mighty tempting. Without any apparent commotion, she fixed lunch for twelve of us! She had fresh black-eyed peas cooked in a heavy iron pot with salt bacon for two hours; hot blueberry muffins, a mixed green salad, *Garlic Cheese Grits and oven-fried chicken. On the biscuits we spread peach preserves and Dewberry Jelly she had put up last year, and we drank iced tea in tall thin glasses. Everything tasted just *right!* She then brought out the heavenly light dessert, a *Torte filled with fruit. I do hope all of you will make this just once, it's easy and you'll be so glad you did.

★

Cheese Grits

1 cup grits
1 pkg. (4 oz.) garlic cheese
1 stick butter
2 egg yolks beaten in a cup measure which is filled up with milk
Parmesan cheese

Cook 1 cup grits. Cut up 1 pkg. garlic cheese, and add with 1 stick butter. Add egg yolks, beaten, and milk. Put in a greased casserole and bake 20 minutes in a 300-degree oven. Sprinkle with Parmesan cheese and serve.

★

Rosanne's Divine Torte

Beat until peaked:

8 egg whites
1½ tsp. vanilla
1 tsp. vinegar

Add:

2 cups sugar, gradually

Spread in two pans lined with brown paper. Cook at 300 degrees 1 hour and 15 minutes. Cool in pans and turn out on plate. Fill and frost with the following:

1 or 2 cans crushed pineapple
¾ cup Maraschino cherries
2½ pts. whipping cream

Another easy and very delectable cake Rosanne makes:

★

Sugar Cake

1 cup butter (2 sticks)
2 cups sugar
5 eggs
2 cups flour
Pinch of salt
½ tsp. almond
1 tsp. vanilla

Cream butter and sugar. Add eggs, creaming after each. Fold in 2 cups sifted flour and salt. Add almond, vanilla. Bake in tube pan for 1 hour in 350-degree oven. Ice with:

SEVEN-MINUTE ICING

2 egg whites
1½ cup sugar
5 Tbs. water
1½ tsp. corn syrup
⅛ tsp. cream of tartar
1 tsp. vanilla

Cook in double boiler.

There is a mellow feeling of contentment after a lunch like that and I can surely understand why everybody takes a nap after lunch in Columbus. It would have been the natural thing to do, but I was anxious to see the old houses of Columbus. Columbus is especially noted for its beautiful old oak trees; their huge green branches make dense shade and a cool and peaceful-looking countryside. Everyone admires the lovely magnolias around the courthouse. We went to several of the old houses which have been restored by descendants of the original owners. Even though street signs have recently been installed in Columbus, directions are still given as "It's right across from Miss Ida's house," or "Catta corner from the Hahn House." We stopped first by Levelia Haastadt's. I wish this were a storybook and not a cookbook as there are so many fascinating stories in the history of this house. Levelia had a big crock of sweet pickles "working." I came home and made some, they sounded so simple, and are they good! Crisp and nippy!

★

Levelia's Pickle Recipe

1 gallon sour pickles
5 lbs. sugar
1 clove garlic
1 pkg. (3 oz.) pickle mix
6 oz. tarragon vinegar

Slice pickles in crock or large jar. Mix remaining ingredients and pour over sliced pickles. Let stand in refrigerator 10 days. They will be very crisp and delicious. You can store them in quart or pint jars after the 10 days if you choose.

If you think this recipe is too large, you are wrong. The pickles are good to have on hand and add a special touch to any meal. They also make very coveted hostess gifts when put up in fancy little jars (not too little)!

We went back to the site of the Anniversary Party to examine the log house on what was once the Sylvania Plantation but is now the Tait ranch, nine miles south of Columbus. It clearly shows the year of its construction: the date 1847 is carved on two of the logs. Narrow windows were made by leaving out one log that the occupants could shoot through with safety. The Tait family installed a tower at the ranch to house the bell that was used on the steamboat *Moccasin Belle* which plied the Colorado River and hauled cotton to Galveston from the Tait ranch and the ranch of Lawrence

Washington, grandnephew of George Washington, who once lived in Colorado County. Later, we also visited the Taits' house in town which was begun in 1856 by slaves who molded, baked and laid bricks for the chimneys and cut the lumber by using a saw run by the motor rescued from the *Moccasin Belle*. The two-story mansion is furnished with lovely family heirlooms, and the attic resembles a museum, as it contains numerous mementoes of former days.

Alice Tait and her family continue the hospitable and gracious traditions of their ancestors and do a great deal of entertaining at both places. Her daughters bring many college friends home with them at Easter, Christmas and other holidays. I know of no better place, particularly for foreign students, to get the true Texana image! Alice gave me the recipe for an *Oyster Pie she often serves on Friday night when they all come in.

★

Oyster Pie

- 2 cups sifted all-purpose flour
- 1 tsp. salt
- ⅔ cup shortening
- 5 Tbs. water

Prepare this pastry and line a pie pan with one-half the dough. Then prepare the following:

- 2 shallots, finely chopped
- 1 clove garlic, minced
- 2 Tbs. butter

Sauté shallots and garlic in butter until golden in color. And prepare ingredients below:

- 1 pt. oysters, drained
- 1 cup crumbled crackers
- 1 tsp. Worcestershire sauce
- ½ tsp. Tabasco
- ½ tsp. salt
- 2 Tbs. lemon juice

Put oysters in prepared pastry shell. Scatter crackers on top. Add Worcestershire, Tabasco, salt, and lemon juice to shallots and garlic. Pour over oysters and crackers. Cover with top crust. Bake 10 minutes at 400 degrees; reduce heat to 350 degrees and bake 40 minutes longer. Serve hot.

Another of Alice's favorite recipes is this Shrimp Casserole. She served it to a couple from England who were looking over the ranch and comparing notes on Brahman and Hereford cattle.

★

Shrimp Casserole (serves 5 or 6)

2 Tbs. butter
1¾ Tbs. flour
1 cup milk
3 tsp. catsup
¾ tsp. Worcestershire sauce
½ tsp. dry mustard
Salt to season
Pepper to season
2 Tbs. sherry wine
1 lb. cooked shrimp

Prepare and cook sauce over double boiler. Mix together the following: melt butter in double boiler, then stir in flour. Blend in milk gradually and stir until thick on a low heat. Add catsup, Worcestershire, mustard, salt and pepper, and sherry. Add shrimp, and heat on a low fire. Pour over cooked rice and place the casserole (which held the cooked rice) in the oven at a low temperature until serving time.

It was nice to have Miss Kitty Bridge-Gunn along, for she kept us cued in on all the history, all the delightful people, events and houses. She came to Columbus as a young girl to teach school, fell in love with the young dentist, married and has lived there happily ever since. She and Laura Brasher had started the PTA years ago and seemed to always be on the hot dog committee at the school carnivals. They wanted the children to get their nickels' worth so they made this sauce to put on the hot dogs, and the kids really like it. For a very small amount, the following recipe may be used:

★

Hot Dog Sauce

1 can tomatoes
1 onion cut fine
A little bacon fat
1 tsp. chili powder

Drain and mash 1 can tomatoes. Add to onion, cut fine and sautéed in a little bacon fat and one tsp. chili powder mixed with a little of the tomato juice. Let this simmer for 20 minutes and pour over hot dogs.

As I said earlier, the men really like living in Columbus; besides that noonday meal and an afternoon nap and being able to run over to Houston for a baseball game, fishing is mighty fine all along the Colorado River. Hunting is also excellent — deer in season and lots of quail and doves. I didn't realize that there were so many deer around this country. We saw many standing under the shade of trees trying to keep cool. During the hunting season nearly every hunter gets his quota, and believe me, the gals really know how to fix venison. Strange as it may seem, many of the families living in this quiet little town also have quieter weekend houses down on the Colorado River. These are the scene for some mighty gay fish fries. Big black iron wash pots are placed over the fire, half-filled with vegetable oil. When the oil is smoky hot, they drop the fish in; the fish have been cleaned, cut, seasoned with salt and black pepper, then dipped in cornmeal. It comes out golden brown, crisp and juicy. A second pot, also with hot oil, is used for frying the Hush Puppies (hot-water corn bread). This is a mighty fine combination on a moonlit night along the Colorado under the pecan trees. When everyone has eaten his fill, they lean back in their comfortable chairs and discuss politics, world travel, old times and how thankful they are to have such a spot as this.

I had really "called" myself trying to start for Austin and home several times, but was always delayed by some other interesting invitation. May West said to be sure and stop by her house on my way out of town, as she wanted to give me some of her Pappy's *Homemade Bread to take home, and to have a bowl of her *Lemon Cream Sherbet. It seems her mother always made this bread — her daddy would never eat any other kind. One of the little granddaughters agreed with Pappy. On one occasion she looked over a bountiful table and remarked, "Don't we have any decent bread?"

One day, May's mother told Pappy (for that is what he is lovingly called by everyone), "Pappy, I'm going to teach you how to make this bread, because if I should die before you do, I don't know what you'd do for bread." So he willingly took instructions and got to be a first-rate baker. A few years later, his wife did pass on, and Pappy still makes the bread at the age of eighty-three! In fact, he really loves to make it in large quantities and brings in loaves to all his friends when he comes to Columbus. We think this is a wonderful recipe, and if eighty-three-year-old Pappy can make it — so can you!

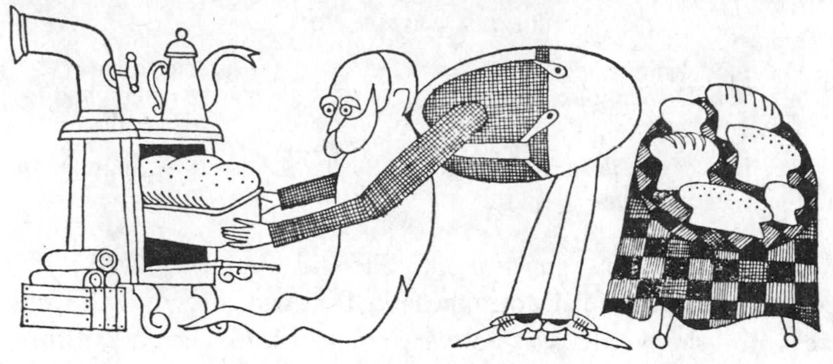

★

Pappy's "Decent Bread"

2 yeast cakes
4 cups lukewarm water
6 cups flour
3 eggs
9 Tbs. sugar
9 Tbs. shortening

Beat together until very smooth. Pappy uses the electric mixer for this part after he stirs it well with a wooden spoon. Let rise, out of draft, until double or a little more. Add:

2 Tbs. salt
6 cups flour

Work a long time — this is very important, he says, to work until it "pops a lot." Cut into 6 even parts and shape into loaves. Put into greased bread pans and brush melted shortening on top. Let rise again and bake 35 minutes at 350 degrees.

A beautiful ending to my day in Columbus was that bowl of *Lemon Cream Sherbet. May makes a one-and-a-half-gallon freezer and keeps it in the deep freeze. I can think of *no* better dessert on a summer day.

★

Original Cream Sherbet (1890)

1 qt. rich milk
2 cups sugar
Vanilla to flavor
4 lemons
1 pt. heavy cream

Put milk in freezer and half freeze (sugar and vanilla added). Add juice of lemons. Turn crank a few times and add heavy cream. Freeze hard.

RECIPE AS MADE NOW

1½ cups lemon juice or 2 cans frozen lemon juice
3½ cups sugar
1 pt. cream (heavy)
7 cups rich milk
1½ tsp. vanilla

Mix the lemon juice and sugar thoroughly. Add other ingredients, and proceed as above.

This is a recipe May "grew up on." She said when they lived in the country, she loved a hailstorm, because it provided them with ice to freeze this sherbet. Ice was not very accessible, so when a hailstorm would come up, the children would stand on the porch and cheer their father on as he ran to close the chicken house, dodgin' hailstones, but turning up a bushel basket to catch them.

THE LBJ RANCH

One person who has changed the least through the years is Lady Bird Johnson. I can remember when Lyndon Johnson was still in Congress and Lady Bird invited Olga Bredt, Bess Jones, Mary Love Bailey and me to come up to the ranch for lunch.

The LBJ ranch house is spacious, and it has a beautiful setting under huge live oak trees by the Pedernales River, but it really isn't a mansion as most people think of that word "mansion." The Johnsons built it for comfort and a heap of living, adding onto and modernizing the old stone part, that was sighing and sagging when they bought the place from Mr. Johnson's aunt (Mrs. Clarence Martin) in 1951. The living rooms, which have large wood-burning fireplaces, get plenty of use, but the actual center of the house, I think, is the kitchen, just as it is in all ranch homes. For many years, while Mr. Johnson was senator, the standard procedure for dispatching outgoing mail was to put it by the Mixmaster near the kitchen door. Then the first person going to town picked the letters up and took them to the post office. The system worked just fine.

We had such a pleasant day. They had just newly papered the upstairs bedrooms and one of the neighbors had embroidered some dresser scarfs for Mrs. Johnson. She was so proud of everything and took pleasure in showing us all around the house, giving a little history and telling little amusing stories as she drove us around the small ranch in a jeep.

A number of years later, when LBJ was Senate leader, in 1959, Bird called one morning and asked me if I could come up to the ranch to help plan a party for a very important visitor, Adolfo López Mateos, President of Mexico. We sat in the dining room and started making plans. Lyndon came striding through the dining room, and Bird very solicitously asked if he had any suggestions or special requests.

He said, "There's only one thing, I want the very same kind of beef S. B. Whittenburg gave us at the dinner in Amarillo last month."

"Was it sirloin strip?" I asked.

"No, it wasn't a strip, and I don't know what it was, but find out, because that's what I want to have. It was the best piece of beef I ever put in my mouth!" So we got Mr. Whittenburg on the phone, and he told us they had served Chateaubriand! We planned the formal dinner around that. There was to be a big barbecue at noon and a small, more formal, seated dinner in the evening.

The guest list for the big Texas-style barbecue was made up of county, state and government officials plus many of the Johnsons' personal friends and ranch neighbors. This was a new and interesting experience for me, a small town caterer. We had several meetings with Warren Woodward, who was general chairman of the affair, and Mrs. Johnson; after all, this was somewhat a new experience for her too. Mrs. Johnson was doing "research" to find out what Señora López Mateos and her sixteen-year-old daughter would most enjoy on their trip to Texas.

Hundreds of people came, some of them from Texas points five hundred miles away and some, of course, even farther. It was truly an international gathering, with Texas, United States and Mexican flags rippling in the warm, bright October sunshine and a red carpet spread for President López Mateos when he stepped out of the helicopter that had brought him and Mr. Johnson from Austin.

Mexican mariachis (musicians) and singers in colorful costumes strolled through the crowd; everything was festive and gay. And amid the flags and bunting and banners one sign stood out in particular, I remember. In Spanish it said, "*Lyndon Johnson sera presidente*" — Lyndon Johnson will be President. It was a prediction we all believed . . . though it did not happen in the way we expected.

One thing that had to be arranged for President López Mateos, as for every visiting head of state, was a direct telephone line from wherever he stayed to the White House, as well as to his own Executive House.

I got Dale Baker, a local barbecue man, and his crew to come do the barbecuing. They went to the ranch the day before and dug a long pit, approximately three feet deep and twelve feet long. Very early the next morning, they started the oak and mesquite wood burning. Then a heavy wire-like grill was placed over the entire pit. Dale put the fine heavy strips of brisket at the end opposite the fire. He does not place the meat directly over the coals, but cooks by the reflected heat, very slowly. The meat is swabbed with his vibrant barbecue sauce on both sides as it is turned; and, when almost done, he covers it with a sheet of corrugated tin to hold the smoke as well as to ensure thorough cooking without burning or drying the beef or the spareribs. The aroma is so tantalizing it draws the guests to the picnic spot a good while before the dinner bell rings, and guests watch with mouths watering while the finishing touches are being made. It was a perfect spot for such a splendid occasion; the green banks of the Pedernales River under a grove of tall pecan trees made a very lush setting. The tables were covered with red and white checked tablecloths. A speaker's platform was festooned with red, white and green bunting for Mexico; Mexican and American flags were placed at intervals all along the roadway. The day was sunny and clear; a pleasant breeze rustled the pecan and oak leaves and put the flags to fluttering. We served the barbecued spareribs and cold beer to the guests as they arrived from all over the country.

In fact, there was such a stream of helicopters over the hill country that Sunday, bringing former President Harry Truman, Speaker Sam Rayburn, ambassadors, Cabinet members, State Department people, many other dignitaries, press, radio and TV, that spectators said it was like seeing a formation of Canadian geese flying in the sky.

After the last helicopter load landed, carrying former President

Harry Truman and several Cabinet members, we started serving lunch. From four buffet tables the typical Texas barbecue menu was served:

Barbecued Beef Brisket
* *Ranch Beans*
* *Potato Salad*
Thick-sliced, garlic-buttered French bread
Trays of cold crisp onion rings and thick slices of home-grown tomatoes
Bowls of pickles
*Beer, Coffee and * Pecan Pralines*

Everyone ate heartily! We had made considerable effort to select only the choicest beef and choicest of each item on the menu, but the pièce de résistance must have been the *Pinto Beans, as a few days after this occasion we received a letter from the senator's office, as a result of a letter from the Mexican Chief Executive requesting the recipe for the beans. Our Amy at Green Pastures beamed broadly, as she was the one who cooked the beans.

★

Amy's Beans (serves 150 people)

30 lbs. pinto beans

Pick over by putting a few at a time on white paper; then wash and soak overnight in a large heavy iron pot with enough water to cover well. The next morning add:

6 lbs. salt pork diced | **1 cup salt (approx.)**

Let cook and simmer slowly 8 to 10 hours, adding more hot water if needed. After about 6 hours of simmering, add:

¼ cup cumin seed | **6 Tbs. sugar**
2 6-oz. bottles of catsup | **1 cup chili powder**

Make a smooth, thin paste with chili powder and some water, then add to beans.

Of course, these seasonings can be altered or others added to suit the taste.

Ellen Erickson, long a member of the Green Pastures staff, makes this salad.

★

Ellen's Potato Salad (serves 150 people)

40 lbs. white California potatoes

Boil in skins 25 to 30 minutes in salted water. Drain, peel and slice ¼ inch thick while warm. Add:

2 lbs. onions, sliced very thin

Mix:

1 cup salt
4 Tbs. black pepper
8 Tbs. sugar
2 cups vinegar

Add seasonings and pour over potatoes. Then add:

3 dozen hard-boiled eggs chopped coarse
1 lb. green bell peppers, chopped medium fine
4 lbs. celery stalks, chopped medium fine
14-oz. pimento, chopped medium fine
1 cup parsley, chopped fine

Add last, approximately 1½ gallons mayonnaise. However, it is best not to mix over 10 lbs. of salad at a time if possible.

A large white cake adorned with a replica of the Mexican flag was presented to President López Mateos. He cut the first piece, and the remainder was cut and passed to the guests by the President's daughter, assisted by Lynda and Luci Johnson and some of their young friends. There was the usual exchange of greetings between the President and LBJ, the introduction of Cabinet members and other VIPs. Mr. Truman asked if he could have a couple more pecan candies "to put in my pocket to take home to the Madam." They were individually wrapped in cellophane, so probably traveled well. I had made *Pralines by the recipe I used when I made and sold them during the war to all Mexican restaurants in Austin:

★

Pralines

4¾ cups sugar
4 cups pecans, broken in large pieces
2 cups water
⅛ tsp. salt
2 Tbs. butter

Put 4 cups sugar, pecans, water and salt in a pan and bring to a boil; meanwhile, melt ¾ cup sugar in an iron skillet and let it brown slightly but not scorch. When it is caramel-colored, pour it into first mixture. Cook until it forms a firm ball when dropped in cold water. Put wax paper over newspaper laid out on a flat surface or table. Add butter; beat until it cools a little. Then drop by spoonfuls any size desired on the wax paper. When cool and hard, Pralines will easily lift from paper.

In the afternoon the guest of honor enjoyed a siesta and afterward, with Senator Johnson, a ride around the ranch to look at the herd of white-face cattle. The dinner that evening was really very lovely:

French Onion Soup with croutons
Mixed green salad with French dressing
Chateaubriand
Red wine
Chantilly Potatoes
* *Spinach Soufflé*
Heart of celery and colossal olives
Hot rolls
* *Stonewall Peach Ice Cream made in individual rose molds*
Champagne
Demitasses

★

Mrs. Johnson's Spinach Soufflé

¼ cup chopped onions
Butter
½ cup thick white sauce
3 eggs, separated
1 cup chopped cooked spinach
½ cup grated cheese

Sauté onions in small amount of butter. Make white sauce of 2 Tbs. of butter, 2 Tbs. of flour, 1 cup of milk (rich milk or light cream), ½ tsp. salt and ⅛ tsp. of pepper.

Beat yolks until thick and lemon-colored. Stir into white sauce and add spinach and cheese. Fold in stiffly beaten egg whites and turn into greased casserole. Set in pan of hot water and bake in moderate oven (350 degrees) about 50 minutes. Serve at once.

For the ice cream we also used Mrs. Johnson's recipe:

★

Mrs. Lyndon B. Johnson's Peach Ice Cream

Make a boiled custard of 1 quart cream, 1 pint milk, 3 eggs, 1 cup sugar. To this, when cool, add ½ gallon of soft peaches mashed and well sweetened. This makes one gallon of ice cream which is most delicious. When this was frozen it was scooped into individual aluminum rose molds and placed in upright freezer until serving time. They looked very pretty and were garnished with fresh rose leaves.

We served Champagne with dessert, and Senator Johnson rose to read a toast to President López Mateos, but once on his feet he disregarded the planned speech and gave a very warm and moving tribute to this great leader, his country, and the hope that strong and friendly relations would always exist. President López Mateos was obviously touched by the senator's remarks and responded without the aid of his interpreter in an equally sincere manner.

In the spring of 1961, after LBJ had become Vice President of the United States, entertaining at the LBJ ranch took on a bit faster tempo and a more official pattern had to be followed. The chief of protocol had a great deal more to say about the planning for the next important visitor, Chancellor Konrad Adenauer of West Germany. The LBJ ranch is in the heart of the German communities of Stonewall and Fredricksburg, so there was much excitement when the news of Adenauer's visit was announced. Simon Berg, president of the Stonewall Chamber of Commerce, said that they would like to host the barbecue for the Chancellor. Stonewall people had just celebrated the centenary of the first settling of Stonewall, and the ladies already had on hand costumes used for this occasion to wear for the Chancellor's visit. We followed the traditional barbecue menu we had served at the López Mateoses visit, but added the famous bread made by Mr. Dietz of Fredricksburg. (It was so delicious that Mr. Winthrop Rockefeller now sends his plane over from Arkansas to pick up a load for his parties!) We also added a huge crock of cole slaw, and a bowl of stewed apricots and peaches which are often served in the hill country at barbecues.

Every detail of the planning is gone over with a fine-tooth comb by the heads of various agencies involved. Warren Woodward was again "general chairman" of the whole affair, and we had meeting after meeting with security agents, transportation and communication people, checking and double-checking the timing of the schedule for each event. We had thought the Chancellor would enjoy being met at the plane in a horse-drawn surrey and driven down to the picnic grounds by one of the men in Western attire. This we rehearsed too, so that the horse would get used to the surrey, the flags which were on each side of the road, and the Stonewall committee waving and shouting welcomes in German. All was set; everything was going according to schedule. The plane was coming in — the excitement grew greater — and just as the plane landed, the horse broke and ran as fast as he could. We had not rehearsed the noise of the plane's motors! The Chancellor was greatly amused and immediately started in shaking hands and conversing in German with everybody as he moved along the enthusiastic crowd. A life-sized portrait of the Chancellor festooned with bunting in the German flag colors hung on the upstairs porch banister, and underneath was a huge sign: WELCOME CHANCELLOR ADENAUER!

We were familiar with the barbecue routine, but where to have the seated formal dinner for fifty in the evening presented a problem. The dining room at the LBJ ranch would only take care of fourteen to sixteen at the most, and we knew not one of the carefully selected guest list could be seated anywhere else. I suggested the hangar — have the decorators and florist disguise it with flags and flowers; but the Vice President put an emphatic No! on that, saying it was too near the barnyard! Then I suggested getting a big party tent from Houston and setting it up on the lawn. LBJ didn't much go for that idea either. However a few days later he attended a beautiful party at Mount Vernon given by President and Mrs.

Kennedy for which a tent was used, so he finally okayed the tent. It turned out lovely, with a soft green carpet on the floor, banks of palms and urns of yellow roses around the side and soft lights. We used round tables of five, covered with white damask cloths, and each one was centered with an antique baroque candelabra holding long white tapers and beautiful yellow roses. We used place cards with the Vice President's crest. The Chancellor and Mrs. Johnson sat at a table on one side of the "room," and the Vice President with the Chancellor's daughter sat on the opposite side, "to give the room balance," explained our protocol man. Menus engraved in both German and English were placed at each plate. The Chancellor was a real connoisseur of wine; Mrs. Johnson specified in detail the kind and the vintage of each wine we should serve with the dinner. We had to be instructed as to the protocol on who should be served wine first, the Vice President, Mrs. Johnson or the Chancellor. Mr. Duke said it should be done simultaneously. This brought to mind a wedding I had attended at the Friendly Will Baptist Church when the little flower girls walked along and counted one-two-three-drop, one-two-three-drop! So with this rhythm in mind, I asked my waiters to do precisely this: altogether, one-two-three-pour . . . well, one would have thought them to have been experienced wine stewards for royalty! We serve fresh Texas gulf shrimp with a Red Rémoulade Sauce from a large snow table in the front yard. This informality and unified service seemed to intrigue the Chancellor. He also ate with great relish the miniature hot chalupas we passed. After hors d'oeuvres the guests proceeded to the improvised dining room and were served a five-course dinner consisting of:

Bouillon
Grapefruit and Avocado Salad
Breast of White Guinea Hen with Artichoke
Baked Barley and Fresh Mushrooms
Snow Peas
Dinner Rolls
Meringue Swans filled with Ice Cream and Fresh Strawberries
Champagne
Demitasses
Yellow Rosebud Mints

The Chancellor and Admiral Nimitz were very enthusiastic about the dinner and ate heartily, which is the greatest compliment the cook or Koock can have.

Just a few months after the Chancellor's visit, we started preparations for Mohammed Ayub Khan, the President of Pakistan. We felt like old hands at this official entertainment by now! But each event was different. This time we got Mr. Walter Jetton, barbecue king from Fort Worth, to come take care of the barbecue at noon. He is truly a master of this type of food and a great character to have on hand for such an occasion. He put on the usual spread but added hot barbecue sausage and chickens with the barbecued briskets. For each of the barbecues there has always been an abundance of entertainment, including sheep dog demonstrations, cutting horses, roping techniques, and charros from San Antonio, just to mention a few.

Ayub Khan enjoyed the horses especially, as he is a fancier of horses, and looked more natural in the saddle and in the ten-gallon Stetson the Vice President had presented him with than had the two previous visitors. He spoke beautiful English and enjoyed all the jokes and humor of the Vice President, who was master of ceremonies for the occasion. Cactus Pryor kept the guests in gales of laughter with his Bob Hope type of humor. Mrs. Johnson thought perhaps it might be more comfortable for the visitors to Texas to have dinner around the pool on a warm Texas night, so we set the long buffet table with both hot and cold dishes, and provided glassine covers for the guests' plates to protect the hot food from the river breeze. The menu was:

Hors d'oeuvres
Shrimp and Crab Fingers on Ice
Nachos passed with drinks (President Ayub Khan drank only fresh orange juice)

BUFFET

Hindquarter of U.S. Prime Beef, Kingsville
Texas Gulf Red Snapper, charcoaled
Huge Luling watermelon bowl filled with Rio Grande Valley fresh fruits
Kerrville Leg of Lamb, Mint Glaze and Fresh Pears

Stuffed Eggplant and Squash Donna
Fredericksburg tomatoes
Bastrop Potatoes Allidi
Rice and Mushroom Beaumont
Stonewall Peach Melba
New York State Champagne
Demitasses
Mints
Brandy

Mrs. Johnson had arrangements of fresh flowers in all the rooms, upstairs and down. It was quite a chore to care for all the guests and their entourages. She also had fresh fruit with fruit knives and jars of Lamme candies in each room, and every morning coffee arrives in each room in thermo pitchers. A real country breakfast is always served in the dining room. Very often these *Popovers are served with Venison Sausage (see page 360).

★

Mrs. Lyndon B. Johnson's Recipe for Popovers

1 cup sifted flour
¼ tsp. salt
2 eggs, beaten
1 cup milk
2 Tbs. shortening, melted

Mix and sift flour and salt. Combine eggs, milk and shortening; gradually add to flour mixture, beating about one minute or until batter is smooth. Fill greased sizzling hot pans three-quarters full and bake in very hot oven (450 degrees) about 20 minutes — reduce heat to moderate (350 degrees) and continue baking for 15 or 20 minutes.

Lady Bird served these the day we were there for lunch. They are wonderful!

During the day Zephyr makes cookies by the thousand, which can be smelled a far piece, and quite often the aroma draws Secret Service men and other personnel to business near the kitchen area!

When Mr. Johnson became President, people couldn't just "drop in" unannounced the way they used to do. Security rules had to be enforced. But family friends and any number of VIP visitors still come in the back door and troop through the kitchen, sniffing its wonderful smells and often as not snitching a cookie on the way.

Let it be said for the help that they seem to enjoy all this traffic through their domain, and never get cross, not even when a soufflé is in the oven!

★

Mrs. Lyndon B. Johnson's Recipe for Texas Cookies

Blend together ½ cup of butter and 1 cup of sugar. Add 1 egg and 1 Tbs. of cream. Grate rind of lemon and ½ tsp. of lemon flavoring and add to mixture. Add 1½ cups of flour, ½ teaspoon of salt and 1 teaspoon of baking powder. Chill from 2 to 3 hours — better when chilled overnight. Roll very thin and cut with cookie cutter shaped like the map of Texas. Bake 8 to 10 minutes in 375-degree oven.

Mrs. Johnson has taught Zephyr many of the President's favorites, such as *Pecan Pie and *Pedernales Chili.

★

Pecan Pie

½ cup (1 stick) butter
1 cup sugar
1 cup dark corn syrup
½ tsp. salt
1½ tsp. vanilla
3 eggs
2 cups coarsely chopped pecans

Flute unbaked pastry shell in a 9-inch pie pan or plate. Allow the butter to stand in a covered medium mixing bowl at room temperature until it is extremely soft. Add sugar, corn syrup, salt and vanilla; with a sturdy hand rotary beater or mixing spoon, beat until thoroughly blended. Add eggs and beat gently just until blended. Fold in the pecans. Pour into pastry shell. Bake in a moderate (375-degree) oven on the rack directly below the center rack until top is toasted brown and filling is set in center when pie is gently shaken — about 40 to 50 minutes. Pastry edge should be browned and the bottom pastry a pale gold. If top of pie gets very dark toward end of baking time, place a tent of foil over it. Cool on wire rack. If desired, serve with unsweetened whipped cream.

★

Pedernales River Chili

- 4 lbs. chili meat
- 1 large onion
- 2 cloves garlic
- 1 tsp. ground oregano
- 1 tsp. cumin seed
- 6 tsp. chili powder (more if needed)
- 2 cans tomatoes with green chilis
- Salt to taste
- 2 cups of hot water

Put chili meat, onion and garlic in large heavy boiler or skillet. Sear until light-colored. Add oregano, cumin, chili powder, tomatoes and hot water. Bring to a boil, lower heat and simmer about one hour. As fat cooks out, skim.

This recipe was given to the First Lady by their very dear friend Mrs. Dale Miller. It is popular at the White House and at the ranch. It was also featured on the Lady Bird Special whistlestop campaign tour during the 1964 Presidential campaign.

Chili has always been a favorite of Lyndon Johnson's. He recalls what a treat it was when he was a young boy to stroll into the Johnson City Café and get a bowl of their "homemade chili" for ten cents — with *crackers!* He was in San Antonio one day and ordered a bowl of chili. When he saw the sign that read CHILI — FIFTEEN CENTS Lyndon walked out; he refused to pay such an inflated price. He said, "Why, anybody knows a bowl of chili costs ten cents!"

★

LBJ Chili Dip (*serves 100*)

- 6 lbs, lean ground beef
- Bacon or beef fat
- 2 Tbs. fat
- 1 cup flour
- 2 cans beef consommé
- 6 large onions, chopped
- 6 oz. chili powder
- 2 tsp. powdered cumin seed
- 1 Tbs. oregano
- 2 Tbs. salt
- 6 lbs. cheddar cheese
- Fried tortillas

Sauté the ground beef with bacon or beef fat. When cooked, add 2 Tbs. fat to skillet and blend in the flour. Heat 1 can of consommé and pour it in, stirring until mixture is smooth. Put it in a large pan with the beef and add remaining ingredients except cheese and tortillas. Simmer for 30 minutes, stirring often. Turn up heat and stir continually until it becomes thick. This can be frozen. When time to use, heat in a double boiler with the cheddar cheese. Mix well and see if it needs salt. Serve with fried tortillas.

Favorites with the Luci group who so often gather at the LBJ home are the *Peanut Brittle and *Wheaties Coconut Cookies.

★

Mrs. Lyndon B. Johnson's Recipe for Peanut Brittle

1½ cups sugar
½ cup water
½ cup white Karo
1½ cups peanuts (raw or parched)
1 heaping Tbs. butter
½ tsp. salt
½ tsp. soda (level)

Cook in large skillet until the sugar, water and Karo form a hard ball in cold water. Add peanuts. Cook until rich golden brown, stirring all the time. Add butter, salt and soda almost together. Stir and pour immediately into buttered pan.

★

Mrs. Lyndon B. Johnson's Recipe for Wheaties Coconut Cookies

1 tsp. soda
½ tsp. baking powder
½ tsp. vanilla
2 cups Wheaties
1 cup shortening (½ butter)
1 cup brown sugar
1 cup white sugar
2 eggs, beaten
2 cups coconut
2 cups flour (or 2½)

Sift and measure flour. Add soda, baking powder and salt and sift again. Blend shortening and sugar. Add beaten eggs, coconut and vanilla. Stir flour mixture into shortening, sugar and egg mixture and add Wheaties. Form small balls. Place on buttered cookie sheet and bake 12 minutes in 400-degree oven.

Favorites with all age groups are *Spinach Parmesan, *Baby Lima Beans, *Strawberry Icebox Pie, *Chess Pie, *Apple Pie and *Cream Pie.

★

Mrs. Lyndon B. Johnson's Recipe for Spinach Parmesan

- 3 lbs. of spinach
- 6 Tbs. Parmesan cheese
- 6 Tbs. minced onion
- 6 Tbs. heavy cream
- 5 Tbs. of melted butter
- ½ cup cracker crumbs

Cook the cleaned spinach until tender. Drain thoroughly. Chop coarsely and add the cheese, onion, cream and 4 Tbs. of butter. Arrange in a shallow baking dish and sprinkle with the crumbs, mixed with the remaining butter. Bake for 10 to 15 minutes.

★

Baby Lima Beans

Cook 2 lbs. baby lima beans in salted water until tender. Drain thoroughly. Add 3 Tbs. butter to a skillet, and sauté ½ lb. sliced mushrooms for 5 minutes. Sprinkle with 3 Tbs. flour, and stir into the butter mixture. Pour in 1 cup heavy cream, stirring continuously, until thickened. Season to taste with salt, freshly ground black pepper and 1 tsp. chili powder. Add lima beans, and let them heat through. Finally stir in ¼ cup of grated sharp cheese.

★

Lady Bird's Strawberry Icebox Pie

- 1 17-oz. pkg. of marshmallows
- 1 box frozen strawberries or 2 cups fresh, sweetened to taste
- 1 cup whipping cream
- 1 baked 9-inch pastry shell

Put marshmallows in double boiler. Add 2 Tbs. of strawberry juice. Cook until marshmallows are dissolved. Mix strawberries and marshmallows thoroughly. Chill about 2 hours. Fold in whipped cream to marshmallow mixture and pour into baked pastry shell. Chill until firm.

★

The President's Favorite Chess Pie

- 2 cups sugar
- 1 heaping Tbs. flour
- ½ lb. butter
- 4 eggs
- ½ tsp. vanilla

Mix sugar and flour together and add to butter and blend until light and fluffy. Add eggs one at a time, beating after each addition. Add vanilla and pour into unbaked pie shell. Bake in 300-degree oven until knife inserted comes out clean, about 1 hour.

★

LBJ's Apple Pie

6 Winesap apples
1 cup sugar
2 Tbs. flour
Juice of 1 lemon
1 stick of butter
Pastry for 2-crust pie

Dice apples into pastry shell. Sprinkle with sugar and flour, that have been mixed. Add lemon juice and dot with ¾ of the butter. Top with crust and sprinkle with sugar and dot with remaining butter. Bake in 350-degree oven about 1 hour or until brown.

★

Cream Pie

1 cup sugar
½ cup flour or 3½ Tbs. cornstarch
½ tsp. salt
2 cups scalded milk
3 eggs, separated
2 Tbs. butter
1 tsp. vanilla

Mix together ⅔ cups of sugar, flour and salt; gradually stir in milk and cook over boiling water 10 minutes, stirring constantly until mixture thickens. Stir small amount into slightly beaten egg yolks; then gradually pour into thickened milk and cook about 2 minutes, stirring constantly. Add butter and vanilla and cool slightly. Turn into baked pastry shell. Cover with meringue made by gradually beating remaining ⅓ cup of sugar into stiffly beaten egg whites. Brown delicately.

FOR LEMON PIE

Use 1½ cups of milk and ½ cup lemon juice. Add lemon juice to egg and sugar.

Lady Bird says Lyndon used to be able to smell this to the far side of the ranch and timed his return to get a piece of hot bread just as it came out of the oven:

★

White Bread (makes 2 loaves)

Cream 3 Tbs. solid shortening and ½ cup sugar. Pour 1 cup scalded milk over mixture. Dissolve 2 yeast cakes in ¼ cup warm water. Allow to cool.

Combine both mixtures, and using egg beater, add 1 tsp. of salt and 1 egg, beaten until light.

Add 4¼ or 5 cups of flour (1 cup at a time), just enough so that the dough can be worked by hand.

Put dough in a large greased bowl — grease the top part of the dough and allow to rise until double in bulk.

Cover with hot damp cloth several times — it takes about 2 hours for it to rise in a warm spot — not too near the stove.

Toss on board with enough flour to keep it from sticking to the board, knead bread for 5 minutes — working outside edges in — kneading with the ball of the hand, repeating until dough no longer sticks to the board, is "bubbly" and puffs right back up. Divide into 2 equal loaves and place in two greased Pyrex baking dishes. Let dough rise again until double in bulk.

Bake at 450 degrees for 10 minutes; reduce to 350 degrees and bake for 30 more minutes (40 minutes in all).

Bake until bread is brown and shrinks from the sides of dish. Remove and turn out to cool on wire tray. Slice when bread is cold.

Can be baked a day or two before — wrap in wax paper. It is delicious sliced, buttered and reheated.

Served often for breakfast with the famous *Venison Sausage is:

★

Mrs. Lyndon B. Johnson's Spoon Bread

1 scant cup cornmeal
3 cups sweet milk
3 eggs
1 level tsp. salt
3 level tsp. baking powder
Butter the size of a walnut, melted

Stir cornmeal into 2 cups of milk and let mixture come to a boil, making a mush. Add balance of milk and add well-beaten eggs. Stir in salt, baking powder and melted butter. Bake 30 minutes in oven at 350 degrees.

A piece-no-one-can-resist at the LBJ ranch is the fabulous *Venison Sausage. It appears on the breakfast table often, and the question is invariably asked by first-timers, "How do you make this delicious sausage?" Well to begin with, that sausage is made in "sausage country," for long have our citizens of the hill country, and especially around Stonewall and Fredricksburg, been known for their fine sausage. The President started by saying that you take a half a deer carcass and half a hog. These may seem rather large proportions, but not when you know how good it's going to be. Actually, the sausage made may double or triple that amount before the season is over. Everyone has his own idea about venison sausage, and to get an *exact* recipe is next to impossible. I can only tell you how Tom Weinheimer, neighbor and friend of the President, told me he made it. He has often made it for the LBJ ranch. It sounded very simple, if you can just bag a buck!

★

Venison Sausage

3 parts venison **1 part lean pork**

Grind coarsely. Season to taste with ground dry red Italian pepper, garlic, salt, and ground black pepper. (Actually this sausage isn't "too hot" in the hill country.) This is stuffed into casings and hung in the smokehouse. A fire is made in a five-gallon can with holes punched in the top. The can is filled with both damp and dry green bark of mesquite and oak to make a good smoke. The fire is kept burning for several days.

Some people like to leave the sausage hanging and aging, just cutting down a link when needed. Others wrap each link in foil and store in a deep freeze. It is powerful good either way!

We felt like "old pros" now in handling state dinners, having experienced the preparation for three world leaders. Even so, we had never had "our own President of the United States." This would be an occasion different from all the others. We were getting ready for someone we all considered our very special personal friend; President Kennedy and his wife would be arriving at the ranch as soon as the big Banquet given in their honor at Austin was over.

Mr. Kennedy spoke in Austin during the 1960 campaign and spent a night at the Executive Mansion as the guest of Governor and Mrs. Price Daniel, but his tight schedule did not permit him to go to the LBJ ranch. He came back after the election, however, and stayed with the Johnsons overnight, going deer hunting the next morning. It was a successful morning, for he bagged a buck.

So on November 22, 1963, he was to be making his first visit there as President, and it was also to be Mrs. Kennedy's introduction to the ranch — something Lyndon and Lady Bird Johnson had been looking forward to for a long time.

Preparations were made for weeks in advance. The Johnsons wanted to do everything possible to make their visit to Texas and to the ranch a happy and memorable one; Western entertainment, their favorite food, time to relax, a beautiful horse for Mrs. Kennedy to ride, gifts they would treasure, and always the peace and beauty of the ranch.

The tragic news reached the ranch as the entertainers were rehearsing and the favorite food of the Kennedys was being prepared for a small "family" dinner. Mary Davis, one of the cooks, was just taking three pecan pies from the oven as everyone stood stunned stiff listening to the grim news casts. She asked, "What will I do with these pies? These were to be *his* pies, for my President," then left the kitchen weeping.

Throughout the years and through all these great and tragic events, Lady Bird Johnson has stayed the same. She is as genuinely interested in the president of the Stonewall PTA as the president of a great nation.

To her friends whom she has known through the years she never changes. She greeted me on the third floor of the White House recently with the same warm hospitality as she did when I first visited her at the ranch in Stonewall. Only this time, instead of dresser scarves, she showed me the Lincoln Room, the Queen's Room and the handiwork of some other First Ladies, and told little bits of history and charming stories of the White House!

HOUSTON

Houston is undoubtedly one of America's most exciting cities and is one of the crossroads of the world. It seems incredible today that once this city was almost abandoned. For in 1836, Mexican General Santa Anna hurried his troops across this site, stopping only long enough to burn Harrisburg, which was the lumber-port town on Buffalo Bayou where Houston now stands. It was also on this ground that Texas General Sam Houston and his volunteer army of nine hundred Texans clashed with Santa Anna's trained troops of more than twelve hundred. However, the Mexicans suffered a disastrous defeat in this battle which lasted only a few explosive minutes! History calls this one of the decisive battles of the world, as it not only freed Colonial Texas, but gave Texas a vast domain from which one-third of the state would eventually be carved and added to the Union. Today this battleground is a state park and is marked with the nation's tallest monument.

Hardly had the smoke of the battle cleared when two New York real estate men, brothers, John K. and Augustus C. Allen, decided to establish a city at the headwater of Buffalo Bayou, eighteen miles upstream from the San Jacinto battleground. They paid $1.00 per acre to the pioneer family of Stephen F. Austin for the townsite, and named their daring and hopeful venture after the heroic General Houston. The Allen brothers began to promote Houston prospects with great flair in newspapers circulated throughout the North and East. Success was slow; at first only a trickle of immigrants flowed into the Southwest, then a stream and finally a wave of populace flooded the area. The Allen brothers' most extravagant promises have long since been overshadowed by the extraordinary stature their infant city has attained, as today Houston ranks seventh in population among cities in the United States. It blends rich traditions of the Old West with the freshness of a modern, youthful city — like the colorful rodeos and livestock expositions and the new six-million-dollar Performing Arts Hall.

Practically in the heart of this bustling city is the home of Miss Ima Hogg, Bayou Bend. It is a large wooded estate situated on the historical Buffalo Bayou in Houston's beautiful residential section, River Oaks. The house is New Orleans plantation style and is surrounded by an arboretum and formal gardens which run down to Buffalo Bayou. The gravel driveway curves through the fourteen-acre estate of tall pine trees and dogwood trees, and the sweet smell in the air comes from the blossoms of pink magnolia trees. The graceful wisteria and giant oaks are accented by pieces of statuary.

The greatly beloved and dynamic person within the house on these acres gives her guests a privileged experience when they come to visit. When the Garden Club of America (sometimes referred to as the Mink, Martini and Manure Set) were entertained at Bayou Bend, they were simply "carried away" by its beauty. The Hogg family has always played an important role in Texas, and Miss Ima herself is recognized as the perpetual First Lady of Texas. Miss Ima has long been identified with the cultural world of Houston: she was a founding member of its symphony, the great force behind the mental health movement, and is a member of the Board of Directors of Houston's Museum of Fine Arts, to whom she will ultimately give Bayou Bend and all its rare antique furnishings, her art collection, eighteenth-century porcelain, and her library, which contains much about Texas history.

Besides being a great benefactor, she is an accomplished pianist; some of the world's musical, literary and artistic greats have dined at her table, which explains, in part, why Bayou Bend is more than a collection. It is the beautiful, lived-in, period home of a great lady who understands that a gracious home is far more than the sum of its make-up. As in all her roles, Miss Ima has established herself as a hostess *par excellence*. She prepares her menus and plans details of parties as though she were writing a poem or painting a picture; everything blends harmoniously and each occasion is one always to be remembered. Her collection and use of rare porcelain and china also add great beauty and interest to her parties at Bayou Bend. For instance, the antique Chinese Canton service with green Bristol stemware is always used for a special *Curry Dish and makes an incredibly beautiful table. Two runners of Milano lace are used for the luncheon service, with napkins to match. This curry recipe was given to Miss Ima years ago by an old friend of the family. This gentleman, a real gourmet, experimenting with fine dishes, perfected the following:

★

Curry Dish

Cold baked leg of lamb or venison
3 slices of ham, 1¼ inch thick, from center cut of lean ham
4 large onions
5 cups beef broth, diluted
1½-oz. bottle curry powder, or to taste
2 pkgs. raisins
4 cups tender celery (diced)

Dice meat evenly and trim off all fat. Cut onions fine and fry in grease from ham fat. After well cooked (not brown), sauté ham in same grease, but after the onions have been removed. Pour in 2½ cups diluted beef broth. Use ½ bottle curry powder. Return onions to pot, add raisins and allow to simmer. When cooked down, add venison (or lamb) and pour in more liquid and rest of curry powder. Simmer again until liquid is right consistency. All ingredients should cook together slowly, about 2 hours. This should be cooked in a Dutch oven or covered iron pot. Just before serving, put in 3 or 4 cups cold, crisp celery, and as soon as it is heated through, serve immediately.

This should be served on a large silver platter, preferably one with hot water chamber underneath. This is bordered by a ring of flaky well-cooked rice, surrounded by halves of lemons and decorated with parsley. Each serving of curry should have ½ lemon squeezed over the meat and be served with such condiments as chutney, slivers of toasted almonds and shredded coconut, either fresh or frozen (after frozen coconut is defrosted, squeeze out water), crumbled crisp broiled bacon. (Toasted almonds are preferable to peanuts.)

The first course is Bortsch, a delicious beet soup with sour cream and a dash of chives. The butler next places the huge silver platter of Curry before the hostess. After the plates are served, he is followed by the maid or second butler with the condiments. The originator of the recipe disapproved of serving wine with Curry, preferring tea as a better complement. Neither did he serve bread with this dish, but Miss Ima knows her guests like bread, so she serves sliced, buttered toasted French rolls. Tossed salad is served on the side with the Curry. A combination of whatever luscious fruit might be in season is for dessert. It is served from a large silver bowl, the flavor being enhanced by a sauce made with either currant or raspberry jelly which has been melted in the top of a double boiler; a couple of jiggers of Kirsch are added and sometimes thin slivers of blanched almonds (not toasted).

When Dimitri Mitropoulos first came to Houston as guest conductor of the Houston Symphony, Miss Ima entertained for him at a small seated luncheon (the number of guests never exceeds ten for seated affairs). After a champagne cocktail in the library, lunch was announced. As the maestro entered the dining room, he stopped still and with misty eyes whispered, "I am overwhelmed by such beauty." The dining room walls, in delicate greens and whites, are covered with shimmering gold leaf and hand painted with flowering dogwood and a few whimsical birds, including a hummingbird, which is indigenous to Texas. Miss Ima used her exquisite white porcelain musician figurines in the center of the table, with white camellias and dainty little white snowflake flowers which grow along one of the garden walks. The table was set with her white salt-glaze eighteenth-century pottery and her emerald and gold Bristol goblets. It was a leisurely and happy occasion which the maestro reveled in; and when the green Bristol finger bowls containing rosewater were brought in after the duck course, he plunged both hands in the bowl with much gusto and wiped over his face as well! This was the menu that day:

** Crumb Pancakes with Sour Cream and Caviar*
** Cold Breast of Duck, Orange Slices*

Large White Asparagus with Hollandaise Sauce
Green Salad with small bits of Crisp Garlic Toast
** Drop Biscuits*
** Light Frozen Lemon Crème*

★

Crumb Pancakes with Sour Cream and Caviar

1 cup stale breadcrumbs (inside of bread, cutting off all crust)
1 cup sweet milk
3 eggs
Butter size of egg, melted
Enough flour to make thin batter
Scant tsp. baking powder

Take 4 slices of stale bread and cut off crust. Crumble and scald with hot milk. Add well-beaten eggs and melted butter, then enough flour to make thin batter, to which is added scant teaspoon of baking powder. Fry in hot skillet, making pancakes very thin. When ready to serve, use stacks of 4 pancakes and cover with hot melted butter. Pass sour cream and caviar, with quarters of lemon. Lemon is to be squeezed over caviar.

★

Cold Breast of Duck with Orange Slices

1 medium-sized wild duck
Garlic clove, uncut
Freshly ground pepper
1 bay leaf
1 small onion
½-¾ bottle French dressing
Pâté de foie gras or good liver sausage
Orange Slices (below)

Wash duck and parboil 1 minute. Drain off water and put in pot of boiling water, slightly salted, with garlic, pepper, bay leaf, onion or any other favorite herbs. Let simmer until duck is tender. Remove from fire and let stand in the same cooking water with herbs until cold. Remove from water, pat dry and pour a good rich French dressing slowly over duck, patting it gently into the meat. Let marinate overnight. Remove breast of duck from bone with sharp knife; trim edges well with scissors.

Serve on oval pieces of toast which have been brushed with melted butter and spread with pâté de foie gras or a good liver sausage. Serve with orange slices prepared like this:

ORANGE SLICES

Take thick-skinned seedless oranges and cook whole until tender in water. Remove at once and cool, then make a syrup of sugar and water and candied red cinnamon drops. Cook until thick. Slice the oranges and return to hot syrup and cook about ten minutes.

★

Drop Biscuits

Make a standard biscuit recipe, only drop by teaspoonfuls in pan instead of rolling. Butter and pass piping hot.

★

Frozen Lemon Crème

1 qt. milk
1¼ cups sugar
1 cup lemon juice (2½ lemons)
Grated rind of 2 lemons
1 pt. whipping cream
Green vegetable coloring

Scald milk, add sugar and let cool. Then add juice of 2½ lemons, with grated lemon rind. Let this freeze until mushy, then fold in whipped cream. Color with green vegetable coloring. Return to freezer and stir often until hard. It freezes quickly.

Another popular and hearty luncheon menu that Miss Ima serves is:

Gazpacho (Cold Tomato Soup)
Waffles spread with cream cheese and a broiled pineapple slice, topped with Turkey or Chicken Hash
Tossed Green Salad
Prune Soufflé topped with Thin Boiled Custard and a homemade cookie

---

It is fun being a house guest at Miss Ima's, for here, too, everything is to perfection. She likes her guests to feel free to relax, not to have to rush to dress or meet a time schedule, so she always sends breakfast to their rooms. She has the guests tell her what they prefer for breakfast, and it is sent on a beautiful tray with fresh flowers and a delicate china service. Of course, Miss Ima adds little surprises, like *Pear Marmalade.

★

Pear Marmalade

1 lb. pears
¾ lb. sugar
1 lemon slice
1 orange slice
¼ tsp. powdered ginger
Pinch of salt
1 cup white raisins

Wash and core pears, but do not peel. Chop with coarse grinder on meat chopper, saving the juice. Add sugar, lemon and orange slices, ginger, salt, raisins and pear juice and cook until pears are clear. Put in sterile fruit jars; seal.

Preceding her dinner parties, her choice of cocktails includes the famous and popular *Bayou Bend Special. A long-sought secret, this is how it is made:

★

Bayou Bend Special

1 thick-skinned seedless orange
1 Tbs. honey
1 fifth Bourbon

PER DRINK

Half orange slice
Stemmed cherry
Jigger orange and lemon juice, mixed
Dash bitters
Dash orange-flower water
2 jiggers prepared Bourbon

Slice orange and add 1 Tbs. honey to whole orange. Put in top of double boiler and let steep 5 or 10 minutes over low heat. Transfer orange slices to a jar (you can use an apothecary jar, as Miss Ima does); cover with a fifth of Bourbon and let stand at least 12 hours, but after 24 hours remove orange slices (if orange is left too long Bourbon will be bitter). Use the Bourbon for mixed drinks. For each drink add a fresh half orange slice, 1 stemmed cherry, a small jigger fresh orange and lemon juice mixed, a dash of bitters, and a dash of orange-flower water to 2 jiggers of prepared Bourbon over cubes of ice.

For dinner the menu is:

** Oyster Broth*
** Roast Duck*
** Stuffed Turnips*
Whole Red Glazed Apples simmered in simple syrup and red cinnamon candies
Wild rice or lye hominy pressed into individual ramekins to form a mold well seasoned with salt, pepper, butter
Dessert

★

Oyster Broth

1 qt. oysters
1 pt. water
½ tsp. red pepper
Pinch curry powder
2 Tbs. lemon juice
Pinch salt

Simmer all ingredients slowly about 15 minutes. Put 2 Tbs. chopped oysters in each cup. Serve with slice of lemon and piece of parsley.

★

Roast Wild Duck

1-1½ lb. wild duck per person
Salt
Grated orange rind
2-3 sticks celery (with tops)
½ cup concentrated orange juice
1 cup chicken consommé

After cleaning duck thoroughly, rub with little salt and grated orange rind and place celery in the cavity. Pour orange juice and consommé over the duck and cook in 350-degree oven approximately 1 hour, basting during cooking.

★

Stuffed Turnips

Small white sweet turnips
Salt, butter, heavy cream
Season with small amount of sugar
Buttered crumbs

Wash, peel turnips and simmer in slightly salted water until tender but still firm. Remove from water. Scoop out the middle of the turnip, mash and season with a little salt, butter, heavy cream and sugar. Put seasoned turnips back in the whole shells, sprinkle with buttered crumbs and reheat in the oven. Place around duck on the platter, alternating with cinnamon apples.

Miss Ima loves to reminisce about her family's glorious past, and her eyes twinkle when she talks about the days she lived in the Governor's Mansion in Austin, when her father, Stephen Hogg, was the Governor of Texas (1892-1898). The New Year's Day Open House was the biggest social occasion of the year. The dining room table was covered with hand-embroidered damask cloths, elaborate drawnwork and handmade drawnwork napkins to match the tablecloth. Flower centerpieces were usually a low decoration and Miss Ima, as a child, would watch them being made. A low three- or four-inch-high tin form in the shape of some flower, heart or star was packed with wet sand, and then heads of the flowers were stuck into the sand to make a solid design. It rested on a wide linen centerpiece, elaborately embroidered with realistic silk flowers. Invitations to the Open House were sent to the wide social circle in Austin and towns nearby.

Miss Ima remembers the making of Beaten Biscuits in great quantities for the parties. The help would let her hammer on them every once in a while. These were served with the Virginia Ham or Smoked Ham. Also on the table would be an ever-present big tray of Chicken Salad garnished with Brandied or Pickled Peaches. Green olives, then a new import to Texas, created quite a sensation. One night a guest leaving the Mansion reached in his pocket and brought out an olive and said, "I didn't know what to do with this." His companion pulled out one also and said, "I didn't know either." So they both flipped them over the fence as they left the grounds! Salted toasted almonds, hearts of celery, and homemade potato chips, then called Saratoga Potatoes, were additional features on the table. These potato chips had been made famous at the Saratoga Springs Hotel in New York and were all the rage. They were made from very large potatoes sliced very, very thin, placed in ice water, then patted dry with a towel and dropped in hot fat. When very light brown, they were lifted from the hot oil and drained on absorbent paper and salted generously.

On beautiful cake stands around the table would always be four or five kinds of cake: Fruit Cake, Lady Baltimore Cake, Marble Cake (white loaf cake with blended chocolate and strawberry batter), Pound Cake and a traditional delicacy I had forgotten about, the Rosettes (a paper-thin crisp sweet waffle-like dainty, dusted with powdered sugar). Thin mints (made by Lamme Candy and Ice Cream Store of Austin) were also popular treats. Even today the Lamme candies are still a "special treat" and are very popular with Texas hostesses. One of Governor Hogg's favorites was salt-rising bread and butter sandwiches, which were always on the menu. Also a cut glass bowl of strawberry preserves to put on the bread. I would think one could make out with this "light refreshment!" Three varieties of punch: Fruit Punch, Champagne Punch and *Eggnog, Southern Style, eaten with a spoon. (See recipe in Abilene chapter, page 262.)

Houston, along with its many recognized citizens, has innumerable attractions. Rice Institute, a university covering three hundred acres, was opened in 1912 by William Marsh Rice as a tuition-free institution. After the hot summer and the first inkling of a "norther," all of Texas seems to break out in parties. In the fall when the football season comes, one of the most popular games of the Southwest is the Texas-Rice game, which is played alternately at Austin and at Houston. When the game is at Houston, one of the main attractions is the great big wonderful party the Harry Holmeses have before the game! The festivities take place at their home, where all their old schoolmates gather. Harry and Carolyn live in a handsome white Colonial house across the street from the River Oaks Country Club. (The two places are sometimes confused!) They started out by having some of their out-of-town friends over for lunch, but you know how it goes and grows — friends bring friends — so finally Harry had to move out into the yard. Carolyn says that this is Harry's party, and she just lets him take over completely, as it truly is a man-sized job. Invitations are not sent; friends just know the party is going on and stop by. As a matter of fact, there were more than eight hundred who "just stopped" last year!

A few years ago, Harry was all set up for the party in the yard, and the night before there came a terrible rain. The next morning the yard was standing in water. He aroused one of the house guests, some young executive not accustomed to a shovel, and told him to get up and start shoveling sand. Then they went over to his lumber yard and got some cinder blocks, with which they completely covered the yard, and the party went off as scheduled. As the guests arrived the calliope merrily played "It Ain't Gonna Rain No More, No More!" After that harrowing experience, Harry bought an enormous party tent, which he now stretches up two days before the party. A long table is simply loaded with food, such as barbecued ribs, a big steamboat round of beef; potato salad; pinto beans; green salad; assorted breads and spreads; and his special *Charcoal-Broiled Hamburgers in miniature. For these, he puts a can of chili in every five pounds of hamburger meat; makes it into small patties and charcoals them; as they flow off the grill everyone dolls them up with a variety of condiments. In addition, there are two oyster bars, one on each side of the yard, with oysters on the half shell — these go like hot cakes — and of course there are two or three bars for drinks. This selection of delicious food sustains his guests during the lusty cheering at the game. Harry built an old-fashioned band-stand to accommodate the music; Carolyn made fancy orange corduroy vests embroidered in white for the boys in the band. Cleverly arranged on one side of the yard is a dramatic waterfall splashing onto a big block of ice and down to chill the soft drinks in the pool below.

Carolyn leaves the Big Party to Harry; she takes care of her own continuous party of her five lovely children, who love for her to cook her *Chicken Speciality, which is:

★

Chicken Speciality

2-lb. chicken cut for frying
½ envelope dehydrated onion soup
½ cup raw rice
½ cup water

Place cut-up chicken in a shallow baking dish. Sprinkle with approximately ½ envelope of onion soup and add rice and water. Cover tightly with foil. Bake in 350-degree oven for 45 minutes. (Of course, Carolyn quadruples this recipe when preparing it for her family!)

Texans do most of their entertaining in their homes. It is a great temptation in Houston, however, to use one of the beautiful clubs, or one of the excellent restaurants. Mr. and Mrs. A. G. NcNeese are busy in many civic affairs and are in the line of fire for entertaining many VIP's, as Houston attracts visitors from all over the world. Catherine McNeese prefers seated dinners to buffet types, so if there are more than ten or twelve to be seated for a formal event. the McNeeses go to the Coronado Club on top of Mac's Bank or the Southwest. Catherine plans the menu in detail with the chef and maître d'. She uses candelabras and elaborate flower arrangements down the center of the table. One of their guests was His Highness Sri Jaya Chamarajendra Wadiyar Bahadur, Maharajah of Mysore! His visit to Houston came at the time when much publicity had been given The Great Impostor. When His Royal Highness deplaned, Mac and a welcoming committee were out to meet him. Mac got a glance of the King and wondered if this dowdy man could be the world's richest. He was just about to call the FBI, but it was quickly confirmed that this was the "genuwine" King, and he just happened not to be concerned about his crumpled clothes and bedraggled appearance. He turned out to be a most delightful guest and brought his hostess an exquisite pair of *ruby* earrings!

When Catherine does have less than ten for dinner, she seats the guests at her dining room table. Often the entrée is her *Stuffed Crab. This was a tried and true recipe of her mother's.

★

Stuffed Crab

2 Tbs. butter
1 small onion (diced)
3 tsp. flour
1 cup milk or water (prefer water)
4 eggs (hard boiled and sieved)
1 tsp. lemon juice
Pepper to taste
Salt to taste
1 lb. can fresh lump crabmeat
1 small can diced mushrooms
Crab shells
Breadcrumbs

Melt the butter in a saucepan. Add onion, don't brown; flour. Stir until smooth; add cup of water and stir until thickened. Add eggs, lemon juice, seasoning, crab meat and mushrooms. The mixture shouldn't be too soft. Fill shells, add bread crumbs, dot with butter and brown in 350-degree oven. Serves 6.

One Houstonian who has made a very fine reputation for himself with his extraordinary French cuisine is Camille Berman. When he first opened his restaurant, Maxim's, he couldn't find many takers for his French food, but now one can hardly get a reservation at all! Camille says that he has seen a great change in the taste of Texans. He feels they know now much about food and can be called real connoisseurs. In fact, Camille said, he had learned a lot about cooking from Texans. For instance, a seventy-five-year-old Texan taught him to put the juice of two oranges and the same amount of Old Taylor Bourbon over steaks and let them marinate 2 to 3 hours before putting them over the coals. He loves being in Texas, where every kind of food is available, and Camille is reputed to have the largest wine collection in America.

On this particular day, he was getting ready for His Royal Highness King Hussein I, of Jordan. The young King had met a Houstonian named John Mecom, and together they had decided to drill for oil in Jordan. John invited him to come to Houston, to visit and to look over his cattle and his sports cars. The Mecoms held a beautiful reception at their home for His Royal Highness, then took him to Maxim's for a formal dinner. Camille was using beef from the Mecom ranch, Corralitos, near Laredo. This was the menu he prepared for approximately one hundred guests:

DINNER
in honor of
HIS MAJESTY KING HUSSEIN I

Palacios Crawfish Bisque

Baked Gulf Trout

Mission Parsley Potatoes
Meursault Blagny 1961

Corralites Rancho Briand
Sauce Béarnaise

Black-eyed Peas *Creamed Spinach*

Gevrey-Chambertin 1937
"Cazetiers"

Jumbo Strawberries from the Valley
à la Maxim's

Magnums
Dom Pérignon 1952

Coffee *Liqueurs*

Maxim's Houston 20 April 1964

Mrs. Albert Jones and I were philosophizing about entertaining — having parties and the many facets thereof. Certainly Nettie is well qualified to speak on this subject, as she fills the role of hostess and guest naturally and frequently. Her guests never suspect that she has worried her pretty head about a thing, but feel that she undoubtedly must just press buttons and everything falls into place for a party, whether it is an impromptu afternoon tea for a distinguished visitor or a buffet for one hundred fifty which has been on the calendar for months. Nettie seems to be on hand for either in the same frame of mind, that of being delighted to see each guest and ready to enjoy their company for whatever the occasion might be.

Indeed, she has not pressed any buttons, but has set out to see that every detail of the party is well taken care of, such as the guest list, the invitations, the flowers, the servants, the food and the cocktails.

When she and Albert had an afternoon reception for Sir Thomas and Lady Beecham, Nettie asked Camille Berman of Maxim's to please contact reliable sources in London as to their preference in drinks. The report came back that Lady Beecham preferred very dry martinis, and Sir Thomas only drank vintage Madeira. So Nettie thoughtfully had this special Madeira, and made sure that there was ample on hand for the party — and that the martinis were especially dry. When the honorees arrived and the waiter took their order — they both asked for orange juice! Nettie said that for the life of her she couldn't remember if there was even an orange in the house, but apparently there was, because in a few minutes Sir Thomas was downing a tall glass of orange juice. The menu that afternoon included:

Chicken Salad
Thin-sliced Ham in Small Hot Biscuits
Lobster with a Tartare Sauce Dip
Large homemade Potato Chips with a Cream Cheese Dip
Bread and butter sandwiches
Cucumber sandwiches
Olives
Broiled Mushrooms
Deviled Eggs with Caviar
*A great variety of cookies, including * Praline Cookies and Lizzies*
Coffee

★

Praline Cookies

1 stick butter
1 egg, slightly beaten
1 cup flour
1 cup brown sugar
1 tsp. vanilla
½ cup pecans

Drop by teaspoonfuls on cookie sheet, and cook at 325 degrees for 20 minutes or more.

The food served at the Joneses' is consistently fine; some of the recipes are Nettie's originals; others she has altered and revised to perfection, for instance, Chicken with White Cherries. With this, the menu would possibly be:

Green Tossed Salad
Chicken with White Cherries
** Baked Spinach Genoese*
Summer Corn
Hot Rolls
Fresh Fruit Compote

★

Spinach Genoese

1 Tbs. chopped onion
1 minced clove of garlic
⅓ cup butter
¾ cup (2 small cans) chopped mushrooms
4 Tbs. flour
2 cups milk
Salt and pepper to taste
1 pkg. frozen spinach
3 chopped, cooked eggs
½ cup buttered breadcrumbs
1½ Tbs. Parmesan cheese

Sauté onion and garlic in butter with mushrooms. Add flour and stir until well blended. Add milk gradually and stir until mixture thickens. Season with salt and pepper. Stir in spinach and egg. Turn mixture into greased shallow baking dish and top with mixture of breadcrumbs and Parmesan. Bake at 350 degrees until brown (approximately 30 minutes).

One speciality she loves to prepare is *Summer Corn — her own brand, as she buys it fresh from the fields in June, cuts the whole grains off the cob, blanches it in boiling water and then freezes it in pint and quart packages. When ready to serve, she simply puts ½ lb. butter with 1 qt. of corn, adds 1 tsp. sugar, white pepper, salt and cayenne to taste and just a little water, in which the corn is simmered gently for only a few minutes.

A lovely luncheon Nettie had for the Avery girls when they visited her in Houston was:

** Caviar and Egg*
** Chicken Breasts in Cream, served with Herbed Rice*
** Broiled Stuffed Tomatoes*
Hot Rolls
Lime Sherbet with Fresh Strawberries
Coffee

★

Caviar and Eggs

Mash a whole hard-boiled egg with salt and pepper, using a fork. Use a small fruit-juice glass as a mold and freeze mashed egg. When frozen, slice and spread caviar between slices and put on plate. Nettie put a fresh pansy on each plate, and passed rye toast rounds.

★

Chicken Breasts in Cream

8 chicken breasts, uncooked
Salt and pepper
Beaten egg
Packaged dry breadcrumbs
¼ cup butter
¼ cup salad oil
2 pkgs. frozen peas
2 cups heavy cream
1 clove garlic, crushed
½ tsp. paprika

Season chicken breasts well with salt and pepper. Dip in beaten egg and roll in breadcrumbs. Sauté until golden brown in butter mixed with salad oil. Place the breasts in large baking dish. Add peas; over them pour cream mixed with ¼ tsp. salt and crushed garlic. Dust with paprika and bake in moderate oven (350 degrees) for 45 minutes to an hour, basting occasionally until chicken is tender.

★

Stuffed Tomatoes

Tomatoes
Butter
Salt and pepper
Onion, chopped fine
Celery, chopped fine
1 tsp. brown sugar
1 tsp. salad herbs
Breadcrumbs

Remove top of tomatoes, if small, or halve if large. Scoop out center. Make a mixture of butter, salt and pepper, onion, celery, brown sugar and salad herbs. Fill tomatoes with this mixture, add well-buttered breadcrumbs, and place in a medium oven to heat through.

One day Nettie gave me a jar of chutney, which I promptly brought home and had with curried shrimp. It was — what shall I say? — I have overused delicious, divine, marvelous, and the chutney was all three. I bribed Nettie for the formula, which she somewhat reluctantly brought out from her secret drawer. It was written in a black notebook, and I glanced over the top of the book, which

Nettie was holding abreast like a prize bridge hand. The page was titled, modestly, "The World's Best Recipe for Chutney." It seems that Nettie and her friend, Mrs. Leslie Coleman, had merged recipes and had come out with this master one:

★

The World's Best Chutney

2½ cups (1 lb.) brown sugar
5 cups hard pears
3 apples
3 peaches
2 lemons, chopped fine
½ orange, chopped fine
1 cup water chestnuts, sliced
¾ cup (3 oz.) crystallized ginger
¼ tsp. cayenne
¼ tsp. allspice
1 Tbs. Worcestershire sauce
2 cups cider vinegar
2 ripe tomatoes, peeled and chopped
2½ cups (1 box) dark seeded raisins (or white seedless)
1 Tbs. powdered ginger
1½ Tbs. salt
1 clove garlic (juice only)
1½ tsp. peppercorns
½ tsp. cinnamon
3 Tbs. mustard seed

Cut up and chop fine. The only thing left is to: add an old tennis shoe! Simmer 2 hours.

I have never looked into the requisites for being an Episcopalian, but certainly one has to be an exceptional cook; I don't know any who aren't! The group that sews every week at the Church of St. John the Divine in Houston is no exception. The girls gather every Wednesday at the parish hall with Mrs. Linsay Russell as chairman. They do needlework that one would expect to find only on the European market: beautiful aprons, tiny stuffed animals, petit point chair bottoms, all sorts of felt toys and articles decorated in beads and sequins. These are sold for the benefit of the Church. One day the ladies were talking about children and grandchildren and at the same time also trying to decide how much they should get for some of the needlework. "By the way, Alice, how old is your little grandson?" and the grandmother answered, "Oh, he's a $1.50!" Mrs. "Cordon-Bleu" Russell plans a menu and the members "take turns" bringing the luncheon. It is always scrumptious! These are some of the featured recipes:

★

St. John's Turkey

1 qt. thick cream sauce
2 cans mushroom soup (undiluted)
2 cans celery soup (undiluted)
2 tsp. salt
½ tsp. cayenne pepper
Juice 1 lemon
2 cups celery (cut fine)
1 can water chestnuts (optional)
½ cup parsley
6 cups turkey (cut bite size)
Chinese noodles

Mix cream sauce, mushroom and celery soup with salt, pepper and lemon juice. Add celery and cook for 10 minutes. Add remaining ingredients (except noodles) and pour into casserole. Heat in oven until hot. Serve over Chinese noodles.

★

Baked Beans

The day I attended the Sewing Bee, this was the *pièce de résistance.*

¼ cup oil or ½ lb. salt pork cut in squares
1½ cups ham (left over or ends)
1 small green pepper (cut fine)
1 small onion (cut fine)
1 tsp. mustard (wet)
½ cup brown sugar (dark preferred)
1 cup catsup
2 lb. small navy peas (white)
Soda

Mix all ingredients together except beans and soda. Boil beans in water with a pinch of soda for 10 minutes; drain. Pour in casserole and add with other ingredients. Mix and add water to cover beans. Cover and cook in 200-degree oven for about 10 hours or until beans are soft.

★

Apricot Salad

This is so tart and delicious made with *dried* apricots.

1 12-oz. pkg. dried apricots
1½ cups water
2 pkgs. orange-flavored gelatine
Hot water or fruit juice
1 small can crushed pineapple
2 Tbs. lemon juice
1 cup fine, slivered almonds

Cook apricots in 1½ cups of water until very soft. Stir until almost a pulp. Dissolve gelatine in hot water (1 cup) or fruit juice. Add apricot pulp, crushed pineapple, lemon juice, almonds, and stir until mixed well. Congeal. Serve on lettuce leaf and top with mayonnaise. (If hot weather, add 1 Tbs. gelatine to recipe).

★

Chocolate Yeast Cake

1 cup butter or margarine
2 cups sugar
3 separated eggs
3 squares bitter chocolate
1 cup milk
½ cake yeast
¼ cup lukewarm water
2¾ cups cake flour
½ tsp. salt
1 tsp. soda
3 Tbs. hot water
1½ tsp. vanilla

Cream butter, add sugar and egg yolks. Melt chocolate in milk. Add yeast dissolved in ¼ cup lukewarm water. Add sifted flour, salt, then beaten egg whites. Cover in mixing bowl. Place in refrigerator for 8 hours. Add soda dissolved in 3 Tbs. hot water. Add vanilla. Pour into pan 13 by 9 by 2. Bake in 350-degree oven for 45 to 55 minutes.

★

Whiskey Nut Cake

1 cup butter or margarine
2 cups sugar
6 eggs
3 cups flour (don't sift, just stir well before measuring)
1 tsp. baking powder
2 tsp. nutmeg
1 cup Bourbon whiskey (or rum if preferred)
1½ lbs. *seeded* muscat raisins
1 lb. pecans

Cream butter and sugar; add eggs. Add 2 cups of flour, baking powder and nutmeg alternately with whiskey. Then mix in raisins and nuts which have been mixed with the third cup of flour. Bake in 2 1-lb. loaf pans for about 1 hour and 20 minutes at 350 degrees. (Start the cake in a cold oven. This one keeps well in foil in a tin box. You can pour additional whiskey on top.)

★

Low Calorie Charlotte

Mrs. Russell makes this for her husband's diet and he loves it.

6 egg yolks
¾ cup sugar (½ brown, ¼ white)
1 qt. skimmed milk
1 envelope gelatine soaked in ¼ cup water
1 pkg. Dream Whip

Beat egg yolks and sugar and add milk. Cook until mixture coats spoon. Add gelatine. Cool and add Dream Whip. Make according to directions. Fold this in and put in ice box. Serve plain or with fruit.

★

English Toffee Dessert

For easy dessert!

16 vanilla wafers
1 cup chopped pecans
¼ lb. butter
1 cup sugar
3 eggs, separated
1½ squares bitter chocolate
1½ tsp. vanilla
Whipped cream

Mix crumbled wafers with chopped pecans. Put half of mixture in bottom of 9 by 9 pan. Set aside other half for top. Cream butter and sugar, add beaten egg yolks, melted chocolate, vanilla, and fold in beaten egg whites. Pour in pan. Pour other half wafer-nut mixture over top. Refrigerate overnight. Cut in squares. Serve with whipped cream.

★

Chocolate Upside-down Cake

4 Tbs. butter
¼ cup dark brown sugar
¾ cup light corn syrup
1 cup chopped pecans

Mix well and pour into the bottom of a 9 by 12 greased cake pan. Then make the cake.

6 Tbs. butter
1¼ cups vanilla sugar (Put vanilla bean in canister)
4 oz. bitter chocolate
2 egg yolks
2 cups flour
2 tsp. baking powder
1½ cups milk
2 egg whites

Cream butter with sugar. Melt chocolate over hot water. Beat egg yolks, add to melted chocolate. Mix in flour, baking powder. Add dry ingredients to chocolate mixture, alternating with milk. Beat egg whites stiff. Fold into mixture. Pour over filling already in bottom of pan. Cook in 350-degree oven for 50 minutes. Invert on board while slightly warm and cut to serve.

★

Butterscotch Brownies

- ¼ cup butter
- 1 cup brown sugar
- 1 egg
- 1 tsp. vanilla
- ½ tsp. baking powder
- ½ cup all purpose flour (sifted in)
- ½ tsp. salt
- 1 cup chopped pecans

Melt butter in saucepan. Stir brown sugar in until dissolved. Cool and beat in one egg, vanilla, flour, baking powder, salt. Stir well. Add pecans and pour in 8 by 8 pan. Bake at 350 degrees for 30 minutes. Cool. Cut into 1-by-2-inch bars. May be frosted with simple creamed frosting with butterscotch flavoring.

★

Broccoli Special

Extra good!

- 1⅓ qts. cooked broccoli
- 1 cup mayonnaise
- 1 cup cream sauce
- 1 Tbs. lemon
- Pinch nutmeg
- ⅓ cup sherry or white wine

Mix together in buttered 2-qt. casserole. Bake in 300-degree oven for 20 minutes.

★

Never-fail White Icing

This is Mrs. Russell's, and certainly you can depend on this recipe, especially after seeing the menus she planned and the results she received!

- 3 egg whites
- ¾ cup sugar
- ¾ cup Karo
- 1 Tbs. water
- 1 tsp. vanilla

Put ingredients in double boiler over cold water. Start beating with electric beater and start fire at same time. Beat until it stands in peaks. This varies in time, as some eggs whip faster than others. You can vary this recipe by using brown sugar (dark preferred) or by using 2 tsp. instant coffee instead of vanilla.

GREENVILLE

It is a beautiful drive from Dallas to Greenville, over the rolling north-central Texas farmland. On that June morning everything was fresh and green after a muchly needed rain. We were invited to Greenville as guests for the fiftieth wedding anniversary celebration of Colonel and Mrs. Hal Horton. Colonel Horton's grandfather acquired the family homestead Puddin' Hill, located two miles east of Greenville, in 1839 as payment for his services in the Texas Revolutionary War. The following winter, to provide food for his family of seventeen, he and some neighbors set out on a deer hunt. Five miles out, a Texas "blue norther" struck, forcing them to seek shelter for several days with an old sutler (early day term for storekeeper). Until they could proceed, poker became the favored pastime. As a result of one game, Hal's grandfather won the entire stock of the store. Packing the horseshoe nails, needles, pins, buttons, beeswax, flint and spices in his saddle bags, he rode home, dumped his winnings on his wife's bed and said: "Now Mary, we will open a store of our own and lead society in this part of Texas for a while."

Gertrude's family has also lived in Greenville for six generations. Her grandfather Briscoe organized the First Baptist Church in Greenville and other North Texas towns. Her mother was the first woman to hold public office (county clerk in 1902) in the state of Texas. It took a Supreme Court decision to make it legal in April 1902. When the children were asked, "What nationality is your family?" they would reply, "Greenville." In 1914, when Colonel

Hal and Gertrude Horton were married in Greenville, the late speaker of the House of Representatives, Sam Rayburn, was the best man. The reception had been held in the white cottage over on Park Street. Gertrude told us how she and her friends decorated the house with garlands of ivy and pink roses over the doors and windows. In the center of the table she placed the bridal bouquet of white roses that Hal had sent her. On every wedding anniversary thenceforth, wherever he is, Hal always sends Gertrude a duplicate of that bouquet.

The Anniversary Party was to be the next evening, but Sam Lauderdale, the husband of one of the Horton daughters, said we should come the day before, as "the fish always bite good on Tuesdays," and we'd have a fish fry. Well, it turned out to be not just a fish fry but a fish festival! Sam and Mr. Hal had caught two beautiful bass that must have weighed between three and four pounds each. After he cleaned them, Sam cut them into steaks and put them into a marinade.

★

Sam's Charcoaled Fish

- 2 lbs. fish steaks
- ½ cup melted fat or oil
- ½ cup sesame seeds
- ⅓ cup lemon juice
- ⅓ cup Cognac
- 3 Tbs. soy sauce
- 1 tsp. salt
- 1 clove garlic, crushed

Place steaks in a single layer in a shallow baking dish. Combine remaining ingredients. Pour sauce over fish and let stand for 30 minutes, turning once. Remove fish, reserving sauce for basting. Place fish in well-greased hinged wire grills. Cook on a barbecue grill about 4 inches from moderately hot coals for 8 minutes. Baste with remaining sauce. Turn and cook for 7 to 10 minutes longer or until fish flakes easily when tested with a fork and sesame seeds have browned. Serve any remaining sauce with fish. Serves 6.

He had the fire going for quite some time, for the coals were gray and glowing. (It is important that there be no flame.) Potatoes wrapped in foil had been cooking in the coals for almost an hour. Sam had also made up a bowl of the green salad for which I am sure one day he will be famous. The recipe will come later in this chapter, when we talk about the church supper where Sam is forbidden to show up unless he brings that onion and lettuce salad! It was perfect with the fish. Mary Jane, Sam's wife, brought out a delicious asparagus casserole and hot rolls and we "fell to" the moment the golden fish was lifted to our plates. I urge you fishermen and fish eaters to try fish prepared thus. The sesame seed gives a nutty, toasted flavor. You'll never eat anything any better — and don't forget Sam's salad with it and Mary Jane's casserole. It is a recipe Mary Jane got from her friend Mary Frances Turner.

★

Asparagus Casserole

- 1 cup cracker crumbs
- 1 can mushroom soup (8 oz.)
- ½ cup asparagus juice
- 1 large can green, cut asparagus, drained, or 2 lb. fresh asparagus
- 1 cup grated cheddar cheese
- Salt to taste

Line casserole with cracker crumbs. Dilute mushroom soup with asparagus juice. Salt to taste. Make layers of asparagus, mushroom mixture, cracker crumbs, and grated cheese. Repeat and top with grated cheese. Bake at 350 degrees for 30 to 40 minutes.

We moved to easy chairs as soon as we felt like moving after such a feast. Later, just at the right time, they served sort of an Alexander à la Forest as a very pretty complement to a fish dinner.

★

Alexander à la Forest

½ jigger of rum
½ jigger of crème de cacao
Several scoops of a good quality vanilla ice cream

Mix in a blender with crushed ice so it will be thick, and serve in Champagne glasses.

The next morning, after touring the beautiful little city of Greenville, admiring its homes both new and old, stopping to see its industrial area and to visit here and there, we drove over to Bonham, which is just a short distance from Greenville. Mrs. Horton wanted me to see the Sam Rayburn Library, and meet Mrs. Bartley, Mr. Sam's sister.

About four miles west of Bonham, in a grove of very beautiful old trees, stands the home of Sam Rayburn. Its tall, stately white columns rise to the full height of the two-story farmhouse. They seem to symbolize the life of its owner, who rose from a simple beginning to one of the highest positions in our nation.

As I pushed the doorbell beside the state historical marker on the front porch, Mrs. Horton remarked that, often as she had been there, it was the first time she had ever entered by the front door! Mrs. Bartley replied, "Yes: all our friends come to the back door. We are very informal and are always delighted to have company."

Mrs. Bartley served us fresh lemonade which had the best little twang — she put a large green olive in each glass. While we sipped our drinks she had many delightful stories to tell of the VIP's that visited there, and how much she enjoyed each guest.

Often, Mr. Sam brought home Cabinet members, foreign dignitaries and, on several occasions, a President of the United States, Harry Truman and Mrs. Truman. All their distinguished visitors were made welcome and enjoyed the informal hospitality of Mr. Sam's family, with his sister, Mrs. Bartley, as hostess.

Reared in this section of Fannin County, Mr. Sam dearly loved to come home, to see his family and numerous friends. He also longed for that good old home cookin' which could not be equaled elsewhere. Mr. Sam had very simple tastes, especially where food was concerned. He often said, "A fellow can change his place of voting, but he can't change his appetite for good old turnip greens, salt pork and corn bread."

Born on a farm, he still held that farmers should "live at home," which the Rayburn family have always done. Wish you could see the size of their deep freezer — and a peep inside is something to behold: chicken, all kinds of vegetables, fruits and berries. At one time they cured their own pork, and often froze a big fat steer from Mr. Sam's place on Red River.

According to Mrs. Bartley, his favorite menu at home never varied — fried chicken and fresh vegetables; from their garden in season, other times from their freezer. Mrs. Bartley's chicken is reputedly "the best." She told me she dips her chicken in slightly beaten egg, no milk, then flours and fries in a heavy skillet in the usual way. This gave the chicken a very thin, crisp coating that is extra good.

Mr. Sam's favorite supper was "Crummin" (Corn Bread crumbled into sweet milk). I might add that this was also a great favorite with my father. When I asked Mrs. Bartley for the recipe, she replied, "I just cook and stir, adding what seems necessary." Those who have had the privilege of dining there will attest to the fact that this is so right.

Mr. Sam dearly loved company, big or little, old or young; and especially children. The family never knew how many guests to expect. The most company he ever brought home was when they dedicated the library. They spent days preparing for about three hundred invited guests. All the neighbors helped, not only from Bonham but from Sherman, Denison, and in fact from miles around, even from Greenville, forty miles away. Gertrude and Hal Horton brought a gorgeous cake in the form of an open book; Gertrude made the cake and decorated it with a facsimile of Mr. Sam's signature and the seal of the new library on one side, and "Fond Memories — Best Wishes — Gertrude and Hal Horton" on the other. There were big baked turkeys, hams, and all kinds of delicious salads and cakes. The Bonham folks had all turned up their noses at the suggestion of having someone out of Dallas cater this big event — *never* for food like this! This is true Texas-style hospitality. They served over six hundred people, as Sam kept inviting everyone who stopped by to stay for dinner! But even with that influx, when it was over there was enough food left to fill the twelve Biblical baskets.

We came back to Sam and Mary Jane's with radiant appetites. Mamie, who has cooked for Mary Jane since she married Sam, had just put lunch on the table; there were individual yellow casseroles in straw containers at each place. I couldn't resist lifting the lid to peek in, for its aroma was glorious. When Mary Jane told me that it was simply called Shrimp Stew, I insisted that such a pedestrian title did it an injustice. A daisy decorated the center of each casserole. The petals were cut from whites of hard-boiled eggs, and a center was made from the yolks, well-seasoned, mashed, and rolled into a small ball. This is how Mary Jane made her *Shrimp Stew:

★

Shrimp Stew

2 lbs. shrimp, cleaned and peeled
1 lb. scallops
1 lb. crabmeat
1½ cups white Rhine wine
¼ lb. butter
5 white onions, chopped fine
2 tsp. paprika
2½ cups breadcrumbs, soaked in 2 cups milk
3 cups cream
3 tsp. salt
1 tsp. pepper
Dash orange bitters

Combine the shrimp, scallops, crabmeat and 1 cup of wine in a saucepan. Bring to boil and cook over low heat for about 10 minutes, stirring every two or three minutes. Strain, reserving the stock; chop the shrimp and scallops fine. Melt the butter in a saucepan. Add the onions and paprika and sauté for about 15 minutes, stirring frequently. Squeeze the excess milk from the crumbs and discard milk. Add the breadcrumbs to the onions; add the reserved stock and mix well. Add chopped shrimp, scallops and crabmeat, cream, salt and pepper. Add ½ cup of

Rhine wine and cook over low heat for about 15 minutes. Add a couple dashes bitters. Serves 12.

This also can be put into a casserole, sprinkled with Parmesan cheese, cooked in a slow oven until thick and used as a fish dish on a buffet table.

Broiled curried fruit complemented the Shrimp Stew to perfection.

★

Curried Fruit

2 No. 2½ cans fruit salad
3 Tbs. butter
1½ cups brown sugar
3 tsp. curry powder
1 bottle red cherries (with stems)
1 bottle green cherries (with stems)

Drain fruit in colander 2 hours. Melt butter and slowly blend in sugar and curry powder. Put drained fruit in baking dish, spoon sugar mixture over fruit; add cherries without juice, bake 45 minutes in 325-degree oven (try to serve in pan fruit is cooked in). Serves 8.

Our lunch also included Fresh Green Beans Amandine, hot Sesame Bread Sticks, a tempting relish tray and iced tea. This delightful repast was followed by an equally delightful Greenville custom, a thirty-minute afternoon nap.

The Horton girls, Mary Jane and Sarah, both married and living in Greenville, naturally wanted to have the fiftieth Anniversary Party, but Gertrude said, "Why, half the fun is getting ready," so all together they whipped up the festive affair.

When the great night came, Sam mixed his *Special Cocktail. Less than ten minutes before the guests were to arrive, he spilled two gallons of the mix (before the sparkling water was added) onto the kitchen floor. It was the first time anyone had known of this being used to brighten a tile floor! Even after all the exhaust fans were turned on and windows and doors were opened, it was no surprise to the guests what he was serving:

★

Sam's Special Cocktail

1 jigger Southern Comfort
3 dashes Curaçao
Juice ½ small lime (1/6 oz.)
⅓ oz. lemon juice
½ level tsp. sugar
Fine ice to chill

Mix in blender.

This can also be used for a party by adding sparkling water.

I wish you could have tasted that luscious beef tenderloin, roasted only till the center was a pretty pink. Other delicious dishes were as follows:

★

Shrimp à la Gertrude (*serves 30 to 40*)

5 lbs. boiled shrimp
1 pt. mayonnaise
4 Tbs. prepared mustard
4 cloves garlic, minced very fine
2 Tbs. vinegar
2 bottles of finely chopped capers
Salt
1 stick butter
⅓ cup flour

While shrimp is boiling mix mayonnaise with mustard, garlic, vinegar, capers, salt in blender. When shrimp is done, drain and quickly add butter and flour. Toss with your hands until all shrimp are well coated, then add mayonnaise mixture and continue tossing. Chill several hours or overnight. Serve with toothpicks.

★

Pâté with Chicken Livers (*serves 30 to 40*)

1 lb. chicken liver
2 sticks butter
1 onion (medium)
¼ tsp. nutmeg
¼ tsp. cloves, ground
Salt and pepper
Any dry white wine to moisten
Tabasco

Put liver in baking dish and add butter. Bake at 350 degrees until done. Cool liver. Grind liver and 1 onion (medium). Mix liver, butter and onion, nutmeg and cloves. May need to melt more butter for spreading consistency. Add salt and pepper, heavy on the pepper. Add wine to the liver. Add dash of Tabasco. Place in mold and allow to chill overnight. Garnish and serve with party rye or crackers. *Chicken livers make the best pâté.* Decorate with:

GRAPE ONIONS

Color cocktail onions purple or leave white for grapes. Use whole, stick with piece of toothpick and form bunches of grapes on mold of pâté or salad. Use either fresh grape leaves or cut leaves from green pepper. If using green pepper, mark veins with back of knife.

★

Cheese Ball

- 6-oz. pkg. blue cheese
- 4 3-oz. pkgs. cream cheese
- 2 5-oz. jars processed cheddar cheese spread
- 2 Tbs. grated onion
- 1 tsp. Worcestershire sauce
- 1 tsp. Aćcent
- 1 cup ground pecans (or chopped toasted almonds)
- ½ cup finely chopped parsley

Mix all cheeses (warmed to room temperature) with onion, Worcestershire, Aćcent. Blend thoroughly. Add ½ cup pecans and ¼ cup chopped parsley. Shape into ball and place in bowl lined with wax paper. Chill overnight. About an hour before serving, roll ball into mixture of remaining pecans and parsley. Place on platter and surround by crisp crackers. You may crumble leftover cheese ball into a mixture of mayonnaise and sour cream. Makes a wonderful dressing for head ot lettuce salad. Decorate with two White Mice:

WHITE MOUSE

Cut off the end of a parsnip or carrot of proper shape. Ears are cut from crosswise slices of parsnip (or carrot) and stuck erect in a slit on either side, cloves are the eyes, and black bristles from a brush the whiskers. Shade nose with brown coloring. With a pin, make three holes on each side of nose and stick a bristle in each hole.

★

Chili Dip

- 6 lbs. lean ground beef
- 4 Tbs. bacon or beef fat
- 1 cup flour
- 6 chopped onions
- 2 cans beef consommé
- 6 oz. chili powder
- 2 tsp. powdered cumin seed
- 1 tsp. oregano
- 2 tsp. salt
- 4 lbs. cheddar cheese

Sauté ground beef, just covering the bottom of the skillet with bacon or beef fat. When cooked add 2 tsp. fat to the skillet and blend in 1 cup of flour. Heat 1 can of beef consommé and pour it in, stirring until mixture is smooth. Put it in a large pan with beef and add 6 chopped onions and 1 additional can of consommé, chili, powdered cumin seed, oregano and salt. Simmer for 30 minutes, stirring often. Turn up heat and stir constantly until mixture thickens. Put one half of mixture into top of double boiler with 2 lbs. of cheddar cheese, cut into pieces. In 15 or 20 minutes the cheese will be melted. Mix well and determine if it needs salt. Second half of the meat mixture with its 2 lbs. of cheese can be heating while the first half is being consumed. Serve with Fritos. (This is a recipe given Mary Jane by Mrs. Dale Miller of Dallas and Washington.)

★

Roast Beef with Garlic Apple

To make apple: season butter with garlic juice to taste. Mold butter in two small tea cups. (Do not fill quite full.) Trim smooth and press halves together, molding with hands and smoothing into shape of an apple. Chill. Paint with fruit coloring to resemble an apple. Place leaf and stem in top of apple. Serve on small dish beside platter of roast beef, either hot or cold. Garnish with parsley.

★

French Sesame Seed Sticks

½ pkg. (1 oz.) yeast
2 Tbs. warm water
½ cup shortening
6 Tbs. milk, scalded
2 cups flour
¾ tsp. salt
½ tsp. sugar
Sesame seed (about ¼ lb.)
1 egg, slightly beaten

Dissolve yeast in warm water, melt shortening in scalded milk, cool to lukewarm. Stir in dissolved yeast. Sift flour, salt, sugar together in large mixing bowl. Make well in center of flour, add liquids all at once, beat until dough leaves the side of bowl. Cover and set in warm place to rise until double in bulk. Punch down. Pinch off pieces size of pecan. Roll between palms of hands into pencil-thin strips. Let strips dry 10 minutes. Dip in beaten egg, then roll in sesame seed. Arrange on ungreased baking sheet. Bake slowly at 325 degrees about 25 minutes. Should be golden and very crisp. Cool. Place in tight container, will keep indefinitely.

We also had:

Sliced Turkey with Mayonnaise, in scalloped grapefruit shell
Relish tray with fancy olives
Corn Beef
Fancy breads

★

Rum Sausage

8-oz. package of tiny cocktail sausages
½ cup soy sauce
½ cup brown sugar
½ cup golden rum

Sauté sausages on one side, turn and cover with smooth mixture of soy sauce and brown sugar. Simmer on the other side in sauce; add rum and ignite. Serve cocktail sausages from chafing dish with toothpicks.

★

Olives on a Stick

1 loaf of unsliced party rye bread
1 package Swab Sticks, colored green
2 pkgs. cream cheese
1 bottle plain green olives
1 bottle stuffed olives
1 can giant black olives
1 bottle midget gherkins
1 dozen cherry tomatoes
1 bottle little green tomatoes
1 bottle cocktail onions
A few drops anchovy paste
Lemon juice
Any other seasoning you desire

(For a small party, use any three of the bottled items.)

If loaf of bread is too long, cut a piece out of center and fasten back together with toothpicks. Fasten loaf securely to plate, as the weight of the olives and pickles will turn it over. Use cut-glass celery tray and tie the loaf down with a thread, or very fine wire. (Neither one should show, but if it does, tuck sprigs of parsley around the bread.) Use Swab Sticks or toothpicks to hold olives and pickles. Whip cream cheese, divide into three or four batches, color and season each differently, pipe cheese on olives and pickles. Stick picks in loaf of bread.

The coffee service on the dessert table was kept filled with freshly brewed coffee, and there was one dessert that the guests just couldn't stop eating — a tray of Mary Jane's fruitcake, cut into cubes, each wearing a frilly toothpick for convenience. These were dipped into a bowl of whipped cream with two jiggers of Cognac added! The sweet table was obviously no place for a conscientious dieter to hang around. It also featured:

★

Minted Pecans

1 cup sugar
½ cup water
⅛ tsp. salt
¼ cup white Karo
6 large marshmallows
3-5 drops oil of peppermint
2½ cups pecans

Combine sugar, water, salt and Karo. Cook until it forms soft ball. Remove from heat, add marshmallows and peppermint. Stir until marshmallows melt, add nuts and stir until they separate. Turn out on pan and separate with fork. Store in tight container.

VARIATIONS

Add 2 Tbs. or more of Cognac instead of peppermint. Add 1 square of chocolate to sugar when marshmallow and flavoring are needed. Green coloring may be added to improve appearance of pecans.

★

Alfajores

⅔ cup butter
1 cup sugar
1 egg
2 egg yolks
1 tsp. vanilla
2 tsp. grated lemon rind
2 cups cornstarch
½ cup flour
1 tsp. baking powder
1 Tbs. brandy

Cream butter, add sugar and continue creaming. Add the egg and egg yolks, beating until light and frothy. Add the vanilla and rind. Sift the cornstarch, flour and baking powder and add to butter mixture, mixing well. Add brandy. Blend until the dough is smooth. Chill in the refrigerator until the dough is quite firm — 4 to 5 hours. Work fast. Pat the dough on a floured board to ⅜- to ½-inch thickness. Cut into rounds with a 2-inch cookie cutter. Place far apart on buttered baking sheets. Bake at 325 degrees for 15 minutes. Cookies will spread and get quite brown at the edges. Place on a rack to cool. Spread with *Rose Petal Butter.

ROSE PETAL BUTTER

1 cup sweet butter
2-3 Tbs. coffee cream
¾ cup rose petals, firmly packed

Select fragrant red or deep pink roses. Gather these early in the morning before the sun strikes them. Carefully pick to see there are not any bugs. Clip the hard white tip from each petal (this is bitter). Place petals in blender with cream. Since the petals are so light in weight you may have to stop the blender and push them down several times. Blend well and add butter at room temperature. With fragrant roses this makes a delicious spread.

★

Uncooked Fondant for Rolled Mints

1 egg white
1 tsp. vanilla or few drops peppermint
1 Tbs. cold water
2 Tbs. evaporated milk or 3 Tbs. cream
Confectioner's sugar

Add sifted confectioner's sugar very slowly until fondant is thick enough to knead. Knead and work until it is smooth. A very little coloring may be added. Cover it with a damp cloth and permit it to stand for 1 hour or longer before using. It may be set aside in a sealed jar in a cool place and used when desired.

★

Crystallized Rose Petals

There are two methods, hot and cold. One is to brush petals or leaves with slightly beaten white of egg mixed with a little water. Sprinkle them thoroughly with granulated sugar and lay on wax paper to dry. The other method is to dip petals in rosewater in which gum arabic has been steeped and cooled before using. Sprinkle sugar over all and dry in an oven at lowest temperature.

Store in tin box that can be tightly covered. Arrange petals on wax paper so that they do not touch and between each layer put layer of wax paper. Serve candied rose petal in place of mint. In spring make enough rose petals to last all year. Make a wild rose on a cake by using crystallized rose petals, with sugar colored yellow for center.

The festivities moved merrily along till the wee hours for both the young in years and those who were only young in heart.

The next morning we came downstairs to find breakfast already smiling on the table. Mamie had sliced fresh peaches the night before and sprinkled them with just a touch of brown sugar. Sam made the coffee and Pud, their daughter, set the table while Mary Jane *baked the eggs*. It was very simple — she just brushed a Pyrex cup with melted butter before breaking an egg into it, dashed a bit of salt and pepper across it, then added "The Touch": a tablespoon of slightly salted sour cream right across the top of the egg, before setting it in a shallow pan of water in the 300-degree oven. In six minutes they were just right and served with *Swedish Rye Bread, toasted. Thank goodness she fixed just one for me, because I am quite sure I could not have resisted the second. Mary Jane explained that the Swedish Rye was a Christmas gift from her mother. "Forty loaves for 1964 — installments of ten loaves, four times during the year," the card had read. Mrs. Horton bakes it in small loaf pans, and Sam eats one the day it's baked, while it's warm, getting full benefit of the dark molasses flavor and aroma. Mary Jane puts the other loaves in the freezer to "have on hand." This was her last loaf — weren't we lucky!

★

Rye Bread

- 1 qt. sweet milk
- 1 cup sugar
- 1 Tbs. salt
- 1 cup dark molasses
- 1 cup shortening
- 2 tsp. caraway seed
- 1 tsp. anise seed
- 2 pkgs. yeast
- ¼ cup lukewarm water
- 2 cups rye flour
- 12 cups white flour

Scald milk, add sugar, salt, molasses, shortening and seeds. Dissolve yeast in ¼ cup lukewarm water. When milk is cool add yeast and rye flour. Set aside to rise about one hour. Add white flour, knead and work real well. Let rise until double in size. Knead and make into loaves, let rise, bake 15 minutes at 390 degrees; cut oven down to 375 and bake till done. Time depends on size of loaf.

At the breakfast table, we had so much fun discussing "old times," when Sam and Mary Jane lived with us in Austin. It was during this year they started making fruitcakes to sell, mostly to our Green Pastures customers. It grew into a business, which Sam and Mary Jane have concentrated on since they left Austin, and last year they made and sold nearly one hundred thousand pounds of the most heavenly fruitcake. They have a beautiful modern plant in Greenville, near a little lake where Sam takes off during the afternoon to fish under tall old pecan trees. It is pecans from these trees which they use in their fruitcakes — just as Mary Jane's great-grandmother did when she lived there on Puddin' Hill in 1840.

Our hosts insisted we stay for the church supper, saying that it just wasn't the ordinary church supper at all. At this particular supper, the ladies — and some of the men — take a great deal of pride in preparing their "extra special" dishes. Everyone tries to think of something different and interesting to bring each time. Of course, this results in friendly competition and subtle comparisons. Well, everyone except Miss Nellie, who on each and every church supper night arrives with her same little bowl of cole slaw, covered with a clean white cup towel in a good-sized wicker basket. She places this unobtrusively on the back of the table, and when the supper is over and the ladies are picking up their dishes, Miss Nellie will pleasantly gather up generous remnants for her husband, who never gets to come for one reason or another, possibly because it conflicts with his domino game — it couldn't have been that his health kept him away — he looks very well fed indeed!

Of all the stories I had heard about that supper, nothing had been said which could possibly do justice to the spread that greeted us there. We were overwhelmed by the beautiful array of food brought on silver trays, old ironstone platters and in delicate Haviland vegetable bowls. One great long table held main dishes, meats, casseroles and vegetables. Another was loaded with salads and breads. And believe me, each of these specialties was done to a turn of perfection. They were simple enough to fix for the family, and delicious and lovely enough for favorite company. Desserts were still another table — all sorts of yummy cakes, pies and cookies. The minister was proud of his congregation and the fellowship they projected. When I told him I simply had to have a recipe for *every* dish, he made an announcement to his assembled flock and they all came forth. Some of these may *sound* better than others, but they won't taste better, so why don't you just start at the top and try one each day? Or maybe you'll be as lucky as we were and find yourself in Greenville on Crestview Church Supper Night!

★

Sarah Horton Plunket's Corn Bread and Ham Casserole

Thin white sauce made with 1 qt. milk
1 bottle horseradish mustard
1 lb. American cheese
Pan of corn bread
Chopped ham

Make milk into thin white sauce. Melt cheese and add; add horseradish mustard. Crumble a pan of corn bread. Make a layer of crumbs, a layer of chopped ham, a layer of cheese sauce. Repeat layers, ending with sauce on top.

Bake casserole at 350 degrees until cheese begins to brown and is bubbling.

★

Sam's Salad

2 heads of broken lettuce
1 small onion, chopped fine
Chopped stuffed olives
1 cup Poppy-seed Dressing (below)
1 cup sour cream

Toss lettuce, onions and olives with dressing. (Poppy-seed Dressing may be made or purchased.)

POPPY-SEED DRESSING

1½ cups sugar
2 tsp. dry mustard
2 cups salad oil
3 Tbs. poppy seed
2 tsp. salt
¾ cup vinegar
3 Tbs. onion juice

Combine all ingredients. Shake vigorously before using.

★

Mary Jane Lauderdale's Banana Cake

Grease and flour a cake pan; Mary Jane makes a foil lining for her pan.

½ cup butter
1½ cups sugar
2 eggs
1 cup mashed bananas
1 tsp. baking powder
1 tsp. soda
2 cups flour
2 Tbs. sour milk
1 Tbs. vanilla
1 cup nuts

Cream butter, add sugar, eggs, bananas. Mix baking powder and soda, sift with flour. Mix alternately with sour milk. Add vanilla and nuts.

Bake at 300 to 325 degrees for 40 to 50 minutes. Remove from oven and cool for 10 minutes. Raise oven temperature to 400 degrees.

At end of 10 minutes, spread with following mixture:

1 cup brown sugar
1 cup coconut
¼ cup nuts
6 Tbs. butter
4 Tbs. milk

Return cake to oven and cook until brown. Allow cake to cool completely before removing from pan; it is a very moist cake.

I must not leave Greenville without telling you about Mary Jane's Apple Pie, on which she serves cinnamon ice cream. She simply softens vanilla ice cream, sprinkles it with cinnamon, and returns the cream to the freezer to harden. She then serves each slice of apple pie with a scoop of cinnamon ice cream.

★

Wilhelmina Warren's Alexanderites

1 egg, beaten
1 cup sugar
½ cup melted butter
2 Tbs. flour
¼ tsp. salt
¼ tsp. baking powder
1 tsp. vanilla
1 cup quick cooking oats

Beat egg; add sugar and melted butter. Add dry ingredients and mix well. Add vanilla and oats. Drop in small amounts on greased wax paper placed on greased baking sheet. Bake for 12 minutes in 350-degree oven. As soon as you remove them from the oven, pull the wax paper off onto cool surface. This prevents the cookies from sticking.

★

Bernice Roland's Black Chicken (serves 6)

1 large fryer
1 onion
1 clove garlic, minced
Butter
2 Tbs. Worcestershire sauce
2 Tbs. black molasses
Salt, pepper
1 small can mushrooms with liquid

Cut chicken in serving-size pieces. Sauté onion and garlic in butter. Strain, reserving butter. Brown chicken in the butter; place in baking dish. Put onions on top of chicken. Pour over the chicken the Worcestershire sauce, molasses, salt and pepper, and mushrooms with liquid. Bake at 275 degrees for about 1 hour; or lower to 225 degrees and bake longer. Will hold indefinitely. Thicken gravy with cornstarch and serve with rice.

It is the black molasses that makes this memorable.

★

Mary Jane Vance's Yellow Rice and Chicken

1 frying chicken (3-3½ lbs.) cut in serving pieces
1 medium onion, diced
2 cloves garlic, peeled and cut
¾ cup olive oil
¾ cup tomatoes
1½ qts. chicken broth
1 bay leaf
2 Tbs. salt
2 cups raw white rice
½ tsp. saffron
1 green pepper, diced
1 12-oz. can petit pois peas, heated
2 pimentos

Cut chicken in quarters and fry with onion and garlic in olive oil for 45 minutes. Add tomatoes and broth; boil for 5 minutes. Add bay leaf, salt, washed rice, saffron and green pepper. Blend. Place in baking dish in 375-degree oven for 20 minutes, or until rice is just tender and has absorbed moisture. Garnish with peas and cut pimentos.

★

Gertrude Horton's Larrapin Tongue with Blackberry Sauce

1 fresh beef tongue
Salted water
1 Tbs. mixed pickle spice
2 bay leaves
Dried celery leaves or 2 ribs of celery
Cloves
Salt
1 glass blackberry jelly or jam
1 cup raisins, cooked tender with 1 cup water
Juice 1 lemon

Cook tongue until very tender in salted water containing pickle spice, bay leaves and celery. When very tender remove skin, trim root end and stick solid meat full of whole cloves. Place in greased baking dish, dust with salt. Beat jelly with a fork, add cooked raisins and lemon juice and mix. Pour over the tongue and bake 20 minutes at 350 degrees, basting often. Serve hot or cold.

Larrapin is right!

★

Mary Foster's For-the-Crowd Casserole

2 Tbs. butter
1 cup buttered soft breadcrumbs
1½ lbs. ground beef
1 cup chopped onion
1 12-oz. can whole kernel corn, drained
1 cup dairy sour cream
1 can condensed cream of chicken soup
1 can condensed cream of mushroom soup
¼ cup chopped pimento
¾ tsp. salt
½ tsp. monosodium glutamate
¼ tsp. pepper
¼ tsp. garlic salt
3 cups medium noodles or spaghetti, cooked

Melt butter in a skillet and stir in breadcrumbs; do not brown. Take them out and lay aside. Brown meat; add onion. Cook until tender but not brown. Add the next nine ingredients; mix well. Stir in noodles. Pour into a lightly greased 2-qt. casserole. Sprinkle crumbs over top. Bake in 350-degree oven for 30 minutes, or until hot.

This makes 8 to 10 servings — depending on whom you are serving. Amy made this amount, and it quickly disappeared before four Texas A&M students, including my Bill.

★

Laurieve Young's Green Beans à la Mushroom Sauce

2 cans long cut green beans, drained
1 can mushroom soup, undiluted
½ cup chopped almonds
Bacon, cooked crisp

Place beans in baking pan and cover with sauce of soup and almonds. Crumble crisp bacon over all. Cook in 325-degree oven until thoroughly heated.

★

Juanita McWhirter's and Mary Shepherd's Creole Fordhook Limas

1 box frozen fordhook limas (prepare according to directions)
1 Tbs. parsley, chopped
1 Tbs. green pepper, chopped
1 onion, chopped
1 Tbs. celery
1 Tbs. bacon grease
Red and black pepper
1 tsp. sugar

Precook limas and set aside. Sauté parsley, green pepper, onion and celery in bacon grease. Add red pepper and black pepper to taste. Add sugar. Pour in casserole and put a few small slices of dry salt bacon on top. Bake 1 hour about 275 degrees. If dry, add more water.

We took this dish to a barbecue instead of the usual Pinto Beans, and it surely made a hit!

★

Sarah Plunket's Sweet-Sour Beans

½ cup sugar
½ cup vinegar
1 onion
1 clove garlic
1 can whole green beans, drained
¼ cup salad oil

Bring sugar and vinegar to boil. Pour over beans with one thinly sliced onion and garlic. Add oil. Let stand. Will keep for months in icebox.

Canned kidney beans may also be used.

These beans were all gone before I got there — they seem to be a familiar favorite!

★

Evelyn Riley's Baked Mustard Potatoes

Boil 6 medium potatoes in jackets. Let cool and slice or chunk into a buttered casserole. Sprinkle with salt. Pour medium white sauce over the potatoes. Sprinkle heavily with dry mustard. Top with grated cheese and bake at 300 degrees for about 45 minutes, or until brown.

I couldn't believe this until I ate 'em.

WHITE SAUCE

1 stick butter, melted
3 rounded tsp. flour
3 cups milk
1 tsp. salt
1 tsp. white pepper

Mix butter, flour and milk. Cook until smooth and thick. Extra milk may be added to thin.

★

Annie Lee Gordy's Kosher Cabbage

3 strips bacon
Bacon drippings
1 whole onion, chopped
1 stalk celery
½ green pepper, chopped
½ head medium cabbage
1 can tomatoes
¾ cup water
½ tsp. turmeric
¼ cup vinegar
3 Tbs. sugar
Salt

Fry bacon and crumble. In drippings, sauté onion, celery and pepper. Add other ingredients and cook slowly for an hour. Serve over hot corn bread. With dill pickles and light dessert, makes a nice lunch.

Bacon and Kosher?

★

Annie Lee Gordy's Epicurean Peas

4 strips bacon, chopped
1 Tbs. onion
1 Tbs. flour
2 Tbs. butter
1 No. 2 can peas
1 can mushrooms
1 cup light cream
Salt and pepper

Fry bacon until crisp; remove from drippings and chop. Sauté onions; add flour, butter and peas and mushrooms. Simmer until thickened and add cream; add salt and pepper to taste. Add chopped bacon.

I noticed the children eating these.

★

Mae Shepherd's Curry Chicken Salad

1½ cups cooked rice
¼ cups minced onion
2 Tbs. mayonnaise
½ tsp. curry powder
2 tsp. vinegar

Mix the above and chill. Just before serving, add:

2 cups chilled, chopped chicken
1 cup chopped celery
¼ cup chopped green pepper
¼ tsp. salt
Dash of pepper
¾ cup mayonnaise

Unusual and extra good. Serves 6 to 8 persons.

★

Sarah Plunket's Beet Mold

1 pkg. lemon gelatine
2 cups beets, cut and drained
1 tsp. salt
1 Tbs. horseradish
2 Tbs. lemon juice
2 Tbs. onion, grated or cut fine
¼ cup sweet relish

Make gelatine as directed on package, using 1 cup beet juice. Cool and add the rest of the ingredients. Pour into lightly greased mold. When ready to serve, unmold and decorate with salad dressing mixed with sour cream.

★

Bernice Roland's Lemon Bisque

1 large can evaporated milk
1 pkg. lemon gelatine
Crushed vanilla or ginger wafers
Whipped cream
Cherries
½ cup sugar
Juice of 3 lemons
1½ cups water

Chill milk and whip, add sugar. Mix gelatine according to directions, dissolving it in the water; chill, then whip. Combine with whipped milk. Line Pyrex dish with crushed wafers. Pour mixture into dish; chill. Cut in squares. Place small amount of whipped cream on each, and top with cherries.

★

Joyce Horton's Orange Pecan Cookies

3 cups sifted flour
2 tsp. baking powder
½ tsp. soda
½ tsp. salt
¾ cup butter
½ cup sugar
1 cup brown sugar, packed
2 unbeaten eggs
1 Tbs. grated orange rind
½ cup sour cream
1 cup chopped pecans

Sift together flour, baking powder, soda and salt. Cream butter, then gradually add sugars, creaming well. Add eggs and orange rind and beat well. Stir in sour cream, then blend in dry ingredients. Add pecans. Drop by rounded teaspoonfuls on greased baking sheet. Bake at 375 degrees for 10 to 15 minutes. Frost while warm and garnish with pecan halves.

ICING

Combine 2 cups sifted powdered sugar, 2 tsp. grated orange rind and ⅛ tsp. salt. Add 2 to 3 Tbs. orange juice until of spreading consistency.

★

Pauline Horn's Cranberry Betty (*serves 6 to 8*)

1 cup sugar
Juice of 1 orange
½ tsp. ground cinnamon
2 cups fresh cranberries
½ cup melted butter
3 cups soft breadcrumbs

Heat oven to 375 degrees. Combine sugar, orange juice and cinnamon in small saucepan. Bring to a boil over moderate heat, add cranberries and cook uncovered 2 minutes, until berries pop. Add butter to breadcrumbs and toss to coat evenly. Arrange alternate layers of buttered crumbs and cranberries in buttered 2-qt. casserole, starting and ending with crumbs. Cover and bake 20 minutes. Remove cover and bake 15 minutes longer until top is brown and crisp.

★

Bernice Roland's Sweet 'Tata Pone

2½ cups raw, grated sweet potatoes
1 cup molasses
2 eggs
2 cups milk
1 Tbs. melted butter
1 tsp. ginger (or 1 tsp. grated orange rind)
1 Tbs. brown sugar
½ tsp. cinnamon

Add molasses, well-beaten eggs, milk, melted butter, ginger (or orange rind) in that order to the grated potatoes. Turn into greased baking dish. Bake 45 minutes in moderate oven. Sprinkle brown sugar and cinnamon over top at the end of first 25 minutes. This was always served as a Christmas dinner dessert by the late Mrs. R. R. Neyland.

★

Mildred Tittsworth's Surprise Cake

3 Tbs. butter
½ cup sugar
3 egg yolks
1 cup cake flour
¼ tsp. salt
2 Tbs. baking powder
¼ cup sweet milk

MERINGUE

3 egg whites
Pinch cream of tartar
¼ tsp. salt
1 cup sugar
1 cup chopped pecans
1 cup whipping cream

Grease and flour two Pyrex pie pans. Cream butter and sugar, add egg yolks, mix well. Sift dry ingredients and add alternately with milk, divide and put in 2 pie pans. Make meringue and spread over batter. Bake 20 minutes at 350 degrees. When cool, top with whipped cream.

Delicious with strawberries or peaches. A very light and heavenly dessert.

★

Mary Jane Lauderdale's Blackberry Jam Cake

1½ cups butter
2 cups white sugar
6 whole eggs, beaten separately
2 cups blackberry jam
5 cups flour
½ box seeded raisins, cut
1 cup chopped figs
4 oz. candied red cherries, chopped
1 slice candied pineapple
2 cups pecans
1 tsp. baking powder (sifted with flour)
½ tsp. ground nutmeg
2 tsp. ground cinnamon
2 tsp. ground allspice
1 tsp. ground cloves
2 tsp. soda (stirred in milk)
6 Tbs. buttermilk
½ cup Bourbon

Cream butter, gradually add 1½ cups sugar, beat in egg yolks, add jam, beat again. Sift flour, measure and dredge fruit and nuts with most of flour; save 1 cup. Sift rest of flour, baking powder, spices; add soda to buttermilk. Add some flour mixture to creamed butter, sugar and add yolk mixture. Add dredged fruits, nuts, buttermilk mixture and flour with spices, until all are in. Add Bourbon. Finally beat egg whites gradually, adding remaining ½ cup sugar. Fold egg whites in last.

Grease and paper-line 3 9-inch layer cake pans, each 2 inches deep. Fill pans 2/3 full. Bake in 350-degree oven for 60 minutes.

CARAMEL ICING

- 1½ cups light brown sugar
- ¾ cup flour
- 1 cup butter
- 1 cup heavy cream
- 1 tsp. vanilla
- ½ box raisins
- ½ cup pecan pieces

Mix sugar and flour, blend thoroughly. Cream butter until light, then slowly add sugar-flour mixture to butter, creaming well. Add heavy cream. Place in top of double boiler, cooking over boiling water. Stir constantly as it cooks; cook until thick. Remove from fire and beat. Cool, add vanilla, raisins and nuts. Spread between layers and on top and sides.

Half this recipe makes an average-sized cake.

*

Joyce Horton's Rocky Mountain Cake (chiffon)

- 2 cups sifted flour
- 1½ cups sugar
- 1 Tbs. baking powder
- 1 tsp. salt
- 1 tsp. cinnamon
- ½ tsp. nutmeg
- ½ tsp. allspice
- ½ tsp. cream of tartar
- ½ tsp. cloves
- 7 eggs, separated
- 2 Tbs. caraway seeds
- ½ cup salad oil
- ¾ cup ice water

Sift flour, sugar, baking powder, salt and spices together several times. Combine egg yolks, caraway seeds, oil and water in large bowl. Add dry ingredients. Beat about half a minute at low speed. Add cream of tartar to egg whites and beat until stiff peaks form. Gradually pour egg yolk mixture over beaten whites; fold in. Bake in ungreased tube pan in slow oven (325 degrees) for 10 to 15 minutes. Invert pan to cool.

I didn't realize what a subtle flavor caraway seeds give till I ate this melt-in-your-mouth cake.

*

Gertrude Horton's Lemon Jelly or Butter

- 1 cup sugar
- 5 egg yolks
- Grated rind of 2 lemons
- ½ cup butter
- 3 lemons, juice

Cook in double boiler, stirring constantly until thick. If used as a sauce, thin with whipped cream. As a cake filling, put a generous amount between layers. Ice cake top and sides with boiled white icing. Sprinkle with coconut. Or mix with generous amount of whipped cream, about equal; ice cake. Be sure to refrigerate cake after icing.

Mrs. Horton said that she learned to make this delicious filling when she was nine years old, and has always tried to keep some on hand, for it has thousands of uses.

CORPUS CHRISTI

Corpus Christi is known as Texas's sparkling city by the sea. Its name means the Body of Christ and it is the only city in the world by this name. Its surroundings are lush and semitropical; the white sand beaches along the palm-studded waterfront are immaculate! A boat trip around the bay at twilight is absolutely enchanting! Corpus (as the natives refer to it) is substantial and prosperous in appearance and in reality. It definitely has an air of romance and adventure for all who live there and all who visit there. This is possibly due to its colorful history as well as its beautiful setting. Early in the 1800's Jean Lafitte and his band of pirates plundered and pilfered trading ships plying the waters of the Gulf of Mexico. In 1812 Jean Lafitte and his men aided General Andrew Jackson's troops in the defense of New Orleans. Because of his aid in the defense of New Orleans President James Madison gave Lafitte a full pardon for his crimes of piracy.

Corpus Christi has an annual celebration based on this romantic history.

Over the years the celebration has become one of the largest in South Texas, with Corpus Christi playing host to Texans as well as tourists from all over the nation. Pirate girls sail into the Yacht Basin and capture the mayor, who surrenders for the fun of the thing. They lower the city flag and raise the black skull and crossbones. The mayor reads the proclamation that the city is surrendered to pirate rule and is then made to walk the traditional plank for the pirates.

From that moment on, Buccaneer Days is in full swing featuring an illuminated night parade, stadium show, boat parades, boat races, water skiing, fireworks and a carnival on the waterfront.

Buccaneer Days means gaiety, laughter and music to all!

I have always loved going to Corpus for Buccaneer Days and just to visit. I recently visited there on the day Dele Weaver's sewing club met at her house. Isabelle Critz showed up with her needlepoint, which added to the atmosphere, and Dorothy Blakeney came with a book full of colored snapshots of the club's meetings and parties in the past, which really added to the merriment. There were the ones taken at the April Fool's Christmas Party at Dorothy's house on the Island. The big sign hung over the door said APRIL FOOL — NO PARTY, but there was quite a party, with Christmas tree, presents, roast duck and dressing and all the trimmings. There was also a hilarious picture of the Hangover Party Edith and Arthur Durham gave the morning after the King's Ball, which climaxes the many festivities held during the Buccaneer Days. The centerpiece was a big "hangover tree" laden with bottles of aspirin, ice packs, snakebite kits, and other helpful items. The menu was divine. An enormous English hunt tray was filled with quail and ducks. Beside it was a gravy tureen filled with a luscious brown tomato gravy. There was a chafing dish of hot buttered grits, and lots of other wonderful things. The table was by the wide picture window overlooking the bay.

Pretty young girls were in a picture taken at a luncheon given by Mrs. Walter Lewright. Dorothy explained that the party honored these lovely girls, who had made their debuts while home for the Christmas holidays. This had been a mother-daughter affair. The hostess read a very humorous original poem about the past social season, then the girls cleverly retaliated. Dorothy's centerpiece was clever, too. It was made of stacks of post-dated invitations, a worn long evening glove, a well-filled calendar, and tired-looking orchids. Favors were porcelain birthday angels and a calendar for the new year. Her *pièce de résistance* was:

★

Crab Crêpes

BATTER

1 egg
1 cup milk
1 cup flour
1 pinch salt
1 Tbs. melted butter

Pour enough batter in a 5- or 6-inch skillet to make a very thin pancake, the thinner the better. When it curls around the edge, turn for a half-minute and remove from pan. Stack with wax paper between each one.

SAUCE FOR CRAB

3 Tbs. butter
3 Tbs. flour
2 cups hot milk
⅛ tsp. cayenne
½ tsp. white pepper
¾ cup heavy cream
1 tsp. salt
2 Tbs. dry sherry
White king crabmeat, cut in bite-sized pieces
1 Tbs. (heaping) whipped cream per crepe

Melt butter and add flour. Let simmer for 5 minutes without browning. Add milk. Whip with wire whisk till smooth. Add cayenne, white pepper, salt, cream, and sherry. Add crabmeat cut in bite-sized pieces.

Put approximately ¼ cup of crab mixture in center of crepe and fold over the edges. Put a tablespoon of mixture on top of each one. Place in shallow Pyrex baking dish and heat in moderate oven before serving. Dorothy added a heaping tablespoon of whipped cream seasoned slightly with salt and cayenne to the top of each crepe after it was on the plate.

This Corpus is a fun town, as all the pictures showed. The girls howled at the ones taken at the Weavers' Hobo Party, which was practically a twenty-four-hour affair. The guests arrived in an array of clothes from heaven knows where. The hors d'oeuvre was Mulligan Stew served in the back yard from an iron pot. Then everyone was teamed up for a scavenger hunt, with the clues carefully done in rhyme. When they returned to the Weavers' with their hilarious prizes and stories of their escapades, they got their suppers tied up in red bandana kerchiefs swung on the end of bamboo poles. There were all kinds of yummy things, like Dele's Fried Chicken, enough to make everyone want to be a bum for life. Finally they all dispersed to their own houses to sleep. A couple of the boys had pitched a tent in the Weavers' yard, threatening to spend the night so they would be sure to be on hand for the second part of the party the next morning. It was a glorious brunch, including a whole suckling pig surrounded by broiled pork chops. It showed up adorably in the pictures. I asked Dele what the beautiful yellow mound on the end of the table was — a cake? No, that was her way of scrambling eggs for a party or a crowd.

★

Party Scrambled Eggs

12 eggs
4 Tbs. cream
Salt, pepper and any other seasonings you like
Chopped chives
Tomato slices

Whip together and turn into a large iron skillet over medium flame. Stir constantly till heated through and only partially cooked. Then turn into a round mixing bowl, well buttered. Place bowl in pan of water and in warming oven. Let it set and "congeal" but not become dry. Turn out on round chop plate, sprinkle over with chopped chives, and encircle with peeled ripe slices of tomato.

I could go on and on about the gay parties and wonderful food in Corpus. It would take another chapter to tell about their Travel Club, a unique idea where no one knows the destination except the host and hostess. They give the members a list of "what to bring," time of departure, and arrival home.

The day I happened to be lunching with "the Needlers," Dele used a south of the border theme. Before lunch she served *Margaritas which Dick had made before he left for the office that morning.

★

Margaritas (per person)

2 jiggers of tequila
1 jigger of Cointreau
Juice of 1 fresh lime

Rub rim of martini glass with a piece of fresh lime, and turn the glass upside down on a towel where salt has been sprinkled. When a thin rim of salt stays on the glass, turn it upright. Shake all the ingredients well with cracked ice and strain. Serve in the martini glass.

Dele's centerpiece was a clever ceramic duck filled with gaily colored paper flowers. On the table were:

---

* *Chicken Balls* (in little casseroles which just fit into half a Spanish melon; these melons were arranged in a market basket with bougainvillaea, which grows profusely in Corpus)

* *Weaver Rice*

**Spinach Salad*

* *Olive Bread*

* *Spanish Cream and Buenuellos*

Kahlua

Hot Coffee

★

Chicken Balls

5 slices bread
6 cups cooked chicken
2 eggs, beaten slightly
1 tsp. thyme
¼ tsp. ground cloves
Minced green peppers or chilis
2 Tbs. Angostura bitters
3 cups water with ½ tsp. salt
⅔ cup butter
1½ cups salted peanuts, ground fine

Soak the bread slices with water and press out excess gently. Grind chicken and bread together. Add eggs, seasonings, and bitters, mix thoroughly with a fork, and form into about 60 firm balls. Bring salted water to a boil, add butter, and gently simmer the chicken balls (one-third at a time) for about 20 minutes. Remove final batch and let gravy cook down to about 1 cup. Add ground peanuts to gravy. When ready to serve, place chicken balls in peanut broth and heat thoroughly. Sprinkle with minced green pepper when serving (or fresh green chilis).

★

Weaver Rice (*serves* 12)

7 cups water, plus fluid from mushrooms
2 tsp. salt
6 chicken bouillon cubes
3½ cups raw rice
1 cup sliced mushrooms, drained
2 cans water chestnuts, sliced thin
¾ cup thin sliced blanched almonds
1 cup butter
⅓ cup instant minced onion
1 tsp. salt
¾ tsp. fresh ground pepper
2 tsp. Beau Monde seasoned salt
2 tsp. rosemary, crushed
1 cup grated sharp yellow cheese
2 cups barely cooked English peas
Tomatoes or cherry tomatoes

Bring water and mushroom juice to a boil and add salt and bouillon cubes. Add rice, let come to a boil, reduce to low heat, cover, and steam about 20 minutes.

Sauté mushrooms, water chestnuts, and almonds in butter until golden, then toss with hot rice together with instant onions, salt, pepper, seasoned salt, rosemary, cheese and peas. Reheat in 350-degree oven until piping hot (covered), but do not brown. Serve with quartered tomatoes stuck in top of bowl or peeled cherry tomatoes (fresh) scattered over top.

★

Spinach Salad (*serves* 12)

2 bunches of fresh spinach
1 head of iceberg lettuce
½ tsp. salt
½ tsp. freshly ground pepper
½ lb. of golden raisins
1 cup preserved kumquats, quartered and seeded
¾ cup toasted pumpkin seeds
2 or 3 Tbs. French dressing

Wash, thoroughly dry, and tear into bite-sized pieces the spinach and lettuce. Sprinkle with ½ tsp. salt and ½ tsp. freshly ground pepper.

Add raisins, kumquat quarters, and pumpkin seeds. Add just enough French dressing to coat lightly and toss just before serving.

★

Olive Bread

2½ cups flour, sifted
4 tsp. baking powder
⅓ cup sugar
½ tsp. salt
1 egg, beaten
1 cup milk
1 cup chopped walnuts
1 cup sliced stuffed green olives
2 Tbs. chopped pimentos

Sift flour, baking powder, sugar, and salt. Add egg and milk and stir just until moistened. Stir in nuts, olives, and pimentos. Pour into well-oiled round glass baking dish (8 by 1½ inches) and bake 45 minutes at 350 degrees. Remove after cooling slightly for 10 minutes and cool on cake rack. Slice into quarters and then slice each quarter into 4 or 5 pieces.

★

Spanish Cream

2 cups semisweet chocolate bits
1 tsp. instant coffee
1 or 2 Tbs. water
6 eggs, separated
¼ tsp. ground cloves
2 tsp. ground cinnamon
6 Tbs. sugar
1 pt. cream, whipped

Melt chocolate chips with coffee and water until smooth. Add egg yolks one at a time, beating smooth after each addition. Add cloves and cinnamon to egg whites, beat until frothy, and add sugar gradually. Fold this mixture and the stiffly whipped cream into the chocolate mixture. Pile into a glass dish or individual glass bowls and refrigerate the day before serving. Serve with Buenuellos (Mexican pastries) or Mexican cookies.

Dele is an excellent cook and a wonderful person, and she gave me a number of original "suggestions," such as:

★

Zucchini in Sour Cream

Thinly slice raw, unpeeled zucchini, marinate overnight in good French dressing, drain and toss with salted sour cream. Serve for cocktail buffet.

★

Cold Rice

Rice
Beef bouillon
Canned Chinese vegetables
Thin-sliced water chestnuts
French dressing
Artichokes
Marjoram, seasoned salt, lemon juice, and salt

Cook rice in well-seasoned bouillon. Toss just before serving with canned Chinese vegetables and thin-sliced water chestnuts, which have been well-marinated in French dressing. Pour rest of French dressing marinade over the mixture and be sure every grain of rice is coated. Serve in center of cold artichokes which have been cooked in beef bouillon well-seasoned with marjoram, seasoned salt, lemon juice, and salt.

★

Canned Garbanzo Beans in Salad

Slip off outer peeling if possible. Marinate in French dressing. Toss with halved artichoke hearts, thin-sliced green pepper rings, and quartered kumquats for cocktail buffet salad. Serve piled high on silver tray and sprinkle caviar over top.

★

Corn on the Cob

Buttered corn
Salt, pepper (freshly cracked)
¼ tsp. anise seed

For informal supper. Generously butter ear of corn; sprinkle with salt, pepper, anise seed. Wrap loosely in square of aluminum foil and bake 20 minutes at 400 degrees. Serve hot in foil.

★

Grits Balls

Cook grits in bouillon to which has been added sautéed onions, butter, seasoned salt, ½ tsp. crushed marjoram. Pour into pan. When cool enough to handle (really cold) roll into dollar-sized balls. Chill. Fry in deep fat and serve hot in chafing dish. Be sure grits is well seasoned. Dele comes from Mississippi, where grits *is*, not are!

★

Green Beans (*one portion*)

Place about 12 or so whole blue lake green beans on a slice of bacon. Sprinkle with garlic salt, 1 tsp. brown sugar, and dot with 1 tsp. butter. Wrap bacon around beans and bake 15 to 20 minutes at 400 degrees. This is one portion.

★

Lima Beans (*serves 4*)

Cook 1 pkg. frozen green lima beans until tender and toss with sliced ripe olives, chopped fresh dill, 2 Tbs. melted butter, and 1 tsp. lime juice. Sprinkle crumbled cooked bacon crisps over top.

★

Cocktail Sirloin

Slice beef sirloins (which have been cooked rare) into thin slices and julienne the slices. Marinate in oil and vinegar dressing. Drain and toss with salted sour cream. Serve at cocktail buffet.

The April Fool's Christmas party in Corpus reminded me of Myra Brewster's Fun Luncheon on the same day, when she entertained her Sewing Club.

The first course — to resemble dessert — was Chicken Salad served in a tall compote, with a whirl of whipped cream dressing on top (¼ cup mayonnaise folded in to ½ cup whipped cream, slightly salted) served with thin cheese wafers, resembling cookies.

The second course was a slice of Toasted Pound Cake topped with an apricot half in a meringue nest — to resemble eggs on toast. Ridiculous fun!

But Myra, who is a former concert pianist, is also an excellent serious cook. She has combinations of recipes, and if she is going to make one, she makes the other as well. We took her idea and do the same here — give the Open Forum her delicious Orange Charlotte Russe at noon, using the same number of egg whites as the number of yolks used in her ever-popular *Mississippi Chess Pie, which drew applause from the members of the State Board of Fine Arts Association who came for dinner that night.

We have also used Myra's *Green Bean Salad for many occasions rather than the usual green-tossed, which has to be made at the last minute. This is good with everything — barbecue, Baked Ham and the like.

★

Bean Salad

1 cup yellow wax beans (canned)
1 cup red kidney beans
1 green pepper — rings, cut thin
2 purple onions, cut in crisp rings
1 cup green beans (canned)
1 cup garbanzo beans (canned)
1 small jar pimentos

DRESSING

⅓ cup corn oil
½ cup sugar
Black pepper
¾ cup vinegar
1 tsp. salt

Make ahead of time, keeping the mixture turned at intervals to marinate it *thoroughly*.

Note that 1 cup is the unit of measurement for all the beans. In doubling the recipe, simply use a can of each, well drained.

This will keep indefinitely in covered glass or pottery jar.

★

Mississippi Chess Pie

1 stick butter
1 cup sugar
1 Tbs. cornstarch
4 egg yolks
1 cup warm milk
1 unbaked 9-inch pie shell

In electric beater, cream thoroughly butter, sugar and cornstarch; add egg yolks, beating well after each addition. Then beat in 1 cup warm milk.

Pour into unbaked pie shell and bake at 350 degrees, cutting down to 325 until firm to the touch and a golden brown; this will take about 45 to 50 minutes.

Make the pie crust ahead of time and refrigerate it; otherwise brush it with egg white. Either will help to prevent its getting soggy in the baking.

ALL OUTDOORS

The Bill Kuykendall ranch is indeed one of the prettiest spots in Hays County. Alice and Bill Kuykendall live in the long rambling ranch house which rises naturally out of the green land!

Bill also rises high and naturally out of the land — he would perish I'm sure if he ever tried to live away from it and the Great Out of Doors. His innate knowledge of nature is extensive and diversified. I would say that he is an authority on birds and bees, certainly, but also grass, wildflowers, cattle, horses, polo, hunting — as the rare trophies in his game room prove — fishing, wild game, gardening and camping, and quite expert in outdoor cooking. He is one outdoorsman who could live well with only a rifle, lasso or fishing rod. Some of the food Bill cooks outdoors may seem a little dramatic to some of us — like the calf's head he cooks underground; or barbecuing mountain oysters; or frying fish down by Onion Creek — but to Bill it's an everyday-occurrence sort of thing and he does it with a minimum amount of effort and much to the delight of his company, whether they be ranch hands or CITY SLICKERS!

Now, Bill knows some of the persnickety ladies may repel the idea of the *Roasted Calf's Head — so he unearths it privately, then arranges the delicately flavored meat on a platter and has Julian pass it around without a label for hors d'oeuvres — and without fail, everyone declares it divine! Food for the gods!

★

Roasted Calf's Head

Wash thoroughly with a hose the complete head, tongue, etc. Skin and saw off the horns, but retain the eyes.

Take whole head of celery, separate the sticks and stuff in chunks in mouth and around head; also use onions. Five or six cloves of garlic also improve the dish. Do NOT salt and pepper.

In the old days, the head was then wrapped in cup towels; but now heavy aluminum foil is used instead.

The head, in the towels or foil, is then wrapped in a burlap sack which has been thoroughly wet with a hose. The sack is sewn up with wire, and a wire "handle" is made on the top.

Meanwhile, dig two holes; in one, start a good fire anything up to 24 hours before you want to eat the roast. When the fire is really hot, shovel out into the second hole all but five or six inches of the coals; and place the head (handle side up) on the coals in the first hole. Then shovel back the hot coals round the head, and pile them at least six inches deep on top of it. Then shovel dirt on top of everything. This will effectively cut out the air, and the sack will hardly even be singed. Leave cooking for at least 12 to 15 hours; it can safely remain for 20 to 24 hours.

Use pitch fork to remove head — by wire handle. When opened, the meat will all fall off the bone. It will, of course, contain the brain, tongue, etc.; and can be cut up and served.

Most any way doves and quail are cooked they are delectible. Mama used to smother them in a milk gravy and cook them slowly for an hour or so. This was one of our special fall-morning breakfasts — with lots of hot biscuits. But the very best that doves can be is the way Carl Bredt used to cook them. There was always only one regret, and that was that the limit was only twenty-one! Jay and George and probably other of Carl's compadres follow this recipe — I surely do when the boys bring home their limit:

★

Doves

Salt slightly but pepper birds generously. Take 2 parts of chopped apple and 1 part chopped onion, depending on number of birds.

Stuff cavity of birds firmly. Wrap each bird with a piece of breakfast bacon. Place on wire rack over low coals; turn often until bacon is crisp. Then place birds in roaster, add just a very small amount of wine or water (½ cup), again, depending on number. Cover and place in very low (200-degree) oven to keep warm till time to serve. Place on platter and pour drippings in pan over the birds.

They are so succulent and delicious I can't begin to describe their flavor.

George Bredt runs a very close second to this recipe with the birds he cooks in wine:

★

Birds in Wine

6 small birds or squabs
6 small hot peppers, cut fine
Butter, salt and pepper
½ cup stock
Worcestershire sauce
Juice of ½ lemon
¼ cup sherry
1 cup sweet cream
1 can mushrooms
Flour (optional)

Split birds, put breast down in pan, sprinkle with hot peppers, salt and butter. When butter has melted, pour stock over birds, cover and steam slowly ½ hour. Add mixture of Worcestershire sauce, lemon juice, sherry and mushrooms and cook slowly until birds are tender. Add cream just before serving. Thicken gravy with flour if desired.

George really has the "touch" when it comes to outdoor cooking. I shall never forget the fabulous fish he charcoaled one night on the banks of the Brazos River — and some exquisite potatoes baked with onions in the coals. This is the way he did the fish:

★

Charcoal-Broiled Fish

1- to 2-lb. whole fish (dressed weight)
Salt and pepper to taste
Garlic salt
Lemon
Butter

Cut through the skin diagonally across the fish every inch on each side. Salt and pepper and sprinkle with garlic salt.

Place fish in steak grill so it can be turned often while cooking. Brush frequently with lemon butter.

Cook over hot charcoal 6 inches from coals about 15 minutes.

And this is the way he did the *Potatoes and Onions:

★

Potatoes and Onions

Peel and slice one potato per person, slice it in thick slices, sprinkle with salt, pepper, butter and Parmesan cheese. Put a slice of white onion between each slice of the potato and wrap it individually in foil. Place on side of coals in ashes and turn occasionally — usually takes about one hour to get *really* done.

I'll have to take my hat off to these gentlemen and their great talent for preparing such gourmet dishes as Duck under Hot Sand — Jay Patterson's specialty. Jay, as I mentioned earlier, is primarily a bird hunter and doesn't particularly care about hunting deer but often will go along just for the fun that they always have and cook for the boys. Jay said they were hunting in South Texas last fall down near Uvalde. It was the last day of the season, and the men were away from camp — out to get their last buck. Jay was sitting there cleaning his guns and getting ready to break camp when he glanced over by the trailer and there was a great big rattlesnake, thirteen rattlers! Jay had unloaded all the guns, but it didn't take long for him to reload and unload again on the snake. He said there were lots of rattlesnakes in that part of the country and the hunters always wore long aluminum leggings for safety. They have also seen lots of coyote down there — sure sounds like rugged but exciting hunting.

When the deer hunters returned to camp, Jay had supper already cooked — and what a feast! While they'd been shooting deer, Jay had bagged several plump ducks there on the Nueces River:

★

Duck under Hot Sand

He cleaned the ducks, salted and peppered them well, stuck a cut-up apple and onion inside each duck and a piece of bacon on top. He wrapped each of them in very heavy foil. He also wrapped a big Idaho potato for each in heavy foil, then laid them on the sand and covered them up with about 6 inches more of sand and dirt. He built a fire with some good-sized wood on the ground over them and let it burn. By the time the fire had burned down, approximately 3 hours, the potatoes and ducks were done to perfection.

FORT WORTH

Fort Worth is considered the most typically Texan of all Texas cities. It is a city blended with cattle, oil, business and industry and the greatest of assets — a progressive and friendly citizenship. To the flutter of a flag and the notes of a bugle, Fort Worth was founded by Major Ripley A. Arnold on June 6, 1849. Before that eventful day, this region had had a history, much of it unrecorded. It was a lush and lovely land, with clear streams and blue skies. Game abounded and this was a favorite hunting ground of the Indians, therefore becoming the site of many bloody wars. General William J. Worth, commander of the United States military forces with headquarters in San Antonio, had instructed Arnold to establish a military post for the protection of settlers against the Indians. So Arnold named the post Camp Worth (later to be called Fort Worth) in honor of this gallant commander. Born in New York State in 1794, Worth entered the Army as a private and rose to the rank of major general. He fought in the War of 1812 and played a leading part in the Florida-Indian War, bringing about peace with the Seminoles. In the War with Mexico, Worth displayed great gallantry in the taking of Monterrey and aided in the storming of Chapultepec and the capture of Mexico City. He was buried in New York City, and a monument stands at the corner of Fifth Avenue and Broadway. The greatest monument to the brave soldier, however, is the great city which bears his name. Great herds of longhorns were driven from Texas to the railheads in Kansas. Fort Worth was on the main route, sometimes called the Chisholm

Trail. The lowing herds camped near the town, and cowboys galloped in firing their pistols into the air and even rode their horses into the saloons — Fort Worth is still referred to as Cowtown. "Wild and woolly" characterized much of Fort Worth's life in the 1880's. Most celebrated of six-gun exponents was long-haired James Courtright, who could shoot equally well with either hand and was a master of the "border shift," wherein a pistol was drawn, fired, tossed in the air, caught in the other hand and fired again.

Fort Worth has rightly been called the nation's largest city with a distinct Western atmosphere. It's a place where a person can enjoy the friendliness and atmosphere of the Old West. It's a new sophisticated business frontier that combines the fruits of cattle and oil, industry and technology to make its second century greater than the terrific trail-blazing days of its first hundred years.

In 1906, a young man named Amon Carter came to Fort Worth to work for the newspaper, the Fort Worth *Star Telegram.* Mr. Carter had a most amazing career, which, besides the newspaper, included radio, television and oil. His personality became so entwined in the development of Fort Worth that his very name is synonymous with it. Mr. and Mrs. Carter typified Southwestern hospitality. They did a great deal of entertaining at their Shady Oak Farm on the outskirts of Fort Worth, often honoring some of the world's most distinguished personalities, such as Will Rogers, an intimate friend who considered Fort Worth and Shady Oaks his second home. Also there were Charles Lindbergh, President Franklin Roosevelt, President Dwight D. Eisenhower and J. Edgar Hoover.

The Carters' two children, Amon, Jr., and Ruth, are following in their father's footsteps, not one minute resting on his laurels, but continuing to contribute their efforts to the many cultural and charitable ventures made possible by their father. Ruth is married to J. Lee Johnson III, and they have four very attractive interesting children. Ruth Johnson remembers the big annual New Year's Day Open House her parents gave in the early years. It was a very dressy affair. She said the buffet tables held ham, turkeys, fancy molds filled with shrimp, every delicious dish you could name. Her father bought the bar from the Ritz-Carlton Hotel in New York. It is still used occasionally. The first smoked turkeys ever served in Texas made their appearance at this party, and there was always Southern-style eggnog and huge bowls of Ambrosia. Her father particularly enjoyed hosting stag parties which were less formal, more Western style. He served barbecue and the famous ranch-style beans which are made today by the same recipe and canned and sold by Great Western Food Canning Company, another Carter enterprise. Mr. Carter also loved to get the members of the press together at Shady Oaks. These parties usually went far into the night, with everyone playing poker. Mr. Carter's traditional gesture was to present a five-star beaver Stetson hat in exchange for the hat of his VIP visitor. This always delighted his guest and gave Mr. Carter a fascinating collection of hats, which still hangs on his many-branched hall tree.

Probably one of the most talked-about foods served at Shady Oaks was Amon Carter's original *Slumgullion, an oyster concoction originating with him and Will Rogers.

★

Slumgullion

3 qts. oysters
2 qts. canned tomatoes
1 qt. chopped onion
Lots of Tabasco or pepper sauce

They would make up a good-sized pot of this and serve it with Corn Bread, declaring *nothing* could be better.

The Johnsons live in a very beautiful contemporary house on land not far from Shady Oaks; both places exemplify its own generation. A life-sized Madonna and Child done by Charles Umlaf, Texas sculptor of international note, overlooks the Johnsons' terraced flower gardens, which are in bloom the year round. Broad stone steps lead to the children's play area and the natural landscape which wanders down the picturesque cliff hanging with native shrubs, flowers and trees.

The Johnsons entertain often. With less than ten guests, the dinner or luncheon is seated. With larger groups it is buffet, and Ruth has some lovely "lap" trays which are very useful for serving buffet. The teen-agers like to have their parties outdoors, for which the

Johnsons usually provide a disc jockey to play records for dancing and plenty of food. Something simple, not fussy, and they make certain there is quantity, such as a tray of ham, sliced turkey or roast beef with the complementary condiments. The teen-agers make their own sandwiches. And for dessert, there is great Chocolate Angel Food Cake with Chocolate Sauce and *Praline Brownies.

★

Praline Brownies

¼ cup butter
1 cup brown sugar
1 egg
1 tsp. vanilla
½ cup all-purpose flour
1 tsp. baking powder
½ tsp. salt
½ to 1 cup finely chopped nut meats

Melt butter in saucepan, stir in brown sugar until dissolved. Cool slightly, then beat in egg with vanilla. Sift flour, then resift with baking powder and salt. Stir these into butter mixture. Add chopped nuts and pour into greased and floured 8-by-8-inch pan. Bake in moderate oven (350 degrees) for about 30 minutes. Cut into bars. Makes about 32 thin 1-by-2-inch bars.

For a seated dinner of eight to ten, Ruth sometimes uses this menu:

** Jellied Avocado Salad*
Chateaubriand
** Braised Celery*
** Artichoke Bottoms with Spinach served with * Sour Cream Sauce*
** Ice Cream Molds*

★

Braised Celery

3 hearts celery
1 can chicken consommé
2 Tbs. cold water
2 tsp. cornstarch
¼ tsp. dried basil

Split celery hearts lengthwise into fourths. Simmer in consommé until fork tender. Remove celery. Dissolve cornstarch in cold water and stir into soup mixture. Cook until thick. Add basil. Pour thickened mixture over celery to glaze.

★

Artichoke Bottoms Filled with Spinach Served with Sour Cream Sauce (*serves* 6)

1 8-oz. pkg. fresh mushrooms
4 Tbs. butter
¾ cup thick white sauce (2 Tbs. butter, ½ cup hot milk, 1 Tbs. flour)
1 pkg. frozen chopped spinach
½ cup boiling water
Salt, pepper, garlic salt to taste
1 can artichoke bottoms (usually 6 to 8 per can)

Reserve 6 whole mushrooms, slice or chop remaining mushrooms and sauté in 2 Tbs. butter. Add to white sauce. Drop thawed spinach into ½ cup boiling water, remove from fire and cover. Drain well, dry and add to mushroom and sauce mixture. Correct seasoning. Drain artichoke bottoms and make mounds (approximately 2 Tbs. of spinach mixture on each bottom). Sauté the remaining 6 mushroom caps in 1 Tbs. butter and top each mound. Before serving place in 350-degree oven for 15 minutes. Serve with the following sauce.

SOUR CREAM SAUCE

1 cup sour cream
1 cup mayonnaise
¼ tsp. cayenne pepper
¼ cup lemon juice, strained

Heat in top of double boiler.

★

Ice Cream Molds

Ruth loves to concoct these; they always look impressive, especially when served from a silver tray. There is an endless number of combinations which can be used, such as:

Press chocolate ice cream into a melon mold, filling half way; keep bottom layer hard. Spread a coffee liqueur and nuts over it. Fill the remaining space with pistachio ice cream. Turn out on a silver tray and decorate with fresh flowers. May be sliced by the hostess at the table and served.

Other combinations are raspberry and pineapple sherbet or peppermint and chocolate.

For some of their larger parties, such as a cocktail party before the Symphony Ball or a party for the press before the opening exhibit, Lee and Ruth will use the Amon Carter Museum of Western

Art. It is a handsome structure built of Texas shell stone with an interior of bronze and teak. It holds the work of two of America's most popular frontier artists, Frederic Remington and Charles Russell, as well as many others. The museum also holds an excellent reference library specializing in Texan and Western Americans in the fields of art, history and anthropology. This is indeed a dramatic and fascinating setting for a party, especially when there are out-of-town visitors. For these parties, Ruth usually chooses something like a Seafood Gumbo or *Shrimp Casserole.

★

Shrimp Casserole

1 clove garlic
½ scant tsp. each of tarragon, chervil
1 Tbs. chopped parsley
1 Tbs. whole chopped shallot
½ cup sweet cream butter
1½ cup buttered, toasted breadcrumbs
Other seasonings such as: nutmeg, thyme, mace
½ cup dry sherry
2 lbs. shrimp, cooked in court bouillon

Make paste by mashing garlic, chervil, tarragon, parsley, shallot, butter and 1 cup breadcrumbs. Cream well. Add dash or two of other seasonings according to taste; then add sherry. Add shrimp, coating each shrimp well with mixture. Place in buttered casserole (size to fit chafing dish). Sprinkle with ½ cup buttered breadcrumbs and heat in 375-degree oven for about 15 minutes. Place in hot chafing dish to keep hot while serving from the buffet. This is a delicious way to prepare shrimp for a luncheon and serve in individual casseroles.

No place in the Southwest is more noted for its dazzling and elegant parties than Fort Worth. They are imperishable to the memory of all who attend — such as the party the Robert Windfohrs gave at their gorgeous home when their daughter Ann made her debut. It is interesting to note how any stroke of extravagance is offset by these practical and civic-minded citizens. For instance, the huge metal platform which was constructed for a dance floor to cover the swimming pool was given to the Lena Pope Children's Home. The multi-multiwinkle lights which had converted the grounds to a fairyland atmosphere are used to light the enormous Community Christmas Tree. Louis Armstrong came from Europe to entertain at intermission for the dance. There was another especially designed structure for Satchmo and the orchestra, which was afterwards converted for use in the aviary of the Fort Worth Zoo!

I was reminded by Francis Prinz, who was in Austin for the opening of the University of Texas's fine new art building, that all was not caviar and Chateaubriand in Fort Worth — in fact, between parties they welcome the sight and taste of *plain* food, as do we all. Francis makes a *Pot Roast with Dried Lima Beans, and I can testify firsthand it is powerful good. Besides, we had almost forgotten about dried limas, or dried butter beans. They were welcomed back to the table with "open hearts."

★

Pot Roast and Dried Lima Beans

1½ cups dried lima beans
Salt, pepper
5 lb. pot roast (bone in)
1 medium onion, chopped
Green pepper
Celery

Soak lima beans in 3 cups of water overnight. Season roast to taste with salt and pepper. Sear roast on top of stove until brown on all sides — in Dutch oven. Add chopped onion, green pepper, and celery.

Cover and put in 325-degree oven. Add lima beans, water and all. Cover, bake for another 3 hours. Serve on heated platter surrounded by beans and gravy.

★

Fresh Pears with Raspberry Sauce

4 pears, very firm
1 cup sugar
½ cup water
1 Tbs. vanilla extract or 1 vanilla bean
1 pkg. frozen raspberries
1 tsp. cornstarch
1 Tbs. cold water
1 Tbs. kirsch

Peel, core, and cut pears in half. Bring sugar and ½ cup water to a boil, then lower flame. Add vanilla, then pear halves, two at a time. Let simmer until pears are tender, but not soft. Remove pears; add frozen raspberries and let simmer for about 5 minutes. Strain into a smaller pan. Add cornstarch mixed to a smooth paste with 1 Tbs. cold water. Stir into raspberry mix over low flame, stirring until mixture becomes clear. Remove from fire; add 1 Tbs. kirsch. Serve over the pears.

RIO GRANDE VALLEY

The Rio Grande Valley, which is simply called "the Valley" by Texans, is one of the most extraordinary regions in the state, or I might say in the United States. It is sprawled along the banks of the Rio Grande through four of the southernmost counties in the state, starting up near Roma and along through pleasant, small towns in tranquil and semitropical settings, one right next to the other on down to Brownsville. Tourists flock there at a rate second only to Florida's and California's, enjoying the year-round beauty of its emerald green citrus orchards, vegetable fields, and the nearly always blue skies. It is a botanical paradox.

Its fertile soil produces a variety of forty-seven vegetables and enormous groves of citrus trees. Laboratory tests on Texas oranges and grapefruit show them to have the highest sugar and juice content of any grown in the world. Lemons also exceed in volume of juice. Fred Birkhead of McAllens CC said that if the Valley hybrid onions and carrots get any sweeter the United States won't need any other country's sugar.

One of the padres from San Juan made 125 walking canes from 125 species of trees, vines and shrubs growing in the Valley. The Valley is studded with oil wells, and the town of McAllen receives nearly $100,000 annually from oil and gas royalities from fields under its streets. That is probably why it could afford to buy its own bridge, which crosses the Rio Grande from McAllen to Mexico.

One of the first citrus growers in the Valley was Mr. John Shary.

The Sharys settled near McAllen; the area is now known as Sharyland. The Sharys' lovely white hospitable home is situated in the center of their vast acreage of citrus groves. Tall palm trees grow symmetrically along the roadways leading to the house and through the orchards.

Looking through the guest book at the Sharys' home, names of many "greats" appear. Marialice Shivers, who is the Sharys' only daughter, said each name brought to memory some gala party or dinner given by her parents. One vivid name was President Dwight D. Eisenhower's, when he came to dedicate Falcon Dam. Marialice said the usual procedure of getting ready for "heads of state" really had everyone running in circles for weeks preceding the President's visit. For example, the Secret Service wanted locks on all doors, and until that time the house had none. Mrs. Shary also made generous provision for the Secret Service in a guest house near the main house, sending out smoked turkeys, baked hams, homemade breads, salads and cakes; it was indeed a pleasant assignment for them. For one occasion during this visit an elaborate dinner of Mexican food, which is at its best in the Valley, was served. The visitors were so enthusiastic about it that they wanted more the second night, but the file shows that another menu featuring many Valley foods was used and equally enjoyed. Before dinner and served with cocktails was a bowl of Russian caviar served with lemon wedges and small Melba toast rounds. A beautiful tray of three colorful and delicious cheese balls was also on the table.

★

Red Cheese Ball

½ lb. natural cheddar cheese, finely grated
1 3-oz. pkg. cream cheese, softened
¼ cup pitted ripe olives, coarsely chopped
3 Tbs. sherry
½ tsp. Worcestershire
Dash each of onion, garlic and celery salts
¼ to ½ cup dried beef, coarsely snipped

Several days ahead or day before:

In large bowl with electric mixer at medium speed, beat cheese with olives, sherry, Worcestershire sauce and salts until thoroughly combined. Shape into ball; wrap in foil; refrigerate.

About 30 minutes before serving:

Remove foil; round up ball with hands, then roll it lightly in dried beef until completely coated. Makes about 3-inch ball.

★

Blue Cheese Ball

¼ lb. Danish blue cheese, crumbled
1 Tbs. finely chopped celery
2 or 3 scallions, snipped, tops and all
2 Tbs. sour cream
3 5-oz. jars blue cheese spread
¾ to 1 cup coarsely snipped parsley

Several days ahead or day before:

In large bowl, with mixer at medium speed, beat blue cheese with celery, scallions, sour cream and blue cheese spread until fluffy. Refrigerate overnight. Shape into ball, wrap in foil and refrigerate until needed.

Just before serving:

Remove foil from ball, round up ball with hands, then roll it lightly in snipped parsley until completely coated.

★

Cream Cheese Ball

3 8-oz. pkg. cream cheese, softened
1 cup drained preserved ginger, coarsely snipped
1 5-oz. can diced roasted, buttered almonds

Several days ahead or day before:

In large bowl, with mixer at medium speed, beat cream cheese with ginger until thoroughly combined. Shape into ball; wrap in foil; refrigerate.

About 30 minutes before serving:

Remove foil; round up ball with hands, then roll it lightly in almonds until completely coated. Makes about 4½-inch ball.

The dinner which followed included:

Ruby Red Grapefruit with Shrimp (Alternate segments of the grapefruit removed and replaced with gulf shrimp. Rémoulade dressing was in the center, where the core had been removed)

Breast of Pheasant on a Slice of Ham

Wild Rice

* *Beets in Orange Sauce* (see page 111)

Valley Broccoli

Hot Buttered Rolls, and always

Hot Corn Muffins at the request of Governor Shivers

* *Avocado-Grape Salad*

*Mary Shary's * Tipsy Pudding, which has been such a favorite at so many of the Sharys' and Shiverses' parties* (see page 88)

★

Avocado Grape Salad

Allow half an avocado and 4-oz. seeded and halved grapes per person. Cut the avocados in half and remove stones. Brush with lemon juice to prevent discoloration. Cover and chill. Pile the grapes into each half of avocado. Serve with dressing (below).

SALAD DRESSING

for Avocado-Grape Salad served at Sharyland

- 1 cup homemade mayonnaise
- ½ cup honey
- 2 Tbs. fresh lemon juice
- 1 tsp. celery seed
- ½ tsp. paprika

Mix well and pour over salad.

Mrs. Shary would often have her cook experiment with recipes using the Valley citrus fruits. Her *Chicken Lemon Soup makes a delightful beginning for a dinner or luncheon. Its flavor is a contradiction of sweet sherry and tart valley lemon; wholly delicious.

★

Chicken Lemon Soup (*serves 6 to 8*)

3 lbs. chicken pieces
2 qts. water
2 bay leaves
1 Tbs. salt
¼ tsp. pepper
2 onions, quartered
1 clove garlic
1 cup dry sherry
2 Tbs. lemon juice
6 or 8 thin lemon slices
¼ tsp. crushed tarragon leaves

Place chicken pieces, water, bay leaves, salt, pepper, onion and garlic in large kettle. Bring to a boil, lower heat and simmer (covered) until chicken is tender, about 1½ to 2 hours. Remove chicken pieces from broth. When cool enough to handle, cut meat from bones. Strain broth. Combine strained broth with sherry, lemon juice and slices and tarragon.

Add chicken meat and simmer about 10 minutes.

Serve with a lemon slice in each cup or bowl.

Also, her little *Dessert Pancakes, flavored with *Valley Orange Sauce and flamed dramatically, turns dinner into a real occasion, and they are so simple to make.

★

Orange Dessert Pancakes (*serves 5 to 6*)

Beat with rotary beater:

1 envelope orange muffin mix
2 Tbs. cooking (salad) oil
2 eggs
¾ cup water

Pour batter from tip of spoon into 3-inch pools onto hot griddle. Bake until puffed and full of bubbles, turn and bake on other side. Fold in half or roll up. Keep warm in low oven between towels. Make Orange Sauce. Serve 3 or 4 crepes on each plate with some of the sauce.

ORANGE SAUCE

½ cup butter
3 Tbs. sugar
½ cup orange juice
1 Tbs. grated orange rind
¾ to 1 cup fresh orange sections (3 oranges)

Melt butter in skillet or chafing dish. Blend in sugar, orange juice, and grated orange rind over low heat. Add fresh orange sections.

To flambée, pour one or a combination of liquors, slightly warmed, over top of crepe and light.

Last spring, two young high school girls from the Valley, Margaret Cantu and Carol Ann Myers, went to Washington, D.C. at the invitation of their congressman, Joe M. Kilgore, to prepare, with the help of the executive chef, Ernest Bahm, of the House Restaurant Kitchen, the menu they had just won first prize with in a contest sponsored by the Agricultural Growers Council in the Valley.

It included the following Valley products:

** Cebollas Rellenas*
Sunshine Carrots with Orange-Ginger Sauce
Southern Green Beans
Tossed Green Salad with Avocado Slices
Steamed Corn Tortillas
Homebaked Cracked Wheat Bread
Dessert was Chilled Grapefruit

The congressmen and senators said that it was the best and tastiest meal they had eaten in years. They all took home the recipe for *Cebollas Rellenas, hoping to have them again soon.

★

Cebollas Rellenas

6 onions
1 Tbs. instant potatoes
½ lb. ground beef
¼ lb. ground pork
20 seedless raisins
2 Tbs. chopped almonds
4 Tbs. lard
1 chili verde
1 tsp. paprika
1 tsp. salt
½ tsp. black pepper
6 eggs (separated)
3 Tbs. sifted flour

Peel onions. Place whole onions in boiling salted water. Mix instant potatoes with water. Combine ground meat, pork, raisins, almonds, instant potatoes, and cook until brown in lard. When almost done, add finely chopped chili verde, paprika, salt and pepper. When well seasoned and done, remove from fire and cool.

Beat egg whites until stiff with wire egg whip. Beat egg yolks separately with rotary egg beater until light yellow in color. Gradually add the egg yolks to the egg whites. Beat continually all the time the yolks are being added.

Take out center of onions and stuff with meat mixture. Place on wax paper. Gently dip onions first in flour, then in egg mixture. Fry in a deep fat fryer at 350 degrees until golden brown on both sides, which will be approximately 10 minutes.

Place on paper towels and keep in slow oven until time to serve.

THE HILL COUNTRY

It is always refreshing to visit any part of the beautiful hill country; around Fredericksburg, Kerrville, Comfort, Stonewall or Mason. It is an area which is unique in many respects, due to our German forefathers who migrated from autocratic Germany to find a new home without oppression in Texas. My husband's grandfather, Wilhelm Koock, was one of these German settlers. He established his home near Mason, at Koocksville. The old German-style stone house and store bearing his name are still there as strong as the day they were built.

We go to Koocksville every year to a family reunion, and it is a thrilling experience for us and our children. We have a great feast on the long shady porch of the quaint old house where Aunt Lola now lives. Dinner usually consists of:

Marvin Wagner's Barbecued Beef and Lamb
*Marguerite's Cole Slaw and * German Potato Cakes*
*The Geistweidts always bring * Bread and Butter Pickles and * Sauerkraut in crocks and Peach Preserves put up by Anna Marie and Aunt Lena. And also Aunt Lena's delicate * Homemade Noodles.*
We are usually greeted with the smell of Aunt Lola's big loaves of bread just out of the oven. She also has a good supply of freshly made Schmierkase and Wild Plum Jam and butter, the only freshly churned butter I know of anymore.
** Carlita makes a wonderful Potato Salad in a bowl so large her husband, Marvin, has to carry it in.*
Koockie and Vera furnish vine-ripened tomatoes, cucumbers and onions sliced thin in sour cream and other fresh vegetables all grown in their own garden.
The girls of the younger generation, Joyce, Gaelyn and Gretchen, have an array of prizewinning cakes like I've never seen nor eaten before.

Someone asked me once what did we take, and I had to admit just seven children with hearty appetites! What could I possibly add to that spread? I wouldn't even dare!

After dinner we sit under the trees, and Gertrude Hoffman Ernest reads the fascinating family history of Grandmother and Grandfather Koock and their courageous days of pioneering, the many hardships they experienced when they and the other German settlers finally reached this part of the country and stood on the top of the hills overlooking the Pedernales River Valley with its great post oak forest, fine springs and fertile soil. They knew this would make an ideal homesite where they could live and raise their families.

The history of the hill country, like most of early Texas, is very colorful and full of adventure, and we sit spellbound listening until Gertrude ends with the important events in the family of the past year, such as the births, weddings, and any honors received by the college Koocks or the Ranchers.

★

Aunt Lena's Homemade Noodles

- 3 eggs
- 3 Tbs. milk or water
- 2 cups flour
- ½ tsp. salt
- 1 tsp. baking powder

Beat the eggs, add milk and beat again. Sift flour, salt and baking powder. Add enough flour to make a stiff dough. Knead well on a well-floured board. Roll dough into 2 thin sheets. Set aside to dry from 2 to 3 hours. Turn sheets several times while drying. When dry enough fold them together and cut in narrow strips. Drop into boiling salted water and cook about 20 minutes. Serve hot, topped with bread crumbs nicely browned in butter.

★

Anna Marie's Bread and Butter Pickles

1 gal. sliced cucumbers
8 sliced onions
2 red peppers
½ cup pickling salt
Chopped ice

Place cucumbers, onions and peppers in pan and cover with ½ cup pickling salt and chopped ice for 4 hours. Drain. Combine:

5 cups sugar
4 cups vinegar
1 cup water
½ tsp. cloves
1½ tsp. turmeric
1 tsp. celery seed
2 Tbs. mustard seed

Add cucumber mixture; boil together for 3 minutes. Put in jars and seal.

★

Arthur's Sauerkraut

Shred fresh cabbage and pack into jars. To each quart jar add 1 Tbs. salt. Fill jar slowly with boiling water and seal at once.

★

Carlita's Potato Salad with Bacon Dressing

1 qt. cooked potatoes
2 hard-cooked eggs
½ cup sweet pickles
1 cup celery
½ cup onion
1 tsp. salt
2 Tbs. pimento

Dice ingredients and mix.

DRESSING

2 slices diced bacon
2 Tbs. flour
1 beaten egg
1 cup water
3 tsp. sugar
1 tsp. salt
¼ tsp. paprika
½ tsp. prepared mustard
3 Tbs. vinegar

Fry bacon until crisp. Add flour and blend well. To beaten egg add water, sugar, salt, paprika, mustard. Add to bacon-flour mixture and cook slowly until thick, stirring constantly. Remove from heat and add vinegar. Mix all ingredients and chill before serving.

★

Marguerite's German Potato Cakes (serves 6)

2 cups raw grated potatoes (about 4 large)
2 eggs, separated
⅛ tsp. baking powder
1 tsp. salt
1 Tbs. flour
¼ cup shortening

Peel potatoes and soak in cold water for several hours. Grate and then drain well, so that all starch is removed. Beat egg yolks, stir into potatoes. Mix baking powder, salt, and flour together and stir into potato-egg mixture. Beat egg whites until stiff and fold into potatoes. Heat shortening in heavy skillet until very hot. Drop potato mixture by spoonfuls in the hot shortening and fry until golden brown. Turn and brown on other side.

★

Vera's Cucumbers in Sour Cream (serves 6)

1 cucumber, thinly sliced
2 large sweet Bermuda onions, sliced in thin rings
Few unpeeled sliced, red radishes
Season with: dill, salt, paprika
1 pt. sour cream
2 tsp. fresh lemon juice

Leave half of green rind on cucumber when peeling, to add cool color. Run the prongs of a silver fork down length of cucumber and rind. This gives a scalloped effect to the rings. Combine onions and radishes. Add seasonings. Mix with sour cream and lemon juice. Serve icy cold in glass bowl.

★

Joyce's German Sweet Chocolate Cake

1 pkg. German sweet chocolate
½ cup boiling water
1 cup butter
2 cups sugar
4 eggs, separated
2 tsp. vanilla
2½ cups flour
¼ tsp. salt
1 tsp. soda
1 cup sour milk (add 2 Tbs. vinegar to 1 cup milk)

Melt chocolate in boiling water. Cool. Cream butter and sugar, add beaten egg yolks, creaming thoroughly. Add chocolate mixture and vanilla. Mix well. Sift together dry ingredients and add alternately with sour milk to chocolate mixture, beating well after each addition. Fold in 4 stiffly beaten egg whites. Pour in 3 9-inch cake pans that have been greased and floured. Bake at 350 degrees 30 to 40 minutes. Cool. Frost with:

COCONUT PECAN FROSTING

1 cup evaporated milk
1 cup sugar
3 egg yolks
1 stick margarine
1½ tsp. vanilla

Blend together and cook over medium heat until thickened, about 12 minutes. Add 1½ cups flaked coconut and 1 cup chopped pecans. Beat until thick enough to spread.

★

Gretchen's Cracker Cake

1 cup flour
1½ tsp. baking powder
½ cup butter
2 cups sugar
4 eggs
1 cup soda crackers, rolled
1 cup pecans
1 cup milk
1 tsp. lemon extract

Sift flour and baking powder 3 times. Cream butter and sugar. Add eggs one at a time and beat well. Add flour, rolled crackers, nuts, and milk alternately. Add lemon. Makes 3 layers. Bake 25 minutes at 350 degrees.

ICING

1 cup hot water
1 cup sugar
1 egg yolk
1 lemon
1 Tbs. cornstarch
1 tsp. butter

Combine ingredients in heavy saucepan. Cook, stirring constantly, over low heat until thickened.

★

Gaelyn's Maraschino Cherry Layer Cake

2½ cups sifted cake flour
1½ cups sugar
3½ tsp. baking powder
1 tsp. salt
½ cup shortening
¾ cup milk
¼ cup Maraschino cherry juice
1 tsp. vanilla
2 tsp. almond extract
4 egg whites, unbeaten
18 Maraschino cherries, well drained and very finely chopped
½ cup pecans or walnuts, finely chopped

Sift flour, sugar, baking powder and salt into mixing bowl. Add shortening. Combine milk and cherry juice. Add ¾ cup of this liquid. Add flavoring extracts. Beat 200 strokes (2 minutes on mixer at low speed). Scrape bowl and spoon or beater. Add remaining liquid and egg whites and beat another 2 minutes. Add cherries and nuts, and blend. Bake in two deep 9-inch greased layer pans in moderate oven, 375 degrees, 20 to 25 minutes. Ice when layers are cooled.

FROSTING

2 Tbs. shortening
2 Tbs. butter
1 tsp. vanilla
½ tsp. almond extract
½ tsp. salt
4 cups sifted confectioner's sugar
9 Tbs. scalded cream
Red coloring

Combine shortening, butter, vanilla, almond and salt. Blend, beat in ½ cup sugar. Add hot cream alternately with remaining sugar, beating well after each addition. Add only enough cream to make a nice spreading consistency. Add a few drops of red coloring to tint frosting a delicate pink.

Gaelyn said this came from Mrs. H. C. Hanneman in Fredericksburg.

FREDERICKSBURG

Nearly all the people in Fredericksburg have retained their use of the German language and speak it fluently, and many of the old German customs are still thriving, such as the Sängerfest, and the family dances on Saturday night.

There are often four generations of the same family present at the Saturday night dance. The youngest may be asleep on a pallet or dancing "Herr Schmidt" and "Put Your Little Foot" with a young brother or sister right along beside their grandmother and grandfather.

Fredericksburg has retained so much of its Old World charm with its many early German houses and stone buildings along Main Street. The most picturesque of these are the "Sunday" houses, which are small two-story buildings with an outside stairway, built as a weekend house to be used by the family when they came into town for church services. Most of Fredericksburg's churches have tall spires. Their bells ring in unison as *Abendglocken*, or bells of evening, to summon the worshippers to services.

We try always to get to Fredericksburg at least once during the Gillespie County Fair. The horse races, exhibits of beautiful handwork, intricate patterns of patchwork quilts, hand-embroidered tablecloths and crocheted bedspreads are always intriguing. However, just as much so is the home economics exhibit of beautiful preserves and clear red jellies and all kinds of homegrown vegetables arranged in artistic and symmetrical patterns in glass jars. So many of these items are entered by twelve- and thirteen-year-old girls. I always told my boys that they should try to get one of these cute Fredericksburg girls for a wife.

Another annual attraction in Fredericksburg is the Lighting of the Easter Fires. This is a very impressive pageant at which the Easter Rabbit builds a fire around a giant kettle of water the night before Easter, and the bunny rabbits living in the hills gather wildflowers that bloom in countless numbers and drop the blossoms into the kettles to make dye for the Easter eggs. The story of the Easter Fires is based on legends of the first settlers and the Indians who were there before them. We were there a few years ago, and our children were very impressed with the story and the pageant.

At this time we visited our friends Arthur and Beatrice Stehling. Arthur's grandfather was one of the founding fathers of Fredericksburg. They have just recently restored a charming old house with the aid of their son Jack, a promising young architect, on Main Street directly across from Arthur's ultramodern bank. It indeed bespeaks the traditional German hospitality. Bea served a buffet supper in the enclosed courtyard. While we enjoyed our schnapps, Chester and Arthur started a Sängerfest reminiscent of their college days when they sang together in the St. Edward's Glee Club. The menu was one we'll never forget:

** Whole Fresh Ham, boned, and stuffed with Cranberry Dressing*
** German Potato Dumplings*
Corn Fritters on a big tray circled with orange shells filled with Minted Apple Sauce
** Cottage Cheese Salad*

** Beet Jellied Salad, filled with*
** Thick Cream Dressing*
Cold sliced Fredericksburg Tomatoes
** Escalloped Cabbage au Gratin*
** Pumpernickel Rye Bread, sweet butter*
Fredericksburg Peach Preserves made by Bea's sister, Rose Mary Burroughs
Mustard Pickles

★

Whole Fresh Ham, Boned, and Stuffed with Cranberry Dressing

6 lb. ham (or larger)
Turkey dressing
1 cup ground fresh cranberries
2 Tbs. shortening
Salt and pepper to taste
½ cup brown sugar
⅓ cup flour
8 or 10 cloves

Have butcher bone a fresh pork ham. Make a small amount of dressing (the same as for turkeys, only add 1 cup of fresh ground cranberries), and fill cavity where the bone was removed. Heat shortening in a roaster slightly larger than the roast. Brown roast on both sides, then bake for about an hour at 350 degrees. Remove from oven, salt and pepper; stick with whole cloves; sprinkle with brown sugar and flour to completely cover the roast. Return to oven and bake 2 or 3 hours longer at lower temperature. Baste frequently. Baking time should be figured at 25 minutes per pound.

★

German Potato Dumplings

1 Tbs. butter
2 egg yolks
1 cup breadcrumbs
1 cup mashed boiled potatoes
Lemon peeling
Nutmeg
Salt
2 egg whites

Cream butter, add egg yolks, breadcrumbs, potatoes, lemon peeling, nutmeg and salt. Last, add stiffly beaten whites of eggs. Drop by small spoonfuls into boiling water and cook about 10 minutes.

★

Cottage Cheese Salad (serves 6)

2 cups well-seasoned cottage cheese
1 cup chopped dates or stewed prunes
1 cup chopped tart red apples
Mayonnaise
Paprika

Combine cheese, dates or prunes, and unpeeled apples. Moisten with mayonnaise. Mix lightly with fork. Press in melon mold, chill. Turn out on crisp lettuce leaves. Sprinkle with paprika; garnish with prunes filled with wedge of unpeeled apple.

★

Escalloped Cabbage au Gratin

1 qt. cabbage (prepared as for slaw)
1 tsp. salt
1 qt. boiling water
1 cup sweet milk
3 Tbs. butter
1 Tbs. flour
Salt
½ tsp. pepper
1 cup fine cracker crumbs
½ cup grated cheddar cheese

Pour boiling water and salt on cabbage and boil 5 minutes. Drain well. Heat the milk. Cream 2 Tbs. butter and flour and add to milk. Then add the salt and pepper. Cook this to the consistency of thick cream. Butter a baking dish and cover bottom with a layer of cracker crumbs; add alternate layers of cabbage, crackers and sauce. Top with cracker crumbs. Dot with small pieces of butter, cover and bake in a moderate oven (350 degrees) for 25 minutes.

This bread is baked in the Edgar Dietz one-hundred-sixty-year-old bakery in a brick oven:

★

Pumpernickel Rye Bread (for 3 loaves)

3 cups pumpernickel-rye meal flour
¾ cup dark molasses
⅓ cup shortening
2 tsp. salt
2 cups tap water
1 pkg. active dry yeast, dissolved in ½ cup water
6 to 6½ cups all-purpose flour

Combine above ingredients and let rise for 1 hour and 20 minutes. Punch down, and let rise again for 20 minutes. Place on floured board. Knead and let stand for 10 minutes. Mold and bake in oven at 350 degrees approximately 45 minutes, till done.

For dessert Bea served the greatest assortment of cookies. I have enjoyed making these at Christmas time, too.

★

Fresh Apple Cookies (makes 4 dozen)

½ cup shortening
1⅓ cups brown sugar, firmly packed
½ tsp. salt
½ tsp. nutmeg
1 tsp. cloves
1 tsp. cinnamon
1 egg

Cream above ingredients well.

2 cups sifted flour
1 cup raisins
1 cup chopped pecans
1 tsp. soda
1 cup finely chopped unpeeled apples
¼ cup milk

Combine flour, raisins, pecans and apples. Add to creamed ingredients. Combine soda and milk and stir into mixture. Blend well. Drop from teaspoon on greased baking sheet. Bake at 400 degrees 12 to 15 minutes.

While still hot spread cookie with thin coating of *Vanilla Spread.

VANILLA SPREAD

2½ Tbs. milk
1½ cups sifted powdered sugar
1 Tbs. margarine
¼ tsp. vanilla
⅛ tsp. salt

Heat milk until steaming, remove from heat, add all other ingredients, and beat until creamy.

★

German Pecan Macaroons

1 qt. pecans finely chopped
2 cups sugar
1 tsp. cinnamon (mix with sugar)
2 cups toasted bread cubes
4 large egg whites

Mix pecans, sugar, cinnamon and bread cubes well. Beat egg whites until frothy, add to other mixture. Place small teaspoonful of mixture on well-buttered baking sheet. Bake at 250 degrees until light brown. Place baking sheet on wet cloth a few minutes before removing baked macaroons.

★

Honey Drop Cookies (makes 2½ dozen)

¾ cup honey
¼ cup butter or margarine
⅛ tsp. cloves
¾ tsp. cinnamon
1 egg, beaten
1¾ cups flour
¼ tsp. salt
½ tsp. soda
1 cup chopped raisins
½ cup nuts

Heat honey; add butter and spices. Cool, and add egg. Sift flour, measure and sift with salt and soda. Add to honey mixture with the raisins and nuts. Mix well. Drop by teaspoonfuls on well-oiled baking sheet and bake in hot oven 400 degrees 10 to 15 minutes.

★

Fruit Cookies

- 1 cup butter
- 2 cups sugar
- ½ cup milk
- 3 cups flour
- 3 tsp. baking powder
- 4 eggs
- 2 cups currants
- 2 cups raisins
- 2 cups pecans
- ½ cup orange peel
- 1 wine glass whiskey or wine
- 2 tsp. cinnamon
- Other spices to taste

Make up as any shortening cake. Flour the fruit as for fruit cake. Make a rather stiff dough and drop on pan from spoon. Bake about 15 minutes at 350 degrees.

★

Jelly Gems

- 1 cup butter
- 1 cup sugar
- 2 egg yolks
- 2½ cups flour
- ¼ tsp. almond flavoring

Cream butter and sugar. Add egg yolks, flour and flavoring. Mix well. Form into small balls. Place on greased cookie sheet. Press thumb into each cookie. Fill indentation with jelly. Bake in oven at 400 degrees until brown.

★

Almond Cookies

- 1 cup butter
- 1 cup sugar
- 3 egg yolks
- 4 cups flour

Cream butter and sugar; add beaten yolks and sifted flour. Roll out thin.

Cut with a large round cutter and take out center with a smaller one, leaving a ring cookie. Brush these with whites of eggs and sprinkle with finely chopped almonds, sugar and cinnamon. Bake a golden brown in a moderate oven (350 degrees) for 12 to 15 minutes.

While we were having coffee and the cookies under the enormous oak in the courtyard, Bea, whose poetry has won great acclaim over the state, read us the lovely ballad she had just written and which had been set to music to be sung by the Fredericksburg St. Mary's Choir at the Dallas State Fair on German Day.

BALLADE OF THE TEXAS GERMANS.

When the Germans sailed from across the sea
Bringing skill and strength to a strange new land,
While their dauntless souls sped bold forces free . . .
They had spirit, that valorous Foreign band;
But whenever symphonic lilts press'd hand
Upon strings tuned up taut for a serenade
It seem'd God's purest joy advanced their stand,
For blessed are those Germans who came and stayed!

When despair near threat'ned hope's reveille
And low voices rumbled against command,
The staunch sect of emigrants clasp'd its lea
With high spirit — that valorous Foreign band;
Though tranquility failed and temper fanned,
There evolved a triumphant accolade
As each one bared his heart for our Texas 'brand' —
Thus blessed are those Germans who came and stayed!

Their way profited by constancy,
The keen verve of reasoning, of demand
For each human right with its guarantee —
They have spirit, this valorous Texas band,
Lending greatness to neighbors as God has planned
Yet, in perfect humility, evade
Vain pretense; they steer clear of all contraband . . .
For blessed are the Germans who came and stayed!

ENVOY

So, today, as before, these deeds have been scanned . . .
They have spirit, this valorous Texas band
For they carve a new culture unassayed —
Now, blessed are those Germans who came and stayed!

Beatrice Deen Stehling
August 4, 1964

STONEWALL

A year or so ago Stonewall was best known for its peaches, but of course now its number one claim to fame is THE PRESIDENT. This quiet agricultural and ranching German community has become the hub of world events and history, and while the President's neighbors are very proud of him and to have the summer White House on the banks of their Pedernales River, they go right along with their ranching and peach growing as they have always done.

Most of their social activities take place in the Stonewall schoolhouse, where Lyndon Johnson rode his donkey from the house where he was born, just a few miles down the road. The school gym is where two hundred VIP's were served a barbecue dinner when Chancellor Erhard of Germany visited the LBJ ranch only a short time after Lyndon became President. This is also where gala entertainment takes place during the Peach Jamboree!

Stonewall celebrated its centennial in 1960 and held its first Peach Jamboree! The peach orchards were laden with luscious ripe fruit — even so, the demand is greater than the supply. The then Vice President crowned the Peach Queen. Lady Bird, Luci and Lynda wore frontier dresses and rode in a stagecoach in the Big Parade. The Jamboree goes full swing for three nights. There's always a barbecue, big dance and thrilling rodeo. Cactus Pryor, TV personality, has always been on hand to regale the crowds with his wit and humor and emcee the special events.

Tom and Betty Weinheimer's land adjoins the LBJ ranch. Betty is the voluntary secretary of the Stonewall Chamber of Commerce, and she handles the job like a professional.

Betty and Tom with a few of their friends occasionally get together for supper and a Saturday night dance. Betty and the girls decided the New Year's Eve dance this year would be special. They would have a buffet supper at the Weinheimers' house before the dance, each lady was to bring a favorite dish, they would really go "big town" and even have a bar, forgoing the traditional beer — that is, as much as the menfolks would allow. The girls got new cocktail dresses for the occasion. They decorated the school gym (for that is where all social events take place in Stonewall) and prepared the food. It was really exciting getting ready for a big fancy New Year's party.

Everybody arrived looking sleek and lovely. The party had just begun. They thought everyone was there when they heard a honk outside. Tom and Simon Burg went to the door and there were the President and Mrs. Johnson, with their friends the Jessie Kellams. Everyone came to the porch to call for them to come on in. It didn't take much coaxing, as Lyndon loves this sort of gathering. Quite a contrast to Washington's sophistication perhaps, but few parties could boast of such delicious food or so much fun.

Hors d'oeuvres were small pieces of smoked sausage — thin slices of the fabulous *Smoked Venison.

On the buffet was:

** Roasted Wild Turkey*
Smoked Ham, Düsseldorf mustard
*Angus Beef with * Texas Barbecue Sauce*
** Pickled Peaches*
** Peach Salad*
Homemade Bread
Homemade Pickles
** Red Cabbage with Apples*
Cakes and Cookies
Toasted Pecans
** Mints*
Coffee
** Jam Cake*
** Brown Sugar Spice Cake*
** Potato Fruit Cake*
** Chocolate Pound Cake*

★

Smoked Venison

Cut the tenderloin from a deer into several six or seven inch pieces. Soak in hot water for one-half hour to keep meat soft. Remove from water and drain. Sprinkle these chunks with meat tenderizer. Put in bowl and cover, leaving in brine overnight. Place on closed barbecue grill, with very little heat, and smoke one day. This meat may be smoked longer according to the taste desired.

★

Roasted Wild Turkey (*serves 8 to 10*)

1 turkey, 8 to 10 lbs., ready to cook
Salt and pepper
8 cups partially dry bread cubes
¾ cup finely chopped celery
½ cup chopped walnuts
2 to 3 tsp. sage
1 tsp. salt
¼ tsp. pepper
1½ cups chopped onion
¼ cup butter or margarine
¼ cup water

Sprinkle turkey inside and out with salt and pepper. Combine bread, celery, walnuts and seasonings. Cook onion in butter or margarine until tender but not brown; pour over bread mixture.

Add the water and toss lightly. Spoon stuffing lightly into body cavity. Put remaining dressing in a greased casserole. Cover and bake in oven with turkey during last 30 minutes of roasting time. Truss bird. Cover breast with bacon slices and cheesecloth soaked in melted bacon fat.

Place turkey, breast up, on rack in roasting pan. Roast at 325 degrees 20 to 25 minutes per pound or until tender, basting frequently with bacon fat and drippings in pan. Remove cheesecloth, skewers and string.

★

Texas Barbecue Sauce

¼ lb. butter or margarine
1 cup vinegar
1 cup water
½ cup tomato catsup
2 Tbs. Worcestershire sauce
Juice of one lemon
1 Tbs. dry mustard
2 Tbs. Texas chili powder
¼ tsp. cayenne
1 tsp. black pepper
1 tsp. salt
¼ cup sugar
2 crushed bay leaves
2 garlic cloves, minced
1 large onion, grated

Melt butter or margarine, add vinegar, water, tomato catsup, Worcestershire sauce, juice of lemon. Mix mustard, chili powder, cayenne, pepper, salt, sugar, bay leaves, and add to other mixture. Add cloves of garlic and onion. Cook together for about 10 minutes. Makes about 2 cups, enough to swab 4 to 5 lbs. of meat.

★

Pickled Peaches

Thin syrup (2 cups water and 1 cup sugar)
½ cup vinegar
5 to 10 whole cloves
Cinnamon stick, according to taste

Put spice in cloth bag and boil in syrup five minutes, remove and boil peaches in syrup. Pack in sterile jars and seal. This should be enough for 12 peaches.

★

Peach Salad

6 large cooked peach halves
1 orange
Lettuce
¼ cup finely diced celery
¼ cup finely diced apple
Mayonnaise dressing
6 Maraschino cherries

Drain peaches. Peel orange. Cut strips of peel to form handles. Place one-half of a peach on crisp lettuce. Stick handle into sides of peach to form basket. Fill with celery and apple mixture which has been moistened with mayonnaise. Garnish with cherries.

★

Red Cabbage with Apples (makes 8 servings)

3½ to 4 lb. head red cabbage
1 or 2 tart apples
2 Tbs. butter
1 medium onion, sliced
2 cups water
½ cup white vinegar
½ cup sugar
½ tsp. salt
¼ tsp. pepper
2 cloves
1 bay leaf
Juice of ½ lemon
1½ Tbs. flour

Wash cabbage; cut as for slaw. Peel and chop apples. Heat butter in large saucepan and cook apple and onion slowly 3 or 4 minutes. Add flour, water, vinegar, sugar, salt, pepper, cloves, bay leaf and lemon juice. Stir, bring to boil. Add cabbages; mix well. Cover and simmer 25 minutes. Mix well.

★

Mints

2 cups sugar
¾ cup water
⅛ tsp. cream of tartar
Oil of peppermint

Mix first three ingredients: stir well before placing on stove; do not stir when boiling. Boil to soft-ball stage. When done, pour into buttered dish and cool. Add a drop of oil of peppermint and beat until of a cream consistency. Work with hands until plastic; mold with fingers into the shape desired and place molded fondant on oiled paper.

★

Jam Cake

- 1 cup shortening
- 1 cup sugar
- 4 eggs
- 1 cup jam or preserves
- 1 cup pecans
- ½ cup raisins
- 1 tsp. vanilla
- 1 tsp. lemon extract
- ½ tsp. cinnamon
- ½ tsp. nutmeg
- ½ tsp. allspice
- 2 cups flour
- 1 tsp. soda
- 1 tsp. baking powder
- ½ cup buttermilk

Cream shortening, sugar and eggs thoroughly. Add jam, pecans and raisins, and flavoring. Sift dry ingredients together, add to creamed mixture alternately with buttermilk. Bake in 10-inch tube pan for 1 hour at 350 degrees. When thoroughly cooled, top with following icing:

- 1 unpeeled apple, grated
- 1 small whole lemon, grated
- 3 cups powdered sugar

Mix thoroughly and spread on cake. If consistency is too thick to spread, add more grated apple.

★

Brown Sugar Spice Cake

- 1 cup shortening
- 2 cups brown sugar, firmly packed
- 2½ cups all purpose flour
- 1 tsp. soda
- 1 tsp. baking powder
- 1 tsp. cinnamon
- ¾ tsp. cloves
- ¼ tsp. salt
- 4 eggs, separated (Reserve the 2 largest egg whites for top of cake)
- 1 cup sour milk

Cream shortening and sugar. Sift flour once, measure and sift dry ingredients together 3 times. To the creamed mixture add the 4 yolks and beat thoroughly. Add the flour mixture and milk alternately and, last, the two beaten egg whites. Pour into a large tube cake pan. (Line bottom with wax paper.)

FOR TOP OF CAKE

- 2 egg whites, beaten until they peak
- 1 cup brown sugar
- ½ cup chopped pecans

Add brown sugar to beaten egg white, beating it in. Spread on top of cake batter and sprinkle with pecans. Bake at 350 degrees for 45 minutes. Cool on cake rack before removing from pan.

★

Potato Fruit Cake

½ cup butter
2 cups sugar
4 eggs
4 oz. unsweetened chocolate, grated
1 tsp. cinnamon
½ tsp. mace
1 cup warm mashed potatoes
2 cups flour
3 tsp. baking powder
¾ cup water
½ cup raisins
½ cup nuts
½ cup currants or any other fruit desired

Cream butter, sugar, yolks of eggs; add chocolate and spices, then add potatoes. Add flour, baking powder and water alternately, and last, the beaten egg whites, nuts and fruit. Bake at 325 degrees about 1 hour.

★

Chocolate Pound Cake

2 cups sugar
1 cup shortening
4 eggs
2 tsp. vanilla
2 tsp. butter flavoring
3 cups sifted flour
½ tsp. soda
1 tsp. salt
1 cup buttermilk
1 pkg. German sweet chocolate

Cream sugar and shortening. Add eggs and flavorings. Add sifted dry ingredients alternately with buttermilk. Mix well. Then add chocolate that has been softened in warm oven. Blend together well. Cook in 9-inch tube pan that has been well greased and floured.

Bake 1½ hours at 300 degrees. Place cake under a tight fitting cover while still hot and leave until cool. This makes a crusty top.

Betty said they wanted the party to be extra special but never dreamed their guests would include the President of the United States and the lovely First Lady.

The ladies of Stonewall spend a great deal of their time working out interesting recipes with peaches. They're safe — because anything tastes good with Stonewall peaches! When we drove over to Mr. Simon Burg's peach shed he gave us a collection of peach recipes — so mark this page, and when peach season opens next June try these:

★

Dutch Peach Pie

10 to 12 ripe peaches
1 9-inch unbaked pie shell
1 egg
1 cup sour cream
¼ tsp. salt
¾ cup sugar
2 Tbs. flour
½ tsp. cinnamon
½ tsp. nutmeg

Peel peaches, slice and arrange in pie shell. Beat egg slightly, mix with sour cream, salt, sugar, flour, cinnamon and nutmeg. Pour over peaches. Bake in an even-browning 350-degree oven for 20 minutes. Meanwhile mix together topping as follows:

TOPPING

¼ cup brown sugar
3 Tbs. flour
2 Tbs. butter
½ cup chopped nuts

Mix brown sugar, flour, butter and nuts to make crumbs for topping and sprinkle over pie and bake for 15 to 20 minutes longer.

The National Peach Council suggests this quick, wasteless way to peel fresh peaches for this French-style pie. Cover the fruit with boiling water for about one minute, then chill quickly under running water. The skins will peel off thin as paper with no waste of juices or the melting golden pulp.

★

French Crumb Peach Pie

2-crust pkg. pie crust mix
4 cups peeled, sliced fresh peaches
1 cup sugar
2 Tbs. tapioca
½ tsp. nutmeg
1 Tbs. butter

Follow the pastry directions for one pastry crust. Fit pastry into a 9-inch pie pan. Chill. Mix the fresh fruit, ½ cup sugar and tapioca and pour into the chilled crust. Blend the rest of the pie crust mix, ½ cup sugar and nutmeg, and cut in the butter with a pastry blender or fork to make coarse crumbs. Sprinkle this crumb mixture over the peaches. Bake at 400 degrees for 40 minutes, or until the fruit starts to bubble and the crumbs are a light brown. Cool two hours before serving.

★

Fresh Peach Cobbler

1 cup sugar
1 Tbs. cornstarch
½ tsp. cinnamon or nutmeg
1 cup water
8 to 10 fresh peaches, skinned and halved
2 Tbs. lemon juice
Butter
¼ cup sugar
2 cups biscuit mix
1 egg, beaten slightly (add milk to make ½ cup)
½ tsp. almond flavoring

Combine sugar, cornstarch, cinnamon or nutmeg with water, boil 1 minute while stirring. Arrange peaches in 11½- by 7⅜- by 1½-inch baking dish. Sprinkle with lemon juice. Pour cooked liquid over peaches and dot with butter. Mix sugar with biscuit mix, egg and milk, and almond flavoring, and stir just enough to moisten. Drop the batter by spoonfuls around the edge of baking dish. Then bake in hot oven (400 degrees) about 30 minutes.

★

Prize Peach Coffee Cake

¾ cup sugar
¼ cup soft shortening
1 egg
½ cup milk
2 cups flour
2 tsp. baking powder
½ tsp. salt
2 cups fresh sliced peaches

Mix thoroughly, the sugar, shortening and egg, stir in the milk. Sift together and stir in the flour, baking powder and salt. Spread batter into a greased and floured 9 inch square pan. Top with 2 cups fresh sliced peaches. Sprinkle with crumble mixture.

CRUMBLE MIXTURE

½ cup sugar
⅓ cup flour
½ tsp. cinnamon
¼ cup soft butter

Bake coffee cake at 375 degrees for 40 to 45 minutes.

★

Peach Preserves

1¼ lbs. peaches
¾ lb. sugar

Peel peaches in the evening and cover with sugar. In the morning cook very slowly for about 2 hours or until the fruit looks transparent and the syrup is like honey. A skin will form as it cooks.

When we stopped by the Roy Weinheimers' after Mass on Sunday morning, their twelve-year-old daughter was wearing the pretty dress she had made and won a blue ribbon for, for her fine seams, at the 4-H Club Home Economics exhibit in San Angelo. She should also get a blue ribbon for the Peach Julep she served us.

★

Peach Julep

1 cup fresh peaches, mashed
¼ cup unsweetened pineapple juice, chilled
¼ cup sugar
1 pint vanilla ice cream
¾ cup milk
½ grated lemon peel

Place peaches, pineapple juice and sugar in blender. Blend at high speed till smooth (about 10 seconds). Add ice cream, blend until softened. Add milk, mixing just till blended. Pour into chilled glasses.

These amounts are for one blender load and make 2 servings. To serve the crowd, repeat recipe as many times as desired.

The drive from Fredericksburg to Kerrville is very scenic — but the thing I enjoy most is stopping by to see Hondo and Schotze Crouch and, down the road a little nearer Comfort, the Adolph Steilers — Adolph, dubbed by *Life* magazine "the Mohair King."

Adolph and his wife Tops are the epitome of hospitality. They are synonymous with this part of the country. A few hunting seasons ago, they invited Chester and me to their ranch to hunt. I got a beautiful buck the first morning as I sat in one of the blinds in a tree, but for some reason I have always felt apologetic to Adolph. He really loves every one of the deer — feeds them tenderly the year round — I guess he only has hunters out of necessity, as the deer would almost "take over" his ranch if some weren't killed off each season. Going hunting to some of us doesn't mean going shooting. Being in the hill country these cold crisp November mornings, wearing so many clothes you can hardly climb up in the blind, watching the beautiful, sensitive and spirited deer with their white plumed tails upturned darting over the hills into the safety of dense ravines and all other wild life continuously creeping through the brush, is such an exhilarating experience, and in the evening, sitting around the fire, the wonderful detailed accounts of how the buck was bagged — or just why and how he was missed — is absolutely enchanting. And the *food*, how absolutely magnificent it all is; the same food would never taste the same under different circumstances. With one exception perhaps — when Nell Shelton and I teamed up to go to the far pasture, Tops Steiler gave us a thermos of hot coffee and some of her little *Fried Apricot Pies that seem to just melt away with each bite. I watched Tops make them, and sure enough they are just as fabulous at a dressed-up coffee as they are in a deer blind. This is how she makes them:

★

Fried Apricot Pies

Cover 1 lb. dried apricots with water and simmer until done, mash, add sugar to taste. Continue to let cook slowly until thick. Put aside and cool.

Make pie crust with 2 cups flour and ⅓ cup shortening; cut with pastry blender or two knives until like coarse meal. Add cold milk, 4 or 5 Tbs., to make dough a little wetter than regular pie dough. Roll, cut in rounds, size desired. Tops made hers about 3 inches in diameter; and put only about 2 Tbs. of the apricot mixture in the center. Fold the dough over and press around edges with a fork, then turn it over and go around edge of other side also with a fork — it must be tightly sealed.

When they were all made, she heated about 3 Tbs. of shortening in her iron skillet and placed the pies in the hot shortening (medium hot); browned them just on one side and then the other.

That's all — place them on brown absorbent paper and sprinkle them with sugar.

But — on to Kerrville — over the lovely curving road through the green hills past fields with herds of sheep, Angora goats and grazing cattle to the peaceful town of Kerrville, known as the "Heart of the Hills." Because of its natural beauty and delightful year-round climate Kerrville is a popular and lively resort town and also a delightful place where people come to retire.

Irene O'Connor and I visited her sister Estelle Louy. Mrs. Louy's husband, along with the Rockefeller Foundation, made a very thorough survey of suitable United States cities for retirement, and Kerrville was the unanimous decision of both! The crystal-clear Guadalupe River is lined with giant cypress and pecan trees and affords excellent fishing. Kerrville is also a paradise for thousands of hunters, whose annual take averages over nine thousand deer and twenty-five hundred wild turkeys!

The Schreiner family has been very important in the development of this part of Texas for generations. At one time Captain Charles Schreiner owned over 900,000 acres of land, known as the Live Oak Ranch. Through the years the ranch has been divided. Part was sold to Captain Eddie Rickenbacker, World War I ace. It is here that the most unusual and varied hunting in the world takes place, as Captain Rickenbacker imported foreign deer and antelope of eight different species. Other animals from India, Africa and even Japan were also imported. Since they are not native game, they are not under Texas game laws. Therefore, Captain Eddie lets the sportsmen eliminate the surplus male species. Hunters come from everywhere for the novel sport of sitting in one blind and securing such trophies as only a trip around the world could otherwise supply. Captain Rickenbacker has given this ranch to the Boy Scouts of America. This is just one of the many hunting grounds around Kerrville, and for almost every hunter there is a good cook. The Kerrvillites have really worked at perfecting the preparation of wild game, and I love getting recipes from there and have also enjoyed using them.

Mr. Scott Schreiner, the grandson of Captain Schreiner, owns the sections of the ranch called Black Bull Ranch. This ranch was named Black Bull by Captain Schreiner because a big black bull would come to water there at the huge natural water tank. It was quite a challenge to the ranchers to try to corral this bull, but Captain Schreiner finally caught and branded him.

Dodo Schreiner Parker, daughter of Mr. and Mrs. Scott Schreiner, and her husband Clyde are ardent hunters. They entertain often during the season at the Black Bull Ranch for their friends who come from far points of the country to hunt in this prolific land.

The deer are so fat and well fed Dodo says the meat does not need a lot of "doctoring." She cooks the succulent tender back strap the way her great-grandmother used to. It is simple and tastes heavenly.

★

Venison Back Strap or Tenderloin

Cut the back strip into filets. Sprinkle generously with salt and pepper and lots of lemon juice. Beat into the meat, very well, until the meat is flat. Then quickly pan broil in butter on both sides until brown. Very quickly remove to a warm platter. Add a little more butter to pan juices and 2 Tbs. of water. Pour over the steaks. Sautéed fresh mushrooms may also be added if available.

For a game dinner, Dodo may serve dove, quail and pheasant along with the venison steaks and a delicious rice and green salad.

★

Dove, Quail, Pheasant with Rice (*serves 4 to 6*)

8 to 12 pieces of game
Salt
¾ lb. butter or margarine
2 Tbs. cooking oil
1 large onion
2 medium garlic cloves
1 can mushrooms
3 Tbs. flour
1 can beef consommé, 1 can water
¼ cup white wine (prefer red; optional)
1 small bay leaf
1 whole clove
2 tsp. or cubes beef bouillon seasoning

Wash game, pat dry and salt lightly. Place butter or margarine and the oil in skillet (oil keeps the butter from burning while cooking). Brown unfloured game. Lift out and place aside.

In skillet add the chopped onion, garlic and mushrooms (retain liquid) and brown until golden in color. Add flour and stir well.

Then add the can of consommé and 1 can water, wine, mushroom liquid, bay leaf, clove and bouillon seasoning.

Return chicken to this sauce in skillet, cover and simmer for 1 hour or until tender. No additional salt is needed because of the consommé.

Estelle Louy prepares a *Venison Swiss Steak which is excellent.

★

Venison Swiss Steak (*serves 4*)

1½ lbs. round steak
Flour
Salt and pepper
3 large onions
1 medium stalk celery
1 cup tomatoes
2 Tbs. Worcestershire sauce

Steak should be about 1½ inches thick. Dredge with flour and season with salt and pepper; brown in fat on both sides. Add the other ingredients. Cover tightly and cook at 350 degrees or over low heat on top of range until tender (about 1¼ hours). Remove meat to platter and make a gravy from the drippings in pan.

Some people have more than seven talents and put them all to such exciting uses — like Felix and Lillian Real, who live on a very beautiful ranch out of Kerrville. From the stones on the ranch and various timber, they have built a most stunning and original contemporary house and made most of the handsome furnishings in it. In addition to being a very successful rancher, Felix is a designer, builder, craftsman, artist and sportsman — see, there's six right there and I am not even started. Lillian is co-author of all these and is an excellent cook, too. I guess there isn't any game Lillian can't prepare to the delight of an epicurean! Such as:

★

Fiesta Rollada (*Rolled Venison*)

1 thin-sliced steak of venison (about like veal cutlet)
1 thin slice of ham
1 slice mozzarella cheese
Salt and pepper
Chopped parsley and chives
Oil
Flour
White wine (if desired)
Mushrooms (if desired)

Cover venison steak with slice of ham and cheese, spread with chopped parsley and chives, add salt and pepper. Roll up as an enchilada and tie. Brush with oil and flour and brown in skillet. Add wine and mushrooms if desired. Bake slowly in 350-degree oven until tender.

★

Sauerbraten

Venison roast or ham shoulder
Vinegar
Water
6 slices bacon
1 Tbs. salt
12 cloves
6 bay leaves
2 medium onions
6 peppercorns
½ lemon, sliced, more if desired
Butter

Place meat in crock large enough to be covered with liquid — half vinegar and half water. Add remaining ingredients except butter and leave meat in mixture 2 or 3 days, turning it each day. Remove and drain at the end of this time.

Brown in butter. Gradually add all liquid in which meat was soaked, including all spices. Lay bacon on top. Bake slowly in oven 300 to 325 degrees for 2 to 3 hours, according to size of meat. Remove spices for baking if desired.

When done, remove from liquid, cool, slice and serve. Suggested for serving cold. If served hot with gravy, add ginger snaps (crushed) to thickened liquid.

It was a pleasure seeing Miss Martha Dobie, sister of the late J. Frank Dobie, in Kerrville at her very attractive bookstore just off Main Street. Martha said the deer around Kerrville is so good and tender that she often makes *Venison Scallops.

★

Venison Scallops with Parmesan Cheese (serves four)

1½-lb. venison back strap or venison steaks
Flour
Grated Parmesan cheese
4 Tbs. hot butter
3 Tbs. olive oil
1 beef bouillon cube
½ cup boiling water
3 Tbs. red wine or sherry
1 green pepper

Cut venison into ½- by 2-inch slices. Roll in flour and grated Parmesan cheese. Melt butter with olive oil in skillet and brown venison.

Dissolve beef bouillon cube in ½ cup boiling water. Add to pan and slice in one green pepper. Stir in red wine or sherry while scraping pan.

Cover. Simmer for one hour. When serving pour sauce over meat. Can be served over cooked white rice or plain.

THE CAMPAIGN TRAIL

Politics in Texas has always been colorful and interesting. I can well remember before precinct meetings became fashionable Mama, and Daddy, the Sheltons and the Canions were about the only ones to show up at Crawford Feed Store where the meetings were held. Bales of hay served as seats. What was lacking in numbers was made up for in noise; there was always a great deal of arguing and shouting. But even so, these were somewhat an improvement over the politicking that had gone on before. I remember Daddy telling about a certain judge who was remarkably gifted as a stump speaker and well known for his quick humor. He once was opposed by a doctor who tried to make political gain with the charge that the judge had killed two men in duels. The judge replied, "On two occasions under dire circumstances I have been forced to kill a man." Then turning to his accuser, "But my dear Doctor, tell us, how many men have *you* killed in the practice of medicine?"

Texas has had some pretty barnstorming campaigns including that of W. Lee O'Daniels, a popular traveling flour salesman, who advertised his product on the radio with the accompaniment of a hillbilly band. He received so much fan mail he decided to run for governor and won the election. "Pappy Pass the Biscuits" became a popular slogan throughout the state.

There is no one who has fought harder to keep Politics Pure for Texas than Mrs. Jud Collier of Mumford, Texas. Lillian Collier is one of these get-up-and-do people. She and her husband have always lived in the rich farmland called the Brazos Bottom. Research shows this land is more productive than the Nile Valley! Their white plantation house is the scene of many political gatherings. For one and only one reason, says "Miss Lillian," and that is for good government; one that will benefit the most people. Her first project was to make their two-teacher school an independent school district. Having accomplished that, she started working for better roads. They only had muddy tracks to ride or walk. She is a strong believer in "If a task is once begun, never leave it till it's done." Through the years, she has taught a Sunday school class at the Baptist Church, served on numerous legislative committees, the Good Neighbor Commission, state and national executive boards, and heaven only knows what else, always working tirelessly. She still entertains a great deal, but it is usually for some good cause. She recently had the State Democratic Executive Committee for lunch and served:

Tomato Aspic
** S.J.'s Fried Chicken*
Fresh Black-eyed Peas
** Creole Beans*
Hot Rolls
** Democratic Rice*
Banana Nut Cake
Ice cream made in the hand-turned freezer

★

S.J.'s Fried Chicken

Cut chicken up. Soak in sweet milk ½ hour. Season with salt, pepper and Lawry's seasoned salt. Flour chicken in brown paper bag, using about 1 cup of flour. Fry in shortening (hot) until brown on each side. (Turn only once.) Lower fire and cover for 20 to 25 minutes. Serve with cream gravy and *Democratic Rice.

★

Creole Beans

½ cup onions chopped fine
½ cup diced celery
¼ cup liquid oil
1 can tomato sauce
1 small can tomatoes, chopped fine
1 lb. fresh green beans cooked until tender (20 to 30 minutes)

Sauté onions and celery in oil, add tomato sauce, tomatoes and green beans. Season with salt and pepper to taste. Simmer 15 minutes.

★

Democratic Rice

1 cup rice
2 cups water
1 tsp. salt
½ stick butter or margarine

Cook inside oven in covered casserole for 45 minutes.

Of course, they raise their own vegetables, chickens, beef, pork and guineas, in addition to cotton. Guineas are just like watchdogs, Lillian said. "We always know when someone's coming in or passing by, with their loud 'Potrack-Potrack!'" Occasionally S.J., her cook and man Friday, will shoot one and cook it. They are delicious.

★

Guinea

Season guinea with Lawry's seasoned salt. Cover with water and simmer until tender. Then put in low oven, filled with a good corn bread dressing, and bake about an hour.

S.J. has always lived on the Colliers' farm. There is very little he doesn't know how to do. He learned to cook from Lula, who was a good cook but couldn't read. She'd open the wrong can if there wasn't a picture on it! One speciality of the house on which S.J. gets a mighty lot of compliments is his Minted Iced Tea. He serves it in tall glasses with lots of crushed ice. While the tea is steeping in hot water, he drops in several sprigs of fresh mint, then puts a fresh sprig on top as he serves it. Nothing could be more refreshing on a hot summer afternoon.

Food has become a very important part of the campaign trails, or perhaps I should say it is still an important part of politics. Doris Herring said that her grandparents had told her about the Duck Gumbo it was customary to serve on the courthouse square on election day — perhaps a method to get voters out to vote. Now people attend the coffees and receptions and hundred-dollar-a-plate dinners. Texans rally to the barbecues sponsored by their favorite candidates. Mr. Walter Jetton of Fort Worth has probably influenced more voters with his food than all the speeches put together. Someone said, "Walter Jetton is to the sparerib what Chateaubriand was to the steak." Walter has "campaigned" in every state in the nation. When one constituent was polishing off the delicious sparerib she asked, "Why can't we have food like this at our hundred-dollar-a-plate dinners?" Walter has introduced world leaders to his own brand of barbecued beef, spareribs, and chicken. He has a fleet of specially built trucks which carry charcoal broilers, barbecue pits, and refrigerators. On location, before the mesmerized eyes of the guests, his small army of helpers dressed in Western outfits works quickly; one member of his crew makes quantitites and quantities of old-fashioned sour dough biscuits, while another dips boiled corn on the cob in big kettles of hot melted butter, another stirs the big crocks of cole slaw, and still another cooks apple turnovers. It is quite a production — like setting up for the circus and even more fun, as Walter was at one time leading comedian in amateur theaters in Fort Worth. He always sees that the production of the party also gets lots of curtain calls.

After our congressman Homer Thornberry was appointed district federal judge, Jake Pickle was nominated to run for the office. Morning coffees and evening receptions have become a very popular way for the candidate to meet the constituents of the district. Jake and his attractive wife, Beryl, had lots of fun going around from party to party campaigning.

There were a variety of slogans on banners and posters, such as "Our Pickle is a peach," "Pickle is a dilly," "We don't wanna beet Pickle," "Pickle is not sour," "We relish Pickle for Congress."

At the end of his successful campaign, Beryl's cupboard was filled with jars of homemade pickles Jake had brought home from over the district, and the recipe was attached to many, for instance:

★

Sweet Peach Pickles
(Mrs. J. Robert Thornton, San Marcos, Texas)

9 lbs. peaches
1 qt. vinegar
2 qts. sugar
2 Tbs. allspice
2 Tbs. whole cloves
1 pkg. stick cinnamon

Remove peach fuzz with soda water or lye water, or peel. Loosely tie spices in muslin bag and add to other ingredients, which have been boiled together for 5 minutes. Add peaches and cook slowly until tender and well glazed. Cover with hot syrup and seal immediately.

Mrs. James A. (Zoe) Talley of Beaumont brought me a few of these fabulous pickles, along with the recipe, when I was visiting in Beaumont. We have made them at Green Pastures several times. I serve them very cold next to a platter of Roasted or Corned Beef and they always bring *raves* from the guests!

★

B & B Fish House Recipe (about 8 pints)

6 lbs. green plum tomatoes
½ lb. small hot peppers
3 large bell peppers
5 large onions
1 qt. apple cider vinegar
2½ cups sugar
½ cup salt

Remove small stems and halve tomatoes. Cut hot peppers across in ½-inch slices. Cut bell peppers and onions in about ½-inch-square pieces. Mix vinegar, sugar, salt and heat. Add remaining ingredients and simmer until uniform in color.

★

Jean Kritser's Pickled Okra

1 clove
1 clove garlic
2 small hot red peppers
1 or 2 sprigs fresh dill
Okra (small)
4 cups white vinegar
1 cup water
¼ cup salt

Put in small (pint) sterilized jars: the clove (cut in 2 or 3 pieces), garlic, hot red peppers, sprigs of fresh dill. Wash okra thoroughly, pack lengthwise in the jars. Boil the white vinegar, water, and salt. Pour over okra, seal quickly. Age 6 weeks. Chill in refrigerator before serving.

★

Ellen's Easy Pickled Beets

1 can sliced or tiny whole beets
½ cup beet juice
½ cup sugar
⅛ tsp. salt
Juice of 1 lemon
1 cup vinegar
1 tsp. whole cloves

Drain beets; save ½ cup juice. Bring juice, vinegar, sugar and seasoning to boiling point to dissolve sugar. Pour this over the beets and let stand in covered jar at least 8 hours.

★

Effie Kitchen's Pickled Eggs (for 100 eggs)

Salt
1 gal. vinegar (Combined with 1 gal. water so as not to be so strong. Adjust to flavor desired.)
1 box pickling spices
Mustard seed
Hard-boiled eggs

Heat and pour the salt, vinegar, water, pickling spices and a small amount of mustard seed over the eggs. Beet juice or food coloring may be used to give the eggs more a festive air.

Mrs. Rex Kitchen gave me this recipe. I remember when she served this at a fabulous Gay 90's party she and Rex gave at their country home near Austin. She had added different food coloring to each jar. The eggs encircled a roasted pig and were surely a big hit that evening. They are good just to keep on hand.

Gertrude Horton says she used the liquid from dill pickles to pickle her eggs by just dropping the hard-boiled, peeled eggs into the pickle jar, making sure the eggs are well covered by the liquid. Keep in refrigerator at least three days before serving. But they keep indefinitely in the refrigerator and are so wonderful on an hors d'oeuvre table, split in halves and spread with sour cream and seasoned with salt and a little white pepper.

This recipe of Imme Taylor makes delicious relish:

★

Tomato Relish (makes 12 quarts)

1 pt. salt
½ bushel green tomatoes, chopped
½ dozen green peppers, chopped
24 large onions, chopped
2 heads cabbage, chopped
1 box celery seed
1 box black pepper
1 box white pepper
1 box mustard seed
2 cups brown sugar
Cider vinegar
1 Tbs. cinnamon
1 Tbs. allspice

Sprinkle the salt over and through the chopped tomatoes, green peppers, onions and cabbage. Let it stand overnight. The next morning, drain through a flour sack and press as dry as possible. Season the mixture with the celery seed, black and white pepper, mustard seed, brown sugar, cider vinegar, Tbs. each of cinnamon and allspice. Divide into several pans and cook about 45 minutes.

The following is a marvelous recipe I have used many years. I received it from Miss Alice O'Grady at the Old Argule Hotel in San Antonio.

★

Tiny White Onion Pickles

For 1 gallon of onions:

Peel the onions and soak in strong, salted water overnight. Next morning drain and let stand in clear water for an hour, then drain. Measure enough vinegar to cover and make a syrup as follows:

2 qts. vinegar
1 cup sugar
1 Tbs. whole cloves
1 Tbs. celery seed
1 Tbs. peppercorns
1 Tbs. mustard seed

Tie the spices in a cheesecloth bag and boil in the vinegar and sugar for 15 minutes. Drop in the tiny onions and boil another 15 minutes or longer. Seal in jars and let stand two weeks or longer before using.

For good luck on a New Year's buffet:

★

Pickled Black-eyed Peas

4 cups cooked black-eyed peas, drained
1 cup salad oil
¼ cup wine vinegar
1 clove garlic
1 medium onion sliced thin
½ tsp. salt
Cracked or freshly ground pepper

Add ingredients and mix. Store in jar in refrigerator. Remove garlic after one day. May be kept as long as two weeks in the refrigerator.

Rosemary and Asa Burroughs of Austin have found what many of us are looking for — a weekend house completely removed from the hustle-bustle of our daily routine. It is a real change in atmosphere yet close enough to be accessible. We were fortunate enough to be guests at their house sitting high on a hill, called Ginger Bread Hill, and overlooking the peaceful countryside near Stonewall. It is one of the old early Texas-German houses, so comfortable and hospitable, and in the tradition of this part of the country. When we were ready to leave, Rosemary loaded us with prizes from the smoke house which she and Asa had put up on a weekend. There were links of German sausage, Stonewall peaches and cucumber pickles.

For seven quarts of pickles she put young, tender cucumbers in a jar and poured this solution over them:

★

Cucumber Pickles (for 7 quarts)

2 qts. water	Cucumbers
3 cups vinegar	Dill
1 cup salt	

Bring the water, vinegar and salt to a boil. Then simmer for at least 5 minutes. Place a sprig of dill in each jar. Pack the cucumbers vertically and firmly. Pour the brine into the jars, filling them to one inch from the top. Place *new* tops on jars. Place jars in a water bath on a cloth or trivet. Let simmer until the pickles change color, which is about 10 minutes. Then take the jars out and retighten the tops. Cool and store. Let set for a week.

Judge Herman Jones is another who has done a lot of politicking in his day, having started at a very tender age when he was the youngest member of the State Legislature. Herman has a wonderful collection of campaign stories, one being about a certain gentleman running for re-election for governor of Texas. A friend called him from Waco and said, "Governor, you'd better get up here quick; they're telling lies on you!"

The Governor replied, "I can't! I gotta go to Houston. They're telling the truth about me there!"

The morning coffees staged for favorite candidates by the ladies have become really the thing to have or to hold come election year. When I was in Brownsville, shortly before the Presidential election, the Republican girls gave such a party on the patio of Frank and Mary Yturria's home. An enormous picture of the candidate completely covered the front door. Red, white and blue bunting was draped across the front balcony. A gold elephant was floating in the swimming pool.

The serving tables were covered in bright reds and blues. The coffee was served from Mary Yturria's lovely old brass coffee samovar she had brought back from Hong Kong. They also served orange juice, often referred to as "goldwater," and loads of miniature doughnuts.

I would highly recommend, regardless of your party, that you make these remarkable *Republican Doughnuts.

★

Republican Doughnuts (*about 3 dozen 3-inch doughnuts*)

4½ cups sifted flour
¼ tsp. nutmeg
¼ tsp. allspice
1½ tsp. soda
1½ tsp. cream of tartar
1½ tsp. salt
3 eggs
1 cup sugar
3 Tbs. shortening, melted
1 cup buttermilk
Fat for deep frying

Sift together the flour, nutmeg, allspice, soda, cream of tartar and salt. Beat the eggs until thick and lemon-colored and gradually beat in the sugar. Add the melted shortening and buttermilk, then add the flour mixture. Mix well, chill and turn out on a well-floured board or pastry cloth. Roll to ¼ inch thick; cut with a floured cutter. Fry a few at a time in deep hot fat (375 degrees) for 3 minutes or until brown, first on one side and then on the other.

Candidates never refuse an opportunity to speak. Even if it is to lead a prayer at church, they try to make it count. Such is the one recalled by Mr. Al Lowman when a revival preacher called on Judge Williamson to lead in prayer. In a solemn voice he intoned grandly:

"O Lord, the supreme ruler of the Universe, who holdest the thunder and lightning in Thy hand, and from the clouds givest rain to make crops for Thy children, look down with pity upon Thy children who now face ruin for lack of rain upon their crops; and O Lord, send us a downpour that will cause the crops to fruit in all their glory and the earth to turn again to that beauteous green that comes from abundant showers. Lord, send us a bounteous one that will make corn ears shake hands across the row, and not one of these little rizzly-drizzly rains that'll make nubbins that all hell can't shuck."

INDEX